A TURBULENT DECADE REMEMBERED

Cultural Memory

in

the

Present

Mieke Bal and Hent de Vries, Editors

A TURBULENT DECADE REMEMBERED

Scenes from the Latin American Sixties

Diana Sorensen

STANFORD UNIVERSITY PRESS

STANFORD, CALIFORNIA

2007

Stanford University Press
Stanford, California

Printed in the United States of America on acid-free, archival-quality paper

Library of Congress Cataloging-in-Publication Data
Sorensen, Diana.
  A turbulent decade remembered : scenes from the Latin American sixties / Diana
Sorensen.
     p. cm.
  Includes bibliographical references and index.
   ISBN 978-0-8047-5662-4 (cloth : alk. paper)—ISBN 978-0-8047-5663-1 (pbk. : alk.
paper)
   1. Latin American literature—20th century—History and criticism. 2. Literature
and society—Latin America. I. Title.

PQ7081.S688 2007
860.9'98—dc22

                                                                              2007020499

Typeset by Classic Typography in 11/13.5 Adobe Garamond.

For my mother, Marta Sorensen

Contents

Acknowledgments   *xi*

Introduction: Imminent Times: Structures of Feeling
from a Turbulent Decade   *1*

1. The Cuban Revolution and Che Guevara:
Between Memory and Utopia   *15*

2. Tlatelolco 1968: Paz and Poniatowska on Law and Violence   *54*

3. From Diaspora to Agora in Cortázar:
Exile as Continental Space   *78*

4. Toward a Transnational Republic of Letters:
A Geography of Discursive Networks   *106*

5. The Anxious Brotherhood: Mastering Authorship
and Masculinity   *143*

6. Rereading "Boom" Novels in the Twenty-First Century   *164*

Conclusion   *208*

Notes   *215*
Bibliography   *263*
Index   *285*

Acknowledgments

It has taken me almost ten years to write this book: the debts are many, and it is a pleasure to acknowledge them. Colleagues and students in the United States and abroad have been valued interlocutors in many a conversation about the sixties. I would not be able to list all the students (both graduate and undergraduate) whom I would like to thank for their interest and engagement with this topic, but I want to start with them, and tell them all (at Wesleyan, Columbia, and Harvard in the United States, and at the Universidad de San Martín in Argentina) that our discussions have left many a trace in my thinking.

I am deeply grateful for the intellectual generosity and support of friends and colleagues with whom I have chatted about this book and, more broadly and often as important, about the excitement of cultural and historical exploration in general. To them, my thanks: Gonzalo Aguilar, Daniel Balderston, Janet Beizer, Homi Bhabha, Alicia Borinsky, Joaquim-Francisco Coelho, Gustavo Pérez Firmat, Andreas Huyssen, Cristina Iglesia, Gwen Kirkpatrick, Alejandra Laera, Josefina Ludmer, Tomás Eloy Martínez, Francine Masiello, Christie McDonald, Sylvia Molloy, Graciela Montaldo, Julio Premat, Beatriz Sarlo, Marcy Schwartz, Ann-Louise Shapiro, Doris Sommer, Susan Suleiman, Mabel Moraña, Cynthia Schmidt-Cruz, María Rosa Olivera Williams, and Jay Winter. At Harvard I have benefited immensely from the best reference librarian I have ever worked with, Mary Beth Clack, and from the most intelligent, loyal, and insightful research assistant a scholar could ever find, Sara Kippur. My warmest thanks to both.

The loving support of my family and close friends was essential during the years of this book's writing: I thank my wonderful daughter Lisa; my brother, sister, and sister-in-law, Daniel, Elsebeth, and Irene Sorensen;

and my extended family: Adriana and Tom Riles, Katherine Evans, Joel Papowitz, Silvia Sieburger Cudich, and Alicia Dellepiane.

I dedicate this book to my loving and beloved mother, Marta Sorensen, and, through her, in memoriam, to my father Geert, who never gave up the utopian longings of the sixties.

A TURBULENT DECADE REMEMBERED

Introduction

The term *Latin America*, coined in the nineteenth century, did not represent a fully continental set of relations until the 1960s. Only then did a transnational cultural identity become rooted in the hemispheric imagination; only then was Latin America able to find its own space in the international republic of letters. This book charts some of the material and symbolic conditions of possibility of this continental moment, and the forms of representation in which they were expressed.

"The most difficult thing to get hold of, in studying any past period, is this felt sense of the quality of life at a particular place and time: a sense of the ways in which the particular activities combined into a way of thinking and living."[1] Here is the challenge of this book, as it sets out to articulate and interpret some key scenes in a Latin American decade that we have inherited and transformed in unanticipated ways. Well over forty years later, we look back on this formative period with a sense of surprise at its outcomes, as if we were reading a plot with an unexpected denouement. Utopia and revolution have lost their charge; the dramatic changes and resolutions the sixties expected to usher in often turned out to be the horrors of repression and violence of the seventies and eighties. How, then, can we recapture a sense of the lived experience of that inaugural moment, as well as the underlying conditions of its mostly grim conclusion?

This cultural history of the Latin American sixties eschews linearity and a totalizing sweep so as to study moments of intense interaction between culture and society, in different forms, but always trying to pry open the workings of the intersections, as Walter Benjamin would have it, "only as an image which flashes up at the instant when it can be recognized and is never seen again."[2] The moments I have chosen as the story for each chapter were experienced as the "time of the now," echoing Benjamin again, but a "now" whose fullness conveyed a sense of imminence, as an expectation that Latin America's time was about to arrive.

Imminence as possibility is entwined with the spirit of utopia, which is central to the cultural and political imagination of the sixties. In the vision of a possible world not yet realized but about to come lived the belief that the fulfillment of a future long awaited and postponed was on its way, almost there, making its signs visible, and hence ushering in a spirit of celebration.[3] The transitional stage was sustained by the conviction that the new was to be constructed, that a "new man" would emerge from a veritable change of skin. *Liberation* was one of the key words of the day: its field of meanings was political but broadly cultural as well: it reached styles of dress, sexual mores, intergenerational relationships, religious belief, and educational forms. In politics, the old rigidities of Marxism no longer held sway: in the wake of Stalinism, the New Left sought renewed articulations of the critique of capitalism; this was the time when Althusser revised Marx and read him with Freud and Lacan, offering cross-fertilizations between material practice and the unconscious. In Latin America, Raúl Prebisch's Dependency Theory, first developed in the 1950s, offered a material explanation for the profound economic disparity between the subcontinent and the advanced industrialized economies of the North, showing how the growth of the latter was the result of the capitalist exploitation of the former. A revisionary critique of capitalism seemed to be particularly urgent for the economic future of the region.

Sexual liberation and the women's movement came on the scene partially aided by the development of the contraceptive pill; they were impelled by the prevalent questioning of established social roles and the drive to redress alienating regimes of power. The Catholic Church underwent its own revisionary process in the sixties: "Liberation Theology" was energized by a redemptive critical consciousness that included politics. Revolution and Christianity took on a Latin American and Third World inflexion in dialogue with Marxism, with a commitment to embrace action and to change the plight of the poor. The 1968 Medellín Conference of Bishops ended with a manifesto that proclaimed the hour of action in Latin America, of total emancipation, of liberation from subjection. Liberation was given a theological valence and placed at the center of the Church's mission.

This spirit of liberation went hand in hand with a critique of what existed: old forms were to be superseded and even destroyed in order to inaugurate the new. There was, therefore, an oscillating rhythm between annihilation and construction, between visions that led to destruction and those that adumbrated liberation on the personal and the collective levels. These general claims voiced in North America and Europe took on a particularly intense form in Latin America, largely on account of the Cuban Revolution. The success of the young revolutionaries who made their way from Sierra Maestra to Havana between 1956 and 1959 surprised the world and betokened culmination and possibility. For the young and those on the left, Cuba became a sign of things to come, a force that might sweep the southern part of the continent. This helps to explain the intensity of the decade in Latin America, but in no way does it exhaust the complex causality that obtained in the transnational order.

The dialogue between the Latin American and the metropolitan worlds is particularly fertile at this time, both in its points in common and in its specificities. This book locates Latin America in this transnational dialogue, attentive to the forces at work in a larger system that, while not yet altogether global, was tightly interconnected. It is therefore an intervention in the field of "world literature," inasmuch as it traces the circulation of Latin American works out of their hemispheric locations and into the reading publics of Europe and North America, where they were received with interest and curiosity.[4]

I would submit that the Latin American difference is one of intensity, and that it is framed by the twin rhythms of euphoria and despair. For even as the Cuban Revolution surprised the world, the stark realities of the Cold War worked as the ultimate limit of the field of possibilities.[5] In other words, Latin America in the sixties encapsulates its predicament: a moment of hope and celebration produced a sense of multiple possibilities, only to reach closure and despair in its culmination. At the time of the present writing, well into the twenty-first century, it is hard to avoid a melancholic sense of loss as one contemplates the aftermath of this utopian decade, as if one had reached the end of a plot with a cheerless outcome. For the sixties were followed by brutal regimes and economic crises whose impact has been profound and long lasting.

As I suggested above, it would be misleading to assume that the six-ties' utopian energies galvanized positive impulses only: the very euphoria of creation brought about a certain apocalyptic edge, an impulse to destroy what appeared to be out of step with the times. One can detect this very tension in the philosophical outlook of the Frankfurt School, whose work began to be widely read in the sixties. Deeply marked by World War II, the Frankfurt School philosophers thought in terms of the *crisis* of capitalism and of the entire project of the Enlightenment. Horkheimer and Adorno's *Dialectic of Enlightenment*, written in 1947, began to circulate in translation in the 1960s; Marcuse's *Reason and Revolution, Eros and Civilization,* and *One-Dimensional Man*, written in the forties, fifties, and sixties, respectively, reached more receptive audiences in the sixties, when the horizon of expec-tations was receptive to the kind of critical thinking that combined Marx-ism, psychoanalysis, and traces of surrealism to proclaim the need for new social, political, and cultural forms to be built on the ashes of the old ones. Marcuse's work called for a total transformation in which the utopian char-acter was psychic, political, and cultural. It rested on the Great Refusal: a radical condemnation of a social reality seen as repressive, and the longing for a true, unalienated eros leading to socially constructive forms.

In France, Sartre's philosophy dealt with the "unhappy consciousness" of modern man, trapped in a state of alienation. The revolts of 1968 em-braced this sense of crisis, and the revolutionaries conceived of themselves as a cleansing force that began the systematic decentering of the West. It is that very combination of crisis and creation that produced the conditions of pos-sibility for the emergence of new kinds of thinking: a case in point is Michel Foucault, whose work (he claimed in a conversation with Duccio Trom-badori[6]) was able to find a receptive audience only after the upheavals of the Algerian war and May 1968—until then, Foucault explains, it was met with absolute indifference. Yet before the subject was proclaimed dead, the philo-sophical outlook of the sixties held out hope for a real break in the contin-uum of history and for the reconciliation of contradictions produced by di-remption, the split between man and nature. Spontaneity and enthusiasm went hand in hand with the longing for transformation: in the condemna-tion of apathy and alienation, everything pointed to the energy of reinven-tion. But this energy was both constructive and destructive: it sought the communal celebration of the creative festival and of the abrogation of order. For order and the system were linked to what Horkheimer and Adorno in their exalted *Dialectic of Enlightenment* called the "nullity" of thought, "as far removed from reflective consideration of its own goal as were other forms of labor under the pressure of the system."[7]

One of the interesting contradictions of the period is the fact that it was the very decried "system" that made the expansive utopian thinking possible. Here is a telling disjunction between the material and the symbolic worlds: it was the economic bonanza of the postwar bourgeois world that produced the social context in which a new culture could flourish. Money and exchange came under suspicion, but they constituted the conditions of possibility for the prevailing sense of experimentation, artistic autonomy, and a generalized teleology of revolution. These were the "golden years" of affluence and economic expansion in the West that witnessed the rise of the transnational economy and multinational corporations, when the industrial capitalist economies did extremely well on the basis of mass consumption, employment, and regularly rising incomes.[8] Yet the economic boom brought about a rise of expectations that could not be fully satisfied: demands were greater than could be met, and a desire to rebel found abundant rhetorical and semantic incentives in the ideology of crisis and liberation. An impatient longing for a transfigured world—stripped of the trammels of consumer society and the established regime of power—drew its energies from the very advanced capitalist economy that produced stunning urban growth, new markets, and new consumers. This is the contradictory logic of the system at this time, and, for about a decade, the contradictions remained productive. Capitalism was to finance its own supersession. A culture of critique and negativity postulated other possible worlds about to rise from the ashes of the existing one—a world of liberated subjects who would suture politics and culture, sexuality and play, celebration and work, all as utopian avatars that shared a rejection of the established world in a new regime of sociability.[9] In the developed world, some theorists of postindustrial society with connections to the New Left envisioned a future-oriented system of modern living in which aspirations for reform would achieve more communal forms of economic and political organization, beyond work and scarcity.[10]

Who but the young could take on such an ambitious vision of destruction and renewal?[11] As the authority of age was devalued, predecessors were displaced, and youth as a generational category gained ascendancy. Although the early Romantics had given great shrift to the figure of the young man, it was not until the sixties that youth appeared as the carrier of power and innovation, overshadowing the contestatory power of class.[12] The young man or woman of the sixties was located in a detached and privileged space that replaced the protocols of apprenticeship of earlier times. In the urbanized economies of the fifties and sixties, occupations demanded higher education: the modern economies called for planners, administrators, teachers, and technical experts. The university as a site of training was itself the focus of contradictions: it entered a period of unprecedented expansion; it was structured hierarchically as a system for the production and dissemination of knowledge (with faculty not only constructing programs of study, but also determining grades and requirements), but it was also the purveyor of critical thinking that was to shake up existing structures of knowledge. Hence the university provided the very stuff unrest was made of: those who were being taught were set apart from the rest of society, and they used the tools of analysis to launch a critique of the system, to occupy the space in which that knowledge was disseminated, demanding a radical transformation. The scale of the student population explosion exceeded what even the most affluent economies were able to accommodate, and hence unrest had material (often physical, in the sense that existing buildings were unsuited to the numbers they had to house, and the sheer agglomeration of students led to disturbances), as well as intellectual reasons. Demands for emancipation and better conditions went hand in hand with the desire to displace forefathers: youth was conceived as the culmination of human development.[13] In a way, this is inherent to the university structure: the precondition for its critical power is precisely its separation from the "outer" world. Octavio Paz captures the double valence of this situation: "during the long years in which young men and women are isolated in schools of higher education, they live under artificial conditions, half as privileged recluses, half as dangerous irresponsible youths?"[14]

Yet the young, while seemingly detached from the economy, became a segment of brisk consumers identified by notions of style in dress, music, cosmetics, and related tastes. Led horizontally by members of their peer group, they were both optimistic and impatient, like the decade itself. The optimistic strain was ambitious and expansive; the impatient one was expressed as a sense of boredom, alienation, and, in some cases, as the spirit of rebellion.[15] Mythical visions of young rebels like James Dean, Marlon Brando, or Che Guevara could be made to incarnate romantic aspirations for Messianism that decried a world seen as dehumanized and that longed for the purifying force of revolution. And in the midst of such redemptive longings, a different sense of community to come was being imagined. This mood was often expressed in sympathy and support for Algeria, Congo, Vietnam, and Palestine.

The Latin American inflection of the dominant fiction of this period registered particular intensity: it was experienced as the long-awaited realization of historical struggles. The surprising triumph of the Cuban insurrection furnished regional innovations to the general model of revolution, heightening the sense of emergent regional power. For one thing, it was the achievement of political actors whose class affiliations were heterogeneous and therefore unorthodox: both working and middle class, urban and rural, lettered and illiterate. They worked out a *foco* theory that, while particularly attuned to the specificities of the Latin American context, pointed to a different way in which radical political change might be generally conceived for future revolutionary endeavors. The young *barbudos* had triumphed by dint of their energy, their constant mobility, their imaginative reconfiguration of previous revolutionary programs. For a while, it seemed that the Latin American time had come, and that it could affirm itself as a contributor to the innovative drive of the period. The region was impatient and impassioned in its desire for contemporaneity with the metropolitan center: it wanted to be not only up to date but also simultaneous and international. There was also—and even in significant numbers of the middle class—a certain urgency to act upon feelings of compassion and solidarity with the downtrodden. I would claim that many groups in Latin America shared an anxious—at times optimistic—sense of imminence, of arrival about to take place, or to be voluntaristically ushered in.

Such stirrings had their counterparts in the theoretical ferment of the day, which might be characterized by various alterations of intellectual focus. In Latin America and in the Third World some books added to the impatience for change: such was the case of Frantz Fanon's *The Wretched of the Earth*[16] (bearing Sartre's exalted preface, suffused in a sense of impending violence), and Eduardo Galeano's *Las venas abiertas de América Latina*, which came out in 1971. Even more tempered interventions in the intellectual arena were characterized by the rumblings of a shift from an established paradigm to an emergent one: Sartre's hegemony was beginning to lose ground to structuralist transformations of the field such as Althusserian antihumanist Marxism, or Lévi-Strauss's structuralist anthropology, which attacked Sartre's historicism and proclaimed the goal of "dissolving man." The linguistic model was on its way to becoming the general paradigm in the human sciences, from Lacan to the study of textuality. Marxism had to face the needs of a new revolutionary libido: in Europe the focus became less strategic than analytic; in the Third World it was channeled into clandestine movements that appropriated Marxist theory in versions of their own.[17] It was as if the last flaring up of Marxism as a theory of society and of revolutionary action produced an outburst of intense energy. Yet even in the heat of the emancipatory rhetoric of the student movements of 1968, one can detect the power of a cultural politics moving away from the strictly political projects of earlier decades. Such an investment in innovation contained not only exceptional creativity, but also the seeds of its own supersession, which is one of a number of reasons why the decade's utopian verve came to an end in the early seventies. While the ferment lasted, it was characterized by an intense investment in the future, and in the cultural dimensions of the political.

The temporality of the sixties is therefore profoundly different from ours today in the early twenty-first century: rather than being drawn to the melancholic work of memory—often stalled in a sense of exhaustion—it was utopian, and still engaged in the struggle to find ways in which culture would play a role in social and political transformation. This is particularly clear in the novels of the "boom," whose ambitious sweep culminated in apocalyptic endings that meant to annihilate defunct social and political worlds—from the bourgeois family to the neocolonial nation-state, all in the sweep of an aesthetics of explosion. Witness the ending of *One Hundred Years of Solitude*, which is merely an exacerbated version of the endings of *The Death of Artemio Cruz*, *Pedro Páramo*, *La casa verde*, or *El obsceno pájaro de la noche*. The dominant fiction of the decade subtends novels in which the family—the most fundamental image of unity in the social formation—is in crisis: it is invoked as an organizing principle, but it works its way through the plot as failure. What clearer example than *One Hundred Years of Solitude*, built on the structural support of genealogy and relentlessly making its way to its anticipated destruction? Most of the other major novels work on variants of the same impossibility. Patriarchy and the Law of the Father are still in place, but in the decades that elapsed between, say, *Doña Bárbara* (1929) and *The Death of Artemio Cruz* (1962), or even the earlier *Pedro Páramo* (1955), it became impossible to continue to consider the family as the stable core around which national and international communities cohered. Instead, powerful men like Artemio Cruz or Pedro Páramo opted for the material enticements of the capitalist system at the price of love and family. I would contend that this is the beginning of a crisis that the twenty-first century has inherited in a magnified fashion, with the addition of further instability in the patriarchal gender system. In *Male Subjectivity at the Margins*, Kaja Silverman reads Freud, Lacan, Leclaire, and Lévi-Strauss together to contend that our dominant fiction bridges the contradiction between the Law of Kinship Structure (which upholds the Law of the Father), and the Law of Language (built on the recognition of the inevitability of castration) through an imaginary resolution that disavows male castration.[18] Silverman locates the crisis in Hollywood films made as early as the 1940s, in the post–World War II scene; my reading of the Latin American novels of the boom suggests that such an imaginary resolution is wearing thin at the edges in the sixties. It is, indeed, frayed by its commerce with the critique of capitalism, with the logic of liberation, and with a generalized unease with the very expansive, modernized world in which Latin American writing finally finds its place. Virile alienation and disenchantment are part of the very same structure of feeling that subtends utopian longings. The pervasive sense of imminence anticipates crisis, destruction, and the rumblings of different beginnings. While patriarchy still rules the gender system, its anxieties and *méconnaissances* call for special attention to the question of gender as a category of analysis that has helped me unpack some of the enabling tensions in the works I examine.

Theodor Adorno's aesthetic theory captures the specific qualities of the relationship between culture and society as it played out at this time. For in Adorno, art's redemptive promise retains its transformative power and its intimations of transcendence, relying on critical analysis as well as on the power to produce *apparitions* through images that work as explosions. The logic Adorno works with has the qualities that characterize the decade itself, paradoxically intense and evanescent: "If it holds true that the subjective rationality of means and ends—which is particular and thus in its innermost irrational—requires spurious irrational enclaves and treats art as such, art is nevertheless the truth of society insofar as in its most authentic products the irrationality of the rational order is expressed. In art, denunciation and anticipation are syncopated."

Hence in *Aesthetic Theory* Adorno moves within the *syncopation* or rhythms alternating between critique or negativity and expectancy, working with the age of Enlightenment but also provoking it—much in the spirit in which his collaboration with Horkheimer had denounced the Kantian system in its ambiguities and contradictions.[19] For Adorno art is akin to explosion, and it operates as a catastrophic fulfillment:

Artworks not only produce *imagines* as something that endures. They become artworks just as much through the destruction of their own *imagerie*; for this reason art is profoundly akin to explosion. . . . Appearance, however, and its explosion in the artwork are essentially historical. . . . What appears in the artwork is its own inner time; the explosion of appearance blasts open the continuity of this inner temporality. . . . To analyze artworks means no less than to become conscious of the history immanently sedimented in them.[20]

It is this very explosion of appearance in its Adornian sense that is the gamble of the present book. Each chapter seeks to pry open (since the Adornian "blasting" may be too powerful a claim) a complex knot of relations that coalesce at key moments or *problématiques* of the Latin American sixties between the world (in its social, economic and political dimensions) and the symbolic order that sets out to chart it, domesticate it, or interpret it. Borrowing from Barthes's work on photography, we might compare the scene to the *punctum* in photography: it is like a mark that stings with the forces it gathers.[21] Thus, each chapter will seek to elucidate the structure of feeling of the period through the analysis of meanings and values that obtain in particular configurations characterized by the mode of change. The elements in the "structure" comprise social and political relationships, forms of behavior, forms of production and communication, ethical assumptions and gender relations, cultural and technical innovation, notions of space and time, forms of language and expression, and other factors that contribute to the shape of lived experience as it is represented in different forms of writing. And writing is precisely a field in which the cultural and political contradictions of an era are performed and represented.

The only possible beginning for this book was the Cuban Revolution, which inaugurates the decade in its fullest sense, rife with continental projections and claiming that insurrection was to end the neocolonial stagnation in which Latin America was mired. The chapter discusses the negotiations between the cultural and the political imagination, and the cross-fertilizations among institutions, myth-making, and writing in the construction of a new continental consciousness. Ernesto Che Guevara as myth and as early historian of the Sierra Maestra campaign is at the center of the chapter, as the axis around which memory and utopia turn. His auratic quality *writes* the Revolution as text, as image, and as a model for the "new man," pointing to a new emotional pedagogy that shifts from individual passions to love of community. I contend that the sentimental attachments plotted here are on the cusp of the changes in the plots of the novels noted earlier, and that draw on the bourgeois model of love and family only to reveal their failure or sheer impossibility in the end.

In my reading of the *Pasajes de la guerra revolucionaria*, I unpack the phallocratic contract that underpins Che's writing, erecting Fidel as hypermasculine hero in a new polis regulated by his libidinal energy and sexualized power. My claim is that gender and revolution need to be read together, so that the exchanges between identification, desire, utopian aspirations, and leadership are productively charted. These exchanges are centrally at work in two later works discussed in this chapter, and which draw their aesthetic energy from the same source (Che): Julio Cortázar's story "Reunión," and Walter Salles's film *Motorcycle Diaries*.

It is important to note that in the materials discussed in the first part of this chapter the utopian impetus is articulated by voices that are affiliated with the state: we have cultural production doing the work of dominant ideology. Che's writing seeks to set the path for the future community even as he writes the history of the insurrection in Sierra Maestra: writing memory and utopia had the effect of opening up a vast field of possibilities on the one hand, but, on the other hand, it was part of an enterprise that contained the seeds of control, containment, and eventual repression. Because I chose the moments in which the sense of the possible acted as a springboard to cultural productivity, I have not focused on the turn toward censorship and repression. The move toward the suppression of freedom of expression is a well-known chapter in the history of contemporary Cuba: as early as 1961 Fidel Castro's speech "Palabras a los intelectuales" marked the limits of what was acceptable within the cultural field, dictating a singular and stable vision. These developments, of course, also involve the many tense exchanges between one nation (Cuba) and U.S. hemispheric interests.

Chapter Two deals with another intense scene in the negotiation between writing and political life: the student movements of 1968 in Mexico. If in Chapter One writing was at the service of modeling the new order under the aegis of the revolutionary state, in Chapter Two I trace the power of two specific texts (written by Octavio Paz and Elena Poniatowska, respectively) to denounce the oppressive state as perpetrator of illegal violence against its citizens. The massacre at Tlatelolco marks the end of a pact between Mexican intellectuals and the state, calling into question the legality of the ruling party (Partido Revolucionario Institucional, or PRI) and generating a truly extraordinary discursive war against a government that was responsible for the death of hundreds of students just days before the Olympic Games. The guiding question here is how writing can erect itself as a contestatory force after the brutal crushing of freedom and voluntaristic possibility.

In Chapter Three I pose the question about writing and the world by exploring how one canonical writer of the sixties, Julio Cortázar, worked out different approaches to questions that vexed him throughout his career: the negotiations between aesthetics and politics. My discussion of his writings is centered on a certain deadlock that structures the question of how to remain true to both a radically free artistic enterprise and a politics of Latin American liberation. Rather than try to resolve the impasse, I use it as a point of entry into a scene of what we might call "enthusiastic resignation," characterized by a writing that problematizes and reconfigures the location of the author vis-à-vis community, and of the intellectual vis-à-vis political commitment. Cortázar's attachment to the Cuban Revolution was an abiding one, and it inflected his writing beyond changing positions in the sphere of politics and literature: he remained convinced that aesthetic and political revolution could become intertwined, without relinquishing critical vigilance. His story is paradigmatic of the vexed location of the intellectual in this period of intense negotiations between culture and politics.

Chapters Four and Five shift into the material and symbolic forces that contributed to the construction of the literary culture of the sixties. In Chapter Four the focus is interdisciplinary: I deal with the powerful convergence of economic and political factors that made it possible for the sixties to become the time for the emergence of the so-called boom of the Latin American novel. I take the term *boom* as shorthand for the acclaimed group of writers who attained an international readership in this period, and who represent both the culmination of high modernism and the emergence of postmodernism in Latin America. Here what interests me is how a vibrant cultural moment is "made" through a complex network of practices located in a transnational arena that is both hemispheric and transatlantic. In Chapter Five the organizing concept is gender and its role in the configuration of the boom, which was predominantly masculine. Here the key question is what constitutes a literary group, what binds it to a general ethos, and how authorship is constituted. Given the debunking of predecessors, filiation and affiliation were suffused with the anxieties of adequacy that beset the male author in the newly configured literary marketplace of the sixties. While José Donoso provides the textual platform for the analysis, the aim of the chapter is to think about the male group that constitutes the boom in its gender-based aspect. This is a constitutive element of literary history that has been insufficiently accounted for, and the boom scene provides eloquent material with which to begin to unpack it.

The book ends with the analysis of the very literary form whose conditions of emergence are studied in the earlier chapters. Chapter Six proposes a rereading of some of the boom novels in light of their location in the transnational literary marketplace of the post–World War II era. My claim is that the Latin American novel was able to attract not only a national but also—and for the first time—an international readership for a complex set of reasons that are developed in the chapter. Technically adept and filled with stories to tell, great Latin American writers such as Gabriel García Márquez, Carlos Fuentes, Mario Vargas Llosa, and Julio Cortázar succeeded in operating the equivalences of knowledge necessary for reception in the North as well as in their own national and continental territories. Magical realism, surrealism, and ethnography are discussed as complex negotiations between the center and the periphery at a time when the center was being confronted by an explosion of otherness produced by decolonization and "new subjects of history"[22] who were making their way into the metropolis. The logic of plots, together with concepts of space and time, are some of the guiding interpretive foci of my analysis. My concern is less with close textual readings than with the imbrications of an ambitious cartographic imagination and technical know-how as they worked to represent complex human experience and attract audiences near and far.

As I observed at the outset, the book does not set out to be a comprehensive review of cultural production in the sixties. Indeed, a great deal is left out: television and film, music and the visual arts, theater and "happenings," cartoons, and other forms of popular culture. Many boom writers are absent from my discussion, as is the great José María Arguedas, who deliberately avoided the boom's scene. Such an enterprise would be not only encyclopedic but also beyond my guiding logic, which was to alight on scenes of particular productivity in the changing relations between ways of life and different kinds of writing. What constitutes each scene is a sort of emergent intensity—that is to say, the energy of what is coming together to construct something new, be it a "new man," a new sense of national identity, a new location for the intellectual, a new literary school, or new kinds of cultural tastes or configurations for the novelistic imagination. An imagined future unbeholden to the past was privileged in varied realms of activity—hence the investment in invention. The chapters tell stories about the different forms of invention that result from the dense interweaving of the material and the symbolic. With counted exceptions, there has not been a revision of the scholarship produced in the seventies and eighties about this foundational moment. I believe it is time to evaluate said scholarship, and to revise some of the assumptions that guided earlier interpretations.

It is the creativity and the instability of this period's experiments in writing and living that are among their most striking characteristics. The 1960s were less linear history than what Barthes refers to as "points" of history, moments of possibility that, while braided together, still retained their own particular textures. A decade of moments is a decade nonetheless: a time when the horizon of possibilities seemed to overpower, at least for a moment, the sphere of experience. The future in the present weighed more than the past in the present. To be sure, this balance shifted quickly, but later disillusionment has never completely obliterated the upsurge of cultural and political defiance that we know as the 1960s. If this book succeeds in illuminating points along the way in this extraordinary decade, then it will have reached its destination.

The Cuban Revolution and Che Guevara:
Between Memory and Utopia

Around the time when European thinkers—steeped in postwar melancholy—reflected on the impossibility of ending alienation, a group of youthful revolutionaries in Cuba renewed hope in the promises of utopia.[1] Their overthrow of the Batista regime in 1959 produced an intense dislocation unconstrained by the limits suffusing the political and philosophical mood of the time. Instead, the early years of the Cuban Revolution ushered in new configurations of radical practice and ideologies of transformation that occupied much of the social imaginary of Latin America in the sixties. The revolutionaries' boundless belief in possibilities, in the creative verve to fashion humanity and its culture, cannot be separated from the experience of newness and invention that characterizes the writing of the sixties in Latin America. In this respect, the new world and the old drifted apart in the decades following the Second World War.

To be sure, as Barthes noted, dislocation is the source of freedom;[2] together with the liberating effect of radical change, it also creates a powerful sense of beginning. Revolutions, as Hannah Arendt observed, "are the only events which place us directly, ineluctably, in front of the problem of beginnings."[3] The challenge of invention—so central to the literary energies of the "boom"—lies at the core of the first decade of the Cuban Revolution, before the strictures of institutionalization, geopolitical pressures, and domestic political control reduced its early creative impetus and replaced it with a disciplinary regime. With the sense of beginning comes a new sense of time: one that, as Marx claimed, "wrote off the past and created its substance out of the future." In revolutionary thinking, reaching this future requires a certain reworking of the past together with the fashioning of a new consciousness and a new language that herald a sense of novelty and voluntaristic planning. What Hannah Arendt observed with regard to the American and the French Revolutions holds true for the early years of the Cuban Revolution: "Only where the pathos of novelty is present and where novelty is connected with the idea of freedom are we entitled to speak of revolution."[4]

Arising from the utopian ethos of the early moments of the Cuban Revolution is an auratic value connected with the release of new political energies, infusing a spirit of vigorously creative—and even aesthetic—potential. The sense of revelation that impregnated the cultural production of the sixties, I would submit, must be read in conjunction with the inaugural impulses of the Revolution. It is less a matter of origin and causality than a productive conjunction that should be read in unison as a set of conditions of possibility contributing to the quality of interrelated experiences. The structure of feeling of the decade, committed to modernization and with its joy in being up to date, admitted the conviction that human energies could be channeled toward a rediscovery of authenticity, of a messianic potential that was secular and modern, yet touched by residual transcendence. The aura allowed for the apparent resolution of contradictions between the secular and the sacred, the traditional and the modern, the spontaneous and the planned, and the political and the aesthetic, operated by the liberating and constructive dislocation of revolution.[5] In fact, the intensity of the mutations in the early revolutionary days actually created articulations in a force field where politics, art, and the reinvention of humanity coalesced. Limits were blurred as myths of change and transformation flourished;[6] reoccupations of the social imaginary replaced earlier belief systems as ideologies of radical social transformation imposed their demands on the cultural field as well as, obviously, on the political one. The energies released by this process had a suturing effect that helped overcome the paradoxes and disjunctions between a commitment to anti-imperialist pronouncements on the one hand, and, on the other, an apparent renunciation of the historicity of Latin American reality. With respect to the latter, Chapter Six will elaborate the claim that a reading that is not arrested by the prima facie claims of magical realism can best account for the ways in which magical realism itself represents a particular—and formally inflected—engagement with history. In other words, magical realism and the fantastic will be seen as allegorical and aesthetic solutions to the condition of Latin American history, not as its disavowal.[7]

A question to ponder, then, is how to explain the far-reaching effect of the Cuban Revolution beyond its national boundaries in the early 1960s. Here again we are faced with a powerful convergence of heterogeneous factors, and a brief overview of them is in order. To begin with, the group of revolutionaries who, led by Fidel Castro, set sail on the Granma in November 1956, fashioned themselves as an exemplary community held together by strong horizontal bonds, led and united by a powerful leader. With a few exceptions,[8] this community was structured as a phallocratic brotherhood based on a spirit of egalitarian solidarity; the national community is imagined by the early writings of the revolutionaries as an extension of this fraternal one. Among them, it seems to me, can be detected homosocial bonds that negotiated the relationships of power and meaning in a subtle play of desire and identification. The libidinal energy released by political power, by the enterprises of liberation and soldiering (which, needless to say, involves killing), and by the will to transform society produced veiled sexualized social and political relations. In Chapter Five I shall argue that there are echoes of this homosocial energy among a few of the boom writers, as can be seen, for instance, in José Donoso's *Historia personal del "boom,"* which describes sanctioned literary partnerships among males.

It is in the fundamental notion of liberation that we find the ruling force in the structure of feeling that informs the decade. Its connotations indicate a qualitative shift distinguishing it from liberty and freedom—appropriated by the capitalist powers—while linking it with the discourse of decolonization of the time. The term *liberation* not only impugns imperialism: it also alludes to the transfiguration of independence movements by transpersonal and transnational forces that can overcome fragmentation by acts of collective will and solidarity. Moreover, liberation is collective; liberty is individual. As noted at the opening of this chapter, it is remarkable that at this time, important European thinkers such as Georg Lukacs (whose *History and Class Consciousness* appeared in French translation in 1960) and the members of the Frankfurt School were commenting on the effects of capitalism as marked by reification and fragmentation, by the loss of community and of an integrated vision. For Lukacs, only when a lonely mind managed to join another and imagine a common bond could some form of reconciliation be reached: the construction of a nonadversarial community was the only way out of the aporias produced by capitalist atomization. Hence, liberation in the sixties, as inflected by the thinking of what was then called the Third World,[9] takes on multiple valences—philosophical, political, personal, and aesthetic—folding into its semantic weave the power of the collective to operate the leap away from the individual. The representation of community in the early texts of the Cuban Revolution, as shall be discussed below, provides a matrix that strengthens its exemplarity.

The young men who surprised the world with their unlikely success in 1959 bore the stamp of exemplarity for another compelling reason: they were not trammeled by the purely utopian dream of revolutionary change or the merely negative critique of the intellectual left. They embraced action, took up arms, and took on the challenge of constructing anew at the personal, national, continental, and even universal levels. In the political climate of the 1950s, clouded by the grim, atrophied sense of despair that emanated from Stalin's rule, by the smashing of the Hungarian revolution, and by the uninspired consumerism of Eisenhower's Pax Americana, the astonishing victory of Fidel Castro's revolutionary effort turned the tables on anticipations of failure, renewing hopes for the left. If Hollywood can be an indicator of popular North American worldviews, one can detect a fascination with the southern border as provider of physicality and violence in films like Elia Kazan's *Viva Zapata* (1952), in which a dashing Marlon Brando takes up arms to defend his people from injustice, leading a utopian peasant insurgency, or the earlier *Treasure of the Sierra Madre* made by John Huston in 1948. No wonder in the early years of the Sierra Maestra exploits, Fidel Castro was photographed admiringly by magazines like *Life* and *Time* as if he were a very macho *caudillo*, riding on horseback and daring to go beyond merely playing the rebel.[10] A young freelance journalist found no better way to describe him than as "a combination of Robin Hood, George Washington and Gregory Peck."[11]

The discussion of the "new man" below is intended to chart how the impetus to invent was represented and, in some cases, mobilized into action. The overall effect up until the beginning of the seventies was the belief that there were ways in which the left could avoid the dead end of mere speculation and embrace praxis. The propulsive infusion of theory and militancy also permitted an affirmation of universalism as the culmination of self-liberation: the collective impetus of the Cuban socialist experiment of the 1960s offered a continental solution to the impasses of previous attempts.

This continental dimension can be summed up by a statement of Fidel Castro's claiming that the Andes were to be seen as the Sierra Maestra of the Continent. The new political consciousness soon spread over progressive sectors in Latin America, promoted by ideological forces and by a complex array of institutions designed not only to consolidate the Revolution within the Cuban nation, but also to exert its influence beyond its borders to the subcontinent and, beyond it, to the Third World. An emerging consciousness of transnational scope announced the possible end of alienation, dependency, and failure. This had to do not only with the transnational dimension inherent in the theorizing about Marxist revolution, and the expansive plans of the Castro regime, but also with the symbolic forces set in motion by the revolutionary moment, which issued a renewed sense of Latin Americanism.

While some scholars have claimed that, despite Batista's dictatorship, Cuba's social and economic situation did not seem to offer the most likely environment for a socialist revolution, the particularities of its historical experience favored a future-oriented and even utopian imaginary. Cuba's insular condition has deeply marked its sense of nationhood, creating what Lezama Lima called "una tradición por futuridad,"[12] bolstered by Cuba's lengthy colonial past, which fostered dreams of emancipatory redemption as well as what Albert O. Hirschman has described as "a rhetoric of intransigence."[13] The 1959 Revolution was able to portray itself as leading the nation to a long-awaited, messianic culmination. Rafael Rojas notes that Cuba's history can be seen as sharing some of the agonistic qualities of Greek tragedy, with the forces of good and evil drawn in a long struggle that the young revolutionaries inherited from earlier attempts at liberation in 1868, 1895, and 1940.[14] In January 1959, Fidel Castro announced, "The road has been long and hard, but we made it. This time the Revolution won't be stopped," claiming both a providential arrival and a heroic genealogy in which José Martí was to play a seminal role.

The powerful coexistence of a sense of ending and of beginning that Cuban history produced in response to the specificities of its own condition was to be appropriated and developed by the Latin American cultural imaginary of the sixties. The metafictional ending of *One Hundred Years of Solitude* can be associated with this Cuban teleology, for the end of a century of solitude is the precondition for a beginning that will erase the failed attempts of the past. As well as producing this concomitance of ends and beginnings, Cuba's extensive colonial past encouraged, Rojas argues, a perceived need for constant invention ab ovo, a kind of Adam-like impulse to be fleshed out in the *hombre nuevo* of Che Guevara's writings and Fidel Castro's speeches, but also, I would submit, in the daring imaginary of some of the boom's story-telling. The temporality thus engendered is founded in the periodic closure of cycles and the rearticulation of the symbolic inheritance in a series of ruptures with a forward-looking effect. One could, indeed, argue that "the Cuban condition" enabled not only its own revolutionary process in 1959, but also a kind of exemplarity whose efficacy can be detected in the political and cultural stance of the Latin American sixties.

If this argument can be made in terms of temporality, it bears development in the configuration of space as well. And here we turn to the meaning of insularity as both bounded and utopian (after all, Utopia is an island[15]), with a clearly articulated sense of its difference: in the minimal space of this Caribbean nation, other Latin Americans located not only a new stage in history, but also a site for the reconciliation of modernity's tensions between technical know-how and emancipatory values. Cuban territory could therefore be construed as a metaphor for origin and destiny; one might venture to see the permutation of this metaphor in the spatial configurations that obtain in many of the boom novels, but also in the decade's articulation of the Latin American difference. This reconfiguration of the categories of space and time appealed to a political unconscious that decried the alienating effects of capitalism and its focus on individualism, consumption, markets, money, and private property. For many intellectuals, the Cuban experiment in the early years of the decade represented an alternative route bearing the promise of community and redemptive integration while encouraging discursive experimentation and renewal. Here again we see the suturing effects of the coalescence of political and cultural renewal. They were to be short lived, however, for by the late 1960s the fissures carved by the *caso Padilla*,[16] Che Guevara's death, and the resolute adoption of the Soviet models had eroded the force fields.

In the mid-1950s Castro's uprising against Batista could be placed alongside a string of successful rebellions that had brought an end to notoriously brutal despots: Peru's Odría in 1956, Colombia's Rojas Pinilla in 1957, and Venezuela's Pérez Jiménez in 1958. And the coup that toppled Argentina's Perón in 1955 called itself "La Revolución Libertadora." It seemed

that the time had come for Cuba's Batista and for the Dominican Republic's Trujillo. Fighting against despots was seen not only as a just cause, but
also as the recognition that the Latin American moment was reaching its
historical culmination.

It hardly needs to be stated that the continental effects of the Cuban
Revolution did not entirely stem from generalized symbolic affinities that
Latin American intellectuals were prepared to assimilate. For there were,
also, institutional forms set up by the Castro government early on to foster
an inclusive, continental community whose political impetus would be furthered by cultural means. Central among them was the founding of *Casa de
las Américas* in April 1959, heir to a much earlier Sociedad Colombista
Panamericana that had planned the creation of a *Casa de las Américas* in
each one of the Latin American nations back in 1933, when it had celebrated
its seventh Conferencia Internacional Americana. Now in Cuba in 1959,
one of its founders, Haydée Santamaría, explained: "We think that an institution could be created that would be both Cuban and Latin American,"
and, indeed, its impetus confirmed its name: *Casa de las Américas* was to
constitute itself as a site for charting a renewed sense of continental identity
whose course was set by Cuban values.[17] It defined its genealogy within the
discourse of liberation, as part of the foundational enterprise of the Revolution. But it also meant to displace other "homes" for the intersection of culture and politics in Latin America: according to Antón Arrufat, its first director, it was conceived as an alternative to the powerful Fondo de Cultura
Económica of Mexico. It succeeded in gathering writers and in constructing a transnational audience by establishing an important Latin American
literary prize that bore its name, and whose jury and recipients included
Latin American as well as Cuban intellectuals. *Casa de las Américas* devoted
entire issues to various Latin American nations, emphasizing the cross-fertilization between culture and politics while celebrating newness in literature and, more specifically, in the novel.[18]

Two of the most persistent discursive strategies pursued by this journal are the definition of the role of intellectuals on the one hand, and, on
the other, the outline of the possibilities for revolutionary change to be set
in motion across Latin America. Regarding the former, there was a con-
sistent march toward the subordination of the artistic to the revolutionary cause, punctuated by Castro's famous speech, "Palabras a los intelectuales" of 1961, the Congreso Cultural de la Habana organized in 1968,
and the so-called Padilla affair, which became strident by 1971. The terms

of this subordination were articulated by Roberto Fernández Retamar when he took over the direction of *Casa de las Américas* from Antón Arrufat as of issue number 30 (1965), with a stronger emphasis on the discussion of political issues from Cuba, Latin America, the Third World (often referred to with the adjective *tricontinental*), and Europe. Of particular interest is number 45, of 1967, devoted to commemorate the October Revolution, with essays by eleven Latin American writers from ten different nations. Here we note a space in which diverse views coexisted within the spirit of solidarity for revolutionary aspirations. Even though the function of the intellectual was being restricted, it was still possible in 1967 for Cortázar to insist on the primacy of personal joy or suffering in the creative process, or for Vargas Llosa to locate the origins of artistic production in a writer's rebellious discomfort with the world he inhabits. Mario Benedetti could still proclaim the centrality of artistic freedom even as he contended, in a tellingly ambivalent gesture, that in Latin America the era of the pure, uncontaminated writer had come to an end. A year later, at the end of the Congreso Cultural de la Habana, the journal adopted a principle articulated by Regis Debray in an earlier, more radical piece of 1966 that was to set the tone for the years to come: "The secret to an intellectual's worth resides not in what he thinks, but in the relationship between what he thinks and what he does."[19]

Despite the progressive restrictions on intellectual freedom, *Casa de las Américas* represents a powerful field of force for the consolidation of a continental discourse affirming the importance of culture in the new political consciousness, and insisting on a new collective as a counterpoint to the individualism of particular writers and artists.

In language that tends to reanimate images of familial and fraternal kinship bonds among the Latin American nations, *Casa de las Américas* proclaimed the emergence of the new novel as if it were folded into a renewed mentality. Invoking Martí, the journal dwelled on the opposition between *nuestra* América and the enemy's to the north, mapping as its own the territory that extends from the Río Grande in the north to Patagonia in the south. And the stronger the North's opposition to Castro's regime, the more insistent the claims to continental identification: as early as 1962, when Cuba was excluded from the Organization of American States, *Casa* reasserted itself as the home in which the Latin American family could retrace its shared origins through language, cultural development, and—even more significantly—the search for justice and liberation. In this search lies the temporal impulse toward a utopian future: "If America exists, it is not the destroyed and superficial one we find each day, but the political one that has shown that utopia can become real" (1:2). The *nueva novela* was located within this home and given a genealogy that tended to exclude outsiders: its authors, whatever their nationalities, shared "our" America's concerns, in which the artistic and the political coalesced. A particularly revealing intermingling of influences and origins is plotted in the following remarks by Fernández Retamar in his study of Carlos Fuentes:

> For as different as Fuentes's novelistic style is, in some respects, from this latest work [*Rayuela (Hopscotch)*], this is his family, his expressive tone, especially that of Carpentier. Perhaps one could say that Fuentes' is the first significant product of Carpentier's style; curiously, this style has appeared in Mexico, not in Cuba: certainly an indicator of the transnational nature of our literature, in which Vallejo, Neruda, Borges, or Carpentier has a direct influence—even in idiomatic expressions—on the entire continent. (*128*)

This series of connections, outlined in 1964, is central to the intellectual energy of the boom writers. Its personal account can be read in José Donoso's *Historia personal del "boom"*; *Casa de las Américas* produces it as part of its own construction of an intellectual community whose task is to locate Cuba at the gravitational center of an expansive movement.[20] As the decade wears on, and the political inflections of the journal become the dominant ones, the spatial reach of this articulation is extended even beyond the allusion to Bolívar's dream: in an editorial of 1966 Fernández Retamar includes Asia and Africa in the "tricontinental" configuration of struggling peoples, anticipating Che Guevara's famous speech: "Only one historical project seems more beautiful to us than the old Bolivarian dream of continental unity: the new dream of tricontinental unity."[21] (34:3)

   The early *Casa* added to its integrative force by drawing into its *concejo de redacción* (editorial board) writers from near and afar: together with the Cuban members, we find such names as Julio Cortázar, Mario Vargas Llosa, Mario Benedetti, and Angel Rama, so that the very voices produce a continental choir.[22] As to the *Premio Casa de las Américas* and its continental reach, the Ecuadorian critic José Enrique Adoum summed up the effects of *Casa de las Américas* in the Latin American cultural imagination:

> *Casa*, a true fortress of culture housed in a sort of old temple of yesteryear, has been faithful to its vocation for forty years: if the Cuban Revolution—and since then, the perspective of our history since our separation from Europe—made it possible to begin to consider myself Latin American before Ecuadorian, *Casa*

reminded our forgetful selves that non-Hispanic literature from the Antilles and from Brazil were part of our Latin American archipelago, and showed us the superior power of culture in the face of threats to thinking: no blockade, no resentment of any power, no matter how tremendous, tenacious or vindictive, has succeeded in impeding the regularity and expansion of this contest, or the edition of prizewinning works, or even their diffusion in Latin America and the world.[23]

Che Guevara and the Construction of the "New Man"

In the complex process outlined above, Che Guevara played an emblematic role. One could make the perhaps startling case with Alma Guillermoprieto that Che was "the century's first Latin American."[24] If in Cuba he did not manage to shed what he himself called his *complejo de extranjero*, or foreigner complex, it was that very mixture of foreignness, transnational identity, and marked Argentinean idiosyncrasies that made Che so uniquely local and continental, as if his travels produced an identity that promoted integration with his own growing awareness of the political and economic alienation of Latin America.[25] His early letters showed the emergence of this consciousness: he will tell his mother as early as 1953 that he feels "American in a uniquely distinctive way." Like Martí (with whom he will be insistently compared), Che constructs an America that is deeply "nuestra," but he also goes beyond it to reach out to humanity. This way of shuttling from displacement in space to an all-encompassing concern for the collective spreads in concentric circles that begin with the solitary self. Here it is in a letter to his father: "A feeling of the collective in opposition to the personal has been developing inside of me. I am the same solitary person that I was before, searching for my way without personal help, but I now have a sense of my historical responsibility."[26]

The Che Guevara myth that grew upon his death cannot be merely attributed to self-fashioning, but rather, more important, to his becoming a model for experience and for living based on the compelling mixture of striking individualism and unconventional personal style on the one hand, with the will to collective integration on the other. What Che Guevara exemplified was metonymical of the manner in which the Cuban Revolution wished to represent itself, thereby offering a possible resolution to the sixties' growing sense of alienation and the disenchantment with "unidimensional" man decried by Herbert Marcuse and by his colleagues in the Frankfurt School. This also accounts for the immediate international appropriation of Che as myth immediately after his death, and his symbolic value in the Paris of May 1968, articulated in the following observation made by Jean-Michel Palmier in *Magazine Littéraire*: "Dead, everyone wanted to appropriate his reflection, to approach his shadow, to forever imprint in their memory the features of this corpse, with its wide open eyes, riddled with bullets."[27]

The spectral quality of the disembodied Che seemed to expand his presence and secrete a magical force that combined holiness with violence, austerity with celebration, effort with joy, fragility with power, unsullied heroism, and defeat. Not until 1997 were his remains found, so that the spectrality had the haunting effect of the disappeared, occupying a space infused with longing for a body that had been withheld but might one day be found.[28] As has been the case with other heroic figures, the absent body encouraged the myth of the eternal return.[29]

This is not the place to add to the already vast literature on the Che myth, except to comment on the exceptional effects of two photographs that contributed to it. The haunting, Christ-like qualities of the Freddy Alborta photograph taken after his death in Vallegrande has been perceptively analyzed by Jorge Castañeda, who has identified the disjunction between his captors' desire to proclaim and verify his death on the one hand, and their unwitting creation of an everlasting icon, both heroic and martyr-like.[30] Jean-Michel Palmier's observation quoted above deals precisely with the effect of this will to memory that had so deep an impact on the *imaginaire* of 1968. Equally powerful, but with different inflections, was a 1960 photograph taken by Alberto Díaz Gutiérrez (known as Korda, after the famous film director) at a ceremony to mourn eighty-one people killed by explosions in Havana harbor—a tragedy that was, according to Fidel Castro, the work of the CIA. Che's face may have expressed a mixture of anger and sadness at the event; it was captured by Korda's lens even though on that occasion there were distinguished foreign visitors—Jean-Paul Sartre and Simone de Beauvoir—whom he was intent on photographing. At the time, the photograph was not chosen by the government magazine *Revolución* that covered the rally; seven years later, in May or June 1967, Korda gave a print to the Italian publisher Giacomo Feltrinelli, who turned it into a poster after the news of Che's death was divulged. The photograph was to have an illustrious life in its extraordinary circulation, as can be seen in a twelve-minute documentary film made by Pedro Chaskel in 1982, and by a more recent one by Héctor Cruz Sandoval, first shown in 2004. In Cuba, Korda's photograph was enlarged to cover the entire facade of the Interior Ministry that faces the Plaza Revolución, where a mass rally was held when Che's death was publicly announced, on October 18. Later, it was appropriated by the young marchers of 1968 in such cities as Milan, Paris, London, and Mexico City. The process of "posterization" was suited to street rallies: the form contributed to their spirit of freedom and, at the same time, it had the boldness of design to express the widespread sense of discontent of the spirit of '68.[31]

The gravitational pull of the Che myth produced a space for the representation of fullness; it allowed the reordering of elements that existed in dislocated form in the social imaginary of the left. The force of integration contributes to the utopian impulse, suturing tensions and prefiguring an alternative society. It is a power derived not only from the magic of his face, but also from what was known about his character, his behavior, and the considerable body of writing he left behind. Che's face had the spontaneity and versatility of expression associated less with political figures than with actors. Asthma intensified the awareness of his body, marking it with fragility and willpower at the same time. His devastating asthma attacks play an ever-present role in the representation of a Che who had to overcome their crippling effects by dint of will, as if illness offered an opportunity for mastery through sacrifice, echoing Hegel's pronouncement: "We must bring to history the belief and conviction that the realm of the will is not at the mercy of contingency."[32] Self-sacrifice and determination were key to the production of self exemplified by Che, as central elements in the *hombre nuevo* to be created after the Revolution. This view of self-fashioning as a conscientious and continuous labor echoes the "saints" studied by Michael Walzer in his book about much earlier builders of humanity: the puritans of the English Revolution.[33] Like the Calvinists of the seventeenth century, Che came to represent a utopia in which radical politics was developed as a constant process of invention and experimentation, in which the pursuit of personal power was transformed into a collective enterprise by means of passionate effort, discipline, self-scrutiny, and industriousness. The radical politics thus produced was the creation of the saints-turned-revolutionaries: at one and the same time personal and impersonal, regulated by collective endeavors as an army of oppositional men whose primary task was the destruction of traditional order. Che epitomized the "new man" as the model the decade aspired to in its revolutionary inflection—as the subject whose self-definition rested on the politics of wrecking and building, hard at work on changing the world. If the saints of the Puritan revolution were inspired by religious zeal, Che was imbued with an emotion that was its secular equivalent: deeply idealistic, uncompromising, with a private passion for the collective. The frailty of his asthmatic body was transformed through discipline and sheer will into an idiosyncratic, self-made power whose aura has expanded into myth, where self-assurance can bring the end of alienation as a triumph of character formation. The emerging sensibility of the period found in Che a repertoire of forms through which a new masculine social identity could be worked out: less driven by the all-encompassing narratives of the American Century, less competitive, more defiant and hip, reluctant to identify adulthood with conventional grooming, career, or marriage.

In what follows, I will attempt to show that in the construction of the Che myth, his style, his behavior, and—more important—his writings, were all deployed toward an important aim of the early years of the Cuban Revolution: finding ways for the transition from individual passions, such as love, to the collective and social dimensions of the state. A new vision of community and the bonds that link it is negotiated by Che's model, one that supersedes the earlier paradigm that rested on the bourgeois family. Better suited to the mood of liberation of the sixties that infused the younger generation was his fervent espousal of a citizenry united by horizontal ties of equality and solidarity. Love was to be located in the spirit of *compañerismo* or camaraderie vividly described, embraced, and advocated in his writings and in his life. This configuration of the social allows for the fusion of the socialist ideals of the Revolution with a new political unconscious predicated on the notions of liberation and contestation—one that impelled the young to take to the streets in 1968. This "imagined community" is organized around a different kind of desire, no longer galvanized by the reproductive aims of the bourgeois family unit and its private values. It espouses the grammar of fraternity, apparently disavowing patriarchy while fostering the conditions for utopian growth. And yet, as we shall see, in its center is located the revolutionary leader and hero, Fidel Castro, who performs exacerbated masculine values in his relationship with the body politic.

How does Che (the construct derived from the myth and the writer) fashion this project for the "new man"? Speeches given at commemorative festivities, at factories, high schools and universities, peasant gatherings, and inaugural ceremonies construct a force field that attains an alchemical fusion of personal and collective, secular and religious. Che maps the terms for the definition of the "new man" in language appropriated from religion, his eyes set on the ideal revolutionary as he works out a new social pact. Notions such as self-sacrifice, discipline, and moral commitment underscore the sense that each individual is inventing himself (and, indeed, the masculine denotation is pervasive and telling) in order to construct both self and community. The result would be a completely new body politic founded on love, moral principles, and solidarity. In the relationship between the leader and the collective, exemplarity and guidance coexist with complete fusion, as if the one and the many were distinct and yet intertwined. Hence what emerges from these writings allows for the disavowal of the individual in favor of the collective, yet it is outlined as the result of a unique enterprise that can only be undertaken thanks to the idiosyncratic guidance of Che, pointing to Fidel Castro as the leader.[34]

The vocabulary that shapes the project is resolutely religious: it is steeped in love and the moral principles of the Judeo-Christian world. Che manages to preach even as he defies the "traditional" principles whose demolition he urges: he strikes a pose that is both rebellious and disciplinarian.[35] The particular inflections of his style enact a compelling self-confidence with admonitory force:

Any real man must feel on his own cheek the slap given to any other man's cheek.[36]

Economic socialism, without Communist morals, doesn't interest me. We fight against misery, but at the same time against alienation. . . . If Communism overlooks our conscience, it can be a method of distribution, but it no longer is a revolutionary moral.[37]

Either we are all redeemed, or we all sink.[38]

We must fight every day so that love for humanity transforms itself into concrete facts, into acts that serve as a model, as motivation. . . . All and each one of us punctually pays his quota of sacrifice, conscious of receiving the reward in the satisfaction of the finished deed.[39]

The gendered language of brotherhood creates community and erases difference: *hermanados* and *igualados* are terms that reoccur. The utopian impulse privileges a language of movement and marching not merely toward a better place, but significantly, to a superior form of humanity. Echoing Martí, Che repeats, "Let's march toward Cuba's future," but his teleology culminates less in the construction of a nation than in the nascent revolutionary, defined as "the highest step of the human species, [that] also allows us to graduate as men." The aim to be attained is *el reino de la libertad.* Joy is the pervading spirit: the leap that combines revolution with holiness produces a magic that figures the state and, beyond it, a superior condition that announces redemption. Here we come to the aporia that the efforts of critical theory as developed by the Frankfurt School never quite resolved, but whose way out was glimpsed by Walter Benjamin in his less secular moments: happiness as indissolubly bound up with images of redemption; freedom and reconciliation as utopian and possible only if our earthly existence is transformed into a superior form. Che seemed to suggest that these aspirations might be realized, and his death arrested the dream while creating the conditions of possibility for its perpetuation. Herbert Marcuse's hortatory *One-Dimensional Man* was to point in the same direction: "society will be rational and free to the extent to which it is organized, sustained and reproduced by an essentially new historical Subject."[40] That true goal would seem to lie beyond the limits of the state, to prefigure a new form of celebratory, masculine sociability in which voluntary work took on a festive air, much the same as it did among the Puritans studied by Michael Walzer.

How these powerful forces find their way into writing is a matter of considerable complexity. I have chosen one particular text that Che wrote—originally in serialized form—for the revolutionary journal *Verde Olivo,* later published in book form as *Pasajes de la guerra revolucionaria* and translated into English as *Reminiscences of the Cuban Revolutionary War,* with the eloquent interpretative adjustment that translation often provides.[41] It is of particular interest because it allows us to think about how utopian aims constitute an enabling form for narrative, and about how the belatedness of writing deals with the double bind between the future of utopia, on the one hand, and a past that is recovered through recollection and reminiscing, on the other. In reconstructing the steps of the revolutionary campaign that culminated in the overthrow of Batista, Che is working out a national narrative project: how to construct the future of a new Cuba in the telling of the past. The temporal complexity is in part the work of memory, but it is furthered by the scene of reading invoked by *Pasajes*: the reader in question is experiencing the new revolutionary society; he is being modeled by the text in his hand as he traces the origin of the nation to be reconstructed. Hence narrative structure and style are deployed to attain a bidirectional effect, as if in the to-and-fro, the back and forth, the past and the future were sutured together.

Of course, the suturing effect cannot obliterate a deep anxiety that hangs over the revolutionary movement—the fear of defeat. A look at the cultural landscape of the early sixties in Cuba reveals that the underside of exhilaration is a lurking sense of anxiety at the possibility of failure. Even as success is celebrated, the odds against it are never entirely neutralized. This is acutely evident in the periodical literature of the time, where the alternation between celebratory and cautionary articles is strikingly evident.[42] In fact, one could understand exhilaration as the giddiness of having managed to avoid defeat; the long history of revolutionary failures has always been a call to arms against the "the enemy." Facing such ever-present danger requires vigilance, and also writing, for even in the unthinkable face of failure, the production of revolutionary history will be a gift for future generations—a literary life insurance of sorts.[43]

Che's ostensible purpose as set down in the prologue is to help preserve the memory of the Revolution, protecting it from the ravages of oblivion, and addressing a question posed by the revolutionary leaders themselves—namely, "cómo hacer una historia de nuestra Revolución."[44] The effort of retrieval (what the Greeks called *anamnesis*, as opposed to the more spontaneous or passive *mneme*) is central to Che's writing, which we could describe as an ethos of remembering, marked by the concerted attempt to be self-critical and accurate:

The years pass, and the memory of the insurrection is dissolving in the past. We have not yet definitively set down these events, which already belong to the history of America. For this reason I am starting a series of personal reminiscences of attacks, battles, and skirmishes in which we all participated. It is not my intention that this fragmentary history, based on remembrances and a few hasty notes, should be taken as a full account. On the contrary, I hope that each theme will be developed by those who lived it.[45]

Hence this is presented as the beginning of a collective work to be executed by a community of memory workers. In the very writing, the project had a collective dimension: Che would begin by recording the first draft; then, when the typed version was produced by his secretary, he would not only rework it, using his diaries to achieve greater accuracy, but he would also review the text in meetings held at the Ministry of Industry with his old comrades-in-arms, who shared their own reminiscences to correct and discuss Che's.[46] The completed effort was to belong not only to the Cuban people, but to all of *América* (Martí's, of course), as befits the continental reach of the revolutionary movement.[47] Che claims to be taking only the first steps, issuing an invitation essential to the success of the project: "There are many survivors of this battle and each of them is encouraged to contribute his recollections so that the story may thus be filled out"[48] (30, *6*).

The ethos of remembering is not fulfilled until the tasks of recalling and writing are submitted to scrupulous self-criticism and editing: the author is to remove any word that may not be strictly true, or of which he may not be entirely certain. Thus the impulses to remember and to commemorate—central indeed to Che's *Pasajes*—to forge a brotherhood linked by a shared past, are scrutinized by a will to truth that is forward looking and vigilant. The writing is shot through with this productive tension between a longing to evoke, with feeling, and the inner call for reticence and self-censorship. In the interstices the reader may detect a passion whose traces have been withheld, but not altogether erased.

Memory as will and as the duty of the revolutionary community enacts, in an exacerbated way, Maurice Halbwachs's claim: "on ne se souvient jamais seul."[49] In fact, the project set down by the *Pasajes* plots the effort to construct collective memory as the passage towards collective identity, which would result in some measure from a gradual construction of memory blocks. The Janus-faced conjunction of past and future is bridged by the present of Che's writing as the site of victory, which produces intelligibility and guarantees meaning. From his own enunciative present in the Ministry of Industry, Che inhabits the double temporality of the act of recalling, evoking the presence of that which is absent in order to establish a number of distinctions around the notions of failure and success, loyalty and treason, strength and weakness, self and community, honesty and deceit, courage and cowardice, weakness and strength. His readers are to take his cue by paying tribute to the positive terms and characters, while giving the negative ones cautionary force. The manipulation that regulates the economy of tribute and condemnation is what Paul Ricoeur calls "instrumental memory": it is markedly ideological because it exists in the crossroads between the problematics of memory and the problematics of identity—in this instance, essentially political identity.[50] Thus, the teleology of victory informs this particular soldier's tale and wrests it from the ravages of chaos that tend to rule the stories of men at war.[51]

Precisely because Che's ideal reader is learning as he follows his tale, *Pasajes* is structured along the topoi of errors, becoming and beginnings. Since the victorious outcome is its very presupposition, it eschews the predictably epic tone and triumphalist rhetoric, replacing them with the rhythms of learning and transformation—better suited to narrative form, to the persona cultivated by Che, and to the mood of his youthful admirers, who were drawn to his informality and lack of pretense.[52] The opening *pasaje*, entitled "Alegría de Pío," is a case in point: it is built as an exemplary story in which the inventory of missteps is meticulously described, the better to avoid them in the future. Like schoolchildren who have yet to draw the unforgiving distinction between game-playing and war games, the eighty-two youthful rebels who disembarked on December 2, 1956, were soon to learn the dire consequences of inexperienced campaigning. Wearing ill-fitting boots, having lost their way at sea and on land, leaving traces that allowed the enemy to detect their whereabouts, lacking the judgment needed to tell friend from foe, they fell prey to an air raid that left many wounded—Che himself among them—and inflicted their first defeat. Time and again they were forced to confront their mistakes: a night spent at a house instead of hiding in the brush, cooking with the revealing traces of fire and smoke, all make for easy detection by the enemy.

The pedagogy of mistakes is but the reverse of the process of learning and transformation that leads to becoming a revolutionary army in this particular version of the bildungsroman. Che's narrative is punctuated by moments of evaluation that keep marking beginnings: this master plot is reenacted at every occasion when the rebels seem to be on the verge of becoming an army: at the end of the *pasaje* entitled "El refuerzo" (the eighth in the Ediciones Unión edition; "Reinforcements" in the English translation), just before one entitled "Adquiriendo el temple," Che concludes: "Our troop reached a new excellence" (90, *51*); much later in "El combate del Hombrito" ("The Battle of El Hombrito") the job is still to be done: "The men were still very green and we had to prepare them before they faced really difficult situations" (151, *115*); toward the end of the little book two rebels respond to the army's attack "con sus casi infantiles armas," and at the battle of "El Hombrito," narrated in the penultimate chapter, Che notes: "This battle proved to us how poorly prepared our troop was" (155,

118). He ends his memoir with an account of effective—though minor—accomplishments (*pequeñas hazañas*) that began to drive Batista's troops away from the Sierra Maestra, as if what constituted a desirable coda were the vision of a promising beginning, in which the rebels have become a fully fledged army and the process of learning that particular lesson has come to fruition. Thus, the significance of *Pasajes de la guerra revolucionaria* lies in the narration of learning from mistakes, which is at the center of Che's construction of the "new man": if this lesson is learned, the task of vigilant self-fashioning can begin again and again, much in the same way as each arrival of reinforcements enacts the pattern of transforming the newcomers into true revolutionaries. This scene of beginning can be illustrated in "El refuerzo," which deals with the addition of fifty new men: "We saw in the new troop all the defects that those who had landed on the Granma had had: lack of discipline, the inability to adjust to major difficulties, lack of decision, the incapacity to adapt to this life" (87, *58*).

A reading attune to literary echoes detects in Che's writing two quite different forms that work together to address questions of ethics. One of them—the picaresque—is inscribed in the rebellious register: it flouts normativity and opts for an irreverent contestation of the doxa. Conversely, the other one—the exemplum—invokes normativity in a didactic manner, making the story subservient to the lesson. This particular mix is perhaps the writerly version of Che's style: carefree and moralizing at one and the same time. It makes the text hover on an interestingly unstable edge that mitigates the heavy imprint of teaching. In the emplotment provided by the economy of mistakes and learning there are picaresque echoes infused with humor and a penchant for the ridiculous. Like the subject of picaresque novels, the young rebels sometimes resort to tricks when their own military callowness makes their wits more reliable than their soldiering. This lightens the narrative tone, and in the pleasure provided by humor the reader can catch a glimpse of the youthful spirit of camaraderie that blurred the boundary between living and dying, danger and fun, soldiering and playing. Early on, a brilliant ruse played by Fidel Castro on Chicho Osorio (an infamous *mayoral* or foreman who terrorizes the peasants on behalf of the local landowners), yields valuable information about the whereabouts of the army headquarters and the possible allegiances of the rural population. Che tells the story with obvious delight not only at Fidel's daring and inventiveness, but also at the process of astutely giving the unwitting Osorio his just desserts. Tricking and tripping up the enemy are narrated tongue in cheek, and the narrated encounter is not always lethal—as is the case with a captured soldier who never suspects that he is being fed the very horse he is intent on looking after.

Not always is the fun poked at the enemy, though: Che himself occasionally poses as a veritable *pícaro*, running away with unusual speed when his machine gun fails to work: "I don't really know how Israel came out of this alive. I only remember what I did under the shower of bullets from the soldier's Garant: I ran with a speed I have never again matched and turned the corner to reach the next street. There I put my Tommy gun back into firing order" (144, *112*).

On another occasion, Che's insouciance and playfulness almost cost him his life: wearing the helmet of a soldier in Batista's army as a victor's trophy, he becomes the target of friendly fire by Camilo Cienfuegos's vigilant shooting. Che is saved by Camilo's defective weapon; while a tragic outcome is averted, the incident reveals multiple shortcomings and offers an opportunity for self-ridicule and humor. Picaresque echoes are also present in the economy of scarcity that the rebels are subjected to. Lack of food and proper weapons is the focus of narrative concern; where food is concerned, Che sometimes depicts himself as a latter-day Lazarillo de Tormes, lovingly evoking the ingestion of four *butifarras* (sausages) as one of the greatest banquets of his life, or acknowledging that the most lamented aspect of a defector's departure was his absconding with a can of condensed milk and three sausages. For Che's readers in 1963, this regime of shortages—of making do and doing without—may have helped them negotiate experiences they were confronting in their daily lives.[53]

More powerful than the picaresque traces in the *Pasajes de la guerra revolucionaria* are the vestiges of an earlier narrative form that has been essential to the transmission of learning: the medieval exemplum. Interspersed in the reminiscences are numerous tales whose exemplarity lies in their presentation of a gallery of heroes and traitors through their actions, complete with codas that explicate and develop the interpretative and didactic value of the passage in question. The result is a veritable study of human potential, ranging from the model provided by heroes such as Frank País, to traitors such as Eutimio Guerra, Felipe Pazos, and Raúl Chibás. But Che's task is not simply hagiographic or demonizing: he is also sketching the embrace of community, for which it is important to offer a spectrum of acceptable forms of behavior and degrees of political commitment. This may help explain the proliferation of names and characters noted in this brief book: its original readers were to recognize them, having been provided with an inventory of those citizens whose role in the foundational effort had to be acknowledged. So together with the exemplary and the execrable, Che offers portraits of charming liars like the "Vaquerito"—who, despite their inability to distinguish truth from fiction, turn out to be courageous fighters—or of illiterate peasants like Julio Zenón Acosta—who, while mistaken in his conviction that reality could be anticipated in dreams, was an indefatigable fighter whose practical knowledge provided valuable help. When driven by fear, defectors may be treated with a certain humorous detachment, as if the frailties of the human condition might be taken into account in this forgiving community—provided treason and ulterior deceit were not at work. Che's pedagogic efforts try to include all those who might eventually join the Revolution's ongoing project, and so he commemorates even those who may not have stayed in the fold, confident that their example may have something to teach his readers. Referring to the *mayoral* David who once helped the rebels but might have left Cuba with his masters when their lands were confiscated by the Revolution, Che advances the following sermon:

The history of the Revolution is made up of many sincere efforts on the part of simple men. Our mission is to develop the goodness and nobility in each man, to convert *every* man into a revolutionary, from the Davids who did not understand well. . . . The Revolution was also made by blind and unrewarded sacrifices. Those of us who today see its accomplishments have the responsibility to remember those who fell by the wayside, and to work for a future where there will be fewer stragglers. (125, *90–91*)

Che's tribute to community relies on the proper name to recognize all those who participated in the early days of the struggle, as if in this list of acknowledgments his readers could identify the foundational citizenry. One can even imagine some of them looking for their own names in the text, verifying the signs of belonging and appreciation. Like Walter Benjamin's storyteller, Che the narrator evokes the intimacy of direct contact in the shared space of the *Pasajes*. The very ability to read is staged as proof of the merits of the Revolution, and he picks a few characters whose story he tells in the hope that the literacy campaigns will allow them to find themselves in this work of remembrance, as if he were sending them a gift, or a message in a bottle: "Popa must know how to read, and if he sees the magazine *Verde Olivo* he will remember that night when three sinister-looking rebels banged on the door of his *bohío*" (94, *56*).

It is, therefore, in the specific temporality produced by the writing of the *Pasajes* that memory and utopia are folded into each other: those who read the book in the sixties might be part of the *edificio revolucionario*; for outsiders following the "passage" from remembrance to commemoration, a sense of fulfillment together with the promise of the future could be experienced with the text. The original violence of the actual *guerra revolucionaria* might appear justified by the temporal folds contained in a text that is speaking to history about origins as well as paths to be followed.

Key to the utopian impulse derived from Che's personal style and writing is the model of humanity it proposes. In *Pasajes* one can detect a productive tension between the self constructed by the narrative voice, and the other observed and admired in the heroic figure of Fidel. The "I" who tells the stories is self-effacing and modest to a fault, reluctantly assuming the protagonist's role and careful not to indulge in emotional self-expression unless he is recording the frailty of his asthmatic body. The pursuit of exemplariness is embraced as modesty: this first-person narrator wants to resist the temptation to flaunt his subjectivity by becoming, instead, the voice and the witness of the collective: "These notes have attempted to give an idea of what the first part of our revolutionary struggle was like for all the men involved; if in this section, more than any other, I must refer to my personal participation, it is because it is connected to the later episodes and it was not possible to separate the two without losing the continuity of the narrative" (81, *42*).

The pursuit of truth is staged as what will validate Che's testimonial authority and act as an example of the righteousness and trust that are to be imitated. This is performed as the insistent gesture of a writing always concerned with the duty of memory retrieval in phrases such as *creo recordar,* which underscore the scrupulous evaluation of the authority of his own memory in its narrative reconstruction. It is, moreover, explicitly formulated as a practice that requires collective vigilance:

Out of curiosity I took note of all the enemy soldiers supposedly killed during the battle. There were more enemy corpses than there had been enemy soldiers. This kind of experience taught us that all facts *must* be validated by several persons. . . . Preoccupation with the truth was always a central theme in reports from the Rebel Army, and we attempted to imbue our men with a profound respect for truth. (119, *84*)

Despite the display of self-effacement and self-doubt—or perhaps due to its appeal—Che the narrator becomes as seductively intriguing as Che the myth, almost coyly allowing his readers to peek at moments of interiority that trace his progress toward the attainment of authority and the status of *Comandante*. One effective practice is the performance of weakness. Central to it is the representation of his body, which was to play such a crucial role in the construction of the myth. Che's stories often deal with the memory of suffering caused by asthma attacks that deter him from doing what his will craves, and so he becomes the character the reader is drawn to with feelings of sympathy and identification. These stories characterize the narrator more than do heroic ones, which are reserved for the *Ejército Revolucionario* as a whole or Fidel Castro individually. Where Che's own participation is concerned, the misery of asthma is represented not only as the body in pain, but also as what stops him from belonging. Time and again he lags behind because he cannot march as fast as the others; in addition, he burdens whomever stays with him with the weight of the equipment he cannot carry:

Everybody was able to reach the peak easily, and go over it; but for me it was a tremendous job. I made it to the top, but with such an asthma attack that, for all practical purposes, to take one more step would have been impossible. I remember how much Crespo helped me when I could not go any further and begged to be left behind. In the usual way of speaking of our troops he said to me: "You— Argentine! You'll walk or I'll hit you with my rifle butt!" (83, *45*)

This passage reveals the double condition of estrangement that Che narrates: that of the frail fighter, and that of the foreigner or "argentino de mierda" (to complete the phrase without Che's sense of decorum) contained in his nickname, in what he himself calls elsewhere his *complejo de extranjero*. Asthma is also a mark of loss and, paradoxically, of distinction. Because it stops him from performing as a soldier, he is forced to give up his treasured machine gun, and he experiences some of the bitterest moments of his revolutionary days; it also is the reason for his being awarded the best kind of hammock a rebel could have before he had actually earned one, for Fidel breaks the rules so that Che can be spared the use of the allergy-inducing *hamaca de saco* (cloth hammock). The instability between gain and loss, belonging and alienation is characteristic of Che's self-presentation in the *Pasajes*: in the interstices between strength and weakness might lie the appeal of the kind of masculinity he represents, less epic in its actual achievements than in the nobility of his efforts and the longing to reach them.

The sense of frustrated desire produces a certain instability that constantly hovers between attempting and achieving, failing and succeeding, doctoring and soldiering. When he allows himself the role of protagonist, Che seems to prefer to tell stories in which he fumbles his way out of trouble, running away from situations in which he could well have portrayed himself heroically: "my participation in the battle had been minimal and not in the least heroic (since I had turned my back to the few shots I encountered)" (146, *114*), or in which he misjudges situations, barely averting serious consequences, as he does by suggesting to Fidel a mistaken course of action when the revolutionaries are about to embark on the Battle of El Uvero, or failing to exert his authority with Jorge Sotús, whose treachery was to be discovered later on. As will be discussed below, the staging of mistakes fulfills two connected purposes: on the one hand, it performs the learning process; on the other, it highlights Fidel's aura of infallibility and contributes to the construction of the hero.

The narrative voice in the *Pasajes*, modest and self-effacing in its presentation and in its actual telling, eschews fixity and completion even in the construction of its own identity. The book itself is focused on becoming: the inexperienced rebels of the Granma become the *Ejército Revolucionario del Pueblo*; the population is gradually undergoing ideological transformation; Che is moving from troop doctor to *Comandante*. The developmental nature of identities underscores the liminal position and evokes the linearity of the bildungsroman. Che joins the Granma group as its doctor, and he elaborates the significance of moments when he has to choose between one condition and the other. Although the force of events will demand that he occasionally perform medical duties, the narrative values soldiering as a higher condition. The difference is emblematically enacted in one of the earliest scenes, where Che's choice is staged. Upon their disastrous disembarkment at Alegría de Pío, as the rebels face *un huracán de balas*, Che is evoking their dismayed confusion with sure-footed literary aplomb as his memory reconstructs scenes "a veces dantescas y a veces grotescas" (*10*), offering the following insight into a personal epiphany of sorts: "This was perhaps the first time I was faced with the dilemma of choosing between my dedication to medicine and my duty as a revolutionary soldier. At my feet were a pack full of medicines and a cartridge box; together they were too heavy to carry. I chose the cartridge box, leaving behind the medicine pack, and crossed the clearing that separated me from the cane field" (44, *9*).

The choice seems motivated less by the pressing medical needs of the encounter with the enemy, than by the teleology of the story itself. Che is penning a narrative reconstruction in which the self is a metonymy for the collective, and the shared path is determined by the shared goal. For Che, the goal is attained when, toward the end of the book, Fidel very casually promotes him to *Comandante*. The rebels are signing a congratulatory letter they have all written to Frank País: "The letter was signed in two columns, the second being for rank. When my turn came, Fidel ordered simply: 'Put down *Major.*' In this informal and almost oblique manner I became major of the Second Column of the Guerrilla Army, which would later be called the Fourth Column" (138, *105*).

Despite the greater value attributed to fighting, Che's double-voiced narration as doctor and soldier offers a plurality of perspectives: the clinical inflections of his vocabulary allow him to describe killing and dying with the distancing provided by scientific knowledge; the health problems he diagnoses as he attends to the peasants' debilitated bodies provide further proof of the pressing need for radical change in Cuba. When circumstances press him into service as a dentist, he characteristically turns this into an opportunity to poke fun at himself by staging the comic stereotype of the *sacamuelas* (ill-trained dentist). Perhaps more important, the healer's voice offers the register in which the narrator uncharacteristically allows his emotions to reach the page. One memorable instance in which the economy of restraint in the representation of battles contrasts with the intimacy of affection is in *El Combate de El Uvero,* when Che takes up the duties of a physician and tries to help *compañero* Cilleros, who has been mortally wounded. Forced to leave him behind under the care of the enemy's doctor, the deeply moved Che acknowledges: "I was tempted at that moment to place a farewell kiss on his forehead"[54] (118, *83*).

The temptation is kept in check, and the fraternal kiss is never given, but it is emblematic of the embrace of eros and polis that keeps the rebels united in a libidinal attachment rooted in a shared experience of pain and a shared belief in the future. And while Che goes out of his way to name the women who have made heroic contributions to the Revolution,[55] this foundational community is essentially phallocratic. Women were eventually allowed into guerrilla camps to perform tasks traditionally allotted to women, such as washing clothes and preparing meals, but Che himself was aware of the low esteem in which they were held.[56]

But the horizontal bonds of this "collective singular," as Reinhard Koselleck calls this kind of community, can figure the state only if the dynamics of egalitarian solidarity is organized around a higher authority. This, of course, is Fidel Castro, the leader whose representation occupies the space carved out by Che: wherever he has noted a lack derived from physical frailty or military ineptitude, poor strategic thinking or faulty judgment, Che has filled it with a totalizing presence—the leader—whose strength rests on features wanting in others. Furthering the heroic representation of Fidel is a framing based on distance that connotes infallibility. If Che can be construed as a possible model for an emerging kind of masculinity, inviting identification through the acknowledgment of weakness and the compensatory effort that accompanies it, Fidel can be seen instead as the emblem of a certain hypermasculinity performed as infallible leadership. The construction of the foundational community rests on the aura of his presence: the horizontal bonds constitute the base of a pyramid that he rules from above, charting its impulses and its path. Fidel is constructed as hero and leader through a meticulous narrative syntax in which he is the agent of verbs that denote ordering, leading, deciding, pronouncing. His infallible judgment provides a principle of organization and the guarantee of order. In Che's writing, Fidel suggests the plenitude of the origin: "Fidel" is indeed the unmistakable forename; the surname "Castro" is unnecessary in a community that has him at its center, and hence it is pronounced only by the enemy.[57]

Such is the power of Fidel's persona in *Pasajes* that there is a barely veiled fear of loss in the text, as if his aura rested on a certain magic sustained by anxiety. One of the most dramatically narrated events in the book is the night spent by Fidel next to Eutimio Guerra, the traitor whose mission it was to kill him. The story itself offers an instance of the homosocial nature of the power relations that rule the group: Eutimio Guerra, the traitor, goes to Fidel asking for a blanket; Fidel suggests that they share the blanket so as to maximize the heat: "Fidel answered that both of them would be cold if he gave Eutimio his blanket. He suggested that they sleep under the same blanket and Fidel's two coats. So Eutimio Guerra spent the whole night next to Fidel; he had on him a .45 pistol with which to kill Fidel" (72, 32).

In the heat offered by the hero, the murderous act is stopped: the magic of Fidel kindles the libidinal political energy that sustains the revolutionary community and helps prevent danger. As for Eutimio Guerra, his treacherous embrace echoes Judas's kiss, and his execution later on is narrated in religious terms that underscore the dramatic connotations of the event. Not only does Eutimio fall on his knees and ask to be executed, but the natural world puts on its own son et lumière to heighten the significance of the act of justice. Thunder and lightning produce deafening sound and dazzling illumination just when the shots end Eutimio's life, as if nature joined forces with the Revolution, on the side of the just. The execution is not without its redemptive potential: Eutimio's dying wish was that his children would be looked after by the Revolution and, indeed, Che devotes a lengthy passage to a reflection on the better life his children have led, stripped of the shameful name associated with their father and educated in one of the many schools founded by the Revolution. In the economy of Che's *Pasajes* not even treason is a complete loss, for the Revolution knows how to straighten the crooked timber of humanity. Yet it all requires Fidel's presence, which regulates the narrative organization as that which provides troop morale when difficulties multiply, and as a gravitational center toward which the numerous reunions converge.

Fidel is constructed in Che's writing as the ultimate authority who regulates desire in social exchange. When he is not around, Che finds it hard to keep up troop morale, because it depends, as he puts it, on "direct contact with the Leader of the Revolution." There is an indisputably libidinal representation of Fidel's *contacto directo* with the people; his political power is sexualized in terms that make him not only the repository of superior male humanness, but also capable of inspiring intensity of feeling that reverberates through the body politic. Striking for its eloquence in this regard is a well-known text that Che wrote for the Uruguayan weekly *Marcha*: "Fidel and the masses pulse in an increasingly intense dialogue until they reach their climax in an abrupt finale, crowned by our cry for battle and victory."[58]

Could there be a more explicit orgasmic embrace in Fidel's rapturous bonding with the crowd? The passage not only bespeaks the indisputable sexuality of power, but it also signals Che's need to carve out a space in his writing for the erection of the supermasculine hero in a discourse with coital resonances. It is as if the unspoken pact that made the writing of

Pasajes possible involved a subtraction of Che's authority, the better to add to Fidel's power. The result is that Fidel takes on the fullness of presence, and his gravitational pull draws in not only the revolutionary brotherhood and then the new Cuban nation, but also the pulse of Che's writing, which beats to a tune focused on Fidel's movements and directions even as it narrates Che's memoirs. His subtly deliberate undermining of his own authority for the sake of underscoring Fidel's is amusingly encapsulated in an anecdote conveyed with obvious delight by Guillermo Cabrera Infante:

The late comandante Duque used to tell a story of a shooting match in Sierra Maestra that he witnessed. Castro and Guevara were engaged in a war against general tedium doing practice against some dangerous empty beer bottles. Castro was hitting all the bottles but Guevara hit none. Later Duque asked Guevara, who was a sharpshooter famous all over the sierra, "Why, Che, you could do better than that!" Guevara answered with a sneer and a true confession: "You want me to make our leader lose face? You should know better than that!"[59]

A Lacanian reading of this little anecdote would see it enacting the confluence of the Imaginary and the Symbolic: the one as the self that obeys the Law of the Father, postpones satisfaction, represses desire (the civilized subject who deliberately misses as he shoots); the other glimpsed in the telling gesture of missing all the time, and in the revelation made in answer to Duque's question. But only if the Law of the Father is proclaimed can the story be told: this bespeaks the silent pact that seems to undergird the writing of the *Pasajes de la guerra revolucionaria*.[60]

The Tribute of Rewriting

Che's writing had the power of sheer historical momentum and forward movement that followed the birth of revolution and the ensuing construction of a new order. Che was offering his curious readers a view into the inner workings of guerrilla warfare, and into the aspirations of those who waged it. And yet—as if *Pasajes* stood in need of rewriting—a short story by Julio Cortázar would seem to make the claim that only artistic reworking can completely convey the significance of Che's writing. "Reunión," published in *Todos los fuegos el fuego* (1966) is a tribute to Che that—ironically enough—suggests that there was a lot left unsaid in Che's own writing. Both paying homage and cannibalizing, Cortázar's writing adds aesthetic value while at the same time, and perhaps less ostensibly, borrowing from Che's writing to engage with levels of experience unknown to him. "Reunión" itself as a short story has not received the critical attention given to others in *Todos los fuegos el fuego*, but it is highly revealing of the complex relationships between art and experience, literature and revolution, history and fiction.[61] Further, it is an early instance of Cortázar's long-standing concern with the thorny question of his revolutionary commitment as a writer.

Cortázar was one of the Latin American intellectuals most intensely transformed by the Cuban Revolution. As a recent biographer has pointed out, it constituted a "fundamental hinge" in his life, the cause of profound changes in worldviews and in his own conception of Latin American history.[62] His allegiance to the Castro regime was so abiding that at times it seemed to bespeak an anxious desire to remain in the fold and not to stray from the official party line: numerous letters sent to Roberto Fernández Retamar, Antón Arrufat, and Haydée Santamaría attest to his solicitous solidarity. Hence he constitutes a paradigmatic case of the intersection between the aesthetic and the worldly in a writer who struggled to articulate codes of intellectual and moral behavior that allowed for responsibility in the midst of artistic freedom. The tensions of this negotiation are addressed in Chapter Three, devoted to Cortázar.

That Cortázar's first trip to Cuba in 1961 was a defining moment in his life has been made amply clear by various declarations he made over the years. In a 1970 conversation with Francisco Urondo, he explained the effects of the trip in terms that echo his writing about the fantastic:

So, when the Cubans invited me to go as a jury member for the *Casa de Las Américas* award, I remember quite well the impression it had on me. It is curious (once again I must invoke the poetic dimension): I had the feeling they were knocking at my door, a certain sort of call. . . . I felt in some irrational way that this was a sort of encounter, a sort of date . . . with something in the dark.[63]

As noted earlier, *Casa de las Américas* played an important role in bringing together intellectuals from different parts of the continent, and in Cortázar's case the journal remained as a point of contact and as a way of engaging in the debates about the relationship between literature and the Revolution. Cortázar's loyalty was so anxiously scrupulous that in 1966 he turned down Emir Rodríguez Monegal's insistent invitations to publish in *Mundo Nuevo* when it became clear to him that Roberto Fernández Retamar resolutely rejected the journal on the grounds that it had U.S. financial support;[64] in 1970 he refused to participate in the creation of *Libre*, a journal to be published in Paris—originally the brainchild of Octavio Paz—if Guillermo Cabrera Infante (an early opponent of the Castro regime living in London) was invited to participate. His "Policrítica a la hora de los chacales" (published by *Casa de las Américas*) could be seen as Cortázar's anxious statement of support after the tense exchanges between the Revolutionary government and the intellectuals over the Padilla affair.

"Me he enfermado incurablemente de Cuba," he wrote in a letter to Antón Arrufat in 1963, and that disease was experienced as Cortázar's estrangement with his own surroundings as well as with his contribution to the revolutionary cause: "Ever since we returned from Cuba I have been assaulted by enormous bouts of the unreal; that was too real, too warm, too intense, and Europe all of a sudden seems like a crystal cube, and I am inside of it, painfully moving around, searching for less geometrical air and less Cartesian people."[65]

His *dépaysement* is, of course, more than geographical: it has to do with a longing for a fulsome life, for that quality of experience that the intellectuals of the left like Cortázar achieved only vicariously, through writing and the imagination. Cuba was hot and intense because it was ignited by the powerful combination of arms and letters, of planning and doing. Like Bruno in "El perseguidor," or the meticulous critic in "Los pasos en las huellas," Cortázar is drawn to the vitality of an experience that writing can only approximate or plunder.

Given the emotional power of this attachment, it is not surprising that Cortázar should have put his pen to the service of the Revolution, and there are many pages that attest to the fervor of his commitment. "Reunión" gives this reader pause, though, not because the sincerity of the tribute should be called into question—a slippery matter anyway for literary and critical studies—but because of the assumption that the supplementarity of Cortázar's text itself constitutes the tribute, as if Che's were not quite enough. Resting on the very belatedness of his own writing to return to Che's, Cortázar works on the principle of addition to elaborate, increase, and adorn—while, as was observed above, Che works on the basis of implacable subtraction. Cortázar's platform is Che's own remembrance of a literary text in the face of death, which Cortázar locates in the epigraph to "Reunión," as if in Che's invocation of Jack London's story lay the authority to write his own. Thus the word *cuento* in the epigraph acts as a passageway into the literary sphere, as a safe-conduct into the world of the Sierra Maestra rebels: if Che turns to the models provided by fiction to learn how to die with dignity, why not put the tools of fiction to further use?

In the effort to amplify, the narrative voice undergoes a fundamental transformation: Che's self-conscious laconism is replaced by an expansive first-person narrator who gives vent to the frustrations derived from the difficulties of the ill-planned Granma voyage, the miserable seasickness, the asthma, and the generalized discomfort. In fact, the story opens with a complaining narrative voice: phrases like *Nada podía andar peor* (Things couldn't be worse), *maldita lancha* (damn yacht), *hechos un asco* (filthy dirty), *asma del demonio* (infernal asthma attack), and *y yo como un idiota* (and me like an idiot) seem to want to say what Che never wrote in his memoir, and therefore radically change the narrative tone: interiority conveys the frustration and exhaustion that Che's own *Pasajes* temper with exemplary stoicism. But there is another register in the fictionalized Che, one that seems to be the festive counterpart of the voice of frustration, and which is characterized by playfulness and laughter. In the midst of the ordeal, Cortázar's Che is beset by *ataques de risa* (peals of irresistible laughter), he laughs *hasta herniarse* (until it hurts), and, when he is finally reunited with Fidel, the greeting is an exchange of jokes followed by laughter. Here is Cortázar's celebration of youthful joy and insouciance, mixed with a longing for innocence, so often expressed in his prose with a carefully wrought footloose air, and detected with admiration during his visits to Cuba. Writing to Paul Blackburn in 1963, he expressed it as inherent to the Cuban condition: "Cubans . . . are in many respects like children: they play, they laugh, they sing while working, they dance. . . . The nation itself has a feeling of happiness and safety that mesmerized me."[66]

Rewriting here goes hand in hand with the expansion of the emotional register, as if the license of fiction allowed for a peek at the inner feelings of the hero, at the frustrations and the joys mostly silenced in the laconic, stoic "we" of Che's narrative voice.

One fascinating index of what has been called "the distinction of fiction"[67] is its ability to supplement by the addition of formal and semantic complexity. Cortázar's reworking of Che's *Pasajes* is fertilized by a deep reading of the carriers of meaning in the original text, which are in turn recodified in the short story with the use of aesthetic devices. Aníbal González's study looks into the workings of allegory in "Reunión," convincingly analyzing the manipulation of numbers to add to the significance of the allusion to Mozart's quartet in pointing to a cosmic order, described in the story as "the new, apocalyptic order produced by the Revolution."[68] And, as I will add below, this desire for significance writ large, in cosmic terms, is one of the impulses animating the story. But aside from the allegorical weight of the numerical indices, "Reunión" has succeeded in identifying through its title and its narrative syntax, one of the anxieties with which *Pasajes* . . . is riddled: the fear of losing Fidel, or of not finding him in the maze of the Sierra Maestra—that essentially menacing Latin American terrain where the anxiety of loss is symbolic as well as concretely geographic. This is the fear that structures the story and that allows Cortázar to gather in one single, emblematic *reunión* a number of different ones referred to in Che's text. The joy of the final meeting provides the "sense of an ending" that comes from overcoming the foreboding developed as the story traces Che's interior monologue. By means of condensation, Cortázar can intensify the significance of the search for Fidel and hence his centrality to the Revolutionary enterprise. If Che Guevara subtracts from the centrality of his own achievements to highlight Fidel's, always circling around the fear of losing him, Cortázar's character resolutely locates the pervading dread of Luis's (Fidel's fictionalized name) death in the very center of the narrative machine: "Nobody mentioned Luis, the fear that they had killed him was the only real enemy, because its confirmation would nullify us more than the pursuit, the lack of weapons, or our blistered feet."[69]

But there is more: together with this fear of Luis/Fidel's death, Cortázar adds a resolute association with the image of god as *pantocrátor*, alluding to the representation of Christ in the Final Judgment. Fidel as judge and model urges his men to follow him and, even more significantly, to be like him, in a passage that is redolent with Old and New Testament allusions: he is the judge as *pantocrátor*, but also, like Moses at the Red Sea, he parts the land from the water: "separa las tierras de las aguas." The additive impulse in the work of rewriting reaches here a certain hyperbolic quality that evokes Freud's observations about the function of the image of God in unresolved libidinal attachments. The text is as haunted by the fear of Fidel's death as by his godlike presence. Given his unique status as leader, judge, and *pantocrátor*, the representation of Fidel can be read as echoing Freud's claim that monotheism is the first religion to recognize the father behind the image of God, and—perhaps more provocatively—that that very image allows for the expression of homoerotic attachments to the father that otherwise must be repressed.[70] Without turning the question of social change into an unresolved Oedipus complex (which would have the unfortunate effect of flattening the complexity of the issues the text is grappling with), it is important to come to terms with Cortázar's choice of symbolic forms to complete and elaborate what Che had already written. By inserting the image of God, Cortázar could be translating Che's *ur-text* and providing a context for radically interpreting its libidinal energy: Fidel is godlike as "the signifier of signifiers," phallic and dominant as the ultimate generative source of all meaning.

This might also provide a clue for the fear of Fidel's death: the *deus absconditus* evokes not only a libidinal deadlock, but also the complexities of the death drives embedded in the Oedipal knot. "Reunión" grapples with this source of instability by once again turning to fiction to suggest what cannot be altogether spelled out. Cortázar's Che has what he uneasily calls "a sort of vision" in which Fidel, surrounded by his closest aides, slowly moved his hand toward his face and removed it as if it were a mask. The vision is unsettling in its symbolic idiom:

[Luis] slowly raised his hand to his face and took it off as if it were a mask. With his face in his hand he approached his brother Pablo, myself, the Lieutenant, Roque, asking us with a gesture to accept it, to put it on. But they all refused one by one, and I also refused, smiling myself to tears, and then Luis put his face on again and I saw in him an infinite weariness as he shrugged his shoulders. . . . We would all try to get up there, but none with Luis' face. "The Diadochi," I thought, already half-asleep. "But it all went to pot with the Diadochi, everybody knows that." (52, *66–67*)

Why a mask, we wonder. Is it that even if Fidel's death called for a successor, he would be accepted only if he bore the leader's face, erasing his own and taking on the only emblem of leadership? Or might Fidel's face itself be a mask, one that could be removed and transplanted? In the undecidability of this vision we might locate the ambivalence produced by the drive to proclaim Fidel's triumphant supremacy as it runs into the possibility of a spectral, elusive pseudo-materiality. A reading pliant to Cortázar's expressed admiration for the Cuban Revolution would be drawn to the representation of Fidel's irreplaceable leadership, but perhaps we could detect a slippage in the all-powerful image of Fidel. In his desire to heighten the expressive power of Che's text, Cortázar may have created a vision with a mask that might contain the secret of the supplementarity of his own text: that, as Žižek claims—in discussing precisely the question of ideology—"there is no reality without the spectre, that the circle of reality can be closed only by means of an uncanny spectral supplement."[71] Reminding us with Lacan that the elevation to the status of symbolic authority has to be paid for by the death of its empirical bearer, Žižek may help us understand the complex and unstable semantic layering of the godlike elevation of Fidel and the concomitant spectrality of his masklike face.

As the fictional Che falls asleep, the question of Fidel's replacement or successor is linked to the four Macedonian generals who divided up Alexander the Great's empire upon his death—the ill-fated Diáconos. Here again, Cortázar works on the principle of aggrandizement, suggesting a parallel with the greatest leader of antiquity by focusing on the question of replacement. The literariness of "Reunión" ends up affirming not only the double bind between the Diáconos's unspeakable desire to replace the leader (and the sublimation of this drive, posited by Freud in *Totem and Taboo*), but also the more unsettling possibility that there is no way in which symbolization, like a mask that does not quite fit, can ever succeed in "fully 'covering' the real," as Žižek notes. Hence the short story is saddled with fields of conflicting force whose regulation cannot quite be achieved. It reads as an exorbitant gesture, as telling excess: the work of rewriting may end up saying more than it originally bargained for.

In the bargain, of course, Cortázar was longing to find an impossible resolution: by borrowing Che's voice and enlarging it, he was hoping to find the language of redemption. Cannibalizing Che, he tried to find the way out of the unresolved antagonisms that the sixties grappled with, and so he allowed himself to write in a messianic vein shot through with longings of transcendence. Striving to reach the register of the beautiful, he invites his reader to follow the story with the harmonious sounds of a Mozart quartet, while the heightened literariness of his prose etches a perfect design of foliage against the early morning sky. The final paragraph is unrestrained in its vision of redemption and, once again, cannot forego intimations of the sacred. Cortázar's Che is led back into the realm of the aesthetic as he daydreams about musical resolutions of visual designs. To close with perfection, he locates a star in the very center of this drawing. He has it shining in the adagio, but he dares to acknowledge that his narrator does not know whether it is a star or a planet. The dazzling blindness induced by its otherworldly light is meant to connote its redemptive power; a less reassuring reading would prefer to focus on its uncanny status as mask or chimera.

In a short and highly emotional piece he wrote for *Casa de las Américas* to commemorate Che's death, Cortázar returns to the complex relationships that obtain in a borrowing that doubles as tribute:

I ask for the impossible, the most undeserved, what I dared to do one time while he was alive: I ask that it be his voice that surges here, that it be his hand that writes these lines. . . . So use my hand one more time, my brother, nothing will have come of their having cut off your hands. . . . Take the pen, write: what I have left to say and do I will say and do with you forever by my side.[72]

Like Neruda addressing the dead Incas at Machu Picchu, Cortázar claims that his voice and his hand can continue Che's work. With stunning self-assuredness, he affirms he can obliterate death ("de nada les habrá valido cortarte las manos"), but he begins with an invocation and a request ("pido que sea su voz la que se asome aquí, que sea su mano la que escriba estas líneas"). Alluding to the brutal act of cutting Che's hands committed by his killers in 1967, Cortázar ends up engaging in an odd exchange of body parts: he takes Che's voice and hands, and then makes his own do the work of speaking and writing. Who is the ghost, one wonders—the revolutionary leader or the intellectual? In this double bind between affirming and requesting, between proclaiming power and asking permission, lies an explanation for the unsettling effect of "Reunión." It needs Che's voice and hand to justify its existence, but it also affirms the authority of the intellectual as the one who can complete the unfinished job. This tension may lie at the center of the text, like the unidentified star at the center of the adagio. On the one hand, the writerly accumulation proclaims a lack in the original—as if it could be remedied by a "literary fix." On the other hand, the writer longs for the "real thing" as he strives to overcome the impossibility of ontological recuperation that saddles the work of art. In more personal terms: is Cortázar revealing to his readers Che's religious recoding of Marx's teleology, or is he using Che to translate and adorn his own conversion into the revolutionary struggle? Is the fusion a tribute, or does the language of the gift conceal a benign form of cannibalism?

In his famous polemic with Oscar Collazos, Cortázar proclaimed the need for "more Che Guevaras of literature," thus justifying his own choice of literary experimentation and freedom of the imagination. In becoming that "literary Che Guevara" he underwent the transformation he himself described as a calling, a meeting in the dark: "una especie de llamada, . . . una especie de encuentro, una especie de cita, una especie de cita en la oscuridad con algo" (a kind of call, a kind of meeting, a kind of date in the dark)[73] he explained, as he grappled with the difficulties of expressing religious or mystical experience. "Reunión" was written in the spirit of this kind of experience, in the hope of achieving utopia and transcendence: hence the revelation at its end, and the distant star, with its own version of the music of the spheres. Cortázar reminds us of one of the many comparisons Adorno proposed in order to get at the status of art in the modern world. In his discussion of art beauty in *Aesthetic Theory*, he likens the phenomenon of artworks to fireworks, because they appear as "a sign from heaven, . . . an ominous warning, a script that flashes up, vanishes, and indeed cannot be read for its meaning. . . . It is not through a higher perfection that artworks separate from the fallibly existent but rather by becoming actual, like fireworks, incandescently in an expressive appearance."[74] The spectrality of the distant star may announce the radical impossibility of that totalizing moment, but the power of art as epiphany, as apparition, as heavenly vision, was a weapon against alienation even for the disenchanted theorists of the Frankfurt School.

The light completely disappeared in later stories that also grapple with the intersection of literature and politics: the darkness of mourning is like a pall in "Recortes de prensa," "Segunda vez," or "Apocalipsis de Solentiname." But in the glow of the early years of the Cuban Revolution it was still possible to believe in utopia, and to write about it in the unrestrained language of cosmic possibilities. As the decade wore on, and as the repressive regimes of the seventies ushered in the horrors of torture and the disappeared, the somber opacity of mourning, loss, and alienation clung to a discourse that could no longer even glimpse transcendence at a star-studded dawn, trusting in the final allegro that announced victory.

"Che, Man of the Twenty-First Century"

So read the Havana banners marking the thirtieth anniversary of Che's death in 1997, a year when commemoration and nostalgia produced a veritable Che "hauntology," in Derrida's sense of the term.[75] Its most successful form was Walter Salles's 2004 film *Motorcycle Diaries*.

It was not the first time that the Che myth had been appropriated by film: only two years after his death, in 1969, a film entitled *Che!* featured Jack Palance as Fidel and Omar Shariff as Che; Antonio Banderas sporting a beret played an unlikely Che in Andrew Lloyd Weber's *Evita*; Italian filmmaker Gianni Mia settled on a documentary version of the trip featured in Salles's film. More recently, Bolivian filmmaker Fernando Vargas made a documentary about Vallegrande, the place where Che was killed, using the password given to order the assassination as its title: *Di buen día a papá* (Say good morning to daddy).

But it was Brazilian director Walter Salles who most effectively rendered the filmic version of Che as the incarnation of a promise without the burden of its radical political implications. *Motorcycle Diaries* is based on Che's account of his eight-month trip through South America with his friend Alberto Granado in 1952, before his revolutionary ideology was fully articulated—before the beard, the beret, the fatigues, and the armed struggle. The choice of this early period is not only the key to the film's success; it could even be seen as its very condition of possibility in the twenty-first century. The film was produced by Robert Redford in conjunction with Film Four and South Fork Pictures; when Redford chose Walter Salles to direct the film, he was picking someone with a cosmopolitan background (born in Brazil and raised in France, Salles had achieved international recognition with *Central Station* and has recently done *Dark Water*, a Hollywood film based on a Japanese terror classic) who insisted on having the actors speak Spanish. Salles picked Mexican García Bernal and Argentine Rodrigo de la Serna to play the main roles; his scriptwriter José Rivera was Puerto Rican, his cinematographer French, his co-producers Argentine. *Motorcycle Diaries* gathered this global array of talent to offer a story of learning and the attainment of political consciousness with thc backdrop of continental geography.

Star Gael García Bernal's handsome face reinforces the mythic quality of Che's. Gael and Che do not look at all alike: what connects them is not physical resemblance, but the aura of good looks. The youthful romantic who undertakes the continental exploration with his Sancho-like friend elicits the sense of forgotten possibility in a story of beginnings.

The road-movie genre fulfills several functions: it is a sort of bildungsroman that constructs a continental vision: Che's and Alberto's eyes guide the viewers through a trip that tends to cancel the fifty years separating Che's diary from Salles's filming. We, the viewers, undertake a Latin

American journey at a time when we are taught to watch with pan-Latin eyes.[76] The American film industry is conveying several messages through Che/Gael's eyes: an idealistic vision of a beautiful territory, a kind of holy tourism that elicits the viewer's awareness of the timeless Southern predicament. It also traces an embrace of Latino identity through the mediation of the myth of youthful idealism.

The *Diaries* end in an epiphanic moment whose historical consequences are suspended: we are left with Che's proclamation of his newly discovered continental identity in the midst of the leper colony—metonymically inscribing the downtrodden he was to fight for in Cuba, Congo, and Bolivia. In this re-creation of the myth, time comes to a standstill: in the logic of spectrality, Che as reincarnated in Gael García Bernal becomes pure spirit. Thus, utopian longings reach today's neoliberal malaise. We never get to see Che pick up a weapon or kill a man. In the *Pasajes de la guerra revolucionaria,* Che the writer had gone out of his way to mark the moment when he left behind his doctor's satchel, picked up a rifle, and became a fighter. Salles's film opts for the medical student ministering to the sick.[77]

The film was more successful than expected; Focus Features raved, "We're completely blown away by this massive, record-breaking opening. We expected success with this film, which we're so proud of and we've had incredible reviews on, but its weekend box-office was unimaginable, even by the most optimistic outlook."[78] Its impact rests on Che's iconic quality, and its power to revitalize energies in the present. The elision of later political actions and programs allows for a sense of timeless, messianic promise. We are left with the sense that what Eric Gautier's cinematography captures is no less true of Latin America in the early twenty-first century than it was in the 1950s: a mixture of beauty and pathos materialize on the screen and point to a fullness that will never be achieved. The truly revolutionary period of Che's life is omitted in the *Motorcycle Diaries*, but his redemptive dreams are articulated by Gael's Che in his birthday, at the leper colony. The continental dream—as watched by Latinos in the United States, Latin Americans in Latin America, or Northerners vicariously traveling with the two young men through a poorly known, distant continent—remains suspended, out of time, in the energy of aspiration. The fullness of revolution as veritable emancipation (defined, in Ernesto Laclau's terms, as "the crystallization and synthesis of a series of contents such as the elimination of economic exploitation and all forms of discrimination, the assertion of human rights, the consolidation of civil and political freedom"[79]) is not achievable. It was not so then, despite the triumph of Fidel and his men in 1959, and it remains even more elusive now: its power as continued promise rests on its radical undecidability.[80]

Latin American film is reaching international recognition today much as the boom did in the 1960s;[81] in the case of the *Motorcycle Diaries* the enchantment derives from peripatetic youth and idealism managing to eschew overt political statement while showing, as director Walter Salles declared, that it is possible "to believe in something again."[82]

2

Tlatelolco 1968: Paz and Poniatowska on Law and Violence

> The task of a critique of violence can be summarized as that of expounding its relation to law and justice.
> —Walter Benjamin

The literature on the massacre at Tlatelolco in October 1968 is formidable and complex. We have studies of its political consequences, as well as overviews of the numerous works dealing with it from varied disciplinary perspectives. Crucial documentary evidence on the decision-making process leading to the massacre is finally emerging from years of secrecy. The violence of 2 October had a powerful set of political and cultural echoes lasting to this day: to some extent, Vicente Fox's electoral triumph in 2001 rests on the fact that he promised he would make information about the massacre available to the general public, for it was a critical turning point, the beginning of the erosion that would lead to the PRI's defeat in 2000, after more than seventy years' rule. This chapter addresses the scene of Tlatelolco at the intersection of aesthetics, violence, and justice, scrutinizing the kinds of formal and discursive strategies whereby two very different writers have addressed the ethics of reading and writing. It sets out to contribute to the scholarship on this traumatic event by taking up the question of violence and the forms of writing that have constructed its memory.

Benjamin's observation helps us to think in different ways about the tragic events at the Plaza de Tlatelolco on October 2, 1968. Violent state repression of a peaceful demonstration in Mexico City caused many deaths; it also called into question the legality of the Mexican state as represented by the PRI, opening up a powerful debate on the question of justice. What follows is an attempt to chart the discursive war unleashed by this tragic event, to map responses articulated by intellectuals who set out to denounce and account for a repressive apparatus that violated justice by invoking state power and law. A whole generation considers the massacre to be the central event in its intellectual formation, "a brand, a scar that has never healed," as Elena Poniatowska declared in 1988.[1] A situation that marked the limits of a pact between the state and civil society generated a wealth of signifying practices that attempted to understand social and political activity in the articulation between experience and cultural representation. The case of this massacre has the urgency tragically conveyed by pain and death. It represents the crisis of a social and political formation: according to Octavio Paz, it marks the moment when the system fractured. The intellectuals' responses to it construct a complex intertextuality with ideological inflections, located in a network of discursive and nondiscursive practices. Its traumatic memory is central to Mexico's national identity. Carlos Monsiváis declared it in lapidary fashion in 2002: "34 years after the Student Movement of 1968, a consensus has been reached: that '68 is the most significant event of the second half of the twentieth century in Mexico."[2]

The texts produced as a result of the massacre of October 2 denounce a spectacular form of punishment with echoes of a premodern era. For while the state may have (in a Weberian sense) the monopoly over violence, its legality is called into question when the use of force is brutal and it forecloses the public sphere. The massacre revealed an archaic form of domination[3] just when Mexico was preparing itself for the inaugural celebrations of the Olympic Games, and presenting itself to the world as a modern, democratic nation. What ensued was a crisis of legitimation that affected not only the state and its control of the public sphere, but also the problematic relationship between might and right. As Derrida notes, "might can never justify right, precisely because the establishment of right can never be fully rationalized."[4] Law as violence opens up the thorny question of the origin of authority—a question the Mexican state has answered by recourse to a complex discursive machine of legitimation set in motion at the end of the Mexican Revolution with the foundation of the PRI. If for Derrida "the establishment of law is violence in the sense of an imposition without a present justification,"[5] its force can be deconstructed as mythical in the sense that the origin of legal authority can never be established beyond the violence of its own foundation. Brutal violence becomes a dramatic mise-en-scène for such a deconstructive enterprise.

After the massacre, what was denounced was not only the repressive brutality of the army and the police, but also the silent pact that undergirded state authority in its very foundation.[6] Those directly involved in the killings of hundreds of peaceful demonstrators were never brought to justice. To this day, even after the archives pertaining to the massacre were opened in 2001, a secret remains: who ordered the attack. As of February 2005, former president Echeverría faces charges of genocide, but much of the crucial information was blacked out before the archives were opened. The mystery remains in place, and its memory has never faded: hundreds commemorate the massacre every October 2 at Tlatelolco Square, and books continue to be written about it.[7] Public reason had to be regained by the critical effort through which the present and the past were scrutinized and unmasked in a radical hermeneutics of suspicion.[8] Violence in the hands of the ruling authorities of the state threatened to turn it into a repellent criminal whose claim to authority had to be deconstructed. Octavio Paz's *Postdata* is the most radical attempt to do this; in other ways, Carlos Fuentes, José Revueltas, Elena Poniatowska, Carlos Monsiváis, and many other prominent intellectuals contributed to the construction of an exceptionally powerful discursive field that proclaimed that in the violence perpetrated in Tlatelolco lay something ignominious. As Benjamin saw it, "the 'law' of the police really marks the point at which the state, whether from impotence or because of the immanent connection within any legal system, can no longer guarantee through that legal system the empirical ends that it desires at any price to attain."[9] Indeed, even as it asserted its might, the government of President Díaz Ordaz was in fact acknowledging its incapacity to rule within the law. The striking disjunction between this incapacity and the hyperbolic rhetoric of modernization and democracy that adorned the preparations for the Olympic Games—the first ever to be held in Latin America—incited numerous portrayals of the government as barbarous, unable to resolve conflict within the space of negotiation and legality. Hence 1968 in Mexico has gone down as a scar, a deeply disruptive break in the landscape of Mexican political life.

The events at Tlatelolco epitomized the collision between the forces of authority and the student movement that had been gaining momentum in the course of the decade. Back in 1959, then President López Mateos had brutally repressed labor unrest headed by the railroad workers union and their leader, Demetrio Vallejo, had been imprisoned. By the time Gustavo Díaz Ordaz reached the presidency, the apparatus of state repression was consolidated, and the fear of communist insurgency was wielded as its justification. Censorship extended to topics considered unflattering to Mexico's image: in 1965 Arnaldo Orfila Reynal was fired from the directorship of the Fondo de Cultura Económica—the nation's most prestigious publishing house—for having published Oscar Lewis's *Children of Sánchez*.

As with similar student movements of the time, the Mexican one was propelled by the quest for social reforms and for greater participation in university governance.[10] An acute sense of the urgency of economic and political issues galvanized mass support for the student movement. In July 1968, after the convulsive European spring, the confrontations within and between the Movimiento Estudiantil and the police reached a critical pitch. Brutality had been the police's most frequent response to the Movimiento's marches and to its occupation of high school and university premises: a bazooka was thrown into an occupied college; a student strike in Hermosillo was bloodily dispersed; riot police frequently intervened even when peaceful marches were organized. In July violence escalated. On the 22nd, a fight between rival student groups turned into a bloody affair when the *granaderos* (riot police) stepped in; on the 26th a demonstration commemorating the 1953 Moncada Barracks attack in Cuba voiced claims against police brutality, only to be met by its full force, resulting in several deaths and hundreds of wounded. By the end of the month a strike kept all schools and universities in Mexico City closed. August witnessed further marches, strengthened by the solidarity of professors and university authorities in the face of police occupation. By September a full-scale military invasion of the university had taken place. A distinctive feature of the struggle in Mexico is the support of the student movement by university authorities: unlike most European university officials, Rector Barros Sierra denounced the violent repression with which the student movement was met.

The peaceful march organized in the Plaza de las Tres Culturas in Nonoalco-Tlatelolco resulted from President Díaz Ordaz's refusal to make public the government's negotiations with the Consejo Nacional de Huelga (Strike Council), which had formulated six demands on behalf of the Movimiento Estudiantil assembling at the Universidad Nacional Autónoma de

México (UNAM) and the Instituto Politécnico Nacional (IPN). Their aim was to negotiate relaxation of repressive measures by disbanding the brutal *granaderos* and senior police officials, releasing detained students and political prisoners, compensating injured students, and repealing two articles from the penal code that outlawed public meetings of three or more people. A vast crowd assembled to pressure for the disclosure of the dialogue with the Strike Council: among them were student leaders, rank-and-file activists, professors, blue-collar workers, and parents and schoolchildren— a veritable cross-section of the civil body. Army troops and police surprised the crowd by trapping them in the square, opening fire on the crowd, pursuing the demonstrators into a surrounding apartment building, and laying siege on them.[11] Hundreds were killed, and thousands wounded, detained, or tortured. The student movement was destroyed; ten days later, Mexico celebrated the opening of the Olympic Games on the "Día de la Raza," in the year proclaimed as the Year of Peace in Mexico. Official reports minimized the casualties, the city was made to regain an appearance of normality, but the repressed returned with a vengeance. The powers of language and representation in their varied forms were deployed by intellectuals in an extraordinary number of essays, poems, testimonials, and novels, so as to sustain collective memory, encourage critical vigilance, and proclaim the horrors that were being silenced officially.

A brief comparison of these events with those they resembled (and, some would claim, emulated) in the European and North American spring of 1968 underscores the difference in outcomes, but also striking parallels in their beginnings and motivations. Like all the student movements of the sixties, such events were the result of new subject formations of the postwar era. A subculture defined in generational terms spoke in a new collective voice—a youthful one that also took stock of the needs and demands of subject peoples. If in the metropolitan nations this implied a self-conscious awareness of decolonization movements in British and French Africa, of the struggles of the Cuban Revolution and Vietnam, of the authoritarian structures of power that stood in the way of the gains of the newly constituted consumer society, in the Third World there was an exacerbated sense of the circumstances of oppression that had been tolerated by the working classes and students alike. Young Carlos Fuentes was an enthusiastic participant in the May events in Paris: his *Paris: la revolución de mayo* is a passionate account of those heady days and nights that proclaimed the cross-fertilization between politics, morals, and the erotic.[12] Writing as if he were immersed in the movement, he proclaimed the student views in a voice that conveys festive injunctions and condemnations. Consumer society is the great evil ("We live in a spiritual Dachau surrounded by the perishable goods of a consumerist Disneyland"[13]); but on the other hand, he celebrates the events as producing an international community that welcomes Latin Americans and offers them a mirror of their own ideals. The community of young rebels considered itself international—whether occupying Berkeley's Sproul Hall in 1964, Columbia's Hamilton Hall in 1968, the London School of Economics in 1967; or introducing international initiatives via the Students for a Democratic Society in Germany, the United States, or Italy; or organizing marches to oppose the war in Vietnam or to mourn the deaths of Martin Luther King (1968) or Che Guevara (1967).[14] A generalized desire to overthrow hierarchical structures was expressed through marching, singing, demonstrating, and occupying, discovering the festive, trancelike solidarity of crowds. But, as Kristin Ross has pointed out, the contestatory impulses—their festive mood notwithstanding—were not devoid of political thinking in France, and they were powerful indeed in Latin America.[15] The generalized "third-worldism" of the decade made for solidarity across boundaries and across oceans: shared concern for struggles in Bolivia, Vietnam, Algeria, or Congo produced new figurations of the social and the political in transnational arenas.

Local differences cannot be effaced, of course: in the Mexican case it is problematic to affirm the existence of a consumer society at all levels—given the generalized poverty of the underclasses. However, access to higher education and the demographic boom contributed to the formation of a youth market and culture that became the site for new forms of contestation. The student demands arose from pressing material needs and the repressive ways of an authoritarian regime that had left its painful marks in earlier decades. Nevertheless, accepting the material disparities that set the Mexican case apart from the French or the North American one, it is clear that the participants shared a generational awareness of the need to question existing power structures and the role of the university in society, while occupying public space in order to make claims, establish some form of conversation with the government, and work out an agenda for public discourse.[16]

But the central difference lies in the question of violence and in the relationship between the state and the citizens' bodies. For while in the turmoil of May '68 in France the total number of deaths is estimated at five, in the Mexican case it is generally estimated that over three hundred students lost their lives on October 2. The contrast is sobering: the greatest concern experienced by Maurice Grimaud, the Paris prefect of police was, as he put it in a 1998 interview, a provocation that would have led the police to turn to their weapons.[17] In fact, the general approach to the student movement as far as the minister of the interior (Christian Fouchet) and the police prefect were concerned was to let it run its own course, even at the risk of appearing slack.[18] At Tlatelolco, instead, the violence of the armed units was unleashed against unsuspecting crowds. Elaine Scarry has noted that "the attributes of a particular political philosophy, its generosities and its failures, are most apparent in those places where it intersects with, touches or agrees not to touch, the human body";[19] the injuring performed during the massacre can be read as a mark of failure that deeply scarred the social contract. Writing became a form of fighting back and of resisting the official silence imposed from above.

Thus, brute force was met by Mexican intellectuals with a symbolic struggle that deploys language and voice. It is as if the exchange of representations stems from a tragic flaw in the mimetic system through which power is enacted: the Mexican president allowed the *granaderos* to shoot at the crowd gathered at the square, he committed a crime, and he revealed his inability to attain the symbolic domination that is achieved only through successful representations of force. Looked at in historical perspective, he acted as if he belonged in the preclassical social space, where brutal struggles had not yet been replaced by a signifying system that conveyed the force of legitimate power. Borrowing from Louis Marin, we might say President Díaz Ordaz and his army were without "the institutionalized forms through which 'representatives' visibly incarnate, make present, the coherence of a community, the force of an identity, or the permanence of a power."[20] Hence he had to resort to the external manifestation of power, to brutalizing bodies instead of abiding by the legitimacy of the social contract, as Grimaud, Fouchet, and Pompidou had done only four months earlier. As Marin has shown in the case of France in the seventeenth century, the shift from brute force to symbolic representations of power was an important contribution to the eradication of violence, for the instruments of symbolic domination fulfilled two related functions: "the negation and conservation of the absolute of force: negation, since force is neither exerted nor manifested, since it is at peace in the signs that signify and designate it, and conservation, since force through and in representation will give itself as justice, that is to say, as law that obligatorily constrains."[21]

In fact, the very deployment of force produced the crisis of legitimation: what was lost by the government of Díaz Ordaz was authority, as Hannah Arendt notes: "Since authority always demands obedience, it is commonly mistaken for some form of power or violence. Yet authority precludes the use of external means of coercion; where force is used, authority itself has failed."[22]

Paradoxical then, is the fact that repressing the student movement succeeded in restoring order in time for the inauguration of the Olympic Games, while at the same time it weakened the foundations of State authority. Yet it is precisely the negotiation of this apparent contradiction that the State must manage effectively: to enforce the law it must be able to turn to force, but doing so can reveal that authority has been lost. Pascal had acknowledged this: "Justice without force is impotent."[23] But then force can end up undermining justice, in a double bind foregrounded and elaborated by the writing about the massacre of Tlatelolco.

Indeed, the violence deployed by the Mexican government on October 2, 1968, led to the production of texts that set out to code, rework, and transform the very fabric of lived experience by not merely critiquing the events themselves, but also by scrutinizing the concepts of culpability, sacrifice, legality, and even the foundation of the state. If on the one hand President Díaz Ordaz restored a semblance of normalcy in the capital city shortly after the events, on the other hand the government failed to articulate the legitimation that was necessary in order to justify the recourse to violence. In part, this had to do with the unexpected nature of the brutal reprisals: although the *granaderos* had deployed repressive force on previous occasions, everything seems to suggest that the crowd was surprised by their sudden intervention and—most notably—by the participation of the Olympia Battalion, an undercover paramilitary police force infiltrated in the crowd's midst.[24] They wore white gloves or handkerchiefs around their hands, but when the firing was taking place their identity was confusing, they had a spectral quality, as if their phantom occupied the very space they were trying to empty of their presence. Benjamin notes this spectrality in its relationship to law and the state, speculating on how even in democracies the police occupy and take advantage of a sort of no-man's land of violence between the making and the execution of the law, showing how the very invisibility of security forces reminds us that the monopoly of violence belongs to the state. The haunting quality of this hidden but lurking presence had a ritual dimension that demonized the PRI as represented by the government of President Díaz Ordaz even as it delegitimated it. The boundary violated by the *granaderos* and the security force is the tenuous one that separates foundational force from conservation: if, harking back to Benjamin, foundational violence has a revolutionary quality that legitimates it, the violence of conservation unmasks its alliance with the preservation of the state. In Mexico in 1968, this meant undermining the PRI's claims to representing populist aspirations.

The work of writing came on the heels of violence: taking the floor and the word, writing and denouncing, actively engaging in action—verbal and otherwise—were attempts to sustain collective memory. Faced with bloody, wounded bodies, with corpses, and with bodies in confinement, Mexican intellectuals affirmed the power to speak and to represent the unthinkable. The response they produced proves that even in the face of repression they held on to the power of the word as an instrument of resistance, and they did so in most varied registers, deploying the protocols of literary genres—novels, poems, essays, personal memoirs, *testimonios*. I have chosen two particularly powerful and different texts, marked by the category of gender and by alternate visions. *Postdata*, by Octavio Paz, is ruled by his unifying vision to interpret the tragic events from the vantage point of his privileged gaze. Elena Poniatowska's *La noche de Tlatelolco* instead opts for fragmentation and plurality, attempting to convey the often conflicting voices of civil society as they address the traumatic experience of Tlatelolco. My analysis scrutinizes the literary—and hence writerly—forms that are put to work in order to represent and interpret the relationships between violence, justice, and aesthetics.[25] The textual practices to be studied raise important questions about the ethics of reading—about the ethics of producing the kind of critique I am attempting: one needs to ponder the dialogue elicited by the representation of violence in verbal or visual terms. If repression and murder challenge the codes of the thinkable and the representable, we need to think about our response to the events at Tlatelolco in terms that attempt to do justice to the pain and the horror suffered on that night. I hope to keep my eyes on the thorny relationship between the bodies in pain and their representation: the challenge remains hard to meet, yet never dismissed.

One of the paradoxes that haunts the study of some of the writings on the Massacre of Tlatelolco is that the violence it unleashed entailed the possibility of a revelation. Indeed, we are forced to confront the possibility that violence may unmask not only its foundational presence, but also the fact that its power may yield epiphanic results. Octavio Paz's *Postdata* may be the clearest instance of this double bind: the book denounces the events of October 2, 1968, while at the same time it discovers in them some of the answers to questions posed in *El laberinto de la soledad* (*The Labyrinth of Solitude*), as if the brutality opened up the secrets of the origins.[26] For Paz, Tlatelolco holds the key to the genealogical code that undergirds the Mexican state, laying bare the continuity of authoritarian violence that connects the PRI with the Aztec rulers. *Postdata* is thus no mere afterthought to Paz's inaugural *El laberinto de la soledad*, but its reformulation, finding the answers in the origin and hence eschewing the future-looking strategy of a modernist interpretation in favor of a historicist move that privileges the past as a source of understanding. For Paz, the repetition of violence produces a connecting thread that makes the history of Mexico both coherent and terrible, understandable and doomed. October 2 allows for the revelation of Mexico's "invisible history," rendered in terms that leave no doubt as to the epiphany involved: "On that afternoon our visible history unfolded our other history, the invisible one, as if it were a pre-Columbian codex. That vision was shocking because the symbols became transparent."[27]

Violence had the effect of an unmasking. It lay bare what was hidden behind the mask of progress that the PRI had presented to the world at the time of the Olympic Games; it stripped the sheen of modernity from the archaic face of the nation. Paz's language is rife with the imagery of deceit and its unveiling. Bloodshed operates the effect of this *aletheia* or unveiling, not so much as a ritual cleansing but as the revelation of the code and the origin. From the Aztec beginning, Paz draws a line marking the continuity of Mexico's hitherto misunderstood history, showing that the mirage of colonial rule and independence did not sever the powerful link with the Aztecs.

If in "Los hijos de la Malinche" (Chapter Four in *El laberinto de la soledad*) Paz had decried Mexico's break with tradition, now in *Postdata* he notes that the brutality of Tlatelolco has the paradoxical effect of showing the continuity hitherto occluded. It is particularly significant that what is seen as a regrettable break with the past is sutured by violence. The break with the Mother described in "Los hijos de la Malinche" has produced the solitude and the alienation that the earlier book attempts to map out, aided by the codes of historical understanding: "History, which could not tell us anything about the nature of our feelings and conflicts, can now show us how that break came about and how we have attempted to transcend our solitude" (88, *107*).

In *El laberinto* Paz suggests that Mexico has been accruing masks throughout its history and, at the same time, severing the connection with its past: this happened during independence, as well as on the occasion of the mid-nineteenth-century Reforma that abolished communal indigenous property ownership, and of the positivist Porfiriato with its European-looking programs. The violence of the Revolution provided the nation with a revelation of its being. In *Postdata* the revelation takes place again, but this time it uncovers a terrifying past: foundational violence and the violence of conservation are conflated as he argues that the repressive brutality of October 2 mirrored the foundational brutality of Aztec rule. By so doing he strips the PRI of the populist legitimacy granted to it by the rural-based, democratic, and even populist myths of the Mexican Revolution. There is a terrifying yet sublime quality to the demonic trace of the Aztec origin named by the brutal acts of October 2: "This preference for the ancient Mexican name is not accidental: October 2, Tlatelolco, inserts itself with terrifying logic in our history, both the real and the symbolic" (320, *351*).

A great deal has been said about the dooming, deterministic nature of Paz's reading of the Mexican name as the totalizing explanation of its history, and more shall be noted below.[28] But it is also necessary to see how the revelation of this mythic, foundational violence exerts a productive as well as a destructive force. For it is through the awareness of its abiding presence that Paz sees the possibility of a recovery of the intellectuals' critical voice. The crisis unleashed by October 2 restores the intellectuals' presence in the public debate, after the decades that followed the Mexican Revolution, when the spirit of dissent and critical vigilance were muted by their transformation into counselors: "the spirit of accommodation . . . has invaded almost every area of public activity" (158, *191*) he had announced in *El laberinto*. Corrupted by this spirit, intellectuals abandoned their independence. *Postdata* notes the peculiar insight made possible by violence: after Tlatelolco, critical discourse was regained: "The long-kept truce between the intellectuals and those in power, a truce initiated by the Revolution and prolonged by the necessities (the mirage) of development, has now ended. Mexican culture has recovered its vocation as critic of society" (266, *309*).

Hence violence tears the masks that cover the truth, and in so doing it represents a discursive inauguration hitherto blocked. If *El laberinto* denounces the masks, *Postdata* announces their removal and describes a beginning. There is a Nietzschean, agonistic quality to Paz's reading, rife as it is with the sense that the recovery of the will to truth follows the dark revelations of Tlatelolco. And yet, it is not a forward-looking insight, but one that moves full circle to the beginning, tracing a logic that Nietzsche himself called crablike: "By searching out origins, one becomes a crab. The historian looks backward; eventually he also *believes* backward."[29]

The circularity of the crab's trail produces a closed logic of explanation that is part of *Postdata*'s compelling force. In his return to the Aztec past Paz can locate the salient features of a terrifying national secret: "The massacre at Tlatelolco shows us that the past which we thought was buried is still alive and has burst out among us" (236, *282*). While it may have, as he claims, a *repelente* (repulsive) quality, the regression it produces grants him both the power of the recovery of a secret and the circular logic of a perfectly sutured explanation. Its master code is the fixity that he attributes to Mexico's space and time: the central immobility of the pyramid is mirrored in the terrifying presence of the past, which defies any hope of its burial in its perpetual reappearance. Reading not only the code of time but also that of space, Paz weaves a symbolic geography determined by the static centrality of the four-sided pyramid that encloses the beginning and the end even as it contains the four cardinal points. In a dazzling explanation of the Aztec worldview, Paz leaves no loose ends: every element in the structure is held together by the centripetal pull of the conceptual axis he deploys. In the center lies the sun, which demands blood through the centuries, following the rule of continuity that permeates time and space: "The pyramid—petrified time, place of divine sacrifice—is also an image of the Aztec state and of its mission: to assure the continuity of the solar cult, source of universal life, through the sacrifice of prisoners of war" (296, *331*).

Furthering the logocentric organization of the argument is the weight of the name: the repetition of the Mexica name for both the nation and the capital city reinforces the haunting, unavoidable presence of the "terrible dominación azteca."

Toponymy is indeed the key to the origin in Paz's reading: names cannot be erased even when they are covered over by contemporary forms. Just as the Mexica trace lives on in the persistence of the name, the square of Tlatelolco rejects its recently given name (Plaza de las Tres Culturas) as it reveals the inevitability of the buried past. It repeats the pyramidal structure characteristic of Mexico's actual and symbolic geography: it echoes the pyramid of the central Zócalo as well as the whole plateau that makes up the national territory. Paz proclaims: "Tlatelolco is one of Mexico's roots," foregrounding the territorialization of tradition and its invention. Through the process of place-making, the static force of identity is grounded and pulled down by the gravitational force of the Aztec past, which is denied mobile qualities in an endless gallery of mirrors. Repetition obliterates difference; difference is a mere mask that *Postdata* strips away.

Yet part of Paz's explanatory power is paradoxically contained by the relentlessly totalizing drive of his argument. Space and place are the embodiments of the temporal stability that runs through Mexico's past and present. By underscoring the relationship between place and identity that obtains in the Plaza de Tlatelolco, Paz territorializes the events of October 2 and lends them the character of the bloody sacrifices of pre-Columbian times. The fact that it contains markers of the Aztec, colonial, and contemporary identities of Mexico highlights its genealogical power. But there is more to the totalizing power of space conjured up by Paz: its essence permeates and homogenizes the key landmarks of the nation, which are the bearers of the past and its effect. The Plaza de Tlatelolco was a *centro gemelo* (twin center) of Tenochtitlán, and it was strictly dependent on the Aztec central power. This hall of mirrors is multiplied by the Museo de Antropología, which holds the key to the secrets of the past.

It is at this point that Paz razes the spatial and temporal coordinates that he so solidly mapped. *Postdata* ends with a dramatic sleight of hand that debunks the status of the Aztec legacy as it is monumentalized in the Museo de Antropología: it proclaims the falsehood of the version the museum proposes, based as it is on the invention of a false tradition. Having shown how the horrors of October 2, 1968, stem from the spectre of Aztec supremacy, he declares the need to rewrite history and wrench it from the brutal hold of Mexico-Tenochtitlán. The final pages of the essay proceed with dazzling conceptual speed as he avers: "the image of the pre-Columbian past which the Museum of Anthropology offers us is false" (323, 353). For not only could it have been replaced by other equally valid archetypes—Maya, Zapotec, Tarascan, or Otomi—and hence superseded, but it also continues to condemn modern Mexico because of its pathological attachment to murderous ancestors: "the true heirs of the pre-Columbian world are not the peninsular Spaniards but ourselves, we Mexicans who speak Spanish, whether we are Creoles, mestizos, or Indians" (323–24, *354*).

Having emptied the nation of its memory in both space and time, Paz concludes with a new challenge: the exercise of criticism and the imagination. After painstakingly constructing an explanation of totalizing coherence, he turns the tables on it, making of its very unifying force the principle of its own demise. Critique (*la crítica*) as the "acid" that dissolves images is identified as the vehicle for learning anew, for constructing different visions unbound by the weight of petrified images.

Thus, *Postdata* as a return to *El laberinto de la soledad* made possible by the violence of 1968, answers most of its questions and unmasks all its secrets. National identity is revealed by an exercise in national memory. But, as is the case with trauma, memory must be relinquished, freed up into the airy chambers of the critical imagination, and replaced by its future-oriented gaze. Paz's critique of violence has the radical power of a surgical operation and the visionary ring of an oracular voice. As such, it sounds alone, like Benjamin's angel of history with his face turned to the past. In Paz's case the future is not the storm of progress, but the debris of a destroyed vision and the uncertain promise of the imagination.

For Elena Poniatowska, instead, Tlatelolco is an opportunity to let the voices of the people speak. Far from articulating a unified vision with powerful links to the present and the past, her *La noche de Tlatelolco* is a deliberate attempt to explode unity and to relinquish a totalizing vision while ushering in a disparate group of witnesses whose testimony configures a mosaic of splintered pieces. By allowing different voices to speak, she constructs a fiction of civil society, a decentered representation of community anchored in plurality. It is precisely this representation that I want to scrutinize—in terms of both its construction and the effects it produces.[30]

La noche de Tlatelolco constructs what Bataille would call a "limit experience,"[31] which is to say one that goes beyond the limits of coherent subjectivity as it functions in everyday life, and that, as Foucault explained it in his gloss on Bataille, reaches "that point of life which lies as close as possible to the impossibility of living, [attempting] to gather the maximum amount of intensity and impossibility at the same time."[32] Poniatowska produces that articulation between intensity and impossibility by rendering her *testimonios de historia oral* as a collage of transcribed voices responding to the horror of the massacre in multiple registers. Some are shocked exclamations ("I saw blood smeared on the wall"; "I can't stand this another minute!"),[33] others are microstories juxtaposed to fragments of varied generic strands.

This varied archive documents the public sphere and therefore counters the logic of the secret emanating from state repression. At times it reads like a collective trial in which the victims denounce the oppressors as they take the floor. Poniatowska explains that after the massacre, people came to her and asked her to go out on the streets and tell the story of what had happened. Equipped with a tape recorder, she interviewed and recorded scores of people, and even managed to visit military camps and prisons.[34] The claim and the conceit of the book is that it merely collects and transcribes—even as it fragments—the oral testimony obtained from witnesses and participants. And yet, as I will show below, there is a carefully orchestrated composition that wrests it from the chaos of raw information. The logic of fragmentation governs the construction of the book, as if to represent the destruction and the confusion of the massacre and its effects. Within the rubric of oral testimony Poniatowska assembles newspaper cuttings, student pronouncements, official reports, fliers, student chants, petitions, poems, and other literary fragments, as well as a great variety of recorded oral testimonies taken from the people she interviewed. As Octavio Paz noted in his remarks about *La noche de Tlatelolco*, Poniatowska listens to the outside voices, in contrast to the poet, who is guided by the inside ones.[35] As a keen listener, she constructs an archive that counters the official accounts of events and in fact embodies the voices of civil society. Drawing on the conceit of the tape recorder and its transcription, Poniatowska moves from voice to vision to spectacle as she stages both the air of celebration in which the students gathered and marched, and the tragedy of October 2. The final effect of this event as it is read in *La noche de Tlatelolco* is to heighten the sense of the collapse of legitimacy of the Mexican regime not through the singular, internal vision of the poet, but through the multiple voices of the body politic.

While important work has been done on the communal—hence collective, relational—values that underpin testimonial writing in Latin America, I want to eschew the rich debates on it in order to turn my attention to a different question.[36] My reading of *La noche de Tlatelolco* will try to follow the multiple foldings and unfoldings of Poniatowska's writing so as to pry out of them an aesthetic impulse embedded in the plurality of voices and textual practices. My claim is that one can posit a series of links between aesthetics, justice, and an ethics of reading. In her apparently artless, spontaneous, and denunciatory impulse to contest the official silence by producing her *testimonios de historia oral*, Poniatowska is actually creating a work in which readers are to be moved by the power of aesthetics and an attendant desire for fairness, justice, and a sense of lifesaving reciprocity. Here is one of the important ways in which art and culture press upon the real.

Let us trace the reader's experience as she/he engages with *La noche de Tlatelolco*, provisionally suspending the visual spectacle provided by the photographs, to be discussed later. Poniatowska's touch is light but powerful: even on the title page of Part One the voice of the students chanting alludes to the need for union to transcend the fracture about to be represented: "People, unite, don't abandon us, people." Immediately afterwards, by way of written introduction, Poniatowska provides a short text bearing her initials—a gesture that affirms authorship while veiling it. It is encoded as a vision, locating the writer herself as purveying the spectacle of events in a present that is sheer artifice: it is the present of the writer and her readers. Its literariness is powerfully constructed by the lyrical tone, the manipulation of point of view ("they come toward me," she avers, as if movement were unfolded in filmic language), and a system of comparisons that evokes childhood games to suggest the brutal injustice with which the students ("children-targets, wonderstruck children, children for whom every day is a holiday"), as innocent subjects, become the target of fatal shots. The childhood imagery is reinforced by the metaphor of festive celebration that obtains in a fair's shooting gallery, where the row of ducks to be knocked over betoken the vulnerable young people: "the owner of the shooting gallery tells them to form a line, like the row of tin-plated mechanical ducks that move past exactly at eye level, click, click, click, 'Ready, aim fire!' and they tumble backward, touching the red satin backdrop" (3, *13*).

Poniatowska's vision renders the immediacy of the events, underscoring the centrality of the gaze already established by the introductory photographs. Seeing as witnessing is a function that her text multiplies: it is performed by her here—and hence vicariously by her reader—as well as by all the subjects whose voices she scripts. But her authorial gaze is privileged by the power to see the future: she can predict what the young marchers do not know, namely, that in a few days' time they will be rotting under the rain, and their blood will become "young blood trampled underfoot all over the Plaza de las Tres Culturas" (3, *13*). Thus the site of the author is acknowledged from the start, endowed as it is with control over space and time. The passage owns up to the re-created nature of this testimonial, to its own artifice, to its powerful emotive and vindicatory thrust. The "I" that will remain effaced in order to stage the spectacle and transcribe the voices frames the text at the outset. The passage ends by appropriating one of the students' chants, as if to proclaim its own ethical imperative and to cancel out the distance that separates her from them: "Mé-xi-co, Li-ber-tad, Mé-xi-co, Li-ber-tad, Mé-xi-co, Li-ber-tad" (*14*).

Drawing a line below her signature, Poniatowska relinquishes her personal voice and opens up the text to multiple voices. Here again I see the interesting interplay between dissonance, apparent disorder, and randomness on the one hand, and an aesthetic practice with ethical implications on the other. Brief, fragmented accounts of personal or collective experience, followed by a line indicating the name of the speaker as well as his or her affiliation, are juxtaposed one after the other. The effect is to construct the fiction of presence: the reader is immersed in the microstories of the everyday experience of '68, as if through fragmentation and polyphony it became possible to reconstruct the meanings of politics in everyday life. Out of these decentered accounts one can begin to witness the social and libidinal energy that circulated among the marchers, to catch a glimpse of the solidarity whose bonds are the condition of possibility of a civil society necessary for the monopoly of the state to be questioned.

Following Elaine Scarry, I claim that by dint of the double-edged conceit of artfully orchestrated multiplicity, *La noche de Tlatelolco* provides the reader with the rare experience of perceiving actions and social relations that are not usually available to sensory perception.[37] By gathering the numerous *testimonios* even as she interrupts them, Poniatowska makes available what is too disperse to be apprehended directly. It is the orchestrated *dispositio* at work here that produces this effect as she arranges the fragments according to a number of aesthetically inflected practices. Thus, the book is divided into two symmetrical parts, "Ganar la calle" ("Taking to the Streets") and "La noche de Tlatelolco" ("The Night of Tlatelolco"), separated—and connected—by four poems, three of them at the end of the first part and one at the beginning of the second, so that there is a lyrical hinge articulating them. Like the first part, the second one also bears a brief introduction with the author's initials as her signature (E.P.). The rhythms of symmetry are sustained in the suturing of contrasting points of view: Poniatowska deliberately leads the reader into the pendular movement of polarized interpretations, as if echoing the structure of a trial. If, for instance, a passage transcribes the critical views on the student movement attributed to one Gerardo Hernández Ponce, "maestro de la Preparatoria número 2 de la UNAM," bitterly denouncing the young people's destructive behavior and the parents' lack of firmness, the one that follows it expresses the opposing viewpoint of young Gustavo Cordillo, of the National Strike Committee (Consejo Nacional de Huelga, or CNH), opening with the following complaint, which echoes and subverts Hernández Ponce's parental disillusionment: "My father keeps telling me what a good son *he* was and all that. . . . And then I start thinking, 'Good Lord, am I some strange sort of creature, or neurotic, or what?'" (13, *22*) And then, as if to provide an alternative to the older generation's viewpoint, Poniatowska locates a different vision in the words of yet another teacher, Pedro Tamariz, "maestro de la Escuela Erasmo Castellanos Quinto," who not only understands the students' anger, but is also willing to take the blame for it: "They have every reason to be angry. We must humbly admit that this is so, because that is one way of remedying our defects and short-comings. Our traditions are bad; our attitude toward life couldn't be worse" (13, *22*).

The logic of distribution that obtains in this frequent procedure has a number of interrelated effects: it interpellates the reader as a third party or witness confronted with conflicting points of view arranged in counterpointal fashion. As noted by Jean-François Lyotard in *Le Différend*, readers cease to be detached spectators of the different disputes in order to become their addressee.[38] The effect goes beyond textuality: "To convince the reader . . . that thought, cognition, ethics, politics, history, or being, depending on the case, are in play when one phrase is linked onto another."[39]

It is precisely the *enchaînement* or linkage constructed by Poniatowska that achieves the carefully weighted alternation of claims. It exposes the reader to notions of distribution and different points of view that may lead to the consideration of fairness, stemming precisely from the unstable, dynamic equilibrium between opposites.[40] This strategy is deployed in numerous instances, so that it becomes an expectation confirmed and reinforced in the process of reading.

Furthermore, there are instances in which Poniatowska draws a narrative line that connects the deliberately dispersed fragments. Urging the reader to piece together the fragments, she separates them even as she constructs the conceptual suturing provided by the proper name. *La noche de Tlatelolco* creates a circulation of short, interrupted passages that can be assembled under the authority of the speaking subjects. Through the play of difference and repetition, the reader is led to experience the fissures from passage to passage, from speaker to speaker, but also the step-by-step narrative sequence that can be threaded together from the multiple interventions of the same (repeated) name. The conceit of disjunction, paradoxically enough, contains the resurgence of repetition: names like Luis Tomás Cervantes Cabeza de Vaca, Artemisa (and Eli) de Gortari, Luis González de Alba, Sócrates Amado Campos Lemus, Gilberto Guevara Niebla, Eduardo Valle Espinosa (Búho)—many of them members of the CNH—reappear throughout the book and trace stories that, although constantly interrupted, produce dispersion while suggesting the possibility of integrated plots. The storylines are similar, covering the speaker's initial moments of political consciousness and adherence to the student movement, then the events of October 2, and the brutal experience of Lecumberri prison either as an inmate or a desperate relative trying to locate a loved one. Each story and each narrating subject provide the singularity of personal experience, so that the work of reading must apprehend resemblances within dispersion and diversity. Some stories engage us as jurors who evaluate the evidence, as in the case of Sócrates Campos Lemus, accused by the other members of the CNH of being an informant who has revealed the identity of his fellow organizers to the Lecumberri prison authorities. Stories by Luis Tomás Cervantes Cabeza de Vaca, Eduardo Valle Espinoza, Salvador Martínez de la Roca, and Pablo Gómez (114, 115, 118, 119, 120, 121, 130) strongly argue for the accusation; Sócrates Campos Lemus defends himself (120, 122, 157); Roberta Avendaño alludes to the difficulty of judging him ("I would never venture to pass judgment on a youngster who has been tortured"; 124, *121*). Reading—and piecing together—the stories and evaluating their ethical implications go hand in hand: the process involves configurational understanding[41] together with an awareness of the moral significance attached to the events pulled together into a narrative constellation.

Echoing Hegel's introduction to his *Lectures on the Philosophy of History*, I see the very possibility of this kind of narrative representation and reconstruction as founded in a legal system that is being interrogated and shaken by the events of Tlatelolco. The fragments usually combine a brief narrative account with a reflection on how government brutality calls its legitimacy into question, so that the microstories actually contain microtreatises on the ethical, personal, and political meaning of 1968:

You begin to find out what the word government means, what it stands for, when that government sends tanks into the streets. (140, *135*)
—Alfonso Salinas Moya, from the School of Dentistry at UNAM

To me, the most horrifying thing was realizing that such a thing was possible in a civilized country: Tlatelolco, killing people, irrational behavior. (19, *28*)
—Artemisa de Gortari, mother

When I was taken prisoner, I had been through a long series of terrible experiences: eight months of being on the run, of hiding out, of living alone. . . . I was not willing to leave the country because I felt—and still feel—that my own fight is here in Mexico. I had honorable friends in prison whom I could not abandon without compromising my own honor. (138, *134*)
—Heberto Castillo, of the Teachers Coalition, detained in Lecumberri

To depoliticize a nation is not simply to make the administration of the country a magical process. . . . It is also to deprive an entire country of the possibility of making moral choices, of the possibility of expressing its indignation. It means destroying morality as a collective concern. (151, *145*)
—Carlos Monsiváis, "La Cultura en México," *Siempre!* 322 (April 1968)

I don't think the sentences were fair, nor for that matter being thrown in prison. (149, *144*)
—Roberta Avendaño (Tita), law faculty delegate before the CNH

These interventions foreground questions of morality, fairness, justice, personal and political commitment, and hence the multiple ethical implications of the massacre at the personal and public levels. Reading *La noche de Tlatelolco*, assembling and making sense of the multiple, interrupted segments, is grounded in their confrontation.

Aside from her skillful *dispositio*, Poniatowska deploys several strategies that further the productive interplay between ethics and aesthetics. The book can be seen as an archive of intertextual negotiations that heighten the connotative power of different genres (poetry, journalism, performance, the essay), and forms of representation (writing, photography). In her insightful book on Poniatowska, Beth Jorgensen has studied the appropriation of poetic texts as one key aspect.[42] I will comment on two others that fulfill similar functions in different ways: performance and photography.

It is possible to make the claim that the students' *prise de parole*, to quote de Certeau again, is a performance that enacted citizenship by marching on the streets and important plazas occupying them, and staging their contestatory claim to power. They chose spaces whose historical significance underscored their actions, which took on symbolic force:

> our goal was the very heart of the life of the country: the Zócalo. We had to take over one of the most imposing public squares in the world (even de Gaulle had been impressed by it!) and raise our voices in protest beneath the balcony, the very balcony where the President of Mexico presents himself for public adulation on historic occasions. We had to give voice to our indignation, hurl any and every insult we could think of at this paternalistic figure, this giver of life. (23, *32*)

Occupation takes on a ritualistic dimension in a space endowed with sacred connotations, where the president performs his power.

The book also contains references to other kinds of performances enacted in less monumental surroundings, but which exert power on citizens in sites—squares, public parks, cafes, factories, markets—where social exchanges raise political consciousness. Some of the stories told by the actress Margarita Isabel represent the performativity of citizenship elicited by the mise-en-scène of conflicts that engender community. By enacting a feigned fight between a bourgeoise who decries the student movement in a newsstand, and a young woman—Margarita Isabel herself—who defies those critical views, they create a *happening*[43] thanks to which a community of supporters for the students is formed. The aggressive exchange mobilizes public opinion in the students' favor: "The crowd would almost always end up siding with me, and the 'snob' would have to take to her heels: 'You dried-up old maid, shove off, what do you know about it, you tottering old wreck'—and the poor actress would light out with her tail between her legs. She really thought exactly as we did, but she was the willing martyr of the 'happening' we staged" (21–22, *30*).

A community results from the opportunity to hate an outsider—even if that location is contrived. Like several other passages narrated by

Margarita Isabel, this one provides some comic relief and the awareness of how performance and political consciousness can converge. Poniatowska's book itself displays many of the practices that unsettled the state's grip on the body politic.

The book opens with a series of photographs that engender a network of looks with powerful effects. In the scopic field, the reader is not only exposed to the kind of journalistic materials within which the testimonial rests its claims to truth, but is also led to reaffirm the students' experience of community through a number of photographs that portray the often celebratory nature of their rallies. Before even starting to read—indeed, before the title page—the primacy of vision elicits spectatorial engagement while at the same time affirming the irrefutable proof of the existence of the crowds and the armed *granaderos* deployed to repress them. In this way, the events are visually narrated, intensifying the book's message and reinforcing its claims to truth. Vision and knowledge validate each other as distances are controlled by the freezing of time. The photographic representational system produces a kind of topographic memory of the streets, monuments, and squares of Mexico City as they are taken over by the youthful, celebratory crowds and then transformed by the repressive power of the armed *granaderos* and their tanks.

The authority of the photographic proof has a documentary function that Poniatowska employs to multiply the ensuing *testimonios de historia oral*. As propaganda and marketing entities know only too well, the intimacy offered to the gaze can have powerfully emotional effects. Coupled with the text that reenacts the evidence initially provided by the photographs— complete with the faces of many of the speakers the reader will encounter— *La noche de Tlatelolco* turns to voice and image to produce the incontrovertible evidence of what Gustavo Díaz Ordaz's government had tried to deny and forget. Against induced forgetting, the book bears witness to the traumatic events of October 1968 as a series of speech acts introduced and borne out by the photographic prints. It thus helps sustain collective memory as an act of resistance founded in the experience of community. Poniatowska's manipulation of the technology of the lens and the tape recorder both avows and denies authorial agency: some shots can be easily located in the journalistic tradition, with echoes of the revolutionary cinematic frames associated with Eisenstein's work, while others call attention to themselves as artifice. The image-time freeze of an aerial shot of crowds at the Zócalo, for example, creates an auratic luminescence produced by the lens's capturing of the movement of torches. The veracity of representation is here pushed to its limits as the fixity of arrested movement lends the shot a suggestive quality in which light leaps out and is amplified into large, blurred circles. What is foisted at the reader has a dreamlike effect reminiscent of spirit photography, with a potentially diminished mimetic value.

There are in fact three kinds of photographs displayed here: a significant group shows the massive numbers who attended the rallies; a few catch the armed forces manhandling young citizens, pointing their weapons at them, arresting them, pulling them by their hair, searching their clothes for weapons, or forcing them to stand against a wall. The third and most powerful kind contains images of dead bodies, the morgue, and the abandoned belongings—mostly shoes—of people who disappeared. While the first two groups of photographs betoken the confrontation between the body politic and the armed forces, showing the sheer force of numbers making up the "experienced community" produced by the marches, and leaving no doubt as to the brutality deployed by the state, the third group presents the spectacle of bodies in pain and of death. If, as Elaine Scarry reminds us, pain resists language, then its nonverbal communication through sight may be the most powerful way of eliciting spectatorial sympathy. Two shots in particular merit consideration, and they are arranged on the same page: on the left is the morgue, on the right a dead boy of about ten. Snatched from death, they exist in a frozen temporality of pure presentness, eternalized with emotional effects on the reader-viewer. On the left, a distant guard stands in control while parents walk in front of the brutalized bodies, presumably trying to identify a lost son or daughter. The experience of the senses is invoked by a gesture of the woman in the forefront: she is covering her nose as she gazes at the manhandled corpses, so that one is confronted by the diminished experience of death yielded by visual representation. On the right, the angelic dead boy is captured along the vector of horizontality that echoes Holbein's Christ, except that rigor mortis is replaced here by the semblance of sleep. Below him, Poniatowska has chosen a question that seems to be culled from the *testimonios* and is meant to represent collective outrage while charting the reader's reaction: "Who gave orders to do this? Who could possibly have ordered such a thing?"

The transition from these powerful visual experiences toward the realm of textuality informs the reading that is about to begin with a blend of emotional registers and journalistic will to truth. For those readers who in some way experienced the events in question, the book might help locate shared memories and, perhaps by an aggregated individual process, contribute to the construction of the collective memory of Tlatelolco and its powers of resistance; for the rest, it means confronting the powerful traces of a traumatic event that resists an integrated, unified narrative.

One of the many tasks of culture is to address crises, to provide forms and vocabularies that allow for the representation of multivocal experience, individual and collective. The writing on 1968 in Mexico, as represented by the two very different approaches by Paz and Poniatowska, speak to clearly situated conditions of writing and reading that radicalize texts' worldliness, to use Edward Said's term. Paz rises to the heights of philosophical and historical speculation, tracing the thread that connects Mexico's present with its archaeological roots. Poniatowska opts for a fragmented representation of individual experience that strives for social memory. Others followed the path of poetry, fiction, or personal or group memoir.[44] Key questions remain to be answered, now that archives have been opened and secrets begin to be deciphered. The generational utopia of 1968 was met with traumatic closure on October 2; the work of mourning and elaboration has produced impressive intellectual responses that continue to sustain resistance and the fleeting configurations of collective memory.

3

From Diaspora to Agora in Cortázar:
Exile as Continental Space

Like few other intellectuals in the twentieth century, Julio Cortázar stages in his life and in his writing the tensions and contradictions that characterize the relationship between culture and society. Upon receiving the "Orden de Rubén Darío" award in 1983, he praised the Nicaraguan Revolution for pushing culture out on the streets "as if it were an ice-cream or a fruit cart," offering it to the people with the friendly gesture of one who is offering a banana.[1] And yet his texts rarely offer such simple, direct access to cultural forms making their way into the materiality of the world. In fact, Cortázar's fiction enacts a series of cuts and separations setting culture in a world apart. And were it to be ingested like a piece of fruit, it would be of a kind that only a selected few would be able to identify, savor, and digest.

Cortázar can be said to represent in paradigmatic ways the figure of the author in the Latin American sixties—that is why he is present in several chapters of this book. Committed to originality and technical innovation, to literary revolution as an antidote to the prescriptive, conventional ways of the past, he struggled to remain true to both political change and the absolute autonomy of the imagination. Later in his life he let his hair and beard grow, as if Che Guevara's image haunted him like a spectral partner. They had more than a little in common: both remained true to a pursuit of informality and humor that was inseparable from a fierce desire to attain the threshold of utopia.

How does Cortázar negotiate his desire to produce cultural forms of accessible consumption with his almost messianic conception of the intellectual as the outsider who can approach the revelation of transcendence from the privileged locus of distance and isolation? To what extent do his stories and novels dramatize the tensions between exile and affiliation, between the individual as visionary or intellectual, and a group that he (rarely she) becomes a member of? If the imagination is a workshop for elaborating the forms of associative life and the possibilities of civil society, how are they fleshed out in the fictions of Cortázar? Finally, how do all these questions stage the problematic relationship between culture and society, literature and political life, the intellectual and his audience? In Cortázar's case this relationship underwent insistent scrutiny and revision; it seems fair to say he never worked it out in a definitive way. In fact, he kept going back to the question of exile so as to fashion it in a way that would strip it of notions of disloyalty and voluntary separation. "From diaspora to agora," he once proclaimed as he put forward the notion that the choice of geographic separation did not preclude strong affiliation and commitment.[2] And, indeed, his later works reveal his efforts at producing literature that elicited a politics of reading. This chapter will address the questions posed above by way of the logic of plot and character in Cortázar's writing, tracing the *vraisemblable* as the representational system within which his stories and novels operate. True to the literary imagination of the sixties, his plots reveal a crisis in the family as the culmination of the love plot or as the basic social formation.

Cortázar's tales tell the story of multiple exiles and separations, so that "agora" rarely obtains. Even when the characters are firmly rooted in their hometowns, they seldom belong: the narrative trigger that produces the well-known "Cortázar effect" frequently leads to a powerful but solitary confrontation with the "other" marked, indeed, by the elusive experience of transcendence, but undoubtedly also establishing a break with social affiliation. The narrative circuits through which readerly pleasure is produced have a disposition to separation as the precondition for revelation. This may in part have to do with Cortázar's surrealist beginnings, in that aesthetic practice is set radically apart from bourgeois life. It can also be seen as a productive contradiction to be located as both a creative nucleus—in which exile must be transformed into the positivity of writing—and the imposition of distance and alienation. More interestingly, I hope, the questions at hand will be a reminder of the multiple subject positions that constitute what Foucault would call the "author function" in Cortázar.[3] Rather than erase the different positions, I want to suggest that the name "Cortázar," referring to a historically specific figure, helps tie together potentially contradictory discursive strands. Further, these discursive strands are produced in dialogue with shifting contexts of enunciation, so that the author function actually assembles but never resolves statements and positions that stem from the disparity of historical change.

Without attempting to produce a systematic reading of Cortázar's work, I will map some of the ways in which social energy circulates and is negotiated in a few of his short stories and novels, deliberately eschewing the question of the fantastic and its metaphysics of otherness. Perhaps by avoiding the narrative focus of the fantastic—which concerned Cortázar criticism for decades—my comments can bear on the contexts in which it breaks in, rooting it in a social experience that not only makes the fantastic possible but also conveys information on the conception of the collective that underpins it. After all, if civil society can be seen to be molded by and to include cultural and ideologized relationships, narrative would be one of the key reservoirs of forms in which its figuration takes place: like the nation, civil society is a projection of the imagination. As civil society is rehearsed in fiction, its forms are represented and announced in the world.

An early story published in *Bestiario*, "Omnibus" (1951), provides a microcosmos of Cortázar's representation of collective behavior and can help us start thinking about civil society and exile. Means of transportation are not infrequent narrative locations in Cortázar's work—an incomplete list would include the ship in *Los premios* (1960), the metro in "Manuscrito hallado en un bolsillo" and "Cuello de gatito negro" in *Octaedro* (1974), and the airplane in "La isla al mediodía" in *Todos los fuegos el fuego* (1966)— and they tend to provide the centripetal force that gathers characters and springs the stories into action. In "Omnibus" the gathering produces the experience of alienation from the group. The state and its institutions are absent; the passengers assembled in the 168 bus are a collective that has in common nothing but the route—an itinerary that draws the urban coordinates of Buenos Aires from the outskirts (Villa del Parque) to the central Retiro station. This is the space of civil society, where power rests in the bus conductor and the ticket collector, but only to the extent that they provide the service of transportation as mere displacement. Yet this space becomes mysteriously charged with hostility: the young woman who looks forward to a leisurely Saturday afternoon is inexplicably turned into the target of angry looks from the other passengers. It is not perhaps mere accident that the silent aggressors are all on their way to the Chacarita Cemetery, bearing flowers (foul-smelling daisies, black carnations) that are the signs of solidarity against the stranger. The mark of a lack is shared by a young man who gets on the bus, like Clara, without flowers. They are the target of the seething, quiet anger that emanates from all the others on the bus. Not a word is uttered: what binds the society of haters is the presence of the strangers, which echoes Freud's point about the need to hate an outsider in order to establish group identity. Their terrified escape from the bus at Retiro Station leads less to liberation than to anxious conformity: the young man buys Clara and himself a bunch of violets so that they, too, can be equipped with the mark of belonging—even though their destination is not the cemetery.[4]

What is the spectral vision of the social suggested by this nightmarish trip? The fraternity of two comes about as a defense against the larger group: the urban world creates incomprehensible enmities and banishments; anger lurks around (even the bus's movement is conveyed in terms that connote anger); this is not a safe public experience. The space in which association takes place is dangerous because nothing prepares the characters for the incomprehensible fury of their fellow beings. In fact, the community is constituted in and through the act of hating together. Furthering the disconcerting nature of the passengers' aggression is the absence of language: there are no explicit codes with which to master the social networks. The social text is unreadable: neither Clara nor the young man who becomes her ally have any way of knowing what motivates the silent rage in the bus. The gaze, instead, is charged with inarticulate messages that cannot be clearly deciphered but which convey powerful hostility.

It is, indeed, not uncommon for the social relationships in Cortázar's fiction to be regulated by inscrutable whispers, pregnant looks, or strange noises. The well-known example is "Casa tomada," in which the brother-sister couple is banished from their home by murmurs that are neither investigated nor translated. What takes over is a dark, aggressive power whose identity is never revealed: part of its force lies precisely in the impossibility of translating it into language. We are not too far from the world of the "disappeared" invoked in a much later story, "Segunda vez," where, again, a man and a woman (Carlos and María Elena) are drawn together by the frightening qualities of their surroundings. The formation of a small community

bonded by the shared experience of not knowing why they have been summoned to the office on Maza Street suggests that fear may be at the root of
association. On the other side of the door are the officials who have both
the knowledge and the power to decide on the citizens' future. In these stories the "couples" are formed precisely as they confront the aggression of a
group that the fictive text represents as fundamentally alienating: rather
than voluntary association, we encounter a joint search for safety in the
midst of a public existence marked by danger. If, as Adam Ferguson claimed
in his early reflections on it, civil society is a space where the common
good can be pursued, its rendering in these stories by Cortázar would suggest the very opposite: it is a space in which danger obtains.[5] Danger is increased by silence, which weakens the social bond. In "Circe," for example, the character makes his way through the narrated events struggling to
decode incomplete messages about his fiancée Delia: half-heard gossip,
veiled comments, pregnant looks from neighbors underscore Mario's inability to know from the outset: "This time the coincidence of incomplete
gossip hurt him . . . the incredible uneasiness in his father's gestures. . . .
Also the girl from the pharmacy . . . and even Don Emilio, always discreet
with his pencils and oilskin notebooks. Everyone was talking about Delia
Mañara with a trace of shame."[6]

Messages are either unclear or derived from a withheld origin: when
Mario starts receiving anonymous letters, his anxiety is heightened by the
secret identity of the sender and by the deliberate ambiguity of the messages. The reader senses that even the narrator withholds information, so
that she shares Mario's suspicious ignorance in a world of family, neighbors,
and friends who seem to know something they hint at but conceal. Only
the shocking discovery of the cockroach at the end reveals a secret everyone
else seemed to be in on. Similar communication problems within constituted groups (family, friends, neighborhood, nation) often lie at the root of
the experience of the fantastic in Cortázar, as if the social were indeed the
site of dehumanization: "Cartas de mamá," "La salud de los enfermos,"
"Carta a una señorita en Paris," or "Lejana" would be a few illustrative cases.

That said, it would be misleading to suggest that forms of voluntary
association are absent in Cortázar's fiction: one would have to remember
the long nights filled with friends and conversation in *Rayuela* and in *Libro
de Manuel*. The experience shared by friends is one that frequently provides the narrative architecture for his fiction; hence it is necessary to study

the location of the individuals vis-à-vis each other, the forms of affiliation, and the ways in which subject formation is tied in with social codes. The forms of association and the levels of intimacy vary, but identification with the other is eschewed. A story in *Bestiario* provides a point of departure. In "Las puertas del cielo" ("The Gates of Heaven") the relationship between Mauro and Celina on the one hand and Doctor Marcelo Hardoy on the other is based on difference and social distance. The lawyer-narrator becomes the friend of the working-class couple as an ethnographer of sorts; the semblance of friendship barely veils a detached interest in the peculiar texture of the existence of the lower classes combined with a certain boredom with law, music, or horse riding. The narrator frequents the world of Mauro (who works in the Mercado de Abasto, the central market) and Celina (a former cabaret dancer) with a disturbing mixture of curiosity and disgust, condescendingly observing their kind from a distance masked by the protocols of solidarity and friendship. For this reader, the story is decidedly encoded in the discourse of racism: Marcelo goes to seedy clubs in order to observe the "monsters"—the lower classes of Native American ancestry, contemptuously called *negros* or *achinados*:

They heave into sight around eleven in the evening, coming down from obscure sections of the city, deliberate and sure, by ones and twos, the women almost dwarves and very dark, the guys like Javanese or Indians from the north bound into tight black suits or suits with checks, the hard hair painfully plastered down, little drops of brilliantine catching blue and pink reflections, the women with enormously high hairdos which make them look even more like dwarves . . . the women talk loudly so that they'll be looked at, then the gorillas grow more fierce and I've seen one let go with a flat of the hand that spun the face and half the hairdo of a cross-eyed girl in white who was drinking anise. Furthermore there's the smell; one could not conceive of the monsters without that smell of damp powder against the skin, of rotten fruit. . . . They use peroxide too, dark girls raising a rigid ear of corn over the heavy earth of their faces; they even practice blond expressions. . . . Looking sidewise at Mauro, I could spell out the difference in his face with its Italian features, the face of the Buenos Aires docks, with neither Negro nor provincial mixture, and I remembered suddenly that Celina was much closer to the monsters. (106–8, *160–61*)

The fleeting moment in which an otherworldly Celina is seen by Marcelo and Mauro is meant to suggest a fantastic experience shared by both men, but even in the instant of commonality the text opts for distance and disgust.

The heightened prejudice of the character in "Las puertas del cielo" is present in another early text, *El examen*; in his later works it has been erased.[7] It is, of course, to be read in the context of Cortázar's reaction to Perón's manipulation of populism, and in his later years Cortázar revised his position.[8] Regardless of the political connotations, the representation of the social sphere is traversed by separation, deliberate distance vis-à-vis the autochthonous groups that happen to make up the bulk of the proletariat. While the man of letters looks on and down, no solidarity or sense of the commonality of experience can be imagined.[9] In fact, the fictive text utters in an almost hysterical way the discourse of social rejection that has fragmented the Argentine political unconscious. These early texts often read as a turning away from the national.

That the urban space in which the narrator makes these observations should be a *milonga*, a dancing bar where tangos are played, suggests that the proletariat is watched with particular contempt when it is not at work. The long disquisitions about the monsters' bad taste in clothing and in grooming is guided by high culture's bent for distinction: Hardoy's contemptuous gaze goes over the choices made by the *negros* when they have the freedom to construct their own identities, while at work their appearance bespeaks their subordination. Beyond the controlled space of work, in the public space of leisure, the masses of native American stock become more threatening with their animal qualities, as if they were stalking their prey: "with the brutal faces below them, or with the expression of aggressiveness, ready and waiting its hour, or the efficient torsos set on slender waists" (107, *161*). In its powerful tension between curiosity and disgust, "Las puertas del cielo" gives away the deep divisions that bar the constitution of an integrated civil sphere. The early stories do not only exclude the *provincianos*, the *negros*, the *achinados*: the mark of exclusion appears again in the petite bourgeoisie. Like the tango bars, other public spaces like cinemas ("La banda") or theaters ("Las ménades"), become the scene in which the contemptuous, puzzled gaze of a detached subject makes the mark of taste. Distinction in Bourdieu's sense of the concept organizes these stories discursively and marks divisions that fragment the congregation.[10] That this should happen in the public spaces of leisure is particularly significant, because they become the site not of pleasure, but of brutal human energy. "Las ménades" may be the most powerful evocation of the dangers of collective enthusiasm: the story illustrates that even the somewhat educated petit bourgeois ("calm and willing people who prefer known evil to a yet unveiled evil")[11] can be transformed into wild beasts. In "La banda" Lucio Medina finds himself in the Gran Cine Opera, where he expects to see an Anatole Litvak film, only to be surrounded by an audience that does not bode well: "There was something going on that didn't seem right. . . . Predominantly obese women spread out in the stalls, and, like the one next to me, they seemed accompanied by more or less numerous offspring. It surprised him that this kind of people reserved stalls at the Opera, many of such women had the complexion and attire of respectable cooks in their Sunday best" (*348*).

Cortázar's well-known penchant for the sophisticated and not yet known except by a small elite frequently lies at the root of his character construction—hence the disgust with the musical assortment offered by the *maestro* in "Las ménades," the choice of a Litvak film as the only alternative in the Buenos Aires of 1947, *escaso de novedades* in "La banda," and the drunken stupor that allows Hardoy to tolerate the vulgarity of the "monsters" in "Las puertas del cielo."[12]

There is more to this complete absence of identification with the lower class sectors: it also marks the impossibility of belonging. Cortázar's characters flaunt the marks of an exilic marginality as a sign of intellectual distinction that bespeaks the impossibility of social cohesion. The relationship between the individual and the group suggested here locates Cortázar's characters in the vicinity of a Nietzschean conception of superior man as a noble individual who has to stand apart and establish his rejection of any conception of community.[13] Complicating matters is the view of the groups in the stories we have been discussing as potentially harmful (actually destructive in the case of "Las ménades"). In a Hobbesian sense, these representations of the collective body portray it as terrible and terrifying, thereby justifying the need for strong social control. A disturbing mixture of conceptions of the individual and the social emerges from these Nietzschean and Hobbesian strands.

What do we find if we look for other forms of association in Cortázar's fiction? Friendship is certainly present in all its forms and mutations; the paradigmatic examples would be the doppelgängers (Oliveira and Traveler, Marcos and Andrés, Nico and Toto) and the groups of friends that structure much of the action in *Rayuela* and *Libro de Manuel*. Letting the title take the lead, let us start with "Los amigos," which appeared in *Final de juego* (1956). Echoing the grammar of horse racing, the story tersely narrates the murder of a certain Romero committed by Beltrán, an old friend of his from the horse-racing world. Motives are not explained; Beltrán's murder plot hinges on the fact that Romero will stop to talk to him, as an old friend would, thereby providing the perfect target. After the shot, the chilling closing reflection of the murderer is the very inversion of friendship: "Driving calmly, Number Three thought that Romero's last vision had been that of Beltrán, a friend of former years from the hippodrome" (*353*).

If murder and friendship form a striking combination, it would be misleading to give this story a ruling or ordering quality in the Cortázar corpus. More common in his stories are friendships that stage the shift from closeness to separation, mapping misunderstandings and differences that cannot be overcome. Friends underscore the inevitable loneliness of the individual: characters are drawn together only to have to confront some form of loss. Multiple misunderstandings provide the scene of writing for "Sobremesa": between the friends Funes and Robirosa, between the letter writers—and friends—Alberto Rojas and Federico Moraes as to the former's friendship, and between reader and narrator as to the dates and the sequence of the events. Yet Funes's suicide has a brutal impact that transcends the preceding difficulties and also stems from them: something happened between him and his old friend Robirosa that may help explain his death. Even one of the later stories, "La escuela de noche," written when Cortázar deliberately sought the voice of association, opens with the loss of a friendship that frames the narrated events: "I no longer know anything about Nito nor do I want to know"[14]). Greater than the shock of discovering what goes on at school at night, and of suffering the torture and indignity meted out by schoolmates and teachers alike, is the final realization that his good friend Nito (presented in the not unusual doppelgänger pairing Cortázar likes) has become part of the gang of sadists and torturers and is ready to threaten Toto with murder if he gives them away. It is that final turn of the screw that gives the story the added horror of betrayal as it explains the end of a friendship.

If we turn away from separation and examine instead the kinds of social force that draws people together, we might see the possibilities of social formations in Cortázar's fiction. *Los premios* (*The Winners*) is precisely about this: a disparate assortment of people have won a cruise on a luxury boat, and, faced with a problem that affects them all, they create a number of alliances.

The captain's mysterious absence is, of course, an allegory of Argentina as the ship of state with no one at the helm—and the novel is indeed traversed by the discourse of national disillusionment—but in functional narrative terms it provides the opportunity for the construction of power groups to supplement a lack of authority. In the absence of the state, the novel stages the formation of civil society and the possibilities of affiliation. This central theme is lyrically presented in Persio's first interior monologue, in which the social configurations about to be played out are anticipated as a chess game of sorts, but without known rules, "as on an infinite chessboard between mute opponents, where bishops and queens turn into dolphins and toy satyrs."[15] The individuals who have won the cruise are seen as a disparate assortment of isolated people about to be subjected to the social game: "the mixture, verging on the dreadful, of lonely creatures who find themselves stepping out of taxis leaving stations, lovers and offices" (31, *49*).

But the text soon reveals the rules that regulate the game of association: they are structured along the divisions of class, which becomes the ordering principle of the chessboard. The novel's epigraph, taken from Dostoevsky's *The Idiot*, gives away the problematic nature of the attempt to represent the "vulgar" classes: "What is an author to do with ordinary people, absolutely ordinary, and how can he put them before his readers so as to make them at all interesting?" Cortázar attempts to solve the quandary in *Los premios* by means of caricature and contrast. Perhaps, in fact, the sole purpose of the lower classes in the system of aesthetic positions is to serve as a foil, a negative reference point. The *mersas* or petit bourgeois are gleefully portrayed with Cortázar's bent for the satirical imitation of their speech; apart from them he locates an educated group of higher class, endowed with interesting subjectivities and bearing the narrative weight. With one significant exception, the "vulgar" people are not, despite the epigraph, rendered interesting in *Los premios*; they constitute a chorus of sorts, reacting to events and people in their highly coded sociolect.[16] As the difficulties confronting the passengers unfold, the novel organizes the action along a series of axes that produce divisions: active/passive, refined/vulgar, man/woman.

The *mersas* do not take control of the situation, they do not confront the officer on board and directly address the mysteries about the ship's destination, the blocked stern, and the possible incidence of typhus. They merely observe and comment on events with a petty sense of respectability: their petit bourgeois codes of acceptable behavior often lead to outrage.

Hence they constitute a little ghetto of outsiders that the reader soon finds predictable, while his interest is drawn to the self-mocking and perceptive conversational exchanges that construct the pairings of the intelligent and educated. The vulgar/lower-middle-class characters are marked by their names and nicknames, indicators of their self-importance and bad taste: doña Rosita, la señora de Trejo, la señora de Presutti, la Beba, la Nelly, Atilio Presutti (el Pelusa).[17] As inexperienced travelers, they tend to get seasick, making their various symptoms and their cures the subject of long, ill-informed disquisitions; when not contending with the miseries of nausea and green faces, they gossip in an irrelevant patter. Thus, class determines the construction of the subjectivity of these characters, who constitute a distinct social group. And yet it would be misleading to claim that they represent the kind of organizational bond that underpins civil society, for the reader is made aware of the narrator's mocking depiction of their kind, and the various boundaries drawn by their tastes, their manners, and their speech. As in the case of "La banda" or "Las ménades," the collective is constructed as uneducated, naïve, and coarse in their tastes. The *doñas* and the *señoras* gossip about the propriety of codes of sexual behavior—and are therefore shocked at Paula Lavalle's aristocratic bent for flouting such codes; la Beba would like to attract Raúl Costa's attention but is too awkward to dare and, further, has the misfortune of liking a homosexual man who is trying to seduce her brother. Only the most vulgar of them all, Atilio Presutti (el Pelusa)—precisely because he is a noble savage of sorts, quite oblivious to the social anxieties that mark the rest of his class—is valued by both groups. He is vulgar yet active, and the very physical prowess that is associated with boxing plays a positive role at the end. But most of the others are portrayed as living epitomes of Bourdieu's observation that "the manner in which culture has been acquired lives on in the manner of using it."[18] Their patterns of consumption, their behavior-modeling parameters, all bespeak their class origins. More significantly, in *Los premios* the indicators of lower-middle-class status see their way into the text through the critical gaze of a higher-class character.

As noted, the lower classes and their tastes become a negative reference point, a field of encounter for a communication pattern that excludes them in the very movement of drawing together reader, narrator, and sophisticated character. It is a reading stance that mirrors the social divisions and pacts of Argentine society. Mimesis would lie as much in the novel's representational felicities (of which there are many, given Cortázar's ear and his talent for parody), as in the reproduction of a social practice in the very act of reading. Particularly significant is the way in which Cortázar chooses to represent cultural consumption as mediated by class-based relationships, so that every choice depends on what is construed to be of value in the eyes of the upper class; social anxiety marks these options because the desire to belong is foreclosed. Witness, for instance, la Nelly's "learning" of the protocols of the higher classes through magazines:

While she was waiting for Doña Pepa to finish doing her hair, Nelly relished with intense gratification photos of various cocktail parties that had taken place in the largest homes in Buenos Aires. She was fascinated by Jacobita Echaniz' elegant style, as she chatted with her readers, really as if she were one of them, without acting at all snobbish about the best society, but at the same time letting them know (why did *her* mother wear her hair like a washerwoman, for heaven's sake?) that she belonged to a different world, where everything was rosy, perfumed, and gloved. (225, *283*)

Cortázar's ideal reader flouts the codes Nelly admires or, like Paula Lavalle, belongs to the class that sets them. Her/his reading of texts is the inverted image of Nelly's reading of magazines—an exercise in freedom, critical detachment, and independence. Nelly, instead, wants to belong: not to her own class but to another. Hence her disapproving glance at her mother's hairdo, which confirms her own extraction and her distance from distinction. The very discovery that in her neighborhood (Parque Centenario) there had been a garden show visited by Julia Bullrich de Saint fills her with longing to have seen an event touched by the magic of refinement ("And all that had taken place in Centenary Park, just around the corner from where her friend Coca Chimento lived, the girl who worked with her at the store?") (226, *284*).

The other members of Nelly's class are also depicted by their unsophisticated forms of cultural consumption: Felipe and Lucio read *Reader's Digest* because, as Felipe clumsily acknowledges to the amused Paula, it's more convenient, since it summarizes the most famous works; doña Pepa, doña Rosita, Nelly, and el Pelusa discuss boxing films and the merits of such stars as *la* Norma Talmadge, *la* Lillian Gish, or *la* Marlene Dietrich. When the efforts of don Galo and doctor Restelli to promote social contacts culminate in the talent show, Mrs. Trejo plays antiquated piano pieces and Nelly recites cliché-ridden poetry. Whatever they do, they cannot get it right, the novel keeps telling us. Early on, an exchange between Medrano, López, and Claudia establishes the manner of using symbolic goods as the key marker of class and as the boundary of exclusion, to the point that the social game becomes a veritable struggle. Says Medrano: "You can't be offended by these people's ignorance or coarseness when neither of us has done anything to help change matters. We'd rather organize our lives so as to have the least possible contact with them. . . . An excellent opportunity which they unconsciously exploit to throw us off balance. . . . Every time one of them spits on the deck, it's as though they were putting a bullet between our eyes" (95, *127*).

What follows is a recitation of the habits and tastes of the *mersas* (loud radios, clichés, pajamas on deck) that justify keeping distances intact.

In contrast with the *mersas*, the members of the other group are characters whose cultural capital is the result of a validated educational and social origin. It is this very cultural capital that allows them to introduce distance and irony into their perceptions, to transgress the anxious constraints of the petit bourgeois—to acquire what we might call "readerly interest." A significant portion of *Los premios* is devoted to long conversational exchanges whereby their subjectivities are constructed as they explore each other, talking (not unusually in a Spanish peppered with *mots justes* in French or English), sharing their pasts and their interests. Persio, Medrano, López, Raúl, and even two women, Paula and Claudia, are the characteristic Cortázar heroes, working their way in and out of a world that baffles them with its uncanny mixture of petty troubles and hints of transcendence. They are educated, intellectually stimulating, and endowed with a critical as well as esthetic sense that allows for interesting transgressions of the conventional doxa, as well as for what Max Weber called a "stylization of life" that organizes their practice. Paula and Raúl represent this disposition most effectively in their playful seriousness, their flouting of norms of bourgeois sexual behavior, their easy good looks and, particularly in Paula's case—though to an extent in Raúl's nonchalant homosexuality as well—unabashed disregard for respectability. Distance and difference organize the fields of force around them: they establish distance from the constraints of necessity, but above all from the conventional codes of middle-class attitudes. Their vigilant intellectual consciousness is eminently critical: rather than mediate social life and articulate forms of cohesion, its effect is to question, to undermine the discourse of association—especially if it is trammeled by the narrow exigencies of the national. The lucid, incisive discussions about the rhetoric of national belonging are perhaps the best illustrations of this effect: as shall be seen in Chapter Four, this is a time when the nation is superseded by the continental and the international. A case in point is a discussion between Raúl, López, and Paula on the question of the language of patriotism prevalent in the (Peronist) Argentina of the 1950s. They question the cliché-ridden enthusiasm of nationalistic fervor ("the imperishable fatherland, the eternal laurels, the guardsman dies but doesn't surrender. . . . Is it possible they use this vocabulary as reins, or blinders?" asks Raúl) and end up with a variation on a skeptical, detached formula about the very existence of the *patria* (fatherland):

> It doesn't exist, but it's sweet (Paula)
> It exists but it isn't sweet (López)
> It doesn't exist, we exist it (Raúl).[19] (263, *330*)

In their long conversations, they discuss works of Henry James, Onetti, Asturias, Alban Berg, or Picasso with the certainty of possessing cultural legitimacy and with the casual ease (most particularly in the case of the aristocratic Paula Lavalle, whose self-confidence has been handed down by family privilege and time—as if true culture were mere nature, yet, of course, inherited). Their witty repartee ranges from the death of a certain kind of writing to the metaphysical searches embarked upon by the characters. Thus, Paula articulates the sort of poetics that Cortázar tried to achieve in *Rayuela*, defending a writing that forfeits beauty in search of a new one that might no longer be called literary. As the most patrician member of the group, she has the privilege of postulating cultural codes that have not yet been validated by the established system. Like Horacio in *Rayuela*, Paula transforms the basic dispositions of a lifestyle into a system of aesthetic principles, negotiating freely the distances separating highbrow culture from more daring and innovative forms.

Faced with the need to take command of a ship with no apparent control or destination, this group actively confronts the problem, taking risks and power. Yet, as the action unfolds, it becomes clear that as a social formation, the group on board is ineffective. Not only was the stern empty after all—and, indeed, that empty center is a powerful metaphor at various levels of significance—but it also makes action retrospectively unnecessary. The death of Medrano is a high price to pay for this absent center.

One wonders if the passive group might not have been wiser after all. . . .
The novel has the brief brilliance of fireworks: the trip, like the intimation
of exile, suggests that departure provides the scene of writing, which is
foreclosed by the return.

Unlike *Los premios*, *Libro de Manuel*[20] (1973) presents an already constituted group; far from playing with the vagaries of social formation, the
later novel gives the group an action-propelling function. Moreover, this
group is held together by friendship, solidarity, and a common purpose,
which combines the spirit of liberation of the sixties with the clandestine
activities that followed. It would seem, therefore, to offer the conditions of
possibility for meaningful social action and the seeds of civil society. The
group in question is "la Joda," made up of Ludmilla, Marcos, Gladis, Patricio, Loenstein, Oscar, Roland, Fernando, Gómez, Monique, and Lucien
Verneuil. The choice of the name "Joda," which conveys a complex knot
of playful, irreverent, perturbing, and disruptive notions catches the reader's
attention. It seems to hark back to Cortázar's privileging of essentially surrealist qualities in a program for social and political action: la Joda turns
out to be a group that provokes a variety of social disturbances and, more
important, kidnaps a counterrevolutionary leader who may be associated
with the CIA.

Cortázar's representation of the group, its ideology, its forms of action, and its achievements bespeaks the difficulties that trammel the combination of surrealism and political commitment. For in order to construct the representation of a playful, metaphysically curious, humanly
transformative as well as politically efficacious movement, he falls prey to
an irrationalist and ultimately hardly credible rendering of its aims and its
achievements.[21] La Joda would seem to exemplify the possibilities of creation of the "new man" in his political, spiritual, and erotic dimensions,
but it often takes on the appearance of frivolity, sometimes echoing the
Club de la Serpiente in *Rayuela* and its utter neglect of dying Rocamadour.
While Manuel receives more attention and is the future addressee of newspaper clippings that report the horrors of torture, repression, and violence,
his parents and their friends spend their time chatting until the early hours
of the morning, making late-night snacks, joking incessantly, and leading
a life ruled by what it is tempting to call the "playing principle." Their existence resembles the somewhat aimless wandering of teenagers, unbound
by work or obligation. If we observe the forms of subversion they produce,

we notice that they take on the shape of happenings, of theatrical performances that disrupt different forms of practical life without altering them in lasting or significant ways. In fact, they are presented as amusing *microagitaciones* designed to subvert the workings of civil society as it pertains to urban and commercial life: Patricio will stand up and yell in the cinema while a Brigitte Bardot film is being shown; Marcos and Gómez will do the same thing at a Bibi Anderson film or during a Wagner opera; Lucien Verneuil will disrupt a bus ride by thanking the driver profusely for his excellent services; Roland and Patricio act out a miniplay at the green grocer's, delaying the other transactions and making fun of the time constraints of consumer society; Gómez and Susana create a scandal at the Galeries Reunies, complaining about their cleaning practices in a deliberate misinterpretation of advertising that claims that a sale will sweep away the merchandise; Gómez and Marcos disrupt lunch at the elegant Restaurant Vagenande by ordering leeks à la vinaigrette and standing up to eat them, furthering the general discomfort by adducing the intestinal advantages of such behavior. Perhaps the most ambitious bit of mischief involves the coordinated efforts of Gómez, Roland, Lucien Verneuil, Monique, and Susana at a bistro where they damage the packets of Gauloises and the matchboxes sold to the public so as to undermine the confidence not only in a cigarette brand that is a long-standing French institution, but also in the "ship of state."

While it may be tempting to go along with the author's intentions to consider these actions revolutionary, it is hard to ignore the restrictions that obtain in the particular choices made by Cortázar. For what is at stake in the *microagitaciones* described above is the production of mistrust in the social body—mistrust chiefly located in the reliability of commercial transactions and the underpinnings of urban life. If department stores, restaurants, green grocers, and buses become the stage for the irreverent undermining of the business they are supposed to conduct, citizens will inevitably experience anxiety about their everyday dealings with them. While the kind of unrest this creates may have eventual social and political consequences, the immediate effect would be the production of collective impatience and irritation: the members of la Joda resemble mischievous children who are out to test their parents' patience. It is not surprising that the more skeptical Andrés should call these activities *travesuras* (pranks), for indeed they are touched by a childish disrespect for efficiency and expeditiousness. Cortázar's deliberate detachment from the practical aspects of the bourgeois order in favor of a surrealist cultivation of faculties centered on play and the unconscious falls prey to the risk of futility. Is it possible to act significantly upon the social body by irritating a few citizens immersed in their bourgeois concerns? Will such actions have any long-term revolutionary consequences? Will power be obtained by disrupting consumption without affecting production?

The values and practices that la Joda represents are anchored in a festive celebration of youthful life, subordinated to the generational ethos of the sixties. There are contradictory tensions traversing this ethos: Is it out to transform social and political structures, or is it merely the ineffectual subversive ideology of a group of young friends leading a bohemian lifestyle? The question becomes more pressing when we scrutinize the kind of relationships that obtain within the group itself. Were we to take la Joda as metonymical of the future society, we would stumble upon marks of inequality and deeply embedded patriarchal structures. One crucial question is gender, its attributions and the kind of subject formations it charts. *Libro de Manuel* is no exception to Cortázar's writing in that it constructs fields of action and behavior ruled by the most traditionally conceived, gender-specific divisions. In this novel there is no Paula Lavalle, daring to subvert social and cultural stereotypes from the privileged locus her social position allows; instead, Susana, Gladis, and Ludmilla are in la Joda as partners of Patricio, Oscar, and Marcos—not as independently active participants. In fact, the novel describes the manner in which Gladis and Ludmilla join the group, and there is no attempt to ascribe to them a political—let alone a revolutionary—consciousness. In a Paris traversed by desire and playfulness, femininity is valued as a generous, erotic force, willing to embrace danger and pain as the seals of amorous commitment. Reason and conceptual clarity are not imputed to the women as lovers. Thus, Gladis finds herself in the house in Verrieres where the "VIP" will be taken after he is kidnapped, and while Gómez and Heredia play chess, and Susana and Ludmilla prepare sandwiches in the kitchen, Oscar muses as he smokes in the dark next to her: "Oscar wondered why Gladis, how it was possible that finally Gladis there with him, in the final Screwery . . . and Gladis so sure of herself and like someone going to a party in the suburbs among cedars and drinks, that tranquil decision of Gladis knowing that they would fire her from Aerolíneas Argentinas, that everything could go to hell" (302, *301*).

When he asks her why she is there, Gladis can only account for her decision by foregoing knowledge and resorting to the grammar of feeling: "[only after a while] did she tell him that she didn't know, that it was fine that way, that she was afraid, that it was starting to get cold, that she loved him so much" (302, *301*). Likewise, Ludmilla confesses to Susana the reasons for her involvement with la Joda and Marcos while they prepare sandwiches for the group: "you know, I wanted to take care of where he'd been kicked and when I saw him all black and blue, poor thing, bloop" (303, *302*), where the metonymic *bloop* stands for notions Ludmilla can never completely articulate. Susana's reply is as significant as Ludmilla's explanation, for it limits the merits of the decision to loyalty to a man: "Well, now I understand why you're here, said Susana, who really had understood since the word go, you're the kind who puts herself on the line for her man if it comes to that, some girl" (303, *302*).

The distribution of space and action furthers the fundamental division of subject positions between men and women: the men are usually chatting, plotting, and smoking in the living room; the women are in the kitchen. The hesitation felt by Gladis and Monique when they are about to follow Susana and Ludmilla into the kitchen is a case in point: "Gladis and Monique were about to follow them automatically as befit the behavior of the maenads, but something told them that it was better to leave them alone" (301, *300*). It is precisely the notion that it is natural ("befitting") for women to occupy a certain space that bespeaks the traditional structures undergirding this novelistic world; it has the unexamined qualities of ideological material, and it only allows for limited fields of action. When Ludmilla asks Marcos to let her follow him to Verrieres, she is not only adopting the locus of subjection, but also subjecting herself to secondary functions in the struggle for change: "We'll make you men lunch and take care of what hygiene and good habits call for" (298, *297*).

Referring to women as *las ménades* furthers their distance from reason and meaningful action: like the characters in the early short story bearing the title "Las ménades," these are women dominated by powerful enthusiasms—who knows what they might get up to if not subjected to control. The novel ends up reaffirming rational political activity as exclusively male: only one gender constitutes revolutionary meaning and practice, the other's sole creative function is to reproduce the labor force, feed it, look after it, while helping keep the fire of eros burning.[22] Espousing a revolutionary agenda may fail to resemanticize existing gender categories and thus end up falling prey to conservative forms. This is important from the point of view of the logic of plot and its alignment with an era's dominant fictions: Cortázar's revolutionary longings, like those of the era he so eloquently represents, did not take him beyond the strictures of patriarchy. The *vraisemblable* of the sixties rests on a reserve of images and stories that stop short of envisaging gender equality, as if that were a possibility that escaped the revolutionary agenda. This is one of the many significant ways in which Cortázar helps us study the decade, in its expansiveness as well as in the limits of the thinkable.

Cortázar's spiritual and ideological affiliations with the 1968 student protest movements constitute a powerful subtext for *Libro de Manuel*, which is encoded along the discursive lines articulated by the numerous graffiti written on the walls at the Universities of Nanterre and la Sorbonne. The novel's dialogue with that utopian revolutionary moment is made quite clear in several of Cortázar's writings;[23] its traces are patently clear in the ideology of dream, revolt, and festival that permeates the narrated events. Like the student protesters who marched in 1968, la Joda and its young members are part of a generational crisis rebelling against the rigid structures and the authoritarian hierarchies of post–World War II bourgeois society. In a trancelike state, the student protesters in history and in fiction found the way for what Michel de Certeau was to call "the irruption of the unthought,"[24] thanks to which dream and revolt combined to produce a carnivalesque form of subversion drawing inspiration from Trotsky and Marcuse but also from Rimbaud and Breton. "Noticias del mes de mayo," published in *Ultimo Round*,[25] offers a productive intertextual echo revealing the discursive homogeneity between novel and graffiti. In the *Ultimo Round* piece, Cortázar collects the brief apodictic texts that spelled out the erotic, unruly, and festive energy circulating in 1968 Paris: "The restraints put on pleasure / excite the pleasure to live without restraints" (Nanterre); "Down with social realism! Long live surrealism!" (Liceo Condorcet, Paris); "I decree the state of permanent happiness," "Imagination seizes power" (Facultad de Ciencias Políticas, Paris); "Undo your brain as often as your zipper" (Teatro Odeon, Paris); "Love yourselves above others" (Facultad de Letras, Paris). They can in fact be read as the injunctions ruling the members of la Joda, allowing them to plot the kidnapping of the VIP while they unleash the powers of eros and the imagination. Hence the community in this novel has a relationship with the real that suggests the conditions of possibility of a happening,[26] with its fictive combination of theater and action: la Joda is staging a way of living that has tenuous roots in the world of purposive action; it is a performance, a stirring up in order to dissolve habit and convention. Yet, as the end of the novel makes wistfully clear, nothing has been achieved, except for the sacrificial death of Marcos. Some of its members return to Buenos Aires, others share a cigarette lying on the cement floor of what might be a prison jail, Manuel's parents pick him up at Lonstein's after the events at Verrieres and decide to go to the cinema, Andrés talks things over with Lonstein and adds his contribution to Manuel's book. The happening over, the group disbands, its traces to be read by a puzzled future Manuel. The reader anticipates the boy's dealings with the book, constructing a reduced version of the novel that contains only the newspaper clippings. As a kind of surrealist "nonsense act," the novel confirms that politics as representation or even poetic politics may have the power of provocation, but it ends up calling into question its merits as praxis, as the end makes abundantly clear.[27]

As usual, Cortázar constructs a character as outsider, Andrés, to act as a prickly critical voice that moves in and out of the group's activities. Andrés's oscillating position problematizes the solidarity that binds the group together: he is their friend, and enjoys their company, but, like Horacio Oliveira in *Rayuela*, he cannot give up the distance that separates intellectual vigilance from immersion in a social body. Andrés enacts a painful search for connection and commitment that is a constant trek in Cortázar's fiction, and if the reader were to judge him following the ideological thrust propelling *Libro de Manuel*, one would consider him a failure. As Patricio explains to Fernando, his range of action is less than effective: "He listens to a wild amount of aleatory music and reads even more, he's always involved with women, and he's probably waiting for the moment" (24, *29*).

Andrés's amorous entanglements are rather destructive: he is involved with both Ludmilla and Francine, making them suffer not only because of his infidelity but also because he uses the erotic search as the path of exploration in his metaphysical amblings. Perhaps the most violent rendering of this tension is the night at the hotel facing the cemetery, when he sodomizes Francine—an echo of Horacio's sadistic love making with Pola, and of the episode with the *clocharde* in *Rayuela*, where erotic debasement also takes on a Heraclitean turn. But the search is fruitless: Andrés loses the girls and waivers between skepticism and commitment, only to almost ruin la Joda's plan by deciding to join them at the eleventh hour in Verrieres, when he runs the risk of being followed by the police and giving away their secret hiding place. Action is indeed not Andrés's forte. And yet, there is a perverse, involuted justice at work here that is signaled by the fact that at the end of the novel Andrés is alive, cutting more newspaper articles for Manuel, while Marcos (the leader, the man of action) is dead. Lonstein's surprised encounter with Marcos's dead body at the morgue is the novel's final scene; it is immediately preceded by Andrés's reaffirmation of playfulness, art, and critical vigilance as he offers drawings and other materials he has selected for Manuel's future book. This brutal juxtaposition is emblematic of the tension between blindness and insight that ultimately holds this novel together. For despite the deliberate attempt to fully engage in the representation of subversive action as Cortázar's answer to political commitment through writing, it seems to this reader at least that in Andrés's blindness lie more penetrating insights into the relationship between culture and community. Hence one is tempted to affirm yet again that separation remains the privileged locus of understanding, as can be seen in the passages that contain Andrés's meditations on art and its audience, on the nature of the divide between elite art and popular art, on the points of contact between a work of art and reception, and on the very possibility of supra-individual art. The account of Andrés's musings as he listens to Stockhausen's "Prozession" constitutes a probing exploration of the problems facing artistic innovation as it pertains not only to the canon but also to the audience it is to reach. In this text Cortázar uses musical experimentation as a code for artistic innovation in general. True to his integrative understanding of art and subjectivity, the slide from creating new art and creating the new man (sic, alas) is elided: both processes are conflated into a conception of revolutionary action that subsumes every material and spiritual aspect of life:

Corollary and moral: everything should be a leveling off of attention, then, a neutralizing of the extorsion of those outbreaks from the past in the new human way of enjoying music. Yes, a new way of being that tries to include everything, the sugar crop in Cuba, love between bodies, painting and family, and decolonization and dress. It's natural for me to wonder again about the problem of building bridges, how to seek new contacts, the legitimate ones, beyond the loving understanding of different generations and cosmovisions, of a piano and electronic controls, of dialogues among Catholics, Buddhists, and Protestants, of the thaw between two political blocs, of peaceful coexistence. (21–22, *26*)

Intellectual practice is therefore more than disruptive; it attempts to step outside any mandarin space of privilege in order not only to question its conditions of possibility within its own sphere, but also to see its own practice as always situated and occasional, immersed in the materiality of practical life. The artistic enterprise would thus involve not only production but also the forms of anticipating consumption by making it possible. The problem of mediation is conveyed by the metaphor of the bridge: the tension it both resolves and presents is at the core of the critique Andrés's meditation expounds. For the solution lies in the almost impossible conjunction (bridge) between sociopolitical commitment and artistic innovation, and it deliberately foregoes the easy solution of an outmoded socialist realism subordinating artistic production to the dictates of reception, which would be "the intellectual [sic] praxis of stagnant socialisms" (22, *27*). And yet, since the question of communication remains central, we are confronted with an aporia that is the very one *Libro de Manuel* stages: "A bridge is a man crossing a bridge, by God" (23, *27*). The only possible solution is postponed: "out of that baby girl suckling in her mother's arms a woman will come someday who will walk by herself and will cross the bridge" (23, *28*).

It is that future reader of Manuel's generation who can cross the bridge and decode the text that results from the elusive conjunction between art and politics—and one such text is prepared by Andrés at the end. Hence, the artist prevails after all, no matter how well intentioned the attempt to represent a group immersed in commonly shared political goals. To the extent that Andrés can call into question his aesthetic pleasure and principles, and their inevitably problematic dialogue with the social body and its pressing demands, he can offer a self-conscious account of this crucial *problématique* and its endless variations. There is, in fact, a series of explorations on the subject that throw light on some of the possible ways to cross the bridge. One of them, discussed in a jocular vein with Gómez, is an attempt by Terry Riley, a North American composer whose way of establishing contact with his audience is described as "the most immediate, simple, and efficacious that has occurred to anyone since Perotin or Gilles Binchois" (97, *99*). It involves truly participatory composition, allowing members of the audience to take turns producing a few notes at a time. Here again communal art, the art of the people, is an almost impossible alternative: it becomes a populist feast that subscribes to the revolutionary ethos but ends up as a *despatarro universal* (a universal mess). A perverse reading of *Libro de Manuel* would find in the narrative of la Joda's exploits one instance of such *despatarro*, while Andrés's critical distance, even in its least sympathetic rendering, would represent the marginal position enabling a lucid critique. What this reading would salvage in its deliberate movement against the grain would be an articulation of the tensions present in the metaphor of the bridge.

As Cortázar's explicitly political writings make clear, the challenge to be met by intellectuals is precisely epitomized by the emblem of the bridge, for truly revolutionary culture would establish the dialogue between self-conscious, critically informed writing and radically democratic values without relinquishing the force of one or the other. As the detached, genteel critic crossed the bridge, he would retrace the "passage" of Alina Reyes in "Lejana"—but he would be transmuted into a committed writer immersed in the needs of community. Yet the transformation in "Lejana" is made possible by the ruses of fantastic writing, which allow for the suspension of contradictions; in the world, however, crossing the bridge remains a problematic, unresolved passage. For the predicament Cortázar finds himself in has been visited by other intellectuals, who, like many of the fictive characters discussed in this exercise, occupied some form of exile and were not altogether able to transcend the very conditions of possibility that define their work. If, as Habermas notes, intellectuals are the only learning class because of their distance from economic and social reproduction, suspending that distance may have nefarious effects on their ability to construct a discourse of transformation.

The intellectual's perch, then, has the unstable balance of futurity in the fray of material, everyday life. It is a threshold claimed as a site of production, a definitional interstice of long standing in the problematics of aesthetics.[28] In that sense exile may take on a metaphorical quality wherein the intellectual is the outsider, never fully adjusted, or, as Edward Said would have it, "exile for the intellectual in this metaphysical sense is restlessness, . . . constantly being unsettled, and unsettling others."[29] If this position implies—quoting Said again—"both commitment and risk, boldness and vulnerability,"[30] criticism will not be abated even in those cases in which social and political demands subject the intellectual to claims that writing be subordinated to an explicitly political agenda. Early on, the interstitial location was carved out with particular force by Cortázar when he was met by the double pull of imagination and politics. When in 1969 Oscar Collazos wrote "La encrucijada del lenguaje," in *Marcha*, criticizing writers like Cortázar and Vargas Llosa for turning to experimental fiction instead of producing resolutely political writing, Cortázar ardently defended the need to probe unknown territories and linguistic experimentation: "one of the most acute Latin American problems is that we now need more than ever the Che Guevaras of language, the revolutionaries of literature more than the men of revolution."[31]

Thus the challenge was to protect not only the relevance of intellectual production but, also, a separate space in which it could work, borrowing from Aimé Césaire, on "the invention of new souls." Cortázar was not alone in claiming this strategic location; his contemporary Mario Benedetti, who fashioned himself as a committed intellectual without the complicating allegiance to a surrealist aesthetics, also saw the need to stake out and protect a different field for intellectual work. At the 1968 Congreso Cultural de la Habana, he mused: "When someone claims, and not exactly in a metaphorical sense, that a revolutionary writer must either become a soldier or else fail to fulfill his function (which in his particular case is an intellectual function), one has to ask oneself why this peremptory dilemma is forced only on the writer, and not on the worker, the technician, the teacher, or the athlete."[32]

Benedetti's speech concludes with the thrust of proclamation: "The truly revolutionary intellectual will never be able to convert himself into the simple clerk of a man of action; and if he does, he will actually be betraying the revolution, since his natural revolutionary mission is to be a sort of vigilant conscience, imaginative interpreter, purveyor of critique."[33]

Elsewhere, Benedetti focuses even more specifically on the revolutionary powers of the imagination in ways that echo Andrés's vision for the *hombre nuevo*: "A revolution should embrace everything: from ideology to love, from conscience to economics, from the land to the imagination. A writer, an artist, must use his imaginative capacity to defend, within the revolution, his right to imagine greater and better things."[34]

Cortázar's and Benedetti's texts adopt a critical standpoint vis-à-vis the risk of the disintegration of culture into commodified goods; in their own ways they vigilantly point to both the autonomy of art and its integration into the material processes of life.

It is obviously not accidental that *Libro de Manuel* and Benedetti's essays quoted above were written in the spirit of the movements of 1968, which affirmed that beauty could articulate the ideals of civil society. Herbert Marcuse espoused this as early as 1937, when in his essay on "The Affirmative Character of Culture" he announced almost messianically, "Beauty will find a new embodiment when it no longer is represented as real illusion but, instead, expresses reality and joy in reality."[35] Faced with the surrealist practice of the May youth revolts in Paris, Marcuse saw it as the dialectic overcoming of culture through which art was transforming life.[36] Yet the fictive practice in Cortázar's text actually ends up problematizing the abolition of the space between culture and life, and in fact the attempt to aestheticize revolution in *Libro de Manuel* could be seen as deconstructed by the lucidity of Andrés's analytical skepticism, as if the novel inscribed its own critical reading.

How can we work our way out of this impasse without resorting to the vexed polarities that trap us into the impossibility of bridging the gap between culture and society, poetics and praxis, art and revolution, the intellectual and the material producers? If Marcuse's belief in art's power to dialectically overcome alienation no longer inspires the confidence it once did, maybe we can sustain a semblance of dynamic equilibrium in which these polarities might coalesce within the discursive field ruled by the plural subject positions of the "Cortázar author-function." For it seems to me that it is productive to read Cortázar's works by positing a not altogether resolved yet creative dialogue between the subjectivities spanning the producer of fictive texts and the hegemonic intellectual of the seventies and eighties who became a continental spokesperson for the Cuban and the Nicaraguan revolutions and against the brutality of the dictatorships plaguing Latin America. This would be the Cortázar of *Argentina: años de alambradas culturales*[37] of *Textos políticos*, of *Nicaragua tan violentamente dulce*,[38] and, to a limited extent, of *Fantomás contra los vampiros multinacionales*.[39] Let us see how this apparent paradox can be productively articulated.

In the construction of his identity as a public intellectual, Cortázar found a continental voice that allowed him to address some of the tensions I have been discussing. In the seventies and eighties, his literary prominence led to an intense relationship with a reading public that he describes in eloquent detail in the speeches collected in *Argentina: años de alambradas culturales*, and which he finds not only more educated but also more demanding: "In recent years, we have noticed the dizzying rise in the number of readers who closely follow the works of our writers, and among them the majority seek in this reading more than distraction and oblivion. Their reading has become increasingly more critical and demanding, and it tends to incorporate literature into the domain of concrete experience, of testimony, and of action."[40]

The relationship with his audience is one of the central themes of these presentations, in which the immediacy of the speech acts seems to make Cortázar intensely conscious of the illocutionary force of his statements. Knowing that his readers now not only listen to him but also demand a sense of his responsibility as a leading intellectual, he can momentarily suspend—within the frame provided by orality[41]—the disjunctions that have been noted in his fiction, and actually bridge the gap. Within these speeches, Cortázar becomes the future man crossing the bridge envisaged by Andrés. There is more to it, however, than the enabling orality of the context. For Cortázar has come a long way in shedding the obsession with distinction that we noted in his earlier works, replacing it with a keen sense of the pain and collective anguish that spread not only over his own country, but over the rest of Latin America as well. Like Fanon during the Algerian war, Cortázar managed to "universalize the crisis"—a phrase I borrow from Said to convey the notion that the sufferings of one nation are associated with the sufferings of others and given broader affiliations.[42] Hence, what began to emerge as a continental consciousness with the Cuban Revolution was consolidated and expanded in the seventies as Cortázar worked in the Second Bertrand Russell Tribunal, as he traveled to Nicaragua and wrote with fervent solidarity about the achievements of the Sandinista Revolution, as he denounced the brutal disappearances in the Southern Cone. To achieve this, as he explained to Roberto Fernández Retamar as early as 1967,[43] he had had to *desnacionalizarse* (strip himself of his nationality), leave Argentina, and operate his return only via a considerable detour: he first had to settle in Paris (to locate himself "in the more universal perspective of the Old World"[44]) and make that the site of a (re)discovery of Latin America via the ideological commitment to the Cuban Revolution. It is in this sense that he resemanticizes diaspora as agora: it is a peripatetic construction of subjectivity that does more than meets the eye. For the agora that exile turns into has freed itself of the communities needing exclusion in his homeland—the *negros achinados*, the petits bourgeois, the silent alienating aggressors who fractured associative life in buses and in neighborhoods. The continental leap is operated by this paradoxical transformation of exile (and internationalization) into the bridge mediating between hitherto irreconcilable positions. By undergoing a process of denationalization he can erase a class position that had blocked solidarity.

From the locus provided by his continental identity, Cortázar constructs a role for the intellectual that claims to resolve the contradictions discussed in this chapter. The intellectual is now able to negotiate between theory and praxis through actions he alone can perform, as a visionary who transforms alienation in an almost messianic way. The speeches collected in *Argentina: años de alambradas culturales* are shot through with an implicit but powerful belief in the responsible intellectuals' redemptive mediation. Not only can they bring light to those who live in exile ("a clarity of vision," "a solar feeling"), but they can also participate in the mystery of national identity formation. Culture thus enacts a utopian leap as it spreads in an auspiciously contagious way ("culture is more contagious than elephants," he claims in one unconvincing comparison), and it suspends the colonization of minds and the deformation of language that result from repressive regimes.[45] In an unstated way, it becomes clear that this leap is made possible through the intervention of a poetics of transformation that only the writer can produce:

the Latin American writer is to bring the difficult search for and inspection of every fountain of national blood to their ultimate consequences. In order to continue being useful for cultural causes, our literature needs to set itself a sort of catalyzing task; upon submerging itself in our reality, it will transmute it into the verbal flask that in turn will transmute it into its most unitary and totalizing form, since what we call culture is not really anything more than the presence and the exercise of our identity in all its force.[46]

This totalizing enterprise can work the magic that not only turns culture into an object of consumption—the fruit cart mentioned at the beginning of this chapter—but it also enacts communication at a deeper level, thus leading to a revitalized national identity with the power to transcend censorship and even defy repression.[47] It is particularly significant that in order to define this messianic vision Cortázar invokes Shelley, the Romantic visionary who in 1812 tried to convey his revolutionary message by sending it via bottles thrown into the sea and balloons sent up in the air. For the

Romantic hero can enact a mission that the twentieth century has had great difficulty accomplishing.

And here Cortázar's definition of the Herculean task invites a comparison with another great visionary of our times: Walter Benjamin. Both of them were drawn to surrealism early on in their lives, and remained temperamentally affiliated with it, grappling with the contradictions latent in the idea of a politicized art. Like Benjamin, Cortázar wanted to be immersed in history, and his desire for art to have the value of fruit, bread, bicycles, or shoes echoes the loss of aura that Benjamin celebrated as enabling the kind of reception that locates art in the material processes of life. And yet they are unwilling to forego the messianic promise of art, or the possibility of attaining happiness as a mass experience. But, of course, in the material reality of existence, there is a poignantly ironic difference in the forms of exile experienced by Benjamin and Cortázar: the former brought an end to his own life when it seemed to him that the freedom of exile to America was blocked at Port Bou (where the powerful monument by Danny Karavan conveys the impossibility of escape), while for Cortázar early voluntary exile provided the route toward continental reintegration. Indeed, in the agora of his final years, Cortázar believed he was helping find the way to family and home:

> the presence and the spiritual radiation of the best Latin American writers has a positive sense that, united with the political currents of authentic popular liberation, will bring us one day to our common land, to our great Latin American homeland, that enormous house with many rooms in which people will live one day like a family in its home: knowing each other, talking to each other, loving each other.[48]

It is striking that what Cortázar is reaching for as the "great Latin American homeland" is located in a home, a dwelling, in the Lévinasian sense of a "land of refuge," a "human welcome."[49] It is a space of utopian longing, a space that has not yet materialized—and which seemed more elusive than ever in the late seventies, under the dictatorial regimes. But it is also the space of aesthetic experience that, even for Theodor Adorno's relentless critical eye, held the hope for a future habitation in a transfigured world where happiness and virtue would be reconciled. In this sense Cortázar remains crucial for understanding the *promesse de bonheur* that art was bound up with in the sixties.

4

Toward a Transnational Republic of Letters:
A Geography of Discursive Networks

It can be argued that the discourse of Latin American cultural criticism in its current disciplinary dimension was consolidated in the 1960s as the result of powerful convergences of cultural and material forces. This chapter will examine some of these convergences as they operated in the public sphere, and as aesthetic experience met the changing demands of market cultures. From the present vantage point of the twenty-first century, studying the 1960s seems like an opportunity to trace how a new kind of cultural world was actually *made*: the decade is a laboratory for change energized by the pace of modernization and by the coalescence of heterogeneous forces. Literature had a role to play in a new marketplace equipped with educated readers, with the public relations machine necessary to identify and promote new talent, with periodical publications that had the know-how to accomplish this, and with a critical discourse that was making the transition from the journalistic to the academic. In this chapter, I will display some of the material practices involved in the making of the culture that attained Latin American integration as well as an international readership.[1]

The 1960s produced a new culture in Latin America by mobilizing a machine that was economic and political, cultural and social, and whose energies were regulated by the unequal conversations between different loci of the transnational public sphere. At stake was a new articulation of continental identity in the production of high and low forms of cultural consumption, mediated by the emergence of critical discourses that found very strong claims for their own power and relevance in the structure of feeling energized by the Cuban Revolution and the tensions of the Cold War. The strength of the competing claims worked first to build and then to ravage the creative impetus of this extraordinary period: the forces involved, remarkably effective as they were, would ultimately be limited by the underlying political and economic contexts in which they operated.

One of the enabling factors of the emerging culture is the process of transnational integration—a chapter in the long history of globalization. A new kind of continental consciousness was fostered by the fast-paced economic development that reached the subcontinent in the post–World War II era, speeding up communications and economic and cultural exchange, and articulating world markets in a dynamic way.[2] Angel Rama's now classical essay on the central role of market forces in the publishing and cultural fields has definitely established parameters for understanding the relationship between the emergence of an educated reading public, the dramatic growth of Latin American cities, and the "boom."[3] It is, indeed, necessary to locate the boom within the dynamics of consumer society in order to articulate the market-driven as well as the strictly cultural aspects of the phenomenon, since it is in this sense, as was noted above, that a study of this powerful moment in the history of the dialogue between symbolic capital and the social conditions of its production yields its most productive insights. Understanding its configuration as a cultural object may also contribute to an understanding of canon formation at a moment of fundamental importance in Latin American cultural history.

Let us begin by considering the author. He[4] succeeded in fashioning for himself a location in the newly configured cultural scene of the time, claiming that he could occupy a privileged space in the transnational cultural arena of a presumably decentered world. "Todos somos centrales," announced Carlos Fuentes, claiming to erase the boundary between center and periphery in a gesture that proclaimed the end of European universalism.[5] Equipped with an invitation to the feast that allowed them to be on an equal footing with William Styron, Robbe-Grillet, or Calvino, the Latin American novelists arrived with complete control of the technical virtuosity that had earned them the invitation, and—adding to the authority of their credentials—they had tales worth telling. The boom novelists, deeply anxious about the potentially international audience to be reached, had the sense that their cultural archive had the riches to spin tales derived from a world in which very unequal development offered the novelty of rural and traditional worldviews from areas far removed from the metropolitan centers, together with the modernized subjectivities of the urban milieu. The complexity of their intellectual and literary know-how enabled them to write sweeping, ambitious novels that reflect upon the nation in the world context, its history, and its different spaces. Unlike their predecessors (the regionalists who wrote in the service of national and political causes), the novelists of the sixties displayed technical dexterity and proclaimed their autonomy vis-à-vis the constraints of a purely na-tional tradition. In fact, their command of a repertoire of literary tech-niques became a passport into the transnational literary arena.[6] They could even don the critical hat, write about each other's work, and produce dis-cursive parameters for interpretation.

What was truly exceptional in the sixties was that the authors were met by a reading public ready to buy their books. The socioeconomic de-velopments that made this possible have been clearly established by exist-ing criticism, and need only be summarily reviewed here. In Latin Amer-ica, an educated, mostly urban bourgeoisie joined the ranks of consumer society and was guided in its choices by dynamic new magazines that cele-brated modernization while pointing to desirable cultural goods through lists of recent musical recordings, novels, business literature, films, art ex-hibitions, happenings, and plays. Television expanded the diffusion of con-sumer goods and contributed to the growth of the new cultural industry. Urban development went hand in hand with the surge of university en-rollments, which reached stunning growth in the major cities: in the Uni-versidad de Buenos Aires, for example, the Facultad de Filosofía y Letras saw a 146 percent increase in students and the creation of two new *carreras* (fields of specialization): Sociology and Psychology. The Universidad Na-cional Autónoma de México, having inaugurated its ambitious Ciudad Uni-versitaria in 1954, increased its student body from 36,000 in 1955 to almost 67,000 in 1961. Lima, Bogotá, Buenos Aires, and Caracas witnessed the erec-tion of their own Ciudades Universitarias in the fifties; the Universidad de Chile and the Universidad de la República in Montevideo expanded their fa-cilities around that time so as to accommodate new *facultades* and increased enrollments. The new professionals found employment in the developing economy of transnational corporations and state-sponsored institutions;

they became part of a middle-class, educated reading public that differed from the elites that had previously validated literary value. Their interests were shaped by the sense of urgent ideological renewal and interrogation derived from the Cuban Revolution and by the impact of far-reaching earlier movements like the Argentine Reforma Universitaria of 1918.

Vectors of Dissemination

How was cultural capital produced, distributed, and validated at the time under discussion? How was the "production of belief"—to echo Bourdieu—set in motion, articulating the commercial and the symbolic, disavowing economic interest but not the power of the economy in which it operated?[7] In this section I will examine different forms of print capitalism in the sixties, arguing that they made important incursions into the public sphere and the construction of the sense of a new culture within Latin America, leaving the question of the international consecration for Chapter Six. The explosive ferment of the decade contains a persistently sobering revelation: within the very energy of creativity lay the ferment of its eventual demise. Today this little history of euphoria and despair leaves us wondering about the cycles of creation and doom that characterize Latin America's engagement with beginnings.

Let us look at some of the political, cultural, and social institutions that structured relations. In what follows, I will consider different practices of knowledge making and distribution of information, consensus, and the advancement of claims to intellectual authority. I will do so through a series of case stories that chart significant geographies of power in a transnationally interconnected sphere.[8] The rough outline of a map will emerge, and its points of interest are not determined by exclusively literary or cultural factors. Indeed, the central aim of this chapter is to show how complex a web of political, cultural, and economic forces and constraints bring into existence new domains of culture.

An important role was played by publishing houses, which Angel Rama called *editoriales culturales*, whose raison d'être was not merely commercial, and whose editorial leadership was willing to incorporate complex works and accumulate a distinguished backlist, because they sensed the time had come to offer the educated reading public books that met their more sophisticated interests. In my study of *Primera Plana* below, I discuss the taste-shaping function of weekly publications and the ways in which they effectively marketed material and symbolic goods. Less propelled by commercial interest were the *editoriales culturales*, and yet they succeeded in reconfiguring the production of literary value.[9] Not only were they willing to incorporate difficult works: they also steered the public away from the established habit of reading only foreign writers in translation. This shift had significant consequences: readers found themselves delighting in the recognition of their own world represented in new and interesting ways, sparing them the preachy and ponderous rhetoric of writers like Eduardo Mallea, Ciro Alegría, or Eduardo Caballero Calderón. The case of Mexico's publishing house Joaquín Mortiz, studied by Danny Anderson, is particularly revealing of the times' new conception of publishing. Founded in 1962, it operated at the outset with criteria that privileged intellectual merit and originality, and it brought to its readers the works of some of the most prominent writers of the sixties: Salvador Elizondo, Juan García Ponce, José Emilio Pacheco, Carlos Fuentes, Homero Aridjis, Jorge Ibargüengoitia, Gustavo Sainz, Elena Garro, Jose Agustín, Rosario Castellanos, Vicente Leñero, and others.[10] Joaquín Mortiz is an excellent example of the kind of cultural publishing that succeeded in marrying cultural promotion and an economic know-how for the changing conditions of the times in which it operated.[11]

In many cases, the books were massively distributed: a short story collection by Cortázar or one of Eudeba's texts on Argentine history were available at many of the *kioskos* that had previously offered only newspapers and magazines. Mass distribution meant that the print runs multiplied—especially after the exceptional success of *Cien años de soledad* (*One Hundred Years of Solitude*), which had the effect of increasing the sales of other Latin American authors. Angel Rama offers a useful table indicating the increasing print runs of novels that were reedited in the late sixties, riding on the coattails of the commercial triumph of books by García Márquez, but also by Cortázar, Fuentes, or Vargas Llosa. *Los premios*, for example, was launched in 1960 with a 3,000-copy print run, and by 1968 it was republished with a second print run of 20,000; in Mexico, *Pedro Páramo* (originally published in 1955, with a modest print run) had a 1971 print run of 60,000. The readers had at their disposal an ample list of offerings that was enlarged by titles of earlier publication—a phenomenon made very clear by the success of Borges's works in the course of the decade.

New state institutions contributed to the cultural ferment. In Argentina, for example, the drive for development led to the foundation of such varied entities as the Instituto Nacional de Tecnología Industrial (INTI), the Instituto Nacional de Cinematografía, the Comisión Nacional de Investigaciones Científicas, and the Fondo Nacional de las Artes, all dating from the late fifties. In 1961, two entities were founded in order to promote book sales: the Junta Intergremial de Defensa del Libro Argentino, and the Comisión de Promoción del Libro. Private institutions such as the Asociación Psicoanalítica Argentina, and the Instituto Di Tella,[12] did a lot to foster a sense of modernization; more informal associations such as the study groups that proliferated outside the universities offered updated knowledge that satisfied a growing desire to keep up with recent cultural trends. The educated public was confronted with circuits of cultural distribution that guided consumption and created the sense of a constant flow of novelties: the notion of being up to date (*estar al día*) generated the anxiety of being in the know, of not missing the turns of an ever-changing scene. All this was experienced with a sense of joyful surprise and discovery, in a climate of creative—yet tension-filled—ferment.

Primera Plana and the Spectacle of Consumption

Periodical publications helped set the parameters of taste and offered fora for cultural debate. They varied in their format, in their "look," and in their mix of culture, politics, and economics, but they all conveyed the sense of a vibrant scene. Some, like *Marcha* (founded in 1939) had been around for decades; others entered the reading market precisely to participate in and help shape the cultural exchanges. They call to mind what Sarmiento had written about the centrality of journalism in national development, anticipating Benedict Anderson's well-known concept of "imagined communities":

Through journalism . . . nations, like absent sisters, communicate their prosperity and misfortunes to one another . . . through journalism individuals announce their needs and call on others to satisfy them; and through journalism, ultimately, uneducated people who had previously been denied access to culture, begin to take an interest in learning and to enjoy reading material that instructs and entertains them, raising everyone to the enjoyment of social advantages, and awakening talents, brilliance, and industries.[13]

Few of the magazines of the sixties could be said to have had these aims more clearly in mind than Argentina's weekly *Primera Plana*, founded by Jacobo Timmerman in 1962, and closed by the Onganía dictatorship in 1969.[14] It responded to the expansive euphoria with an updated sense of the complex negotiations between offer and demand called for by the times. Its readers were socially anxious, prepared to buy not only books, magazines, and records but also tickets to the cinema, the theater, museum exhibitions, and *caffé-concerts* as well as television sets, washing machines, imported Scotch, cars, clothes, and airline travel. *Primera Plana* made being *au courant* an absolute must, and it put into circulation a code of distinction for the urban bourgeoisie. Its pages produce a festive integration of diverse (and at times even incompatible) experiences, operated by imaginary solutions to the contradictions of the socioeconomic conditions of its production and reception.

For today's reader, the festive, celebratory tone of the magazine has the air of what has been called "a doubly lost paradise, that of youthful years and of a country that offered possibilities for individual and social growth that have been irrevocably lost."[15] It created an imaginary reader defined by youth, and by access to the new. Its air of celebration sought to consecrate the present and displace older forms through the operations of taste making. *Primera Plana* imbricated different reading positions, as can be seen in the coexistence of the new *ejecutivos* or corporate men (a socioeconomic type jocularly portrayed by María Elena Walsh's famous song[16]), and the intellectuals who were at the forefront of cultural and political renewal.[17] The magazine worked out fluid reading positions between and among them that could hardly obtain beyond the imaginary space of its pages. Let us see how some of these heteronomous sites were made to coexist in *Primera Plana*'s dealings with symbolic and material goods.

The corporate man or *ejecutivo* of affluent means occupies one of the reading sites in question. He is interpellated in the news about industry, the economy and finance, national and international politics, as well as in the numerous advertisements. Of particular significance is a playful section entitled "Sir Jonas, el ejecutivo," in which humor is made to skillfully negotiate between identification and ironic distance. Sir Jonas may be prone to erotic indiscretions and to the misuse of English words, but he does represent a new lifestyle with access to travel, power, and amorous adventures. The section includes a "Championship" whose participants were some of the *ejecutivos* of the day, identified by name and by some of their achievements and pastimes. This is one of the ways in which *Primera Plana* astutely interpellated a specific reading public; another is advertising. The business world, its purchasing power, and its tastes were the intended audience for ads selling scotch, cars, stereos, airline companies, men's tailors and hair products, industrial companies (Grafa, Dupont, Atma, Ducilo, Olivetti, Ranser), and insurance. In the advertising discourse of the day, most of the goods were promoted through erotic persuasion: glamorous young women appear to be seduced by the effects of Glostora hair gel, Mustang cologne, or even Dupont plastic bags.

What Guy Debord called consumption's "never-setting sun" shines beyond the space of advertising: *Primera Plana* celebrated the spectacle of abundance in sections (such as "Extravagario" and "Vida moderna") where the implied reader is the subject who judges and validates as the member of a community endowed with new forms of cosmopolitan knowledge. In these early days of globalization, national cultural and consumer goods were recontextualized so as to mix the local (often recovering the autochthonous) and the international. At the newly established Galería del Sol, for example, an exhibition of new mirrors is valued because it reveals the influence of primitive Mexican art, together with "light doses" of Hindu craftsmanship, and art nouveau. Likewise, when Yves Saint Laurent's new styles are presented, we read that they artfully combine elements from both the Congo and France; new tableware from the province of Mendoza mixes local design with the warmth of *gres*. "Renovarse es vivir" (Makeover is life), the title of the decoration section, could well convey the aspirations of *Primera Plana*: it plundered the new and the unexpected in a style of celebration that is informal and flexible while operating various types of cultural and marketing cross-fertilizations.

The myth of the new is at work in different spheres: whether in the launching of consumer goods, or in the review of new books or artforms, it takes on similar features. About Néstor Sánchez's *Siberia Blues*, we read, "he hurls himself along the path that he himself has just opened: torturing syntax in ungodly ways, violently attacking verbal tenses, turning language inside out, like an old sleeve."[18] Julio Cortázar is one of the models for the writer of the times; in a piece entitled "Julio Cortázar at Home" he has an air of studied, youthful insouciance mixed with admiration for Cuba's revolutionary ethos:

Wearing his hair long . . . and exhibiting a disinterest in literature as sharp as his interest in life, the novelist Julio Cortázar returned to his home in Paris after one month in Cuba. "I want to repeat—he said to the French press—that Cuba is the only Latin American country that has found its historical destiny." While finishing a book of short texts, he finds time to define, with a lack of solemnity that seems like wisdom, the reasons for the rebirth of narrative in Mexico, Peru, Argentina, and Uruguay: "We have found our language out of our spoken tongue."[19]

Cortázar as *style* underscores what Guy Debord claims as the *spectacle* of modern society, managing to subsume different forms—even those that appear to be subversive—under the program of the dominant class. By successfully constructing a discursive style that privileges very modern informality as well as plural voices and positions, *Primera Plana* managed to harmonize varied and often contradictory modulations of modernization (economic growth, artistic creativity, dynamism, the discourse of liberation) in a dynamic balance.

While celebrating writers and artists, pride of place was given on its pages to the institutions of the culture industry. The literary boom and the success of theatrical shows were described in both artistic and commercial terms. A case in point is a piece devoted to the rise of new publishing houses, which rose in number from six to twenty in only a few years. Entitled "La danza de los millones," the article explains the publishing bonanza by considering the force of a new linguistic medium deployed to deal with local themes, thereby responding to the readers' growing interest in their own world.[20] But the central character in the success story is the editor as impresario, seen as the protagonist of an adventure that is staged as a dance in step with the modern world, turning, as Guy Debord would say, the accumulation of capital into an image[21]: "the boom or the bibliographical rise unleashed a dance of millions that exchanged the cautious steps of a Gavotte for a massive rock 'n' roll."[22]

The significant shift from the publication of foreign authors in translation to Latin American authors is explained by means of an industrial analogy: the old publishing houses are presented as "dealers authorized to bottle a product that someone else manufactures."[23] In the theater world, the impresario is again the center of the success story: an article about the Buenos Aires scene is entitled "Los dueños del escenario," and its focus is the know-how required to operate in the new theatrical marketplace. The model to be emulated is Broadway, purveyor of successful commercial formulas.[24]

However, when books are reviewed in *Primera Plana*, the literary approach is critically sophisticated, and the repertoire is international. The style reminds us of Cortázar's prose: informal and very polished at one and the same time. In the new best-seller lists there is a mix of national, Latin American, and international authors gathered in a republic of letters with new kinds of exchanges that constitute, in Carlos Fuentes's formulation, "a central eccentricity, without poles."[25] The optimistic presumption in the 1960s was that the world was changing, that the metropolis was being decentralized as the periphery gained centrality. More realistic was the increasingly continental reach of the cultural field that *Primera Plana* was helping to map. In 1967, launching *Cien años de soledad*, the cover announced it as "la gran novela de América," and in a later issue García Márquez was called "el Amadís de Colombia" for having created Macondo, "where the entire history and geography of America find their place."[26] In the same issue there is a complex *mise au point* of Barthes's *El grado cero de la escritura*, published by Editorial Jorge Alvarez. Furthering the cultural crisscrossings are a chapter taken from *Memorias del subdesarrollo* and an article dealing with Che Guevara's Bolivian guerrilla operations, written with thinly veiled sympathy for the revolutionaries.

What needs to be foregrounded here, I submit, is *Primera Plana*'s successful conjunction of reading sites within its heterogeneous discursive strands. The reader it constructed would manage to negotiate between very progressive political views (indeed, left-of-center even by the liberal standards of the sixties), cosmopolitan and sophisticated cultural tastes, *and* the interests of a managerial class anxious to read about the steel industry, foreign trade ("Argentina steps into the world scene" claims an article about exports), railroad workers' unrest, and the possible agreement between President Illia and exiled leader Perón. That reader was interpellated through a knowledge machine able to deal with politics, business, and finance in the ideological discourse of power. Additionally, s/he was expected to defend adolescents who felt antagonized by an authoritarian society—denounced by a discourse produced by the newly minted tracks of Psychology and Sociology of the Facultad de Filosofía y Letras—to celebrate the miniskirt ("this meeting across generations, a triumph of authenticity and a defeat of puritanism"), or to joyfully enter "consumer society"—which comes into existence in Latin America in the sixties—as it was staged by the new advertising agencies (introduced in an article entitled "Un slogan cada día estimula y sienta bien" [A slogan a day keeps the doctor away]). These disjunctive and even contradictory operations were made to coexist in *Primera Plana* because it articulated imaginary solutions for what could only actually be grasped in fragmented (and fragmenting) processes. In its utopian space, and during its short life, it constructed an imagined community kept momentarily together by symbolic resolutions that the world of experience did not manage to achieve.

Mundo Nuevo and the Failed Dreams of Independence

As the Cuban Revolution ushered in *Casa de las Américas*, it led to North American efforts to foster voices opposed to it, in an atmosphere already polarized by the Cold War. Funding was made available for institutions such as the Congress for Cultural Freedom[27] and the Alliance for Progress, seeking to preempt revolution by underwriting development projects and cultural initiatives that might contain the revolutionary spirit of the time. Some enterprises were immediately drawn into debates about their affiliations with the CIA, and the cultural arena became a political battlefield. A first attempt made in 1953 with *Cuadernos por la libertad de la cultura*, initially edited by Julián Gorkin and then taken over briefly by Germán Arciniegas, yielded mixed results and was greeted with little interest. Its publication came to an end in 1965.

Few publications were drawn into the conflicting force fields of the decade more strikingly than *Mundo Nuevo*, a journal established in 1965 in Paris under the direction of Emir Rodríguez Monegal. It came on the scene with euphoric proclamations about Latin America's privileged location in the international cultural marketplace: "Latin America finds itself in the enviable position of a continent that simultaneously inhabits two worlds: the Old World of European traditions, always up to date, always alive, and the still unformed world of emerging nations."[28]

This claim to two different temporalities, seen as a privilege and as the mark of difference, is one of the distinctive features of much of the boom writing. *Mundo Nuevo* actually played down the old—either in the European tradition, or in the Latin American one. In fact, that "world as yet unformed" of emerging nations raises questions about how the editor articulated the relationship between the cultural and the political: the statement seems to value the notion of emergence (so dear to the ideology of the group) while attaching it to a sense of the as yet undeveloped, waiting—one is led to infer—for the sculpting effects of the new novelists' pen. At the same time, though, the notion of Latin American originality was foregrounded as one of the continent's greatest merits, deserving of the mission *Mundo Nuevo* announced: "to insert Latin American culture into both an international and up-to-date context, that allows us to hear the almost always inaudible and disparate voices of an entire continent."[29] Those are indeed the key words: *international* and *up-to-date*, and they undoubtedly rule the tone and the subject matter of the magazine. It focused on Latin American material, but by deliberately mixing it in with European or North American cultural novelties, it produced a discursive space in which the distinction between outsiders and insiders depended less on existing systems of consecration than on *Mundo Nuevo*'s power to endorse the cultural value of its authors: Günter Grass and Susan Sontag were in dialogue with Julio Cortázar, Carlos Fuentes, or Guillermo Cabrera Infante.[30] The magazine located its voice in the very struggle with time and difference that betokens modernization: the newcomers it announced had to push back into the past those already consecrated; they had to always bear the mark of originality and difference, making the Latin American both exotic and so contemporary as to run the risk of soon being out of date. By locating itself in Paris and interpellating the great literary capital, *Mundo Nuevo* sought consecration in the international republic of letters even as it proclaimed to its Latin American readers the universal appeal of their own culture.

At the outset, the celebratory tone was powerful and pervasive. It constructed the image of the writer as more than a man of letters: on *Mundo Nuevo*'s pages the novelists of the boom acquired glamour and star quality. Carlos Fuentes may be the most eloquent example, epitomizing the desirable features of cosmopolitanism, youthful energy and originality, while coming from a Mexico represented as both the space of a "black angel of lost times" and, echoing Breton's phrase, "surrealism's chosen land." In the inaugural "Diálogo" with Emir Rodríguez Monegal, Fuentes was made to metonymically embody the qualities *Mundo Nuevo* promoted:

Carlos Fuentes' personality is almost as incandescent as his novels. Dark-haired and slim, he has penetrating eyes and a sensitive mouth, a nose that is sharpened and is made to leap in vehement conversation . . . the natural fluidity of speech of someone who is comfortable in many modern languages. . . . Whether in his enormous house in San Angel Inn, in Mexico City, or in the middle of New York City, in a modern hotel in Santiago, Chile, or an Italian restaurant in Montevideo, between the ominous ruins of Chichen Itzá or in the geometrical discipline of the Boulevard de Courcelles, chance has allowed me to accumulate over the last four years very clear and lively images of Carlos Fuentes.[31]

Fuentes's very masculine energy not only makes his nose spring into action: it also turns him into a *dínamo humano* (human dynamo), so that he becomes a heightened version of modern man's potency and drive. His cosmopolitanism is also exceptional, with the flair of the diplomatic corps (his father was Mexico's ambassador to Rome at the time of the interview), the command of foreign languages, studies in Santiago de Chile and Washington D.C., and a doctorate in Geneva. Rodríguez Monegal notes that "there are absolutely no chauvinistic roots in his vision," alluding to the earlier regional novel that the boom's writers and critics disparaged. While Mexico is central to Fuentes's preoccupations, his gaze is mediated by surrealism, which acts as an emblem of international validation. It is, indeed, surrealism that provides the unavowed framework for the return to an authorized interest in the national and even the regional, with the additional cloak of a critical concern with the questions of national identity and—not infrequently—failure:

There has always been in our countries a sort of radical intuition, especially in Mexico. You remember that Breton called Mexico surrealism's chosen land, and while it is true that surrealism is always this tension between desire and the desired object, in Mexico the tension is much stronger because the gap between desire and object is enormous. It's a true precipice: any encounter with desire in Mexico must be superreal by force.[32]

Furthering Mexico's claims to conjoin the unique temporalities of the archaic and the *avant la lettre* is Fuentes's contention that all the great areas of contemporary reality preexist in Mexico. This not only underscores a Mexican (and, to a considerable extent, Latin American) difference, but it also privileges this area of the globe with a kind of foreknowledge that has uncannily anticipated surrealism, camp, pop art, and existentialism. It has even led writers such as Artaud, Michaux, Huxley, Lawrence, and Lowry to quasi-hallucinatory processes of creation. It all seems not unrelated to the effect of the fantastic, which was to become central to the fiction of the sixties. And yet, Fuentes's comments evoke a generalized contemporaneity that foreshortens Latin America's distance from a privileged present. Octavio Paz had already proclaimed in *El laberinto de la soledad*, "somos contemporáneos de todos los hombres" (we are the contemporaries of all men) and, indeed, the continental sense of modernization made universalizing claims in its quest for consecration in the agora of cultural value.

Mundo Nuevo's location in Paris (in offices previously occupied by its predecessor under the auspices of the Congress for Cultural Freedom, *Cuadernos por la libertad de la cultura*) attenuated the differences between center and periphery, First and Third Worlds, which had hitherto organized hierarchies of space.[33] It was, of course, not the first effort of its kind: Leopoldo Lugones, for example, had attempted the same venture in 1914, with the creation of the short-lived *La Revue Sud-Américaine*. Lugones's ostensible aim, though, was to reach a European audience while, as has usually been the case, appealing to Latin American readers. Emir Rodríguez Monegal's Paris was in some ways a universalized cultural capital, much in the way that Benjamin saw it in Baudelaire's time. From its privileged vantage point it was possible to produce the effect of a world of cultural ferment with substantial Latin American contributions. Further, it reduced distances, producing a virtual geography that accommodated Paris, London, New York, Santiago de Chile, Montevideo, Buenos Aires, Caracas, Lima, or Mexico City. In this kind of mix lay the possibility of celebrating an interdependent, transnational moment that mitigated earlier exclusions and leveled the superior rankings of the then-called First World. In this spatial configuration, it was possible for Guillermo Cabrera Infante to write a letter from London to Paris, entitled "Desde el Swinging London," to be read in Spanish by *Mundo Nuevo*'s readers in Latin America. Here Cabrera Infante combines topics such as Twiggy, the launching of the English translation of *Rayuela*, excerpts from Susan Sontag's *Against Interpretation*—in which she discussed Cuban singer La Lupe as a camp phenomenon—Borges's acclaim in Europe and North America ("this century Borgifies or Borgesifies, however it should be said"), the Beatles, and Antonioni's *Blow Up* as well as Mary Quant—all in the space of eight pages.[34] In the complex geometry of overlappings produced by this letter from London, multiple cultural trajectories are possible, and the distances inherent in the traditional system of center-periphery, inside-outside, appear to be reassuringly reduced in *Mundo Nuevo*.

Acting as a mediator in the dynamic conditions of change at this particular moment in advanced capitalist society, *Mundo Nuevo* concerned itself with launching books into the literary marketplace. The case of *Cien años de soledad* is instructive, not only because of the mechanisms of promotion that were set in motion, but also because the magazine's relationship with García Márquez was fraught with the conflicts that ultimately led to Rodríguez Monegal's resignation in 1968, offering a view of the thorny articulation between politics, ideology, and symbolic practices during the Cold War. Conflating the appeal of the new and the power of publicity, *Mundo Nuevo* introduced its readers to the novel while it was still being written.[35] A practice associated with the nineteenth century's feuilleton was refashioned and updated to meet the conditions of the sixties: in this particular instance, the magazine paved the way for a future readership, as did many other weekly publications in Latin America. In its second issue (August 1966), *Mundo Nuevo* presented the story about the pirate Francis Drake, and concluded with Ursula's return to Macondo after her futile search for her elder son. Five issues later, in March of 1967, we find the chapter devoted to the plague of insomnia and the announcement that the Editorial Sudamericana is about to publish the complete text. The break with García Márquez occurred in May 1967, but *Mundo Nuevo* continued to promote *One Hundred Years of Solitude*: one suspects that the sponsor may well have been Editorial Sudamericana.[36] A full page was devoted to the book, with a mechanism that rests on the boom's characteristic protocol of consecration by peers: Julio Cortázar, Carlos Fuentes, and Mario Vargas Llosa each wrote a laudatory paragraph with the categories of interpretation suited to the literary values of the decade. For Cortázar, García Márquez's novel signaled the "irreversible eruption of the highest form of creative imagination in the South American novel," together with the end of the "boring obstinacy in paraphrasing the chronicle." Fuentes equated Macondo with a universal, Biblical territory; Vargas Llosa found powerful and vindicatory echoes of medieval masters silenced in America by the Inquisition and metropolitan censorship.[37] The effect was to announce the new while providing protocols of reading, much in the same way that other cultural products were circulated and authorized. The publication of excerpts from important works was not limited to *One Hundred Years of Solitude*: a pathbreaking novel of 1956, *The Devil to Pay in the Backlands*, by Guimaraes Rosa, appeared as a *relato* in 1967, the year of the author's death. *Mundo Nuevo* sought to promote new works and canonize existing ones, locating them within a cultural world with porous boundaries between North and South, proclaiming that it eschewed the conflicts between East and West.

Yet the enterprise was rent apart by the rifts of the Cold War. It turned out to be impossible to accomplish what *Mundo Nuevo* had proclaimed as one of its aims in its "Presentación" of July 1966: "*Mundo Nuevo* will not submit to the rules of an anachronistic game that has tried to reduce all of Latin American culture to opposing and irreconcilable factions, and that has prevented the productive circulation of ideas and opposing points of view. *Mundo Nuevo* will establish its own rules, based on respect for different opinions."[38]

The instability of the material conditions within which writers worked in Latin America gave the lie to the triumphalist rhetoric of *Mundo Nuevo*'s inaugural discourse. A roundtable discussion held at the P.E.N. Club meeting in New York in 1966, under the direction of Arthur Miller—transcribed by *Mundo Nuevo* from the recorded version—helps us discern the fragility of this transitional time. The Latin American writers present (César Fernández Moreno, Carlos Fuentes, Mario Vargas Llosa, Pablo Neruda,[39] Victoria Ocampo, Haroldo de Campos, and Nicanor Parra) all decried the effects of underdevelopment in their literary production: lack of communication with their reading public, economic difficulties, the "anachronism" of their official culture, the debilitating limitations of the book markets, the high rate of illiteracy, the hostility of the ruling classes toward their writers, the inevitability of exile to safeguard their professional calling, political alienation, the cooptation of language by the rhetoric of the powerful elites, the erosion of utopian thinking, the sense of being unknown abroad. The picture was bleak. It is telling that the coda was supplied by Emir Rodríguez Monegal in an attempt to rescue an optimism consonant with the ideology espoused by the journal he was directing. Transcoding the language of despair into a positive form, Rodríguez Monegal had the final say, and he renamed underdevelopment as a condition marked by the displacement of defunct structures and the erection of new ones, accompanied by strong works, filled with stories and themes. Anxiously resituating the pessimistic conversation in the grammar of change and renewal, he concluded: "But I don't want to end this meeting on only a negative note. . . . The Latin American writer is faced with a cruel reality, but now he is confronting this challenge with strong works of art; he is confronting this challenge as a writer and as a human being. This is a very positive sign and I hope that all of you are in agreement with me about this."[40]

Despite persistent efforts to affirm the power of culture to overcome the trammels of underdevelopment, the demise of the journal was to be the result of the power struggles of the Cold War. These very struggles were the silent but unavoidable foundation of *Mundo Nuevo*, marking both its conditions of possibility and its demise, and proving that in the sixties the stark polarizations of the Cold War channeled material and intellectual energies into the undercurrents of conflict and competition.[41] The scene that *Mundo Nuevo* operated in was one of crisis of legitimation for cultural forces operating in a polarized world where the very notion of independence of judgment was called into question. The figure of the "independent intellectual" came to represent either bad faith or naive blindness to the dual tensions of the era.[42] In a complex set of exchanges inaugurated by a series of articles published by the *New York Times* in 1966, it became known that the CIA had provided funding for *Mundo Nuevo*'s sponsor, the Congress for Cultural Freedom.[43] Caught in the fray, Rodríguez Monegal resigned in 1968.[44] Despite its short and agitated life, *Mundo Nuevo* has continued to be associated with the remarkable cultural growth of the boom. In José Donoso's nostalgic appraisal we might find an exalted view of this journal's impact:

> *Mundo Nuevo* was the voice of the Latin American literature of its time. . . . For better or for worse. . . . I am convinced that the history of the boom, at the moment in which it was most united, is written in the pages of *Mundo Nuevo* up to the moment when Emir Rodríguez Monegal abandoned its directorship. Of all the literary magazines of my time, from *SUR* to *Casa de las Américas* . . . none has succeeded in transmitting the enthusiasm for the existence of something alive in the literature of our period and of our world with the precision and amplitude of *Mundo Nuevo* at the end of the '60s.[45]

Marcha and the Politics of Culture

An important cultural journal of longer standing, Carlos Quijano's *Marcha*, founded in 1939, and an active player in the intellectual life of the River Plate area, was, like *Mundo Nuevo*, not immune to the binarisms that defined and constrained the republic of letters in the decade. *Marcha*'s ambitious sweep covered politics and economics with the lens of a democratic, pluralistic left; it reviewed films, art, literature, and other artforms with a lucidly independent, often intransigent gaze, like the vigilant and creative conscience of the times.[46] Its readership extended beyond the Uruguayan public as its cultural authority gained recognition through its exchanges with intellectuals from the River Plate area and beyond.

The conflicts and rivalries that regulated the changing editorial policy of this remarkable weekly reveal the passionate investment in a politics of culture, and its relevance to the fate of *Mundo Nuevo* itself. Between 1959 and 1968, *Marcha's* critical gaze was steeped in the views of the director of its literary section, Angel Rama. Immediately responding to the intellectual impact of the Cuban Revolution, Rama defined a cultural program that was designed to articulate its historical mission:

As is well known, History is written by our own hands, and the year 1958 in which I joined *Marcha* was the year of the fall of dictatorships (in Colombia, in Venezuela, a bit after the Peronist debacle, a bit before the overthrow of Batista), and of an intense continental shake-up leading to many unfortunate events, but also to a multitudinous hope of renewal to which we owe the splendor of Latin American narrative, which would become known as the "boom."[47]

In order to fulfill the demands of such a mission, Rama defined not only what literary texts *Marcha* was to review and highlight, but also the critical paradigms organizing the reviews. Moving deliberately and strategically away from previous editorial policy (under the aegis of his rival Rodríguez Monegal), he eschewed the reviews of foreign books (especially the Anglophone repertoire) in favor of Latin American works of the day. This was an important move that actually produced import substitution in the literary marketplace and contributed to the consecration of Latin American writers. Rama's power of convocation elicited contributions from writers and critics as far flung in the continental territory as José María Arguedas, José Miguel Oviedo, Noé Jitrik, Roberto Fernández Retamar, Sebastián Salazar Bondy, Mario Vargas Llosa, Juan Carlos Onetti, Ernesto Sábato, or Carlos Drummond de Andrade. The aim was to provide a totalizing vision of "la hora que escribía América" (the hour when America was writing). Arnold Hauser's 1951 *The Social History of Art* provided Rama with the critical tools to probe the intersection between the social and the artistic, but many of the opinions responded to a personal investment in a powerful mix of cultural and political affinities and hostilities.

One can see a tense conversation working its way between the lines of *Marcha, Mundo Nuevo,* and *Casa de las Américas,* mapping a triangle whose vertices were the Southern Cone, Paris, and Cuba. The geographic matrix dots spaces and ideologies whose boundaries were not porous: they were, instead, marks of belonging to heavily inflected ideologies of culture, establishing continental links. There were, as well, significant tensions determined by allegiance to or suspicion of the notion of Latin American liberation and its semantic connotations. *Mundo Nuevo* and *Marcha* were at polar opposites in their political affiliations, which were among the many differences separating Angel Rama and Emir Rodríguez Monegal, two towering figures of the critical scene of the sixties. Even without tracing the intricacies of their relationship, it can be averred that the field of possibilities of writing and reading was not unaffected by the avatars of member groups and the tastes and affiliations their names commanded. Rodríguez Monegal had been at the helm of *Marcha* between 1944 and 1957, years of cultural ferment that witnessed the foundations of the Facultad de Letras y Humanidades and of the Cámara Uruguaya del Libro, the creation of literary awards, and the gradual consolidation of interest in national literature. An awareness of the need to fight the dispersion of the literary scene in Uruguay is conveyed by the following call published by Rodríguez Monegal in 1945: "TO NATIONAL AUTHORS: *Marcha* has determined to offer a special place in its pages to information and criticism about any aspect of Uruguayan arts and letters. With that in mind, we are asking national authors to send us copies of each book that they publish in the future, as well as recently published books."[48]

But it was too early to proclaim the centrality of Uruguayan and Latin American writers to the educated reading public: only in the 1960s was the battle cry for lending sustained attention to them loud and clear. During his years in *Marcha,* Rodríguez Monegal's editorial eye was not dissimilar from *Sur's,* focusing on Anglo-American and French literature and criticism, while gradually building a Latin American corpus that included Rodó, Bello, Quiroga, Borges, Onetti, Felisberto Hernández, and a few others. Later, when he took over the direction of *Número,* he continued with a program that brought together authors like Orwell, de Beauvoir, Eliot, or Kafka. In the 1950s, the educated reading public was familiar with writers such as Faulkner, Hemingway, or Proust: their books were easily available and quite well known. The path toward establishing a national and a Latin

American canon was still being carved, and there were occasional acrid debates around matters of taste and tradition: Borges, for example, was admired by Rodríguez Monegal, and given short shrift by Angel Rama, who considered him in a group with "the Malleas, the Ocampos . . . those who have adapted with pleasure into the plaster of their own and conventional statues."[49] Only in the 1960s were conditions favorable for the almost exclusive celebration of Uruguayan and Latin American voices. It is important, however, to note that this shift entailed debates and enmities that were to have lasting effects in the field of cultural production and in the mechanisms of consecration. Literary prizes for poetry and the novel were mired in bitter disagreements: underpinning them were differences of taste that frequently stemmed from ideologically inflected positions. When in 1960 a fellowship allowed Rodríguez Monegal to study Andrés Bello's papers in England, his departure made it possible for *Marcha*'s new leadership to embrace the Latin American literary program as part of its political and cultural commitments.

Responding to the euphoric optimism of the early years of the Cuban Revolution, Rama took over the directorship of *Marcha,* intensifying the focus on awards that addressed continental themes: in 1962, the competition was to deal with novels of "Latin American subjects," while the essay prize would be awarded to the one that best addressed the question of Latin American underdevelopment. Some issues were announced as "welcome to young people," "to new comrades," and devoted to young national writers, who gained exposure thanks to new publishing houses: Arca, Alfa, Banda Oriental, Pueblos Unidos, and El Siglo Ilustrado were bringing out books by Cristina Peri Rossi, Eduardo Galeano, Mercedes Rein, and other emerging figures. Echoing Che Guevara's call for creating the society of the "new man," Rama's program was to take stock of new works, to chart the field of Latin American literary production, and to engage relentlessly in the defense of socialist aesthetics. He defined this latter venture in no uncertain terms, as "the relentless polemic in defense of the 'third position' and the reply to those who leaned on imperialist forces or with whom they appealed for independence from North American financing but, finally, who sought protection in it."[50]

Not surprisingly, Rama's cultural politics in *Marcha* led to repeated confrontations with Rodríguez Monegal: they vehemently expressed their disagreements, flourishing accusations and sparing no verbal aggression.

Even before *Mundo Nuevo* was formally launched, Rama translated their dispute over Carpentier's *El siglo de las luces* and its views of the Cuban Revolution into Rodríguez Monegal's political subordination to the dictates of the U.S.-led Organization of American States: "Any day now the Alliance for Progress will invite him to give classes outside of the country, or the American Embassy will propose to finance his magazine."[51]

When in 1966 Rodríguez Monegal left for Paris to start *Mundo Nuevo*, the intellectuals who supported the Cuban Revolution were ready to disclose the tense exchanges between Fernández Retamar and Rodríguez Monegal over the possible funding of the recently established Parisian publication. Peter Coleman's book on the CIA and the Congress for Cultural Freedom was met with the glee of confirmed suspicion by the intellectuals of the left, turning the end of Rodríguez Monegal's leadership into a kind of political unmasking.

Marcha's decades of active participation in the cultural and political life of the Southern Cone ended in a tragically revealing way, with the signs of censorship and repression that crushed the creative impetus of the decade. Like *Primera Plana*, it was closed down by one of the dictatorial governments of the seventies, and its termination came on the heels of censorship and imprisonment. In February of 1973, shortly before it was definitively closed down, *Marcha* had published the winner of its narrative competition, a short story by Nelson Marra entitled "El guardaespaldas" (the bodyguard). Claiming that the story sought to positively portray the Tupamaros organization, the government of Juan María Bordaberry, in collusion with the army, not only closed down the publication but also sentenced Quijano, the director, to jail as well as members of the jury (Juan Carlos Onetti, Mercedes Rein, and Jorge Ruffinelli—who had left Uruguay before the arrests were made). The penalty exacted was quite brutal: Nelson Marra spent four years in jail, subjected to abuse and torture. *Marcha* was definitively closed down in 1974; publisher Quijano and his family went into exile in Mexico; Onetti had already left for Spain; Ruffinelli had left for Mexico before "El guardaespaldas" had been published.[52] The end of publications like *Primera Plana* and *Marcha* underscores the close relationship between cultural expansiveness and political freedom; repression brought the creativity and vital conversations to a halt. Even *Mundo Nuevo*, which was not closed down by a repressive regime, was caught in the trammels of political strife and did not manage to survive.

The End of *Sur*

Even journals of the standing of Victoria Ocampo's *Sur* were to be jolted by the political, economic, and cultural tensions of the period. Not only did José Bianco's trip to Cuba lead to a break with Victoria Ocampo and bring to an end a twenty-three-year stint as the journal's editor, but it also meant the loss of the cooperation of intellectuals who were closely identified with the Revolution. But the ideological rifts were deepened by changing views on the literary repertoire and the interests of an emerging reading public, which was no longer an elite of highly educated people. With his characteristic irony, Borges summed up the claims made by *Sur*'s critics: "Europeanism or Foreignism, it's the mysterious crime that they tend to impute to *Sur*."[53] At stake was a shift in cultural tastes, which were being molded by trendsetting magazines like *Primera Plana*, whose dynamic journalistic discourse appealed to notions of youth, modernization, and the emerging continental consciousness expressed by the boom writers. Middle-class readers were drawn to the freedom offered by new forms of inquiry consonant with economic development and cultural expansion: fashion, advertising, music, the arts, theater, and film were in conversation with the new literary works. The changing economic conditions of *Sur* and the marketplace made it harder to sustain Victoria Ocampo's internationalist (universalist) editorial policy. She herself acknowledged the problems of maintaining foreign contributions: "As the years go by, with the recent loss of purchasing power of our money, our magazine has been losing the opportunity to buy or take on foreign projects."[54]

And yet, as Carlos Fuentes and Octavio Paz had proclaimed, the very notion of a universal culture was giving way to different configurations, and in Latin America the rise of consumer society, on the one hand, and the teleology of change opened by the Cuban Revolution in its early years, on the other hand, made for a shift in interests that altered *Sur*'s standing despite the valuable work done by Bianco's successors.[55] Victoria Ocampo may have deplored the difficulties of engaging foreigners due to the Argentine peso's loss of purchasing power, but the literary marketplace was steering away from such imports as the value of Latin American writing rose.

I would be missing a significant phenomenon if I did not point out that in the critical writings that appeared in *Marcha*, *Mundo Nuevo*, *Casa de las Américas*, and a handful of other publications of the sixties it is possible to discern the emergence of a critical discourse making its transition from journalism to academic scholarship. Emir Rodríguez Monegal and Angel Rama, the two great critics involved in tense conversations in *Marcha* and *Mundo Nuevo*, might epitomize this transition. They went on to establish themselves in the American academy—though the Immigration and Naturalization Service brought Rama's productive time at the University of Maryland to a premature halt—and to write foundational books in the field of Latin Americanism. One could note similar trajectories in other critics of the period: Noé Jitrik, Roberto Fernández Retamar, Julio Ortega, and several others.

Transatlantic Connections

One could think of the boom as fertilized by a series of sites of encounter and reception in which its powerful seeds could grow and prosper. Or, in a different take on the floricultural metaphor, one could see a series of sites ready to enrich whatever growth would thrive in them, and the hardy, foreign spawn of the boom were the ones that took and flourished. The fact is that the geography of discursive networks that played so vital a part in the coming on the scene of the boom as a transnational event would be incomplete if we did not consider the intellectual and material transatlantic agency of Franco's Spain. It is ironic that a regime that had a deeply negative impact on the cultural life of that nation could have contributed to the growth of the Latin American novel, but then the silences of Spain may have helped make the new voices from Lima, Mexico, or Buenos Aires especially audible.[56]

To be sure, material and cultural factors contributed to the auspicious conditions for the boom in Spanish soil. The editorial business was in an expansive phase thanks to the effects of the "Nueva Ordenación Económica" of 1959, which instituted new monetary policies designed to revitalize the economic scene and decidedly establish consumer society. In the cultural field, goods began to circulate within mass markets; the book trade witnessed the foundation of important book clubs like the Círculo de Lectores (founded in 1962), and of the "El libro de bolsillo" series by Alianza Editorial. Powerful publishing houses were founded: Destino, Plaza y Janés, Santillana, Tusquets, and Alfaguara all date from the sixties. By the early years of the decade it became less arduous to find books of

Spanish American provenance in Spanish bookstores, and publishers such as Mexico's Joaquin Mortiz were presented and distributed by Barral. All this was part and parcel of the *apertura* period of Franco's regime, especially as conceived by the 1966 Printing Law conceived by Minister of Information and Tourism Manuel Fraga Iribarne.[57] Astute developer of Spain's successful tourist industry, Fraga Iribarne understood that attracting tourists and readers might require a certain slackening of the strictures of censorship. With a vast potential readership in sight, both at home and across the Atlantic, the Printing Law tended to make it less arduous for entrepreneurial publishers to sell even some of the authors who were blemished by their support of the Cuban cause. The permissive silence, however, was uneven and hard to predict, and it did not extend to novels by gay writers like Manuel Puig, whose books were detained by Franco's censors until the seventies.

The publishing creativity comes from beyond the central sphere of Madrid and Castille: it is in Catalonia that the conditions of possibility were more auspicious to the reception of the Latin American novel, for reasons that are easy to infer. At a time when the social novel that had survived the Franco regime was in decline, the modernizing developments called for new voices, for a different kind of engagement with the outside world, and for new novelistic techniques. Social realism was beginning to lose its prestige in the Spanish literary world. The long-sanctioned appeal of a pan-Hispanic cultural sweep welcomed the renewal of bonds with the former colonies, where cultural and economic modernization was producing interesting new novels that would be presented to the Spanish reading public as bearing the marks of the exotic.[58] Here was an opportunity to create a new republic of letters with attractive regional differences provided by the different Spanish American nations, and united by Spanish publishers.

When the stifling cultural environment of Franco's Madrid became the *penitencia nacional* eloquently described in Carlos Barral's memoirs, the combination of economic expansion and cultural stagnation, coupled with the modernizing urges of the decade, led to the search for new literary horizons. Entrepreneurial spirits who resisted the inward-looking isolation fostered by the Franco regime—associated mostly with Madrid's hold on the national scene—looked to France, Germany, Italy, Scandinavia, and the UK in much the same way as the Latin Americans who had read publications like *Sur* had sought translated texts in the fifties as a way out of the limitations of the national. Yet now Latin America seemed poised to offer the excitement of its powerful novelistic production, obviating the need for translation[59] while offering its own reading public as consumers, who by 1973, were buying 40 percent of the books published in Spain. The literary crisis was not exclusively Spanish: there was a certain malaise in the European novel in general, a privileging of the formal as a result of not having much to say, as Carlos Barral put it in an interview.[60] The Latin American novel of the sixties, instead, had more than mere command of form: in Barral's words, "it has the will to express itself, and to say it with urgency."[61] Moreover, the ideological commitment of the waning social novel was transplanted to the sociopolitical transformation infusing the Utopian longings of the Cuban Revolution and its aftermath.

This geography of transnational circulation brings us back to Cuba in expanded ways, beyond the Latin American imaginary. Despite the strict censorship of the Franco regime when it came to its own subjects, distinguished intellectuals like José María Castellet and Francisco Fernández Santos accepted invitations to lecture in Havana and participate in *Casa de las Américas* as an institution of transatlantic sweep. For Castellet and Barral, the line that linked the different literary works was, in Castellet's phrase "the Cuban meridian";[62] it acted also as an axis for the articulation of leftist thought, which was constricted on the Southern side of the Pyrenees.[63] In the European space, the sense of the new gravitated away from Madrid and toward the northern side of the Pyrenees. The "Escuela de Barcelona"[64] (in which Carlos Barral played one of the leading roles), while keeping valued contacts with poets from Castille, sought inspiration and models in the literature of French poets like Baudelaire, Mallarmé, and Rimbaud, and in the thought of Sartre and Simone de Beauvoir.[65] National publications coming out of Madrid, like *Insula* and the "Colección Adonais," had to face the challenge of Seix Barral (founded in 1950, by Carlos Barral and Víctor Seix) and other initiatives such as the "Colección Colliure," which launched its first publications in 1961.[66] The ambitions were European as well as Latin American, in an effort to produce antidotes to the perceived decadence of the culture of Castille. This was often expressed in a mixture of dislike for the established literary tradition ("that tradition of worried worry for the supposed essence of Spain with which the '98 generation had infected—it seemed forever—the thought and literature of this country," complained Carlos Barral in *Años de penitencia*[67]), and a despondent perception of the regional landscape of the central plateau:

And I felt an instinctive repulsion for all this foul-smelling papier-mâché. . . . From Lérida to Madrid the bull's skin seemed to me to be a dead or moribund star in which the human collectivity played the residual role of ethnicities in extinction, old without being ancient. Madrid struck me as uglier, but especially more depressing, than what I had expected. . . . It is one of the most unpleasant cities of Europe from the point of view of aesthetic satisfaction.[68]

The Catalan interest in the boom is part of this impulse to turn away from the *astro moribundo* in search of transnational landscapes.[69] In Braudelian fashion, at first the route was Mediterranean, with important outposts in Colliure and Mallorca. The former was the name given to a poetry collection initiated by Castellet in 1960, in Barcelona, and published by Seix Barral. The choice of name was significant: its exilic connotations were meant to script a new path for the revered Antonio Machado, whose pilgrimages, given the civil war, had to be rerouted away from Soria or Baeza and into neighboring France. The territorial connotations of Colliure suggested not only exile, but also the need to shift the national imaginations away from Franco's Spain. It was the place where Machado had died some twenty years before, and where a group that included José María Castellet, Jaime Gil de Biedma, Jaime Salinas, Carlos Barral, and José Agustín Goytisolo met to discuss Castellet's *Antología de la poesía española 1915–1931*, whose aim was to draw new generational lines and to give the Catalan group a prominent location in the modern scene. Appropriating Machado in the Colección Colliure could also mean wresting him away from the central canon, while retaining the intimate colloquialism of his voice and his social consciousness.[70]

The old Hotel Formentor in Mallorca, associated today with the *Prix International des Editeurs*, which launched Borges's international fame in 1961, was the Mediterranean outpost that concerns the boom and its making. A magnificent hotel chosen in 1936 by Joan Estelrich to hold a "Week of Wisdom" crowned by Count Keiserling's presence, it had been picked by Camilo José Cela in 1959 for his ambitious *Conversaciones poéticas*, which gathered the great living poets from Spain, and which received considerable press coverage. It was after the renowned *Conversaciones* that Carlos Barral, Víctor Seix, and Jaime Salinas organized the international colloquium on narrative and the Biblioteca Breve Prize, adding to the remaining foreign figures (Robert Graves, Alastair Reed, Yves Bonnefoy, Anthony Kerrigan, among others) a host of European publishers exploring the possibilities of internationalizing the publishing industry. Here we have a vibrant conjunction of forces in the field of cultural production in which names were "made" as the affirmation of difference and newness. As Bourdieu contends, "to make one's name means making one's mark, achieving recognition (in both senses) of one's *difference* . . . creating a new position beyond the positions presently occupied"[71]: an insular and displaced location (the great islands whose age-old intellectual identity was neither Spanish nor French) in which entrepreneurial publishers were seeking new voices hitherto enclosed in purely national traditions.[72] Is it not significant that two peripheral figures, an Argentine and an Irishman, should have shared the First Prize?

For Seix Barral, the need was clear: "From the inside of a caged literature, we could see the exact inverted image of what we could reflect in the mirrors of international attention."[73] For Giulio Einaudi, Claude Gallimard, and Heinrich Ledig-Rowohlt, who joined Barral in the ambitious venture whose seal of approval played such a fundamental role in the literary canonization of the "new" literature of the sixties, the goal as explained by Barral in "La encrucijada de Formentor"[74] was to create a virtual monopoly of literary information among the publishers so as to mobilize and circulate the names of writers who were in creative command of their craft, but were locked within purely national traditions. For Einaudi, in particular, the publishers' venture should also establish the mechanisms of coordinated consecration that would guarantee the enthusiastic reception of new works and new names across the transnational scene.[75]

Aside from the more internationally visible *Prix International des Editeurs*, Formentor played its role as a "literary agora"—quoting Barral once more—by providing a location for the Biblioteca Breve Prize discussions.[76] Instituted in 1958, in the early sixties the Prize was enlivened by important international conferences devoted to the study of the novel, its form and social perch, its future, and the role of the publisher as a mediator. The doors were first opened to a Latin American novel in 1962, when a unanimous vote recognized Vargas Llosa's *La ciudad y los perros* and paved the way for the enthusiastic reception of Latin American literature, which now came on the scene bearing the signs of technical and formal innovation, political credentials validated by the Cuban Revolution, and the power of "things to say." This event marks a watershed of sorts: it was the moment when the conditions of possibility described above produced a propitious reception for the transatlantic novel.[77] The prize made a best-seller of *La ciudad y los perros*, established Vargas Llosa's international reputation, made translations available, and focused attention on Latin America's creative genius. The route was, again, circuitous: Vargas Llosa's reputation in Lima was enhanced by European recognition, and, more significantly, his name became known in cities such as Buenos Aires or Bogotá through the Prize's metropolitan consecration. In Barral's appreciation, it became "a literary transatlantic bridge [that] traveled across the cultural cells of the other continent and summoned writers cloistered in cafés in faraway neighborhoods or temporarily camped out in Paris."[78]

Barral's memoirs leave little doubt as to the complexity of the machine that awarded the Prize: not only did it require the professional organizational skills of Jaime Salinas, but it also meant disseminating calls for submissions in metropolitan newspapers like Madrid's *ABC* or Paris's *Le Monde*, as well as in decidedly local ones like Toluca's *El Sol*, or, in Barral's words once again, "algún periodiquillo de Oruro o de Iquitos."[79] To that has to be added the distributional apparatus that allowed Seix Barral to place books on both sides of the Atlantic—they even managed to evade the trading blockade with Cuba.

But perhaps it is more interesting to trace the leagues of validation that led to consecration by peers, and to alliances of friendship, loyalty and strife, debts accrued and discharged. Personal tastes and allegiances to language or nation, North or South, Anglo-Saxon or Mediterranean, French or Spanish, as well as an emerging set of norms as to what constituted "new" literary value—they were all brought to bear on lengthy discussions that went late into the night, in an air of festive tension galvanized by generous meals and a collective penchant for drinking. With the exclusion of authors whose novels were under consideration, the community of evaluators was made up of old friends and previous winners. What had begun as a publisher's ambition to consolidate the fragmented literary market in the Spanish language turned out to have a potent effect. For the Latin American authors, the obvious advantage was exposure, international visibility, and even consecration. But there was also an effect of market amalgamation, since when the winners of the Premio Biblioteca Breve were Spanish—as were the cases of Juan Marsé, Juan García Hortelano, and Juan Benet—it was their turn to profit by a Latin American public. The audience was made, and so were the prizes, which were the culmination of intricate strategic moves toward the production of consensus and desirable outcomes.[80] Vargas

Llosa and García Márquez, Luis Goytisolo and Juan García Hortelano, and several others, moved in and out of juries that led to the awards of the sixties. Latin Americans such as Carlos Droguet, Vicente Leñero, Guillermo Cabrera Infante, Carlos Fuentes (*el interamericano*, as we will see in Chapter Five), and José Donoso were launched into this intelligently arranged scene, which had the amplitude to include and revalidate older, important writers of the caliber of Carpentier, Asturias, Sábato, and Rulfo. This machinery of consecration led to the setup of other literary prizes, such as the prestigious Premio Rómulo Gallegos, which began in 1966 and gave a generous monetary award to the best novel of a five-year period.[81] It is a remarkable story that owed its success to the talent of local novelists in need of a politics of literary promotion and, in equal measure, to the vision of entrepreneurial Catalans bent on escaping Franco's stranglehold on an anemic national literature.

These achievements did not, however, manage to bypass Franco's censorship. Indeed, it was so formidable that its system of pervasive surveillance set the parameters of criticism and presentation designed to assuage its readers. In some instances, the offices of Seix Barral were invested with stern censors,[82] but even in more benign moments it controlled the material that reached the reading public. Günter Grass's *The Tin Drum* was not allowed into print, even after Carlos Barral had managed to buy the rights to it through intense negotiations at the Frankfurt Book Fair; Manuel Puig's *La traición de Rita Hayworth*, a finalist for the 1965 Premio Biblioteca Breve, did not appear in the Spanish market until 1971; Carlos Fuentes's *Cambio de piel* became a cause célèbre in the raging debates between the author and censor Carlos Robles Piquer; the presentation of *La ciudad y los perros* was carefully designed to elide the condemnation of the military school Leoncio Prado in favor of praise for the lyrical qualities of the prose and the universal moral values it upheld. Even Borges's *Ficciones* were found problematic because of the theological questions they posed, and certain passages were omitted before they were allowed to reach Spanish readers. It may not have been off the mark for Juan Goytisolo to have declared defiantly that had the boom novels been written by Spaniards, they would never have been published.[83] That full chapter of the literary history of the boom still needs to be written, so as to shed light on the extent to which the texts we know bear the traces of a censor at work.[84] And yet, we close the account of the Transatlantic adventure with Carlos Barral's nostalgic evaluation of the forces that contributed to the remarkable coming on the stage of the boom:

Very quickly, that award of literary cafés, of café buddies, was gaining prestige, especially across [Latin] America; it was converting itself . . . into the axis of a potential literary politics, a politics of true discovery of [Latin] American literature, not only because, through its track record of winners and finalists, passed the majority of those writers determined to return greatness to the prose of the Indies and who were to cause so much surprise outside of their national sphere, but also because it served as an instrument for recovering writers who were already important but not well known.[85]

To this award of "café buddies" we must add the extraordinary impact of the Nobel Prize awarded to Miguel Angel Asturias in 1967—the very year when *One Hundred Years of Solitude* made its stunning way into the reading public.

By the early seventies, Carlos Barral seemed to have lost his touch, and his power of discovering new authors was becoming lusterless in the literary marketplace. Novelties had to be found elsewhere, since the Spanish American authors were stabilized within the regular offerings. The darkening cultural and political prospects of the seventies in Latin America were announced by the *caso Padilla*. In the Spanish economic landscape, the publishing industry offered a changing scene in which the notion of Latin American innovation seemed to have saturated the marketplace. Profound disagreements in Seix Barral in the early seventies, combined with the lack of new discoveries, brought the expansive commercial moment to an end.

An International Modern Master: Borges in the Sixties

I close the chapter with a different kind of story, focused on one author. The story of Borges's consecration as an internationally admired "modern master"—to quote Paul de Man's phrase of 1964[86]—is a worldly affair that involves material as well as literary and cultural factors. It constitutes a literary history unto itself, and it is about the republic of letters in all its domains: textuality and meaning, literary production and circulation, systems of evaluation and consecration, the discourses of literary criticism and of national identity, the rise of structuralist theory, translations and translators, traveling texts and traveling critics, publishing houses and reading publics, lectures, honorary doctorates, and—very important—the power of literary prizes. The internationalization of Borges's reputation can help us think about the conditions of possibility for the entry of a Latin American writer into the Western canon.

In 1961, when the group of European and North American publishers gathered at the old Hotel Formentor chose Samuel Beckett and Jorge Luis Borges to be the winners of the First International Publishers Prize, Borges's standing in Latin America was—while distinguished—substantially contested. Only a few months before the Formentor Prize was announced, critic Pedro Orgambide had written in the *Gaceta Literaria* that Borges was a writer divorced from national reality: "exiled in his house, in his garden. . . . Life and death were missing from his life," Orgambide contended.[87] He was recasting views that had gained prominence some twenty years earlier, when in 1941 Borges's submission for the Premio Nacional de Literatura (*El jardín de senderos que se bifurcan*) had been turned down in favor of *Cancha larga*, a now-forgotten novel by Eduardo Acevedo Díaz. At that time, the controversy over the prize exacerbated the fractures in the discourse on Borges's merits as an Argentine writer. A number of them anticipated Orgambide's negative opinions. They decried his lack of attention to what was loosely called "the human," as well as his predilection for an exotic and obscure subject matter that paid scant attention to the demands of Argentine literature. "Decadent" is an adjective frequently brandished against him, as is "dehumanized." Justifying the jury's decision, the magazine *Nosotros* noted: "It occurs to us that perhaps those who are determined to read the book find their explanation in its quality of dehumanized, complicated literature; of a dark and arbitrary mental game, that could neither be compared with chess combinations, because these respond to a rigorous linkage and not to caprice that at times combines with *fumisterie*."[88]

Orgambide and *Nosotros* had, in turn, precursors as lucid as Néstor Ibarra, a friend of Borges whose *La nueva poesía argentina: ensayo crítico sobre el ultraísmo, 1921–1929* contained a serious study of Borges's three first books of poetry. Despite his admiration for Borges, Ibarra ended up providing the discursive frame for future negative evaluations:

In the final analysis, his lucid scrutiny of any dark deception, his sensual taste for ruses, his refined reticence, his taste for renunciation—they all distance him irrevocably from the nation. They distance him so much that one wonders if that

Byzantine, precious, almost narcissistic man, despite all his talent, is what defines our country; or if, instead, we need less special, more ample, younger, more vital spirits.[89]

Even some critics who participated in the "Desagravio a Borges" included in *Sur*'s July 1942 issue voiced similar reservations. No one's ambivalence is more telling than Enrique Anderson Imbert's, whose evaluation of Borges back in 1933 had been so negative as to consider him quite devoid of interest.[90] In *Sur* in 1942, Anderson Imbert acknowledged that Borges gave Argentine letters nobility and greatness, but he also developed the view that his sphere of interest was becoming increasingly limited, to the point that his readers were becoming asphyxiated.

Given such reservations among some of Borges's self-proclaimed defenders, it is not surprising that the critics of the 1950s (such as the Viñas brothers, Juan José Sebreli, Noé Jitrik, Adolfo Prieto, and Ramón Alcalde) gathered around left-leaning magazines like *Centro* and *Contorno* would launch their Sartrean attacks against a writer they viewed as most uncommitted. In fact, the first book-length study devoted to Borges, Adolfo Prieto's 1954 *Borges y la nueva generación*, recapitulated the preceding attacks and located them within the demands of a literary criticism that claimed to go beyond ideological disagreements. Read today, however, Prieto's attacks appear to be rather feeble literary arguments marshaled to justify attacks against what has gone down as "la ideología liberal" since the nineteenth century.

It is, indeed, significant that Borges's standing in the Argentine cultural scene of the early sixties should be so redolent with the debates surrounding the location of Domingo F. Sarmiento in national culture.[91] The important difference, to be sure, is that Borges was a man of letters, not a statesman whose writings were to become canonical. But similarly inflected ideological debates guided the judgments of literary value, and what they reveal is significant: that critical discourse remained subordinated to concerns that were not text-immanent. Borges's canonization, in fact, offers us the chance to see the gradual development of a critical vocabulary focused on language, textuality, and the architecture of fiction itself. As we will see, the process was circuitous and it required wresting his writing from the demands of representing the nation.

Sur provided the initial ground for the construction of literary parameters for the interpretation of Borges's writing, and it did so with the powerful minds gathered around it since its foundation in 1931.[92] I would venture to claim that without the system of evaluation and the protocols of reading provided by *Sur*, Borges might not have become a prominent international figure. For not only did Victoria Ocampo and José Bianco organize the "Desagravio a Borges" mentioned above; they also contributed as agents for his consecration and internationalization. After the 1942 "Desagravio," the Sociedad Argentina de Escritores (in which the *Sur* group wielded considerable influence) granted Borges its first *Premio de Honor*.

More interesting, in my view, was *Sur*'s command of a cultural network that was to allow Borges's writing to migrate to the north. Here the personal and the institutional become interwoven, and they do so in the figure of Victoria Ocampo, whose connections with Europe led to visits from intellectuals and, during the World War II years, to their prolonged stays in Buenos Aires. One of them was Roger Caillois, a young French writer who had been invited to Buenos Aires to give a three-week series of lectures in 1939, and, choosing exile from the Vichy regime, ended up staying in Argentina for five years. When Caillois returned to France, he acted as a cultural mediator, bringing back to the postwar French scene a few Latin American writers. Borges was to find his way into the French reading public through Caillois, who arranged for the early translations[93] and, later, for publication of his work in a new series published by Gallimard, entitled *La Croix du Sud*.[94] Paul Verdevoye's translation of *Ficciones* launched the series in 1951, with a preface by Néstor Ibarra and book-jacket references to Poe and Kafka. Such references are not insignificant: both Poe and Kafka were outsiders to the Parisian literary sphere, and they were read as such even by those who admired them most.[95]

Early reviews of Borges's book in French publications of the 1950s teach us a great deal about the transnational republic of letters, and about differing standards of reception and evaluation that obtained at the time in the south and the north. In France, Borges was not perceived as lacking vitality, but as strikingly original and powerful. The French reviews published in 1952 are in stark contrast with what could be found around that time on the pages written by members of "la nueva generación" such as H. A. Murena, Ismael and David Viñas, Adolfo Prieto, and Noé Jitrik in *Centro*, *Letra y Línea*, or *Contorno*. The French reception was, instead, akin to the emerging academic, text-based Borges criticism that was being produced by intellectuals such as Amado Alonso, Raimundo Lida, Ana María Barrenechea, and Enrique Pezzoni.[96]

It is both ironic and quite unsurprising that what troubled national-
ist critics in Argentina would work as the passport granting Borges entry
into the European imagination. His texts traveled with ease because of
their extraordinary value—to be sure—but also because if they bore the
marks of alien, fantastic worlds, their strangeness was not an exclusively
Latin American one. Instead, the estrangement of a Borges story bore
identifiable family resemblances with the works of Kafka and Poe, the *nouveau roman* and the early works of structuralist criticism. The Borgesian
text traveled without the trammels of the very national specificity that was
seen as a serious lack by the most vocal Argentine critics of the 1950s and
early 1960s. In France Borges was "cosmopolitan," an open spirit whose
vast sphere of literary allusions placed him in the company of such *hommes
de lettres* as James Joyce, Samuel Beckett, Cyrano de Bergerac, Lewis Carroll, or Jules Verne. As distinguished a critic as Etiemble wrote a provoca-
tive article entitled "Un homme à tuer: Jorge Luis Borges, cosmopolite" (A
man to kill: Jorge Luis Borges, cosmopolitan) that appeared in *Les Temps
Modernes* in 1952 and, significantly, became part of his 1955 *Littérature de-
gage,*[97] a book that represented a break with Sartre's "littérature engagée."
Borges was thus drawn into the discourse of French intellectual life, shaped
by the schemata of reception of postwar Europe.[98] He was transplanted
into a cultural landscape inhabited by towering presences like Bachelard,
Ricardou, Bataille, and Blanchot, all of whom detected in his writing illustrations of the literature *à venir*. Blanchot found in Borges the very mirror images that he was weaving into the concepts of infinite space and eternal reflection;[99] Ricardou delved into the power of the Borgesian labyrinth
to disrupt the deceptive certainties of everyday life.

Works by Borges appeared in most of the periodical publications of
note: *Tel Quel* (whose Philippe Sollers would translate and publish "El arte
narrativo y la magia" in 1962), *Les Temps Modernes*, *Nouvelle Revue
Française*, *Arts*, *Preuves*—which would publish numerous short stories and
poems in the late fifties and early sixties. Given the exceptional enthusiasm
that greeted Borges in France, the Prix International that he shared with
Beckett in 1961 appears as a lucid way of striking a balance between the
new and the established: Borges could be seen as the new cosmopolitan
voice that was launched by the Prize, but he had already been validated by
an admiring press. Like Beckett, he was an outsider who had been brought
into the fold. By 1964 *L'Herne* would publish a five-hundred-page volume
devoted to his work: the first-ever tribute of such magnitude to a Latin

American writer. The extraordinary mark left by Borges in French structuralist and poststructuralist thought is perhaps most clearly inscribed at the beginning of Foucault's 1966 *Les Mots et les choses*:

This book first arose out of a passage in Borges, out of the laughter that shattered, as I read the passage, all the familiar landmarks of my thought—our thought, the thought that bears the stamp of our age and our geography—breaking up all the ordered surfaces and all the planes with which we are accustomed to tame the wild profusion of existing things, and continuing long afterwards to disturb and threaten with collapse our age-old distinction between the Same and the Other.[100]

Genette turns to Borges for illustrations of modern literature: subverting the notion of personhood and verisimilitude, granting the reader the right to "translate" a work into his own terms, and hence to rewrite in *Menardian* terms, and therefore equating writing and reading. Like Blanchot, Genette locates Borges in the literature of the future. To be sure, the selection of Borgesian texts that reached the French critics inspired and validated such appropriations, but it is important to note that they were made possible by their very detachment from their own context of production, and from the complete corpus of his works. This was not the Borges of *Evaristo Carriego*, immersed in the *orillero* poetics of a minor Argentinean writer, nor was he the poet of *Fervor de Buenos Aires*, engaged in creating a criollo literature. The Borges who migrated with ease and even acclaim was—to echo Etiemble—the cosmopolitan one of all-encompassing, uncontaminated textuality. And he was admirably suited to the French cultural sensibilities of the time: resolutely post-Sartrean, structuralist in a text-immanent way. Stripped of the encumbrance of local voices (Argentine, Latin American, criollo, *orillero*), Borges became absolute textuality himself, and in this weightless incarnation he migrated and reached consecration.

While the French (and, eventually, European) acclaim did not obliterate the controversies surrounding the merits of Borges's writing in Argentina, it did help consolidate and develop the growing corpus of academic criticism in his homeland, and it contributed to his canonization back home. This "boomerang" effect is not exceptional: peripheral authors are often validated by external and mostly metropolitan—approval. What made the International Prize so powerful was precisely its transnational dimension, and its reach across the North Atlantic, where the discovery of Borges was belated but immensely enthusiastic.

In the United States he became a writer for and of the sixties and beyond: during the course of the decade, the demand for his books and for his presence grew to a feverish point that culminated in honorary doctorates, named lectures, and even legal squabbles over publishing rights. Grove Press was the first publisher to launch Borges into the English reading public, with the 1962 *Ficciones* in Anthony Kerrigan's translation. New Directions had included two Borges stories in a 1949 anthology, "The Circular Ruins" and "Investigations of the Writings of Herbert Quain," but by 1958 they were determined to bring out an entire book devoted to him. This was to be the 1964 *Labyrinths*, edited by Donald Yates (from Michigan State University) and James Irby (from Princeton), with an introduction by André Maurois. Paul de Man's review of these editions, and of the 1964 University of Texas Press's *Dreamtigers* in *The New Review of Books* starts by decrying the unfair neglect of Borges in the United States, pointing out that he had received critical acclaim in France.[101]

It is remarkable that it all happened within the short stretch of a few years, and decades after the stories had appeared in Spanish. As the rush for permissions to publish more Borges began to create legal tensions among Grove, New Directions, and E. P. Dutton, we cannot but note an irritated but revealing comment by New Directions' Robert MacGregor in a letter dated 1968, the year Borges gave the Norton Lectures at Harvard. Expressing anxiety about Weidenfeld and Barney Rosset's pressing interest to publish more Borges, MacGregor noted: "In fact, Rosset stopped to ask me who Borges was before he went off to that International Publishers do at which Borges won the prize. You will remember that we would have had the book out by then if we had not been held up by your co-editor's introduction."[102] Earlier that same month, Donald Yates (who played an important role in Borges's introduction into the United States) had noted with anxiety, "My how the Borges books are proliferating!! I wonder what this arrangement with Harvard is."[103] By the 1970s, with Norman Thomas Di Giovanni's joint translation venture with the author himself, we begin to see that Borges's consecration led to legal disputes that involved powerful Washington law firms and the Center for Inter-American Relations. The desire to read and teach Borges precipitates anxious notes with the presses to see how soon new printings can meet demand: one such note is caused by NYU's Alexander Coleman's decision to teach Borges in 1971, and the bookstores are said to be "deluged by orders."[104] The Borges frenzy reached television: the year he received an honorary doctorate at Columbia (1971), he appeared on the Today show. His North American celebrity involved different mechanisms of consecration from the French: it rested less exclusively on translations, criticism, and reviews and more on the lecture circuit, the interview, and other forms of public presentation. Borges became a gregarious author, happy to be interviewed, masterfully in control of the conversation, warming up to anxious crowds. With the advent of postmodernism, he was nimbly relocated from high-modernism into postmodernism: self-reflexive and self-ironizing, wary of all totalizing possibilities, it was all too easy to plumb his writing for elegant illustrations of the new aesthetic.[105]

Borges became a celebrity, a true cosmopolitan whose international prestige contributed to the boom's aura: here was a great precursor who was being discovered as his successors were attaining recognition. His prestige encouraged the welcome of other Latin American writers into the bookshops and colleges of the North, helping create his successors.

What I have called a geography of discursive networks in this chapter has been a geography of possibilities, of openings and closures within which the exceptional energies of an epoch circulated until they encountered the barrier of interdiction in the seventies. The actual localizations north and south involved relations between interlocutors that were intense, often enabling, and conflictive, but in their intense exchanges lay the seeds for new systems of interpretation, cultural production, and validation within an expanding cultural marketplace.

5

The Anxious Brotherhood:
Mastering Authorship and Masculinity

Dressed in a white suit that evoked the Caribbean, Gabriel García Márquez finished his Nobel address suggesting a possible rereading of his great novel's apocalyptic end—one that entailed a second chance, a new beginning, defying the constraints of linear history:

Faced with this awesome reality that must have seemed a mere utopia through all of human time, we, the inventors of tales, who will believe anything, feel entitled to believe that it is not yet too late to engage in the creation of the opposite utopia. A new and sweeping utopia of life, where no one will be able to decide for others how they die, where love will prove true and happiness be possible, and where the races condemned to one hundred years of solitude will have, at last and forever, a second opportunity on earth.[1]

This "minor utopia" rewrites the closing line of the novel—perhaps even dissipating the despair of obliteration of "races condemned to one hundred years of solitude [who] did not have a second opportunity on earth."[2] Could one think of the end of the Buendías and their vexed history as the precondition for the opening up of a different temporality, ushering in perhaps the era of resolutions, with the utopian euphoria of beginning anew? Here is an ambivalent tension that traverses the writing of the so-called boom, poised between a sense of arrival and beginning, on the one hand, and a melancholic awareness of the failures of nation building, on the other.

The codas of García Márquez's great novel and his Nobel address, so different in their relationships to ends and beginnings, are central to Latin

American literary history as it can be discerned in the construction of the boom. What this chapter will examine are some of the ways in which this particular moment in cultural history came on the scene as a will to originality and newness, giving itself a beginning—a "minor utopia"—by reinventing its genealogy, erasing its affiliation with existing tradition, and claiming for itself a place in the transnational scene of a world perceived as decentered and ready to welcome the vibrant contributions of Latin American fiction. Such a double gesture of destruction and beginning anew is the enabling move that ushers in the boom, filled as it is with the euphoria of originality and the fear of obsolescence.

To be sure, this combined interplay is characteristic of modernity, which, as Paul de Man observes, "exists in the form of a desire to wipe out whatever came earlier, in the hope of reaching at last a point of origin that marks a new departure."[3] It is this concomitant deletion of origins and erection of itself as beginning that establishes the fraught relationship with history and tradition characteristic of the literature of the sixties in Latin America. While it might be construed as an episode in the long-standing quarrel between the Ancients and the Moderns, the convergence of cultural, political, and socioeconomic forces of the sixties, as discussed in Chapter Four, made it a particularly powerful moment in its cultural history. The impulse to forget the engendering power of tradition is accompanied by a proclamation of itself as an origin, so that it ends up operating within a tension between the power of the present moment as an origin and the radical impossibility of completely severing itself from the past. As H. Blumenberg reminds us, there is a radical break with tradition, on the one hand, but, on the other, "the reality of history can never begin entirely anew," so the past tradition, devalued though it may be, can never be abolished.[4] The boom is both parricidal and Adam-like, but its focus on beginnings bespeaks its own fraught relationship with the history from which it emerges: its writing tends to return to foundations even as it claims to demolish them.[5] At an epistemic level, a principle of differentiation is essential to start an intervention in a cultural field; the boom seemed to need to hurtle itself forward by radicalizing that principle all the way back to foundations. The fiction it produced is revisionary in that it entails a meditation on foundations, yet it tends to want to erase its own reliance on predecessors in its construction of its own literary history.

It seems worth the exercise, then, to examine the conditions of possibility of this disjunction between the engagement with and disavowal of the weight of history in the writings that we group around the problematic category of the boom. My primary goal is to reflect on the construction of Latin American literary history at an unusually productive period, when its commitment to modernization was an act of faith as well as an act of will. The boom novelists produced a great literary revolution: they changed the parameters of writing in Latin America, and, more remarkably, were received as full members of the international literary league. They were recognized by their peers in the north, and several of them found an eager audience in translation. What, then, made this moment possible for the writers it gathered, and through what networks of relations did they operate? How did they work out a genealogy while rendering filiation and affiliation deeply problematic? What were the deliberate omissions and realignments that it might be productive to chart? In other words, how can the belatedness of our own reading, located as it is in the twenty-first century, understand this particular scene of writing?

One of the boom's fundamental features is a certain anxiety of belonging that can be detected in the penchant for making and remaking lists of its members. Who is "in" has never been quite definitively established except for a few canonical names: Carlos Fuentes, Gabriel García Márquez, Mario Vargas Llosa, Julio Cortázar. Around this central core there is a variable constellation of names arranged according to different temporalities and literary features. Precursors were gathered into the fold: Borges, for example, was made to join the boom in an act of recuperation; the same might be said about Rulfo, Lezama Lima, or Carpentier. The tensions attendant upon the constitution of the list stem from the social imaginary at work at this moment of growth and celebration, when exclusion seemed to matter as much as inclusion. Belonging attached emerging star quality to authors precisely when, ironically enough, the discourse of European literary criticism was proclaiming the death of the author: in 1968, Barthes proclaimed that "writing is that neutral, composite, oblique space where our subject [the author] slips away, the negative where all identity is lost, starting with the very identity of the body writing," and yet, as he himself acknowledges, the author is "the epitome and culmination of capitalist ideology."[6] In the sixties in Latin America, the boom author managed for the first time to reach a broad reading public as a professional writer, but he also acquired a transformed, but still auratic, star quality based on a combination of capitalist market strategies and a harking back to more traditional forms of connection with his audience.[7]

How was authorship mastered in this shifting scenario? What forms of filiation and affiliation were invoked when it was time for writing its early literary histories? Despite its thunderous connotations, the boom did not happen—it was constructed, made by discursive and material practices. Moreover, some of the authors themselves were at once elements and agents of this construction, for they were publishing fiction and, at the same time, writing about themselves as boom authors.[8]

One way of dealing with the question of affiliation was to turn the very notion on its head and opt, instead, for a decentered world in which orphanhood was universal. Carlos Fuentes did just that in his *La nueva novela hispanoamericana* of 1969. Shedding the bonds of regionalism for the sake of absolute autonomy from the trammels of nationality, Fuentes detected a generalized malaise—*alienation* was the key word of the time— that afflicted Moravia, as much as Sontag, Calvino, Burroughs, or any of the Latin American novelists. No longer subjected to the demands of regionalism, or even to the fraught continental history, writers like Fuentes, García Márquez, or Cortázar could engage in a craft that was based on myth, language, and structure.

Here was a leveling of differences, a shrinking of distances between Latin Americans and the metropolitan cultures, now seen as existing in a "shared cultural present." Drawing on the structuralist discourse that was gaining ground in the sixties, Fuentes constructs a critical apparatus of considerable erudition, complete with structural diagrams and references to eminent theoreticians of the stature of Claude Lévi-Strauss and Paul Ricoeur. It allows him to make claims such as the following one:

Latin Americans—I would say, expanding on one of Octavio Paz's wise remarks— are today contemporaries of all men. And they can be contradictorily, fairly, and even tragically universal writing in the language of men from Peru, Argentina, or Mexico. Because, once the fictitious universality of certain races, certain classes, certain flags, certain nations is overcome, the writer and the man detect their common *generation* from the universal structures of language.[9]

By dint of text-based critical discourse, Fuentes radicalizes the disdain for regionalism and other forms of strident Latin Americanism, setting up a center-free world of writers who operate in the spheres of language, myth, and structure. His study reads as if it belonged in the pure realm of the writerly, stripped of personal anxieties and allegiances: Fuentes makes his claims with self-assured intellectual authority, showing the range of his readings and his familiarity with the European and North American novel: he is displaying his own technical virtuosity as proof of his complete control over his own *métier* as a writer, as if responding to Alejo Carpentier's admonition of 1931: "llegar al fondo de las técnicas."[10] His voice sounds critically detached, with no recognition of his own interests in the novelistic enterprise, as if beyond the anxieties of marginality.

In a very different vein, Donoso's *Historia personal del "boom"* reveals an acute awareness of the swirling rhythms of success and failure opened up by the new conditions of the republic of letters, and he constructs a genealogy that eschews established forefathers. In attaining authorship and working out a personal sense of belonging within a group that saw itself as distinct from its predecessors, Donoso wrote his idiosyncratic account of the boom. In his contemporaneity with the phenomena he discusses, he offers insights into the forces that shaped the movement, their power to articulate the literary field and its transformations, as well as the inner workings of the collective enterprise at hand. It is a book that deserves closer scrutiny than it has received so far.[11]

The *Historia personal del "boom"* stages the tensions of belonging and affiliation attendant upon the impulse to raze what came before and clear the field for what is proclaimed as entirely new. His title may hark back to Alone's canonical *Historia personal de la literatura chilena*, but it is an invocation that actually underscores distance and rupture: gone is Hernán Díaz Arrieta's bonhomie and acknowledgment of the human factor ("we see above all else human beings, in the flesh, that are born, live and die," Alone claims at the outset).[12] The very first paragraph of Donoso's book, bristling with disquiet, attributes the boom to hysteria, envy, and paranoia, but it also proclaims the "extraordinary high point in the past decade" reached in Spanish American fiction. Adding to the turmoil of the beginning is Donoso's declaration that this extraordinary productivity is inhabiting a hitherto desert space, which has the effect of abolishing the preceding literary history in one fell swoop.

Donoso's book is rife with images of orphanhood and patricide embedded in the discourse of the family and genealogy. The group with which Donoso's "we" identifies disowns its "weakened fathers" (12), but then has to face the consequences of this abjuration: being left homeless, without a tradition. The *Historia personal* reveals the anxieties attendant upon the dismantling of tradition in the name of the new: not only "appalled by the fragility of fleeting literary certainties," but—even more urgently—the "risk of a quick death" (13). Torn between the will to escape and the risk of homelessness, Donoso's personal account dramatizes the anxieties that may saddle such strong gestures of disaffiliation. In Donoso's own terms, the "orphaned sensibility" of the boom novelists rejected attempts by critics and the arbiters of taste to impose upon them "literary fathers" whose statuary weight they were unwilling to accept. In a telling justification of the desire to kill these ancestors, he imputes to the critics who would like to prescribe them the pernicious designs of museum collectors: "With their [*criollistas, regionalistas, costumbristas*] entomologists' magnifying glasses, they were cataloging the flora and fauna, the tribes and the proverbs which were unmistakably ours. A novel was considered good if it loyally reproduced those autochthonous worlds, all that which specifically makes us different—which separates us—from other areas and other countries of the continent: a type of foolproof, chauvinistic machismo" (15, 25).

Difference is eschewed in the move away from the autochthonous, favoring the gravitational pull of the international. In another passage, the national literary heritages are called "cages," as if the young novelists were once again dehumanized by the deadly, exoticizing grip of tradition. Little wonder, then, that one of the early moves of these novelists-turned-literary historians in the enterprise of self-fashioning should be to break such cages, affirm their uniqueness, and proclaim their own orphanhood, in a gesture that was tantamount to proclaiming the death of the Father. The young writers were left free to choose lateral progenitors (Kafka, Faulkner, Joyce, Woolf, Mann) and, perhaps more importantly, to turn their backs on their Hispanic heritage—repeating a gesture that had been flaunted in the postindependence ardors of the nineteenth century. And the escape was to be total: from tradition, from the region, from the nation. Their literature was to be freed from the demands of national belonging. Not surprisingly, the thrill of freedom was not without its attendant anxieties, as shall be seen below.

The "Boom de marras" described by Donoso in his personal history did away with the cage and with its strictly defined parameters of belonging: leaping out of its trammels also meant having no clearly marked ground to stand on. Hence the "angry young men" who were to become the boom had to constitute themselves as a group with their own claims to filiation. And here is where the inflection of gender comes into play, much as it did in earlier literary circles, clubs, or *ateneos*, through which power relationships between men worked out tensions between rivalry and fraternity, competitiveness and friendship. The bonds of masculinity that I discern in the exchanges and relationships described in Donoso's *Historia personal del "boom"* deserve scrutiny in that they played a significant role in the construction of the literary movement itself, and in the plots of some of the novels of the period. One could in fact argue that the authors under consideration (Fuentes, Vargas Llosa, García Márquez, Cortázar, to name the central figures, aside from Donoso himself) established social relationships among themselves that were organized around the dominant fictions of masculinity and, therefore, of the patriarchal order. Reading gender and sexuality in relation to the larger social order, I will chart some of the ways in which the period dealt with the enabling newness discussed above and the anxieties derived from it. The self-proclaimed orphans under consideration had indeed disowned their forefathers—one could in fact posit symbolic parricide and its consequences as the scene that precedes Donoso's anxious writing.

The disquiet that results from this professed orphanhood makes itself manifest in the opening chapters of the *Historia personal*, where the very notion of a boom is called into question. Donoso ventures the thought that the boom may exist only as the product of hysteria, envy, or paranoia (11); that it may in fact be the invention of those very people who call into question its existence. As he manhandles the notion itself, the specter is gradually endowed with flesh and given an identity; by the end of Chapter Four Donoso has taken up even the name "boom" to designate the phenomenon in question. I believe this coincides with the narrative of group formation that he charts as he writes, and with the emergence of new group ties, whose unifying force was the rejection of previous literary forms and the commitment to new ones. The process itself speaks to the origin and dissolution of the male brotherhood in question, and to the kinds of libidinal energy that held the group together. The novelist Donoso presents at the beginning of the *Historia personal* is the epitome of the solitary intellectual, alone in a cultural wilderness filled with dangers—not the least of which are phantasmatic: "The truth is that these detractors, frightened by the possibility of finding themselves excluded or of having to prove that their countries did not have names worthy of the honor roll, threw a sheet over the specter of their fear and, having covered it up, defined its fluctuating and frightening form" (4–5, *15*).

As Donoso unveils the "specter," he fleshes out the emergence of the group, the friendships it depended on for artistic support, the validation made possible by publishers and translators, as well as book sales and even the prospect of success. His personal story traces the slow transnational path followed by the Latin American novel of his time. It starts with the artisanal production and distribution of books (based on the solidarity of family and friends); it moves through the mediation of the *chasquis* (as Donoso calls them, evoking the pre-Columbian messengers who carried mail on foot), to facilitate the exchange of books from one country to another; and it reaches the present of his narration, when there is a recognizable group in place. Like most earlier salons or *ateneos*, the boom was strictly male, and it offered its members a phallocratic embrace made possible by feelings of identification, affection, and rivalry. They read and consecrated each other, often writing each other into their own novels (as did García Márquez and Cortázar, for example), and for as long as the movement lasted they fashioned themselves as friends. Professing friendship did not overcome the anxieties of belonging: there are telling signs of abiding insecurities in Donoso's *Historia personal*, and in some of his fiction.

There are two very significant scenes in which Donoso describes the formation of ties that helped constitute the boom as a group: the Congreso de Concepción in 1962, and a party given by Carlos Fuentes and Rita Macedo at their house in San Angel. In both cases Donoso notes a sense of beginning and consolidation derived from the gathering of writers, although (ever aware of hostile outsiders) he avers that for some, roundtables, conferences, and meetings deserve contempt. Like Carlos Barral in his memoirs, Donoso has fond memories of the parties associated with gatherings of literary groups: "It was very international and modern—with simultaneous interpreters and all the rest—a sort of huge intellectual carnival, with picnics, dips in the ocean, exhibitions, flirting, and meals" (33, 46).

The Congreso's deep impact on Donoso derived in good measure from the impression made upon him by Carlos Fuentes. We read many pages inspired by the dazzled discovery of *La región más transparente*, as a kind of response diary that includes his innermost reactions to Fuentes's stunning acts of narrative daring, but it is the Mexican's personality, flair, and appearance that turn him into Donoso's model. With unabashed and even boyish admiration, he describes the thrill at the prospect of getting to meet him, his humble approach to Fuentes at the airport upon his arrival in Chile, mustering courage to ask him for an autograph. As in the stuff of dreams, here is wish fulfillment in real life: it so happens that it is Fuentes who recognizes Donoso first, calls him by his familial "Pepe," and reminds him that they had been in the same English school together. The coda to the little scene of gratifying anagnorisis is "We became friends" (47, 59). Donoso's portrait of Fuentes is striking because of its unmitigated admiration for his appearance, flair, and cosmopolitanism. Deliberately exaggerating, he claims:

He spoke English and French perfectly. He had read every novel—including Henry James, whose name still did not mean anything in the solitary regions of South America—and he had seen all the paintings and all the films in all the capitals of the world. He did not have the annoying arrogance of pretending to be a simple son of the people . . . he assumed his role of individual and intellectual with ease, uniting the political with the social and the esthetic, and being, moreover, an elegant and refined person who was not afraid to look it. (47, 59)

Donoso opts for the rhetoric of hyperbole: his exaggeration expresses the anxieties triggered by this dashing incarnation of a desirable intellectual life. Like Luis/Fidel in Cortázar's "Reunión" studied in Chapter One, the Fuentes Donoso constructs here looms as a leader: instead of a brotherhood of young revolutionaries, Fuentes galvanizes the energies and aspirations of Donoso and a few others at the inception of the boom.

Fuentes took his own role quite seriously, offering guidance, contacts, and support: he introduced Donoso to his agent in New York, and finally arranged to have Alfred Knopf ("the most important gringo publishing house"; 52, 63) take on the translation and publication of *Coronación*. In ambivalent tribute to Fuentes's leadership, Donoso ends this chapter recognizing his help and the inspiration provided by his writing: Carlos Fuentes has been one of the precipitating agents of the boom. For better or for worse, his name goes on being linked with it as much for his reality as for the legend of his Mafia and his cohorts (53, 64).

And it is impossible not to note that Fuentes's aura infuses the *Historia personal del "boom"* with his flamboyance and savoir faire, with his cosmopolitan ease and luxurious surroundings. For Donoso, Fuentes's aura benefited all the members of the group: he insists that Fuentes *incarnated* the triumph that was associated with the boom ("that fame, that power, even that cosmopolitan 'luxury' which from the isolated Latin American capitals seemed impossible to obtain and which still is connected to the writers of the boom"; 57, 67). It is Fuentes's great party at his and the actress's Rita

Macedo's house in San Angel that marks yet again a beginning for the boom (just as his presence at the Congreso de Concepción had done in Chapters Two and Three): he is represented as the leader who has the editorial know-how and the cultural style needed by the times.

The significance of the leadership qualities attributed to Carlos Fuentes is underscored by the fact that the members of the boom are all, of course, men. Their friendship is short lived; it coincides with the initial years of success, and is threatened by envy and competitive drives. Not surprisingly, Donoso chooses parties as the demarcations of beginning and end: closure is marked by a party held in Barcelona, at Luis Goytisolo's home, on New Year's Eve in 1970–71. Five years are identified as containing the eruption and the demise of the movement, and Donoso's "masculine clique" (72, *84*), is regulated by group psychology, as Freud understood it.[13] For, indeed, the group of men who constituted this literary movement developed ties of solidarity and common interests that allowed for the reversal of feelings of hostility and envy for as long as they remained friends. As Donoso tells the story, the group came together drawn by the shared identification with the drive to reach an international readership, to help one another break the stifling hold of national boundaries and traditional literary norms. Fuentes as leader provides—in Donoso's account, at least—a common tie, a model of success and generous mentorship.

The gender-based nature of the identification leads us to reflect upon the question of masculinity and group formation in the emergence and consolidation of literary movements. In the previous chapter, I described the many different cultural, economic, social, and political factors that helped produce the discursive networks that actually *made* the boom; here I wish to set the power of gender to work so as to probe the emergence of the literary movement, and some of the novelistic configurations themselves. In this regard, Donoso's writing is particularly telling in its more or less veiled expression of the anxieties of masculinity within the group, as well as in the relationships it figures with women and their place in the literary profession. *Historia personal del "boom"* is admittedly a minor book—one that has often been read with different degrees of condescension and amused curiosity—and yet it is revealing of the decisive role played by group psychology and gendered associations in the republic of letters.

According to Donoso's literary history, the novelists under consideration came together in their struggle against stifling cultural and material environments. But there is another side to his personal account, one that is shot through with ambivalence, rivalry, and even aggressive competitiveness. The group has a beginning and an end; the story is narrated from the point of view of the end, obviously after the aforementioned New Year's Eve party at Luis Goytisolo's home in Barcelona. If we take Donoso's account in its critical and literary-historical inflection, it can be read as a rather skeptical assessment of literary value. As to the friendships that led to group formation, they are manifestly precarious: Donoso avers that "friendships among today's Latin American novelists are rather relative—and in some cases nonexistent, sometimes reaching frank hostility" (66, *76*). The comments on the works of his peers tend to be half-hearted in their recognition, with the notable exception of Carlos Fuentes and his *La región más transparente*. Regarding Julio Cortázar, Donoso points out that "the public and critical failure of *Hopscotch* in France and Italy has been one of the great calamities for his Spanish-speaking admirers" (59, *69*), and that his international reputation actually rests upon the fame of *Blow Up*. Behind the "dazzling avant-garde wrapping," Donoso sees in Cortázar a Cartesian mind intent on the vaunting of playful poses. Vargas Llosa's success with *La ciudad y los perros* is described as merely "a great deal of hoopla" (61, *70*); of *One Hundred Years of Solitude* we are told that *Time* considers it a novel much talked about, but hardly read. The friendships that unite them, as we have seen, are not only "relative" but also possible in that they obtain beyond national boundaries, so that the novelists are spared the envy of their fellow citizens. The precarious nature of the group is the closing reflection of the book itself: not only does Donoso diagnose the *crisis* that afflicts the boom, but he also notes a certain exhaustion and disorientation in the critical paradigms, produced in some measure by its very excess: "it is a crisis produced by . . . the loss of order and direction, until finally by the time we enter the '70s everything has been transformed into an indiscriminate conglomeration where it is very difficult to perceive values and to judge" (114, *133*).

The sense of an unstable comradeship infuses Donoso's narrative voice with an idiosyncratic tone: there is an unsettling presumption that the addressees of his tale will be drawn into the unstable rhythms of identification and rejection. The writing itself seems to relish the risk of alienating the reader, who may not be prepared to leap from a dazzled, gossipy tone to utter disenchantment with the fleeting mechanisms of consecration.

The 1987 edition of Donoso's *Historia personal* bears two telling appendixes that, as happens with prefaces and postscripts, frame the new edition and offer a new perch for the reading of the original version of 1972. One is by Donoso; the other one—about which there will be more below—is by his wife, María Pilar Donoso. His is entitled "Diez años después" ("Ten Years Later"), and it has a nostalgic ring for times gone by, while not entirely relinquishing the occasionally embittered remark. The end of the first edition conveyed the embattled sense of a group that experienced the uncertainties of identification and rivalry—to the point that the consideration of its demise is envisioned as a possible end to the aggressive drives of competition: "Perhaps the moment has passed . . . we can stop shoving one another in trying to climb on the ornamented wagon whose journey is still followed by some glittering stars" (115, *134*).

This complex metaphor sums up the fleeting temporality of the group and the precarious nature of the friendships it relied on and produced. Ten years later, the boom had established itself in the literary institution, but the friendships were relegated to the past. The authorial voice is occasionally tinged with nostalgia, as when he acknowledges a certain longing for the pre–Nobel Prize "Gabo de Barcelona," but the ruling affect is no longer identification: its veil torn, the contained aggression is now given freer rein. The second go at the canonical group is definitively critical: not even Carlos Fuentes is left untarnished. In this second evaluation, he remains brilliant, but the ardors of admiration have been cooled: now Fuentes is also "the coldest, the most calculating, the least shrewd" (*223*). Still clear is the energizing effect of the friendships at the boom's inception, acknowledged as "a brief germinating and fraternal moment of cohesion" (*216*). There is a lot to be learned from that phrase—about the engendering power of literary friendships, about their role in the rise and fall of literary movements, about the intricacies of canon formation, and about gendered affiliations. Donoso makes a point of locating the boom within the question of social bonding (and he even advances a tentative comparison with the Bloomsbury group), but he also claims that the production of literary works should be studied as a "mysterious" process that is rooted in the intractable effects of such variables as "daily life, family relations, the social environment of the moment, eating out in a restaurant, going for a drive" (*218*).

Even more revealing is another supplement, the appendix entitled "El 'boom' doméstico," written by Donoso's wife, María Pilar Donoso.

The supplementarity of woman here is not only discernible in the posttextual status of her "domestic" writing, but also in her metonymical standing as woman in the boom. For, like her, women are excluded from this phallocratic brotherhood of writing, since the gender system still dictated the law of female domesticity. If her husband's *Historia personal* is framed by the beginning and the end of the movement, María Pilar Donoso's location at the end becomes a narrative sleight of hand in the later novel *El jardín de al lado*, which marks a turning point in the writerly Law of Gender and the rise of the woman writer in the postboom of the 1980s. In this novel, the anxiety of masculinity shifts away from the spectrum of the male bonds toward the castrating power of women.

Let us start with the suggestive little "boom doméstico" added to the 1987 edition of the *Historia personal del "boom."* The uxorious solicitude of this woman's personal account offers the silenced portion of the "mysterious" factors that contribute to the germination of writing mentioned by her husband in his appendix. Food, clothing, heating, children and their friends, gatherings and their preparation, all take central stage in this modest and conversational piece. The narrative voice is strikingly different from the husband's, as if it bowed to the dominant fiction that regulates the distribution of gender roles. María Pilar Donoso's domestic stories take on an ancillary role: they are added on in the eighties, after García Márquez's 1982 Nobel Prize, when the boom "is no longer a boom"—as she put it—but when the star quality of the established writers guarantees an interested reading public for the personal details and *petites histoires* she provides. Like Donoso's, hers is a memoir, a nostalgic evocation of youthful experiences of shared friendships and hardships. Both texts demarcate beginnings and endings for the boom, now framed by the distance provided by time and firmly established in the canon. Indeed, reading "El 'boom' doméstico" confirms the sense that a literary movement tends to outlive the male comradeships that energized its inception, as the balance between homosocial competition and communion between men—intimate and rivalrous partnerships—cannot be sustained beyond the early stages in which group solidarity can help break the hold of tradition. María Pilar Donoso's account of the loss of bonds at the end has a nostalgic ring:

Relationships and communication have been diluted; the periodical letters from Fuentes with the latest news about the goings-on and events of the group, of the boom, no longer come. The boom is no longer a boom, it is neither a group nor a collective action, nor meetings among friends. They are mature men who write their own books and read others' individually, each one alone in his study in a different country. (*202*)

However, she does acknowledge that the separation is concomitant with the achievement of a definitive place for the boom in the history of world literature.

This woman's writing is significant in its mapping of the literary habitus of a world ruled by the hegemonic myths of masculinity. The duality between women as reproducers and men as producers is heightened by the fact that these emerging writers worked in the domestic space, so that the division of labor is even more striking. In the traditional sphere invoked by the rural town in Aragon in which the Donosos live, a classic Spanish tableau described on the very first page sets the tone for what follows: "Generally a light attached to the ceiling illuminates the group, and the classic scene includes the wintry, Spanish look of the woman with her sewing basket, the man reading the paper and the children doing their schoolwork around the table, welcomed by the warmth of the dark heater hidden by a thick tablecloth" (*140*).

In the Donoso household, the man reading the paper would be the man writing the novels (in 1971 it was the *Tres novelitas burguesas*), but, unlike the newspaper reader whom one can imaginatively locate outside the house while at work, this author has been writing at home. Hence the separation of labor roles becomes striking, when, a few pages later, María Pilar Donoso narrates a return to her home on a very cold winter evening, carrying some logs with which to warm up their home. She bristles at the sight of a rich publisher who is unloading luxurious new heaters for his weekend house—not at the thought of her husband sitting at home. Clearly, the female narrative voice has internalized the roles assigned by this particular, literary inflection of the law of patriarchy, so that she cannot think herself out of this overdetermined complex of everyday life interactions. In his *La domination masculine*, Pierre Bourdieu reminds us that there are limits to the possibilities of thinking that domination imposes on the dominated:

Symbolic power cannot be exercised without the contribution of those who undergo it and who only undergo it because they construct it as such. But instead of stopping at this statement (as constructivism in its idealist, ethnomethodological, or other forms does) one has also to take note of and explain the social construction of the cognitive structures that organize acts of construction of the world and its powers. It then becomes clear that, far from being the conscious, free, deliberate act of an isolated subject, this practical construction is itself the effect of a power, durably embedded in the bodies of the dominated in the form of schemes of perception and dispositions (to admire, respect, love, etc.) that *sensitize* them to certain symbolic manifestations of power.[14]

It is, indeed, hard to read "El 'boom' doméstico" without recognizing a dated form of patriarchy that—even in traditional societies—was beginning to be called into question at that time. María Pilar Donoso assumes her role as mother, wife, and woman, concerned not only with their daughter Pilarcita and the children of the other boom families ("the *miniboom*, as someone nicknamed it"; *154*), but also with town life and Catalan festivals, home warmth and comfort, social arrangements, and friendships. She is vigilant about her own appearance and the need to meet the gaze of others in some sort of sartorial adequacy: she tells us about the transformations of old dresses in order to have something to wear for a Christmas party, or about the value of Mercedes García Márquez's much appreciated hand-me-downs.

It is abundantly clear in María Pilar Donoso's account that the young novelists were seeking recognition, fame, and even glory, writing their novels and talking to one another in a community of unstable exchanges in which the quest for mastery required partnerships with other authoritative males. We read a great deal about extended, often heated, discussions about literature at the dinner table, at times conveyed in the language of wrestling: "they got entangled in literary discussions that always ended in Flaubert" (*165*). Not surprisingly, the women were left out. In a few instances, though, the exclusion of women from the masculine exchanges takes on an openly derogatory form, as when "el Gabo" García Márquez stated that he detested intellectual women, or when Mario Vargas Llosa offers the narrator the following warning, not altogether in jest: "On another occasion Mario buttonholed me, half in jest but also half seriously, saying that I was going to be the cause of his marriage's ruin. Intrigued and also worried, despite the fact that I felt I had a tranquil conscience, I asked him why. He answered that I was 'instigating' Patricia to take Italian classes with me" (*166*).

Shrewdly enough, the "instigator" prefers to quote a comment made by *las feministas*, who made reference to Mario's *declaraciones machistas*.

The male authority of the high-cultural author is upheld in fact by the separate sphere accorded to and assumed by women. The threat of the feminine is kept at bay by explicit interdictions in the sphere of art, which is, in fact, hypermasculinized by the woman's assent. The presence of the wives in fact confirms the aura of the authors, as the former ensure the latter's sacrosanct location in the house, in the protected silence of their writing chambers. In fact, women's literacy is made to be purely instrumental, deployed to spare the men even the concern with food provision. The following little anecdote—redolent with irony—confirms that women's writing is given a purely instrumental role in this world of separate spheres. It takes place at La Font dels Ocellets, a Catalan restaurant where it is the custom for each guest to write on a slip of paper his or her choice from the menu. A heated debate over the Padilla affair kept the group of men from paying any attention to the question of ordering the food. Finally, the owner himself, summoned by a frustrated maître d'hôtel, commanded the group's attention with a peremptory question: "Do any of you know how to write?" (*149*). Julio Cortázar, Gabriel García Márquez, Mario Vargas Llosa, Carlos Franqui (the Cuban poet who had just defected), and José Donoso said nothing, "both unsure and amused." It was "la Gaba" whose assertive answer ("Yo, yo sé") saved the day, writing down all the orders, and confirming that the power of female uxorious writing could be sanctioned for the sake of food and other amenities. The dinner served, the masculine ritual of intellectual jostling continued—this time performed by Vargas Llosa and Franqui in a heated argument over Cuba. On other occasions, comradeship and competition are exercised through the benign mediation of childhood toys, as when Vargas Llosa and Cortázar raced each other with remote control cars: "They fought angrily, enthusiastically, to win a little auto race on remote controls taken out of the bag of gifts for Alvaro and Gonzalo, who, tired, had gone to sleep accompanied by little Pilar" (*158*).

A telling, inverted symmetry can be discerned in the economies of marital and textual authority in "El 'boom' doméstico" appended to the *Historia personal*, on the one hand, and the final chapter of *El jardín de al lado*, published in the postboom years, in 1981. It may be a measure of the coming to terms with the end of the exclusively masculine mastery of the republic of letters, as we shall see, or it may be the case that the later novel is the artful performance of a masochistic scene involving what Deleuze has called the "oral mother."[15] *El jardín de al lado* warrants attention as a novel of melancholic mourning for a lost world: it offers an inverted and exacerbated reconstruction of the representation of the boom in the *Historia personal del "boom."* In fact, I would go so far as to claim that the same narrative and human categories populate both the personal literary history and the fictive world of the novel, as if Donoso had made a fascinating, transformative relocation from one to the other. What in the earlier book is discovery, expansion, partying and celebration, and masculine camaraderie (sublimating envy but leaving anxiety intact) is reconfigured in the novel as closure, exile, depression, and alienation. Place, of course, remains central in its dislocation: the *Historia personal*'s asphyxiating enclosure within the region and the nation, seen as a border that hemmed in and contained creativity, changes its valence when Julio, Gloria, and their disoriented friends are excluded from the national polis, banned from returning, adrift in the doldrums of exile. In that sense, it would be a skillful acting out of weakness verging on victimhood, in a circuitous attempt to reclaim a certain form of authority. In *El jardín de al lado* the ruse of narration rests on the tacit assumption that the interesting and valued role for the disempowered male author is that of the victim of his own crises, which span a vast register: literary, sexual, financial, marital, and, of course, bodily. Julio Méndez is hemmed in between women whose power is represented as threatening phallic authority: Nuria Monclús (clearly based on the powerful literary agent Carmen Balcells) is invested with this power in the novel, as a severe and exacting critic whose withholding of approval (and publication) looms large with the threat of matriarchal punishment. For their part, Gloria and her friend Katy are linked by bonds of identification and solidarity that make Julio feel left out. Desultory Julio deserves the adjective *rimbauldiano*—coined to describe Bijou—for his dispersal often looks like a relentless exploration of the abyss. Self-pity guides the construction of this character: he is made to radiate a negativity inimical to the social order; to display his malaise and inadequacy, prioritizing pain over pleasure. But the very sleight of hand that surprises the reader at the end, as the mastery of writing is transferred to a woman writer may well be an instance of what Barbara Johnson astutely calls one of "the official structures of self-pity that keep patriarchal power in place."[16] Julio remains at the center of this novel, both as presumed subject of narration at the beginning, and as its object in Chapter Six.

What is relevant to our understanding of the boom in *El jardín de al lado* is its refiguration of *Historia personal*: from a mood of anxious emergence to one of melancholy and decline. The "structure of feeling" of the texts shifts from the convexity of growth to the concavity of loss, as if the very same substance were turned inside out, hollowed out. The transition is operated by space and time: the extraordinary convergence of factors that made the boom possible was dissipating by the seventies, when the sweep of history had changed the political landscape, the enabling value of certain countries and cities, the freedom of circulation (the curtailment of which makes exile a cause for fragmentation and loss), and the community of writers. As a case in point, the very Catalan world described by María Pilar Serrano in her domestic *petites histoires* has changed its valence: too many wandering Chileans and Argentineans get in the way. No longer a space for circulation and discovery, the Spain of *El jardín de al lado* is the confining place of those who cannot return home, and who do not belong. The shackles of the Southern Cone dictatorships constrain the plot of the novel: it is the dominant fiction that monitors its logic. Time also has to do with additional factors that pertain to group psychology: as Freud observed, the regulation of identification and aggression at work in a group such as the boom is a delicate balance that is not immune to change.[17] What in the earlier personal history was a tension between longing for inclusion and anxious envy is fictionalized into alienated aggression—one that is performed in a voice that purports to come from those mentioned at the very opening of the *Historia personal*:

I want to begin these notes by venturing the opinion that if the Spanish American novel of the 1960s has come to have that debatably unified existence known as the boom, it is due, more than anything else, to those who have devoted themselves to disputing it; and that, real or fictitious, valuable or negligible, but always entangled with the unlikely carnival that has overtaken it, the boom is a creation of hysteria, envy, and paranoia. (1, *11*)

Julio Méndez's masochistic self-beratement is located as the loss of belonging, not only to the national embrace in the alienation of exile, but also, in an equally painful way, to the group of writers that made up this "mafia," as he again calls the boom in *El jardín de al lado*.[18] Torn between envy and the desire to belong, Julio Méndez is paralyzed by impotence, by an aesthetics of pessimism suffused with negativity. The boom is deprecated as "the consumerist literature . . . of false deities like García Márquez, Marcelo Chiriboga, and Carlos Fuentes" (5, *13*); its passing glory has left only "a whiff of gunpowder and sulfur left in the air after the boom had died away" (21, *30–31*). The wiles of narrative voice locate these bitter castigations within the melancholic fixation of Julio Méndez, the ostensible novelistic voice. But there is an unstable shifting of the I's in the two books in question: from personal history to first-person narration, Donoso is producing fugitive I's that ostentatiously mirror each other in the fictive and referential registers. They stage the anxieties produced by ever-changing conditions of possibility for the mastery of authorship.

That such anxieties are inextricably bound up with gender identity and with the crisis of masculinity is made abundantly clear by the sleight of hand that grants textual mastery to Gloria at the end. Enlightened articles have traced the game of substitution that is operated by the switch from male to female authorship, showing the architecture of verisimilitude and reversal that paves the way for the surprising revelation of Chapter Six.[19] I will focus my comments on the phallic dislocation that the logic of plot in *El jardín de al lado* is predicated upon, and how it may help us think about the economy of gender roles that regulates the rise and fall of literary movements. Oscar Montero and Rosemary Geisdorfer Feal have written very lucidly about the layers of veiled substitutions at work in the novel. The latter notes the shifting nature of the narrative I's: "In keeping with modern functions of the first person, the masculine *I* harbors a latent *she*, who eventually dislocates the unstable *I* to subordinate it as a third person, *he*. The narrative filter is thus a veil that cloaks the shocking, naked reality of the female author at the work's core."[20]

Elsewhere, she points out that the novel is "itself a study of trickery with regard to characters and readers alike,"[21] and indeed it seems at times that the novel has managed to trick even a few critics, who take Gloria's authorial role at face value, trying to read it back into Chapters One through Five. But that drive toward signification tries to suture a gap that must remain in place, for while in the novelistic world Gloria the narrator may appear to supersede Julio, in the sphere of representational hierarchy, Gloria is under the control of the implied author. The game of veils notwithstanding, Chapter Six is a kind of authorial deus ex machina that provides closure, introduces a dazzling sense of surprise, and, I would claim, also manages to slyly address some of the changes that obtained in the republic of Hispanic letters in the latter part of the 1970s, when the boom's command of authorship was facing the challenges posed by women writers whose books were reconfiguring the publishing landscape by the early 1980s.[22]

Hence the novel would perform double duty, addressing the crisis of masculinity on two fronts: one, concerned with the anxiety of all-male

competition; the other, with the rise of castrating females (Nuria, Gloria,
Katy, his own dying mother perhaps). The space in between is actually the
space of a potential implosion. Bijou and the veiled figure in Tangier operate in that fearful in-betweenness, which is as much about homoeroticism
as about the drive toward Thanatos, loss of self. For Julio insists on the dual
nature of the attraction: their young bodies may attract him, but they also
offer the possibility of a loss of self and escape from the sense of defeat:

Envy: I would like to be that man, to crawl into his sickly skin and into his
hunger, to hope for nothing or fear nothing, and most of all to get rid of this fear
that my background and my culture will make me confess tonight . . . the complex story of my defeat: a garden lost . . . my justification for my life, painful roots
in another hemisphere, desertion of the collective project. (217, *239*)

Gender relations thus convey the essential traits of the crisis of authorship
that marks the beginning and the end of the boom. Donoso was admirably
placed to explore the crisis of the boom novelists by way of gender. He had
explored its instabilities with penetrating daring years earlier in *El lugar sin
límites* (1967), tracing La Manuela's relentless drive toward seducing Pancho, the aggressive hypermasculine character whom he does succeed in
captivating in the climactic scene of the brothel dance.[23] In *El jardín* Julio's
dissolution is generalized, but it is most powerfully expressed through the
crisis of normative notions of sexual identity. In fact, the novel's compelling
power stems from its ability to suggest the specters of discontinuity and in-
coherence that gain ground when personal and social upheavals call into
question "the regulatory practices that generate coherent identities through
the matrix of coherent gender norms."[24] I invoke Judith Butler here, who
has reminded us of the political effects of the practices of desire that do not
"follow" the normative paths of either sex or gender. Julio's sally into the
streets of Tangier at the end of Chapter Five, in search of Bijou or the
young man he had been drawn to earlier, represents the crisis precisely in
terms of gender trouble. Donoso succeeds in inscribing the mark of gender in such a crisis.

   And, indeed, the seventies and early eighties were times of crisis. The
world itself became a darker place: the mid-1970s witnessed the end of the
period of economic expansion that spanned the two decades prior to 1973.
The economic downturn put an end to the consumer boom that had begun in the 1950s, and this of course had a deep impact on the material
support needed for the dissemination of cultural production. The political

landscape of the mid-1970s was overshadowed by repressive dictatorships in Uruguay, Argentina, Brazil, Chile, and Paraguay, which, as noted above, canceled not only the freedom of expression and circulation but also the conditions of possibility for writing and reading. Publishing houses were particularly affected by changing economic circumstances, as were the market conditions for risk taking. In this sense the economic boom of the post–World War II period was reaching the end of its eruptive force, weakened in no small measure by the rise in oil prices.

But there is another sense in which the boom had to face its postvolcanic moment—one that is embedded in the life cycle. The youthful eruption of the boom was reaching its autumnal moment: by the late seventies the young men who were anxious to experiment and break the "cages" of nation and tradition were ensconced in their middle-aged, established literary standings and reputations. If Julio Méndez voices the anxieties of decline, then one might suggest that the 1987 Donoso of the Appendix expresses the melancholia of loss: a loss that comes with age, and which *El jardín de al lado* elaborates and explores with a relentlessly lucid eye.

6

Rereading "Boom" Novels in the Twenty-First Century

> Journeys, those magic caskets full of dreamlike promises, will never again yield up their treasures untarnished. A proliferating and overexcited civilization has broken the silence of the seas once and for all. The perfumes of the tropics and the pristine freshness of human beings have been corrupted by a busyness with dubious implications, which mortifies our desires and dooms us to acquire only contaminated memories.
>
> . . . our modern Marco Polos now bring back the moral spices of which our society feels an increasing need as it is conscious of sinking further into boredom, but this time they take the form of photographs, books, and travelers' tales.
> —Claude Lévi-Strauss, *Tristes tropiques*

The boom writers, I would suggest, have been among the "modern Marco Polos" identified by Lévi-Strauss as purveyors of "moral spices" in a Western civilization of contaminated memories and boredom. Their novels' resounding impact in a transnational audience was the result of the confluence of several cultural histories, including those of Europe, North America, and Latin America. It is arresting to trace the path that made such powerful intersections possible, for to do so enables us to chart forces originating in different cultural and political sites, and producing the conditions of possibility for a phenomenon that exceeds the explanatory power of each one of them. In these postimperial times the novels of the then-called "Third World" recaptured politics as a field in which contradictions were culturally inscribed and reconfigured. After 1945, the decolonized world seemed to have the power to find its second chance in history.[1]

Because Latin American literary history is by definition a transnational, comparative enterprise, the emergence of the boom is an eloquent case study of the complexities of the continental and transcontinental exchanges brought about by post-1945 development. When the Argentine weekly *Primera Plana* announced the publication of *One Hundred Years of Solitude* in 1967, its cover extolled it as "(Latin) America's first great novel": I would extend the hyperbole not in terms of rank, but of reach, which was not only continental but also hemispheric and Transatlantic. European and North American—as well, of course, as Latin American—audiences were able to delight in this tale for reasons that stem as much from the world Lévi-Strauss is decrying in the West, as from the "new" world in the South.

At the root of this set of relationships lies the Enlightenment project and its relationship to its Other (savagery, barbarism, primitivism). Modernity, its heir, needs to keep primitivism within reach, juxtaposing the very old with the very new so as to assert its rhythm of shock and revelation. In that sense, the marginal (for our purposes, the world represented by the Latin American novel of the 1960s) as the authentic Other was certified by the great novels of the boom, functioning within what Deleuze and Guattari describe as the value-producing operations that lead to a "generalized systemic institution of equivalences spectacular in its complexity and discontinuity."[2] The boom novel, as we shall see, was coded in a currency that made it possible for its own marginality to operate the equivalences of knowledge leading to reception in the North.[3] At the same time, though, it took charge of the fraught relationship with its own Latin American literary tradition, which it inherited and transformed, commanding a readership anxious to rediscover and reconstruct fictive models of its own world. It is this double-voiced power to negotiate between different cultural needs, and to reach audiences in the South and in the North, that made the boom novel so compelling. It recovered traditional materials that were being threatened by modernization even as it handled them with the technical skills that are its stamp: it reclaimed and revitalized, affirming its difference as periphery's force.

To think about how "cultural needs" were conceived, I will leap back to 1932, when *Transition*, an avant-garde journal published in Paris, formulated big questions and asked some of the most distinguished intellectuals of the day to answer them: "What is your opinion of our time? What can come of it? Can you not give us some advice?"⁴ Among many of the answers, I choose a brief passage from one by Leo Frobenius to give us a sense of the longings that suffused the times:

A man who has devoted a good part of his life to explore the experience of stranger peoples, will have learned to recognize more accurately the superficiality of every simultaneous, every temporal life and experience, and finally to evaluate the little lines of individual existence, historic happenings, the impulses of practical events, the character of party and ethnological formations, from a higher plane, as being the symptomatic play of waves on the surface of the ocean, in the depths of which the paideumatic and psychic currents, as well as the currents of civilization, go their eternal ways.⁵

The desire for "stranger" peoples and experiences came out of a sense of exhaustion prevalent in the modern European cultural and political unconscious. Our usual need for origins and demarcations tends to attribute to the avant-garde the response to this generalized sense of alienation, but one could find the seeds in Blake, Baudelaire, and other earlier seekers of renewed contacts with the currents of psychic depths. And, moving away from beginnings, the extent to which this sentiment spread beyond the exalted proclamations of the earlier decades of the twentieth century needs to be at the center of this exercise in literary history. For it created a gravitational pull toward the areas of the world deemed to be "strange," less contaminated by, quoting Frobenius again, "the greedy pursuit of the corpse-like concepts of a dying materialistic age."⁶ It remains at the heart of intellectual life in the forties, fifties, and sixties, at times wearing the cloaks of surrealism, existentialism, or Marxist critique. Moreover, a European reading public confronted with the *nouveau roman* in France, or the works of Kingsley Amis, Muriel Spark, and Anthony Burgess in Britain, or the novels that managed to survive the stifling censorship of Franco's Spain, might have found a lot to enjoy in the robust imagination that produced the Latin American novels of the sixties.

Renewal and "Stranger Peoples"

Some of the cultural aspirations of earlier decades are expressed in journals founded with the purpose of exploring alternative cultural experimentation. *VVV* (1942–44) and the above-named *Transition* (1927–38) are instructive examples. Edited by David Hare and Eugène Jolas, respectively, they manifest not only a longing for the birth of a new spirit but also the persistence of surrealism well into the middling decades of the century. The earlier journal, *Transition* (which bore the cryptic subtitle "An Intercontinental Workshop for Vertigralist Transmutation"), celebrated its tenth anniversary reviewing its accomplishments, among which were the "construction of a bridge between creative Europe and America," and, most significantly, the creation of "a new narrative in magic realism (paramyth) and a new form of dream-poetry (hypnologue)."[7] In its search for transatlantic cross-fertilizations and magic realism, *Transition* turned to the North and to the South: together with texts by Joyce and Kafka, Martin Buber and Stuart Gilbert, Gertrude Stein and Herbert Read, one finds occasional texts by Luis Valcárcel, Alfonso Reyes, Alejo Carpentier, Luis Palés Matos, and Fernando Ortiz. The journal is all about searching: for a new language (with "experiments in language mutations" that yield lines such as "What a twinklevertigo! / The presses blastcascade into the night"), for insights into and possible borrowings from pre-Columbian cultures (here a poem by Alfonso Reyes, "Yerbas del Tarahumara," deals with *yerbas de salud* brought down by the Tarahumaras, "perfectos en su ciencia natural")[8]—in sum, for renewed forms of human experience. In a section that contains "primitive documents," Alejo Carpentier transcribes two "Cuban Negro" prayers "inspired by a religious sense that invokes . . . all the divine powers for deliverance from the cruelties of daily life."[9] For his part, Fernando Ortiz turns to poetry by Luis Palés Matos to illustrate the extent to which *jitanjáforas* can be construed as "the poetic form of the magical language."[10] No doubt *Transition* can be seen as an indicator of the role played by Latin America in this search: it is seen as a repository of the primitive energy that may render possible the longed-for transmutation. Here the marginal operates as a recognizable differential that the center is anxious to appropriate.

And then there is the short-lived (1942–44) *VVV: Poetry, Plastic Arts, Anthropology, Sociology, Psychology*, edited by David Hare with two main editorial advisers, André Breton and Max Ernst, dealing with the catastrophic events of World War II and their effect on the creative imagination.[11] Here again there is a sense of exhaustion accompanied by the quest for alternative pathways toward what André Breton in his "Prolegomenon to a Third Manifesto of Surrealism or Else," calls "the true flower of life," one that will be found only when the seekers "understand that they have to set sail, and that all preceding pretended voyages were only a decoy."[12] Significantly, one of the dominant fictions of this yearning for change is the metaphor of the voyage—one that has no definite route, but is not without a strong sense of direction. It is away from the center, away from the North and the West, and toward the experience of discovery that awaits beyond. Breton's lyrical writing is illustrated by the Chilean surrealist painter Eduardo Matta, and it is not accidental that one of the drawings displays what could be construed as Noah's Ark. Matta fills it with explosive floral exuberance and plural suns, evoking a Caribbean exploration. In Breton's Manifesto, South America and New Guinea provide glimpses of other forms of humanity: a South American woman's gaze may arrest belligerency; the New Guineans' art "has always subjugated some of us more than Egyptian or Roman art." The poetic voice needed by the times comes from Martinique's Aimé Césaire, whose work is amply featured by the journal. Redolent with images of death and rebirth, Césaire's poems in *VVV* invoke the combined effects of plunging into darkness and awakening into new worlds. Such is the delicate balance of "Conquête de l'Aube," which follows Breton's Manifesto in the journal, moving from an initial "We die our death in the forests" to an attempt to recover a childhood protected by "the diurnal barriers" as the source of rebirth. But what is important to note is that *VVV* sets its gaze not only beyond the canonical names, but also beyond the established geographical and linguistic coordinates associated with the metropolitan axes. There is, for instance, a "Letter from Chile" signed by Braulio Arenas and addressed in Spanish to André Breton, in which he traces the various activities of the surrealist Grupo Mandrágora founded in 1938, and followed by a poem in Spanish by Jorge Cáceres entitled "La mejor parte." Another piece is devoted to "Two Young Peruvian Poets," with works in Spanish by Xavier Abril and Juan Ríos; in a section devoted to new books and journals, one can move from mention of *Arson*, a surrealist review published in London, to Mexico's *Cuadernos Americanos* and Madrid's *Excelsior*. The surrealist gaze is expanding its reach, aided by the mediating power of Ethnography.

This discipline—itself founded upon the traveling seeker of other knowledges—was particularly well suited to one of *VVV*'s aims: "the systematic enlargement of the field of consciousness towards a total view."[13] Pieces by Lévi-Strauss entitled "Indian Cosmetics" deal with the Kaduveo Indians' face paintings' profound effect on all those who see them, affirming the superiority of their artistic power: "the most admirable tapestries cannot rival these native paintings. Actually, never has the erotic effect of cosmetics been so systematically—and no doubt so consciously—developed. Beside this achievement the gross realism of our powder and rouge seems like a puerile effort."[14]

In the same issue, Kurt Seligman writes about the evil eye, tracing its significance through antiquity and focusing on the fascination of terrifying forces. In the cross-fertilization between the familiar and the strange, surrealism and ethnography converged in their participant observation of a defamiliarized cultural environment. While this had happened in earlier periods, the twentieth century's point of departure was a world deeply in question: in the nineteenth century, for instance, it was the temporary thrill of the bizarre, the Orientalist, or the exotic. But for the postwar intellectuals of the twenties, thirties, forties, and fifties, with their ironic and even disillusioned experience of culture (as represented by the writing cited earlier), the *other* (however it may have been available) was a crucial object of modern research.

The rapports with Africa are well known: they link disparate events into a suggestive configuration. Picasso's fascination with African masks, André Breton's collection of objects from Africa and Latin America, the Parisian infatuation with *le jazz,* Josephine Baker, the success of the *Revue nègre* at the Théâtre des Champs-Elysées in 1925, can actually be imagined within a structure of feeling that would also contain the rise of surrealism after Breton's (First) Manifesto of 1924, and the establishment of the Institut d'Ethnologie by Paul Rivet, Lucien Lévy-Bruhl, and Marcel Mauss in 1925.[15] France's first major fieldwork expedition, the Mission Dakar-Djibouti of 1931 was the result of the foundation of the *Institut,* and the participation in it of a man of letters such as Michel Leiris can be attributed in no small measure to his desire to expand his literary reach by pursuing ethnographic research. The grandiose Musée de l'Homme announced by Paul Rivet in 1934 assembled the cosmopolitan urges of the time into the monumental and miscellaneous notion of "humanity," with its longings for a vision that would unite art and ethnography.[16]

Less well known, perhaps, are the links between ethnography, surrealism, and Latin America.[17] We have seen them in the inclusion of works by Latin American writers and artists in *VVV* and *Transition,* and it occupies pride of place in Lévi-Strauss's *Tristes tropiques,* with its sense of the dark entropic currents of European history and the transformative energies of the primitive. Latin America developed in the surrealist and ethnographic imagination among a group of writers who were to exert powerful influences on the Tel Quel group, Michel Foucault, Jacques Derrida, and Roland Barthes. Here one of the central figures was Georges Bataille, whose interest in pre-Columbian art led to one of his first publications. Deeply stirred by Marcel Mauss's thinking on transgression, Bataille became fascinated by the question of human sacrifice among the Aztecs: in his "L'Amérique disparue" he finds in Tenochtitlan the repugnance of a slaughterhouse alloyed with the beauty of a Venice-like city.[18] Striving to wed ethnographic work with forms of subversive cultural criticism, Bataille edited the review *Documents* (1929–30) that drew on the exotic, and the *insolite,* to interrogate cultural assumptions. The ethnographic gaze furnished a non-Western repertoire with which to probe cultural hierarchies and attempt breaks in the metropolitan order of things. It is significant to note that Alejo Carpentier was a collaborator on this journal, as well as of *Bifur* (edited by Georges Ribemont Dessaignes between 1929 and 1931), and his decisive "De lo real maravilloso en América" must be read in consonance with his work in these journals.[19]

The Epiphany of Return

Around those years, Miguel Angel Asturias studied Mayan ritual and religion with George Raynaud. Between 1923 and 1928 the future Nobel Prize winner (1967) followed Raynaud's courses at the Sorbonne, and together with Mexican González de Mendoza, he embarked on a new Spanish version of the *Popol Vuh*. Using Raynaud's French translation, Asturias and González de Mendoza reworked the sixteenth-century version penned by Father Ximénez.[20] This work of translation is integral to his 1930 *Leyendas de Guatemala*, as well as to his later *Hombres de maíz* of 1949. In both books, avant-garde forms of expression that undermine Cartesian rationalism allow Asturias to valorize pre-Columbian forms of thought.

At a time when a longing for reenchantment—or perhaps for a postimperial setting for its "Other"—drove the developed world to its own peripheries, writers like Carpentier and Asturias managed to splice two worldviews: the one from the center and the one from the primitive as purveyor of what Benjamin called a "mythic spell."[21] Arturo Uslar Pietri tells an instructive little tale of origins: he locates the new configuration in Parisian café conversations dating back to 1929, when he, Asturias, and Carpentier gathered to discuss the political predicaments of their homelands, but, perhaps more importantly, what had never made it into the literature of their nations. For Carpentier, it was the African heritage in Cuban culture, in voodoo, in *santería,* or in the magical outlooks of the average Cuban; for Asturias, it was the power of the Mayan legacy in his native Guatemala; for Uslar Pietri, Venezuela had to grapple with the varied signs of a cultural mix that defied clear genealogical classifications, but the powerful influence of which had to find its way into writing. They shared the conviction that the time had come to represent the unique results of a Latin American specificity that amounted to a continental rediscovery even for Latin Americans. Regardless of the accuracy of the reminiscences of the Venezuelan critic (or even of his claims to have coined the phrase *realismo mágico* in 1949), the tale encapsulates the main forces at work in the construction of this new approach to fiction: an enabling distance (Paris), providing the tools and the aspirations for the new, and the recuperation of the archival riches awaiting the writers back home.[22]

They constructed asynchronous visions that reelaborated memory, myth, and history in discursive constructions of heterogeneous strands. While their enterprise responded to the urge to excavate Latin America's riches, it does not remain immune to the originating impulse of their search, and in the long run what became known as "magical realism" was to become reified as the subcontinent's acceptable contribution to world literature. The complex trajectory of these multiple negotiations will be at the center of this chapter. As the preceding pages indicate, the impetus came from the European sense of exhaustion (both cultural and political), and its traces can be detected in the enthusiasm with which it has remained as the passport for reception of Latin American literature.[23] The bridge built by magical realism was meant to transport the primitive energies harnessed by imaginations nurtured by the Latin American experience. The direction of the traffic—to belabor the metaphor of circulation—has been complex and fraught, yet it helped determine the literary fate of the Latin American novel of the 1960s. It expanded the reach of its power by invoking myth, magic, and religion. As for the Latin American writer, he located his own gaze outside, looking in and translating his findings to the outside world.[24]

Strikingly representative of what we might call "the spirit of return" is Alejo Carpentier, whose 1953 *Los pasos perdidos* (*The Lost Steps*) can be read as his own novelistic version of *Tristes tropiques*, published two years later. Like Lévi-Strauss, Carpentier's character is a man in search of origins and meaning. Intent on turning his back on what he calls "such total bankruptcy of Western man,"[25] he embarks upon a journey in which time and space come together, as if the protagonist—an ethnomusicologist—were traversing the *gran sabana* while seeking his own and modern man's beginning. One could say about *The Lost Steps* what Clifford Geertz has said about *Tristes Tropiques*: that its design is that of the Heroic Quest, and that it is an internal journey in search of a rite of passage.[26] When Lévi-Strauss muses about the lessons learned from books and lectures, he reaches a conclusion with striking affinities to those of Carpentier's protagonist. Lévi-Strauss begins by posing a question that has the ring of imminent erasure: "For what, after all, have I learnt from the masters I have listened to, the philosophers I have read, the societies I have investigated and that very Science in which the West takes a pride? Simply a fragmentary lesson or two which, if laid end to end would reconstitute the meditations of [Buddha] at the foot of his tree."[27]

For, indeed, Lévi-Strauss is claiming deep affinities between the cultures he as an ethnologist studies and his own mind, which he describes as "a neolithic kind of intelligence."[28] Carpentier's ethnomusicologist has embarked upon a search that the novelist himself had recounted in his unfinished *Libro de la Gran Sabana*, based on trips he took in 1947 and in 1948. In *Tristes tropiques* and *The Lost Steps*, the observer's gaze is gradually assimilated into the world it studies, so as to undergo a transformation that will color his rendering of the material as well as his quality of mind. Carpentier's ethnomusicologist may not conclude, like Lévi-Strauss, that his intelligence is neolithic, but he shares with Lévi-Strauss a similar revelation about the mistaken assumptions that underpinned the knowledge that the character once pursued:

I saw how unfounded were the speculations of those who feel that they can grasp the beginnings of certain of man's arts or institutions without knowing prehistoric man, our contemporary, in his daily life, in his healing and religious practices. My idea of relating the magic objective of the primitive plastic arts . . . to the first manifestations of musical rhythm, the attempt to imitate the gallop, the trot, the tread of animals, was highly ingenious. But I was present, a few days ago, at the birth of music. . . . What I had seen confirmed, to be sure, the thesis of those who argue that music had a magic origin . . . I thought of all the other fallacious theories, and I began to muse on the clouds of dust my observations would stir up in musical circles in which ideas all come from books. . . . But suddenly I grew exasperated at these ideas running through my head. I had made up my mind to stay here, and I had to lay aside, once and for all, these idle speculations. (199–201, *260–61*)

Like the Buddha at the foot of his tree, the protagonist has distilled and transformed his knowledge so that it matches the world it is intended to explain. Lévi-Strauss's mind approximates the neolithic; the ethnomusicologist in *The Lost Steps* boils down knowledge to magic—wherein lies the birth of music—as if knowledge itself had to find a mimetic relationship with its object, eschewing "vain intellectual speculation." Here is the lesson to be learned: far from attaining the relative autonomy of conceptual constructs from the subject that formulates them, the ethnographers in Lévi-Strauss and in Carpentier claim to reach comprehension at a level that is deeper than and radically different from that which is produced by objective, rational detachment. This is a view of the cognitive and intellectual relationships with the world that values a different kind of engagement with representation. It bears striking resemblances with Adorno's philosophy, which was reaching European audiences in the postwar period, denouncing "diremption" as a wound—produced by the Enlightenment—that marked the gap between the human and the natural worlds. Art, Adorno claims in *Aesthetic Theory*, is the autonomous sphere whose cognitive capacity sets limits to philosophy: Lévi-Strauss and Carpentier would seem to be locating writing in the same sphere, as if it could suture the gap between subject and object in the very move that wrests away the subject's supremacy.[29]

Unlike Lévi-Strauss, though, Carpentier decided to leave *El libro de la Gran Sabana* unfinished, and to narrate the experience of the search by imitating a travel journal in novelistic form.[30] But the logic of plot leads the protagonist of *The Lost Steps* to the inevitable recognition that he belongs outside the world he has tried to seize up, and Lévi-Strauss himself ends his *Tristes tropiques* with a melancholy reflection about the fate of every effort to understand (which "destroys the object studied in favor of another object of a different nature . . . and so on and so forth until we reach the point at which the distinction between meaning and the absence of meaning disappears: the same point from which we began"[31]). Both books lead us through a search that culminates in a renewed conviction of the need to unlearn certain forms of understanding: Carpentier's character begins to see it as a path to be traversed by the unconscious and its portal to the marvelous: "Winnowing the bitter truth from words my companion listened to without understanding, I told myself that the discovery of new routes is embarked upon without realization, without awareness of the wonder of it while it is being lived" (271, *324*).

As for Lévi-Strauss, he leaves his reader with the hope opened up by the possibility of "unhitching," a process described in the radiant beauty of the last sentence of the book:

[It] consists—Oh! Fond farewell to savages and explorations!—in grasping, during the brief intervals in which our species can bring itself to interrupt its hive-like activity, the essence of what it was and continues to be, below the threshold of thought and over and above society: in the contemplation of a mineral more beautiful than all our creations; in the scent that can be smelt at the heart of a lily and is more imbued with learning than all our books; or in the brief glance, heavy with patience, serenity and mutual forgiveness, that, through some involuntary understanding, one can sometimes exchange with a cat.[32]

But the ethnomusicologist in *The Lost Steps* is more than a social scientist and an ethnographer-turned-philosopher: he is also an artist—a composer—and Carpentier chooses to end the novel with a return that contains the promises of art. The novel opens up this promise as conjoining the search for the origin with the anticipation of the future: the protagonist has to return because art mediates between the two temporalities. That is why he cannot go back to the jungle—even when the river waters begin to show the Sign that would have pointed the way.

And here lies, it seems to me, the difference not only of art, but also of the Latin American consciousness of its own cultural position at this time. While Lévi-Strauss will return to his desk in Paris and to the Cartesian forms of structural anthropology, Carpentier is imagining a coda for his novel that is made possible by a sense of the intersections between culture, time, and space which he sees as unique to Latin America. He had worked it out in an earlier essay that appeared in 1948 in *El Nacional* of Caracas, and in 1949 as the prologue to *El reino de este mundo*.[33] This is, of course, the famous "De lo real maravilloso en América," about which so much has been written, often invoking it as one of the founding texts to understand magical realism. Like Lévi-Strauss, Carpentier begins to write by thinking about travel, pondering the equivalences between what is remote, what is distant, and what is different—notions that are imbricated in the imaginary constructions of Latin America. The central moment of this essay is the moment of return, which could be considered to be one of the dominant fictions of the cultural imaginary of magical realism. This obviously presupposes a departure and a separation from the Latin American scene, followed by a going back as recognition. Carpentier writes himself into this circuit, foregrounding the experience of discovery that takes place as he begins to understand his own Latin American world after his travels. Returning involves an epiphany that comes on the heels of the experience of other cultures, as if the Latin American archive elicited allied processes of syncretism, eclecticism, and translation. Carpentier is not claiming, as some critics have argued, that there is a Latin American ontology to be reckoned with, but that the Latin American archive is the result of complex historical sedimentations that have accrued from the coexistence over time of different ethnic groups, and their own layering of myth, narrative, superstition, hybridity, conflict, contradiction, and violence:[34] "A Latin American drags along a thirty-century legacy, but, despite the contemplation of absurd facts, despite many sins committed, it must be recognized that *his style* affirms itself through *his* history, even if at times that style can engender real monsters."[35]

Faced with *his* history, Carpentier sees the simultaneity of the heterogeneous, the multidirectionality of times, and the juxtapositions of modes of production, social formations, and world views, and he decides that they call for specific forms of representation: "I saw the possibility for establishing certain synchronisms that were possible, American, recurrent, above time, connecting this with that, yesterday with the present."[36]

Destabilizing the established categories of space and time, Carpentier claims that engagement with *lo real maravilloso americano* can radically transform the pale attempts of surrealist artists to engage with the marvelous through recourse to *trucos de prestidigitación* (juggling tricks), such as the oft-cited umbrella and the sewing machine. Further, it can help avoid the risk of turning artists into bureaucrats who activate memorized codes to invoke the fantastic. The essay's foundational effect derives from its power to engage the polyphonic contours of a determined material world while sketching a transformative mode of representing it. It is a renewed self-description and a radical assessment of the established categories hitherto deployed. What Carpentier discovers is an opportunity to write in a way that takes stock of the polyphony of cultural voices which coexist in the belief systems to be represented. He fleshes it out in *El reino de este mundo*, a novel that draws on the mythology constructed around the figure of Mackandal. What America has to offer, then, is its extraordinarily rich *caudal de mitologías* (stream of mythologies) seen as an antidote to the worn-out forms the surrealists had invoked as a source for inspiration. Carpentier's return is thus a recovery of materials that might have been missed had it not been for a search he had embarked on with the impulse derived from his years in Europe.

The revelation described by Carpentier in this essay leads to a kind of writing that provides a mode of access for diverse audiences. The artistic maturity reached by the prominent Latin American writers of the sixties allows them to produce works that encompass the double gaze of the insider and of the outsider, of the Latin American and of the European or North American, arranging remarkably varied cultural ingredients, spaces, and temporalities with technical and narrative élan. These novels and short stories inscribe a number of different readings, they plot literary paths for readers North and South, and thereby find their way into an international reading public that is anxious to deal with the fascinating cultural heterogeneity of Latin American spaces and times. They work out a gaze that observes different spaces at the same time: the recondite, the periphery, the country and the city, the North and its relationship to the South, the nation and the world system, all in combinations where the old and the new combine in compelling ways. It is this double articulation that defines magical realism, the "marvelous real" of Carpentier, and the fantastic—all of which, despite their different characteristics, enable this multidirectionality of reception.

The encyclopedic critical efforts to define and classify the different modes and forms of the fantastic or the magically real read today as part of a disciplinary habitus characterized by the drive for typological investigation. Not surprisingly, many of the essays on the subject begin with disparaging observations about the critical disarray that besets studies of magical realism or the fantastic, and proceed to offer the genealogy of the concepts, marking the origin in Franz Roh's 1925 name for an aesthetic category associated with *Nach Expressionismus*. In Latin American criticism the key names include Luis Leal, Angel Flores, Emir Rodríguez Monegal, Angel Valbuena Briones, Klaus Müller-Bergh, Amaryll Chanady, Roberto

González Echevarría, and many others.[37] Decades later we can echo what Roberto González Echevarría noted in an article that appeared in 1974, later to be published in his 1977 *The Pilgrim at Home*: "What deserves to be preserved in magical realism is not the concept since . . . it is a theoretical vacuum and at times an historical nullity, but rather its reflections, which are symptoms of a much more relevant *problématique* in the history of letters and ideas in Hispanic America: the dilemma of positioning America in universal history."[38]

Indeed, what is at stake is Latin America's place in the world system. The writing of the sixties works out different solutions to this quandary, and in all of them there is interest, novelty, adventure, and surprise. Unlike the deplored efforts of the much-decried *novela de la tierra* or regional novel, which was unidirectional in its inward-looking thrust, the novels of the sixties find solutions for establishing Latin America's location by affirming both its difference and its manifold connections with the "center." They display—and even flaunt—the simultaneity of the heterogeneous, the area's time lag and hybridity, but they do so by posing the problem of its own understanding as an exercise in confronting the contradictions of European history and its own. Thus, the incongruous and the peripheral yield insights into the need to read "magical realism" or "the fantastic" as an exercise in dealing with meaning and representation in different ways, no longer under the aegis of the doxa. The rest of this chapter will offer some thoughts on how some of the boom writers elaborate formal and semantic approaches by looking at questions of narrative form, time, and space.

Finding a Voice, a Time, and a Space

I take as my point of departure Gabriel García Márquez's account of how he managed to find a narrative voice to guide him out of the impasse of his earlier efforts, and to write *La hojarasca*. He set about rereading his masters Joyce and Faulkner, and found a technical solution to the question of how to narrate, by resorting to three voices (the grandfather's, the mother's, and the child's) that might approximate the qualities of a Greek chorus and help portray the *epopeya* (epic story) that he was striving to construct.[39] This "discovery" is described as a turning point in his literary apprenticeship, and indeed it allows his texts to appear to emanate from the depths of the represented community's political and symbolic unconscious, carrying with it the intimacy of community. In *Cien años de soledad* (1967) the voice is one: both archaic and familiar, it reads as if it emanated from the community itself, as a kind of complex cultural memory conveyed by a sagelike storyteller who is not far from his own people. That very intimacy translates incommensurable levels of living and meaning to readers near and far, because the communal, choirlike narrative vehicle has the fullness and conviction that can best represent difference.

Instead of confronting relativism and distance, García Márquez's narration offers the priority of voice over writing, seeming to cancel out the anxieties attendant upon the act of grappling with cultural difference. The immense seduction of *One Hundred Years of Solitude* emanates in no small measure from the force of that singular narrative voice that seems to whisper to the reader's ear and assure her that experience can still be exchanged. We are reminded of Walter Benjamin's observations about Nicolai Leskov: "Experience which is passed from mouth to mouth is the source from which all storytellers have drawn. And among those who have written down the tales, it is the great ones whose written version differs least from the speech of the many nameless storytellers."[40]

Like Francisco el Hombre—the two-hundred-year-old storyteller who travels from town to town telling and collecting stories—García Márquez constructs the fiction of shared knowledge and belief to travel from audience to audience. Indeed, *One Hundred Years of Solitude* has the uncanny power to move within a vast range of different positions of reading, in a capacious register that reaches metropolis and periphery in different ways but with equivalent power. This great novel constructs a cognitive map that permits a semblance of recognition within different areas of the world system—a system in which it was necessary to confront the emergence of new "subjects of history" as a result of the sweep of decolonization in the sixties.[41] At a time when the North was confronted by an enigmatic "new" world in which revolutionary and independence movements summoned its attention, and whose inhabitants began to produce a veritable explosion of otherness, the novel lends a kind of epistemological transparency to a hitherto enigmatic world. And it does so through the fiction of an archaic storytelling voice that renders such a world accessible by reducing distance, while at the same time providing reenchantment and a certain tamed reification of savagery. Let us see how this is operated in *One*

Hundred Years of Solitude through strategies of recognition and mediation between different areas of the world system. My point of departure is that García Márquez constructs a series of platforms for reading that accommodate and inscribe audiences located in different regions, with different expectations and competencies. The result is a powerful reading machine whose geographical breadth of appeal lies in the complex and varying narrative interests it ignites.

"No postwar work has been greeted by the Old World with more enthusiasm than *One Hundred Years of Solitude*." So claims Franco Moretti in his *Modern Epic*, as he goes on to argue that the novel succeeds in "solving symbolic problems that European literature was no longer able to work through."[42] What would an old-world or North American reader find enjoyable in this novel, and what are some of the solutions Moretti is referring to? I would suggest that for him or her this is an exotic tale about a remote, dark little Arcadian village in what will become a veritable Banana Republic, complete with passion and lust, violence and magic. Its perfectly circular narrative line ends in decay and destruction—and a lot of it might be seen as self-inflicted. What we might call the tourist's reading is inscribed in the novel itself, providing surprise, delight, and the occasional hearty laugh. Think of José Arcadio Buendía's fumbling attempts to acquire scientific knowledge. He elicits the bemused chuckle of scientific reason as he blindly revisits the history of scientific discovery. Benign ridicule is not without readerly pleasure, and the moments when José Arcadio proclaims that the earth is round, or uses magnets to find gold, offer a rapturous kind of superior amusement to a First World reader.

Then there are multiple instances of political and institutional violence and failure, as Aureliano's thirty-two armed uprisings, the murders, and the executions all prove. Characters are adrift in a world whose meanings they may blindly contribute to, but cannot altogether fathom out. For the metropolitan reader, though, the storyteller acts as a naturalizing agent: his voice is always there mediating and providing the power of the primitive to help justify, perhaps, the time lag that characterizes the Third World. Here, we could claim with Michael Taussig, lies the "aesthetics of violence, and the complex of desire and repression that primitivism constantly arouses."[43] Violence is not only ever present; it is also worked into the nature of this world as a narrative solution, and not simply as the outcome of political struggles. "The only effective thing . . . is violence," claims

Dr. Atilio Noguera, the false homeopath who dispenses little sugar pills while he plots subversive schemes. A similar claim might be made about many a narrative solution. Conflictive situations are seldom negotiated; their outcomes are frequently resolved with the dazzling swagger of wild feelings and their brutal expressions. The family's foundation rests on Prudencio Aguilar's murder; even before the dead man is buried, José Arcadio storms into the bedroom and, "pointing the spear at her," orders Ursula to take off her chastity pants.

The novel remains true to the twin rhythms of sexual violence and bloodshed. Sexual attraction is always violent and tinged with the pathological: when Rebecca first sees José Arcadio, she becomes extremely sick ("she vomited up a green liquid with dead leeches in it"[44]) and reverted to eating earth. When he makes love to her, "a cyclonic power lifted her up by the waist and despoiled her of her intimacy with three slashes of its claws and quartered her like a dead bird" (101, *80*). Many years later Amaranta Ursula and the last Aureliano will do more damage with their lovemaking than the feared carnivorous ants, and it is their love that ultimately brings about the seemingly apocalyptic end of the novel. Then we have Pilar Ternera, who had to leave her town in order to flee from "the man who had raped her fourteen times." When faced with the fear of losing Pietro Crespi, Amaranta threatens to kill Rebeca if she marries the little Italian musician. Nonromantic disagreements lead to brutal acts or to civil war. Examples abound; the very opening of the novel reveals the extent to which the imminence of execution propels the narrative forward. It also suggests that violence constitutes a narrative instrument of intense effectiveness: its very power allows for sweeping resolutions that move the story forward in leaps, with no ambivalent indeterminacies. Moreover, the force of violent resolutions becomes the medium for constructing a world rife with the mysterious and the terrifying, yet made available through the mediation of an intimate storyteller who is in control of it all.

It seems that the effect of the narrative voice is precisely to wrest from the violent events their demonic power, to guarantee their legibility for the metropolitan reader, who can read on in a mood of bemused, occasionally shocked enchantment. For the world of *One Hundred Years of Solitude* is one in which disorder rules, death becomes coterminous with life's unstable surfaces, and at times it even incorporates the disorder of carnival. In its fast-paced turns of frequent reversals and narrative acceleration, García Márquez's writing achieves an almost kinesthetic regime that offers the reader a sensation of immediacy and involvement. Surprises abound; drastic changes such as death can be reversed in the transition from one sentence to the next, and visceral—often libidinal—arousal turn the reading into a kind of joyride. Events follow one another in dizzying speed so as to produce a vertiginous experience of reading that traces fast-paced movements.

For the sake of illustration, let us consider the chapter that begins with the arrival of the "marvelous inventions" and with the Banana Company. While the introduction of modernization and North American capital instantiates accelerated exchange and circulation, García Márquez's narrative rhythm had been proceeding with dizzying speed long before the arrival of the foreign entrepreneurs. In this chapter one of the foci of narrative interest is Remedios the Beauty, her power to inspire not only overwhelming sexual desire (such that it caused death and desperation) but, more alarmingly, daily disasters. These vicissitudes are woven into a plot whose cinematic qualities remind us of the "cinema of attraction" that film historian Tom Gunning studies in early movies whose sensational appeal actively attracted viewers as in a vaudeville show, producing a sensation of immediacy and arousal.[45] It is not just her oft-cited spectacular rise up to "where not even the highest-flying birds of memory could reach her" (255, *193*), but, before that, the extraordinarily timed incident in the bathroom, when a stranger fell off the roof—and to his death—in a desperate desire to soap her after watching her from above. The sight of the corpse leads to a striking experience of perception and understanding among the stunned Macondians:

The foreigners who heard the noise in the dining room and hastened to remove the body noticed the suffocating odor of Remedios the Beauty on his skin. It was so deep in his body that the cracks in his skull did not give off blood but an amber-colored oil that was impregnated with that secret perfume, and then they understood that the smell of Remedios the Beauty kept on torturing men beyond death, right down to the dust of their bones. (251–52, *190*)

Disasters will multiply, and hence the next lovesick victim will have an even more spectacular end: "the kick of a horse crushed his chest and a crowd of outsiders saw him die in the middle of the street, drowned in his own bloody vomiting" (253, *191*). After such sensational deaths, her heavenly rise with the sheets is one more mechanism of rapturous stimulation.

This does not slow down the narrative rhythm, though. As we turn the page we are swept into another succession of vertiginous incidents—the death of sixteen of Coronel Aureliano Buendía's sons. Notice the telling diegetic transition, in which the narrative voice skillfully negotiates the boundary between amusement and horror. Commenting on the Macondians' belief in the miracle of Remedios's ascension, he makes the leap to the next set of dizzying events: "Perhaps there might have been talk of nothing else for a long time if the barbarous extermination of the Aurelianos had not replaced amazement with horror" (255, *193*). And, indeed, the reader is also led from one emotion to the other as the narrative pace explodes in a frenzy of violence that is, to evoke Barthes on Sade, a combinatory based on body parts and language. Witness the following passage, which ends up being about narrative itself and a kind of "concerted 'irrealism'" produced by favoring semiosis over mimesis.[46] A grandfather has taken his seven-year-old grandson out for a soft drink, and in the midst of the brutal violence following the armistice of Neerlandia, he and we are faced with the following harrowing dispersion of body parts:

because the child accidentally bumped into a corporal of police and spilled the drink on the uniform, the barbarian cut him to pieces with his machete, and with one stroke he cut off the head of the grandfather as he tried to stop him. The whole town saw the decapitated man pass by as a group of men carried him to his house, with a woman dragging the head along by its hair, and the bloody sack with the pieces of the child.[47] (257, *194*)

Barthes's take on Sade relates to García Márquez's narrative of spectacular calamities in that both writers can press the code of representation by a successful relay between speech and crime, between rhetoric and violence, that reads as an acrobatics of brutality. Admirably regulating the vertigo of peril with the reassurance of spectatorial distance, *One Hundred Years of Solitude* elicits a sort of titillating engagement that never loses sight of the fact that it is all ultimately synergetic pleasure. The narrative voice enables and reinforces the reader's safe haven with its archaic ring, echoing novels of adventures and folkloric tales. It offers enchantment and novelty embedded in the periphery, and for the urban or metropolitan reader the seduction proved powerful.

And then there is the reading carved for the Latin American reader, with a special furrow for the Colombian one. *One Hundred Years of Soli-*

tude draws on the nation's political unconscious and reaches into its depths to pose questions about the nation-state as a homeland, and about the relationships between its different spaces, as well as between them and the outside world. It does this by offering a variety of different ranges: from the home, to its environs—at first deeply enigmatic, then gradually mapped, grafted onto the national territory and finally facing the metropolitan world as the place to which characters travel, to return or perhaps not. For the Colombian reader this novel offers the symbolic legibility of space by providing openings to national and international worlds, and at the same time rewriting and updating the regional novel. As Angel Rama has argued, García Márquez wrote the culture of the Caribbean coast into the literary map of Colombia, which had been dominated by what Rama calls the "cultural complex" centered around Bogotá or Medellín.[48] Closely connected with the "Grupo de Barranquilla," his writing opts for the lesser-known area, producing a shifting of the ground for storytelling, finding a recondite location and then expanding outward, gradually reaching the recognizable areas (such as Barranquilla, especially toward the end of the novel), in a series of narrative expansions that originate in uncharted territory. In *La vorágine* the main character, Arturo Cova, left the city and moved into the jungle: *One Hundred Years of Solitude* reverses the direction of the narrative trajectory. Macondo is so distant from the capital that a messenger sent by José Arcadio has to face the following daunting journey: [He] crossed the mountains, got lost in measureless swamps, forded stormy rivers, and was on the point of perishing under the lash of despair, plague, and wilds beasts until he found a route that joined the one used by mules that carried the mail (3–4, *9*).

The novel will expand from this original place, and in the process of doing so, it represents the nation from a different point, reinventing it for an urban reader to rediscover the homeland, turning the distant space into a temporal sign, with the power of beginnings. From this initial register, redolent with the foundational energy of myth, the novel ambitiously flows outward in space and in time, allowing the Colombian reader to identify the signpost of the historical novel in spite of its appearance as a tale of marvelous surprises and discoveries. For the national reader, then, *One Hundred Years of Solitude* delineates a journey that involves traveling outward in space and forward in time along the twin axes of national geography and history. Of course, García Márquez does not turn to the traditional form of the historical novel, which is a journey into the past; rather, he works with time in its different permutations while keeping the plot embedded in the sweep of Colombian history. The avatars of the nineteenth-century civil wars, the allusions to General Uribe Uribe, the many conflicts that were partially ended by the Treaty of Neerlandia in 1902, and the events surrounding the United Fruit plantations are easily recognizable.[49]

For urban readers North and South, *One Hundred Years of Solitude* offers ways of confronting the fundamental gap between older and newer forms of production and communication. The arrival of the Banana Company and the events it ushers in are narrated in such a way as to address the following difficulty in translatability: "Modernism can be positioned as a reproduction of the abstractions to which metropolitan phenomena have been reduced at the same time that it seeks to recomplete those afterimages in a formal way and to restore (but also purely formally) something of the life and vitality, the meanings, of which they have been deprived."[50]

So claims Fredric Jameson as he ponders the temporalities of the modern and the postmodern, noting that the modernist writer was still contending with "an only partially industrialized and defeudalized social order."[51] In the novel, the question of technical innovation as a harbinger of change is foregrounded as estrangement, turned into an aesthetic device of *ostranenie*. The inhabitants of Macondo express different levels of puzzled suspicion and amazement at the arrival of the "marvelous inventions" that follow the yellow train, offering the bemused reader a renewed look at the very oddity of the machine, and hence revisiting its novelty. Electricity, the moving image, the phonograph, and the telephone are reexamined and translated from the viewpoint of a premodern observer, distanced from their function and turned into strangely unserviceable objects. Macondo's people refuse to give up on the vitality and meaning of premodern communication: the phonograph, initially met with curiosity, is soon dismissed as "a mechanical trick that could not be compared with something so moving, so human, and so full of everyday truth as a band of musicians" (242, *183*); the telephone, another reproducer of the voice, leaves them all more upset than incredulous. The entrepreneurial agents of modernization and commerce are likened to "ambulatory acrobats" in a circus. Mr. Herbert, one of those "theatrical creatures," leaves the people dumbfounded as he dissects a banana in an intriguing ceremony that makes it impossible for his observers to eat in peace. The enigmatic nature of these technical intrusions contributes to the reading pleasure and to the effective representation of the uneven development of the world system.

Still another inscription of reading in this novel is the reader in the text, mirroring the one with the book in her hand in a system of refractions dear to the 1960s aesthetics of the "open" work and the self-reflexive text. *One Hundred Years of Solitude* claims to be a self-consuming artifact constructed by Melquíades, that other narrator whose parchments stage the scene of reading throughout the generations. Thanks to this old gypsy the narrative voice can sound even more archaic, donning a self-ironizing air with which different visions of America can be carnivalized. While the book we read contains—but exceeds—Melquíades's story, the fiction of his mediation enhances the discursive range of the novel: its parodic registers include the Biblical scene of creation, the narratives of discovery, the Darwinian paradigm, concepts of history, memory and forgetting, the language of myth, and the authority of Anthropology.[52] Its breathtaking conclusion radicalizes the power of violence as narrative resolution: indeed, what can be more stunning than the final sweep of total annihilation?

But there is even more to this spectacular ending than meets the eye: it may be the end of a certain kind of novel, and it may, in a different sense, be an end as a beginning, as a harbinger of things to come. *One Hundred Years of Solitude* is a brilliant family novel that actually enacts the impossibility of the family itself as a bearer of meaning. While the novel rests on the family tree as the conveyor of organization and understanding,[53] its very structural perfection brings about its dissolution. Hence there is a productive tension between the family as narrative order on the one hand, and the family as human disorder on the other. The enigma of identity that keeps the reading moving in leaps and bounds is, at the point of revelation, the operator of destruction and closure as Aureliano learns he is a Babilonia and not a Buendía, and understands that "the city of mirrors (or mirages) would be wiped out by the wind and exiled from the memory of men" (448, *334*). The genealogical code underpins the structure of repetition and difference organizing José Arcadios and Aurelianos, but the characters themselves (with the exception of Ursula, who has occasional sightings of the hidden system that regulates the workings of her family), cannot grasp its enigmatic meaning. In a sense, we might see the family in this novel as a perfect machine of annihilation that grinds to a halt when there is nothing left, without even the hope of "a second opportunity on earth" (448, *334*).

It is tempting to think about what might have made that "second opportunity" possible, and García Márquez offers a glimpse of it in his Nobel speech, where he rewrites the end of his novel and thereby suggests alternative interpretations. Turning to the metropolitan audience gathered to honor him, he affirms the Latin Americans' right to be treated with solidarity and recognition by the advanced nations. Such treatment would enable not only a more just order, but the power of the imagination to create a utopian realm:

> we, the inventors of tales, who will believe anything, feel entitled to believe that it is not yet too late to engage in the creation of the opposite utopia. A new and sweeping utopia of life, where no one will be able to decide for others how they die, where love will prove true and happiness be possible, and where the races condemned to one hundred years of solitude will have, at last and forever, a second opportunity on earth.[54]

Might the prospect of that "second chance" be read back into the end of *One Hundred Years of Solitude*? Would such a move be aberrant, or would it, rather, be attentive to the vision of history adumbrated by the novel? For the destruction of the House of Buendía might be understood as the closure of the cycle of colonialism and neocolonialism in which Latin America was trapped. To entertain such a hypothesis of reading we do well to bear in mind that this novel was written under the spell of another utopian moment—one that, while lodged in the political unconscious of the sixties, was not limited to tellers of tales like García Márquez, but had the continental reach ushered in by the Cuban Revolution. As Gerald Martin notes, "it is a historical era that is over, not a biological line."[55]

Ends and Beginnings

Like *One Hundred Years of Solitude*, other great novels of the boom unfold the connotative possibilities that arise from the doubling of closure as both end and beginning. Not immune to the utopian longings of the sixties, they tend to arrange their plots along sweeping, ambitious designs that encompass a nation's fraught relationships with time and space. One can just think of *La muerte de Artemio Cruz* (*The Death of Artemio Cruz*) or *La casa verde* (*The Green House*), novels that reach urban and remote areas of the geographies of Mexico and Peru: their plots rest on a range of places and historicities that are tied together in the movement toward plot resolution. Indeed, their narrative design would not obtain without them. More on that later; for now let us consider the system of exchanges between ends and beginnings, and the ideology of form that articulates them. The notion of Necessity that underwrites verisimilitude derives from a sense of history that is both utopian and nostalgic: the imminence of transformation (as discussed in the chapter on the Cuban Revolution) coexists with a yearning for origins that might have produced other historical outcomes in national and continental terms. Hence a look back (to the foundation of Macondo, to the Menchaca estate in Veracruz, to the jungle beyond Santa María de Nieva, to the sleepy Buenos Aires of the barrios that were once left for the lure of Paris) acts as a narrative impulse in these boom novels, as if it were a precondition for imagining other possible outcomes. Here is the nostalgic pull. And yet, the look backwards coexists with its opposite: a desire for renewal and reinvention (even re-creation, perhaps) that might lead to something other than annihilation even after the dazzling finale obtained through death and destruction. One could venture to say that the sense of an ending in these novels is poised in liminal spaces and in in-between times, ready to give different configurations a chance to emerge.

Technical virtuosity lends these glimpses of other possibilities the power of form: in *One Hundred Years of Solitude* the exchanges between circularity and linearity in time—between the repetitions perceived by Ursula and Pilar Ternera, and the pace of impending change marked by the dialogue with Colombian history—pry open an alternative temporality, as in the end of a series, to be followed perhaps by other modalities. Indeed, the reconceptualizing power of form in the novels under consideration underpins a desire for history that is both utopian and apocalyptic. Hence these novels might be seen as deploying the aesthetic dimension so as to imagine other worlds, to raise consciousness in the conviction that new modes of aesthetic representation had a role to play in the process of social and political transformation. The Latin American reading public of the sixties—progressive, mostly urban, university educated—found its own writers able to exploit the playfulness and even the anarchy of language without forsaking the possibilities of raising consciousness and speculating about the ways toward change, marrying formal experimentation and political engagement. The interest in ends and beginnings is a sign of a decade poised for change: for Henri Lefebvre it may be an indicator of a transitional time: "What many people look upon as the conclusion of a well-defined period, as the end of this or that . . . or else as the institution of something new and definitive . . . should really be conceived of solely as a transition."[56]

Let us briefly consider the workings of this technical question in another important work of the period: *The Death of Artemio Cruz*, whose narrative design is willfully fractured in terms of personal pronouns and verb tenses, and which also plays with ends and beginnings. In this novel, Fuentes begins with the imminence of death, and locates in that intense moment—in a faint echo of Borges's "The Secret Miracle"—a mosaic of times that move the reader through Artemio Cruz's life to the perfect final narrative convergence of death and birth. The circle is drawn differently than in *One Hundred Years of Solitude*, but the narrative design culminates in the same point. While the world posited by the novel does not disappear in a Macondian sweep when Artemio dies, the narrative machine is brought to closure ("all three . . . we shall die . . . You . . . are dying . . . have died . . . I shall die"[57]) by putting to rest both the pronominal and the temporal operators, bringing discourse to a halt precisely when the story would seem to end, on the heels of birth, narrated just before death. And yet, once again, the sense of this ending has hints of other possible beginnings, as if it were possible to operate a reversal of apocalypse by transmuting it into a desire for other worlds, for other revolutionary outcomes, and other ethics for the nation and its civil society. In that sense, Artemio's memory, which stages the narrated episodes, could be construed as a form of nostalgia for transformative opportunities that were not realized in Mexico's twentieth-century history.

The Death of Artemio Cruz works metonymically so as to erect a character who will stand for the entire nation. Such condensation is enabled by a concomitant expansion of the categories of time and space: the dying Artemio's memories take us over the vast geographic atlas of Mexico: Chihuahua, Acapulco, Mexico City, Veracruz, Hermosillo, and other places appear as the character moves through his life. Artemio also travels to New York, a city in which he knows his way with Fuentes-like cosmopolitan ease. Human and environmental experience brings forth an intense immersion in Mexico's landscape, with its visual and cultural characteristics. The nation-state, too vast to be known directly, with a shape too artificial to be perceived as a natural unit, is woven together by the crisscrossings of

Artemio's adventures in search of power and fortune. Both country and city are incorporated into the novel's cartography, emblematically represented on Artemio's office wall: "An entire wall of your office is covered with the diagram of the vast network of businesses you control: the newspaper, the real-estate investments—Mexico City, Puebla, Guadalajara, Monterrey, Culiacán, Hermosillo, Guaymas, Acapulco—the sulphur domes in Jáltipan, the mines in Hidalgo, the logging concessions in Tarahumara" (9, *15*). The passage expands into a long recitation of Artemio's holdings, which literally cover the entire map: his range of action by the time of his final illness holds much of the nation's riches in its grip.

To the synchronicity of the map, Fuentes adds the diachronic sweep of history, as Artemio's life and movement string together place and time between 1889 and 1959, so as to display the web of relationships between Mexico's history and a subject's agency. As Paul Julian Smith has observed, Fuentes's novel has a "totalizing impulse" as well as "encyclopedic ambitions," drawing a wide arch that spans the reverberations of the Santa Anna regime, the Porfiriato, the Mexican Revolution, and the decades that followed, marked by the progressive decline of revolutionary ideals that had been confused in their very inception.[58] Narrative technique is pressed to the service of a strong and persistent meditation on ethics, freedom, and alienation: the choice of dated passages in the third person and in the past tense is intended to confront character and readers with the moral implications of actions, which are further theorized in the passages in the first- and second-person pronouns. The corrupting effects of power and ambition are narratively and discursively staged, with force that borders on the allegorical. The twin closures of death and condemnation evoke their counterparts: they carve out a space in which to long for rebirth and redemption at some time in the past or in the future, as either memory or utopia. Such would be the effect of the passages devoted to Artemio's childhood with Lunero in the verdant lands of Veracruz, or even his early years in the Revolution. The progressive loss of innocence is an indictment of Mexico's official post-Revolutionary history—one filled with apocalyptic foreboding and, at the same time, with nostalgia for utopian possibilities that were forsaken in the march of history. Here we might recall that Fuentes began this novel in Havana in 1960 when revolutionary fervor was still running high.

As in the case of *One Hundred Years of Solitude*, *The Death of Artemio Cruz* draws its readers into the wiles of the love plot only to stage its radical impossibility. The power of love to draw characters together in configurations that engender family, community, and nation is here again transmuted into failure and loss. The family Artemio builds with Catalina Bernal displays the destructive effects of ruthless ambition on his part and resentment on hers; failed affairs with Laura and Lilia foreclose the narrative potential of the love plot except as defeat. The novel's symbolic universe enacts the demise of the bourgeois model of the family.

A Rhizomatic *Heart of Darkness*

A similar sense of circularity and decline subsumes the narrative movement of *The Green House*, which opens and closes with the "Selvática" Bonifacia. Her life journey—and the novel itself—begins, like Artemio's, when she is wrested away from her birthplace; it ends in that most emblematic of masculine spaces—the brothel. As in *One Hundred Years of Solitude*, the story begins in a remote location in the Peruvian jungle, where some of the characters have not quite joined the national community. Here again we are reminded of the storytelling appeal of unknown and distant areas at a time when decolonization movements were forcing the issue of empire back into the focus of attention. There were few empty spaces left in the globe in the 1960s, no more expanding frontiers or settlements to establish, but the novelistic imagination was ideally perched to plumb the haunting riches of wildness and primitivism. The cartographic gaze offered an unstable, dangerous—yet fascinating—configuration of a natural, social, economic, and moral environment whose dark contours touched global relationships awaiting representation by the sophisticated tool kit of the new novelists.

In this regard, Vargas Llosa extended the geography of the Peruvian novel. In the work of José María Arguedas, the jungle had remained untouched, as the mysterious area that could not be written about: at the end of *Deep Rivers*, doña Felipa escapes the pursuit of the army into the jungle. From there, it was feared, she would return to Abancay heading a dangerous invasive force made up of *chunchos*, or jungle Indians. That was as far as the great Peruvian novel before Vargas Llosa had gone. In *The Green House* Vargas Llosa achieves what Félix Guattari calls a "transversality," which develops multiple interactions and overlapping zones between ecosystems, the social, and the ethical.[59] Its ambitious sweep covers the perceived char-

acter and destiny of a particular geography in its complex—at times secret—interactions with the rest of the world. And it offers it to a readership that, again, is both national and international. The novel retraces and
reconfigures a trip Vargas Llosa took in 1958 with Mexican anthropologist
Juan Comas.[60] Its vivid memories haunted him as a doctoral student in
Madrid and, later, in Paris, when he set pen to paper to deal with the claims
they made on his imagination.

For the growing metropolitan readership of the Latin American
novel of the time, *The Green House* might be seen to be rewriting *Heart of
Darkness* (1899) sixty-six years later, when the imperial vision had given
way to fragments or to new configurations of domination à la Naipaul or
Rushdie, without obliterating its potential for brutality. In all these cases
we see how the plot mechanisms address an entire system of social and natural references, lending it identity and the weight of its ideological force.
My claim is not about influence (in fact, in Vargas Llosa's tale about the
making of this novel, Conrad is absent as a tutelar presence)[61]: instead, I
wish to locate Vargas Llosa's novel in the intersections between worldviews
and the cartographic fictions that are in conversation with them, so as to
better understand the extent to which a novel, as Roland Barthes put it—
echoing Hegel on History—establishes oppositions between a universe of
values (love, justice, freedom) and a social system determined by economic
laws, and does so through the mediating power of form and technique.[62]
Literary form, then, would be the result of productive negotiations between forces working from the outside and from the inside of the novel.

Like Alejo Carpentier, José Eustasio Rivera, and Joseph Conrad—to
mention just a few eminent forefathers in this particular genealogy—Vargas
Llosa writes at a distance, away from the "dark places" that his novel projects. They are writing about the primeval jungle, and, therefore, there are
telling coincidences in their works. Conrad, Rivera, and Vargas Llosa write
immersed in the political unconscious of a particular form of natural exploitation: the extraction of riches from the jungle. The excesses it produced
bear upon the relationship between the quickening of primitivism in the
novelistic fabulation, and the fetishism of commodities. Kurtz's amassed
stacks of ivory in King Leopold's Congo, Barrera's slaves and his warehouses
filled with stolen rubber during the years of Julio César Arana's Putumayo
empire, and Fushía's and Reátegui's rubber smuggling during World War II
are all at the center of the obsessions that propel the narrative in *Heart of*

Darkness (1899), *La vorágine* (1923), and *La casa verde* (1965), respectively. The similarities that link these novels help underscore the ways in which Vargas Llosa's manipulation of form allowed him to address the changing configurations of the world system while remaining within the same *problématique* of rubber and the jungle. Commenting on his readings in the field of the *novelas amazónicas*, he discusses the difference he is striving for—which, I would venture to say, he will not completely steer clear of in his writing of *The Green House*:

> I especially remember the incredible "Amazon novels," with their demagogical fauna and flora: butterflies the size of eagles, cannibalistic trees, aquatic serpents as long as streamers. At one time I thought I would write an essay about Amazon literature, which is almost unknown to people, of little interest from a literary standpoint, but interesting as a symbol for the most common vices in certain Latin American narratives, since it had succeeded in assimilating them all: a predominance of the natural order over the social, a picturesque, dialectical, descriptive frenzy, a certain gruesomeness.[63]

It does not seem outlandish to aver that he does end up writing one of those *increíbles novelas amazónicas*, with their charge of brutality, natural and human horror, and even considerable truculence. How, though, does his location as a 1960s boom writer allow him to avoid the risk of being derivative and, instead, lead him to construct a novel that is dazzling in its novelty and appeal? And, concomitantly, how is his writing tributary to the established archive, which is in constant negotiation between the world and the forms of representation charting it? They are two of the key questions that the novels of the boom address in compelling ways, managing to convey the epoch's contradictions.

    The Green House's geographic imaginary echoes the profound sense of not-at-homeness (the very opposite of topophilia[64]) that accosted José Arcadio Buendía when he set out to explore the territories around Macondo. But in *The Green House* there is no central place, no Macondo, no place to call home. In this lack of centrality lies the dynamic transversality of space in this novel: unlike the ever-expanding concentric circles that have Macondo at their center, and then reach beyond it into the national and international world, in *The Green House* we have spaces of indeterminacy located between two hostile worlds: the windy, sandy area around Piura in Northeastern Peru, and the impenetrable jungle around Iquitos, Santa María de Nieva, and other points along the Upper Marañón and

Amazon rivers. A cartographic trope appears early on, in the voice of old Aquilino, the man who can make his way through the Amazonian labyrinth precisely because he knows it cannot be definitively charted: "Do you remember how we burned your maps? . . . Nothing but junk. People who make maps don't know that the Amazon is like a hot woman, she's never the same. Everything is on the move here, the rivers, the animals, the trees. What a crazy land we've got for ourselves, Fushía."[65]

The burning of the maps by Aquilino and Fushía is not without symbolic value. Unlike the vast holdings recorded in Artemio Cruz's office map, encompassing a stable territory of ambition and corruption, the lands in this novel defy the stability of cartography as much as the aims of human effort. Distance is alienating, and the ever-present likelihood of getting lost daunts those who traverse it. This is not only the experience of the jungle: traversing the windy desert that surrounds Piura involves facing dangers that are both natural and human, as illustrated by the misadventures of young Antonia and her protectors, brutally assaulted by bandits in ways that evoke Sarmiento's sublimely terrifying *desierto*. Anselmo (the newcomer who builds the brothel that ostensibly gives the novel its name) arrives out of nowhere, as if the roads that led to Piura were veiled in mystery.

In Vargas Llosa's twentieth-century heart of darkness there is no "home" to go to: neither Piura, with its sand-bearing winds, nor the Amazonian basin's devouring organic growth, nor even Lima's distant location, which Lituma visits while in jail, and from where army orders emanate— no place (urban or rural) bears the promise of a happy, settled life, marked by affective ties to the environment.[66] Love of place is out of the question here. And there is no place to escape to: unlike the darkening Thames from which Marlow is evoking the distant horrors of the Congo, or the urban ennui of Bogotá that Arturo Cova escapes from, in *The Green House* there is no point of departure to be marked as such, and its very lack determines the geographic density of the novel. As Deleuze and Guattari would have it, this is a truly *rhizomatic* configuration, with no root, no point of order, with bulbous ramifications that defy the linearity of arrangement ordering novels like *Heart of Darkness* and *La vorágine*.[67] In these two novels the voyages are into the inner continent, following a line into the jungle that also traces the story line: Marlow goes to the Central Station and from there on to Kurtz's trading station, further into the jungle; Cova elopes from Bogotá with Alicia, and after a time in the plains of Casanare, they make their way into the Putumayo and Amazon rivers. Unlike Marlow's, Cova's is a trip with no return: the famous "¡Los devoró la selva!" (The forest devoured them!) encrypted in the message from the Colombian consul in Manaus to the Minister seals Cova's disappearance into the devouring jungle. Indeed, Marlow has to go back in order to be able to tell the story to his five companions on the Nellie, whereas Cova's destiny is framed by the conceit through which the story is transmitted: the ministerial request that Rivera edit the manuscript found and delivered by the Consul. Vargas Llosa's technical know-how dispenses with such framing devices for the sake of a kind of writing that is decentered, expansive, perched in multiple and movable points in space and in subject positions. Hence, the circularity of the beginning and end is, to echo Deleuze and Guattari again, bulbous, with *lignes de fuite* and *lignes de segmentarité*[68] that eschew unity. And yet, in what I think is a productive paradox, the sense of closure emanating from Bonifacia/la Selvática's life journey is not without that longing for a different order (perhaps perceived as imminent in the 1960s?) that emanates from the endings of *One Hundred Years of Solitude* and *The Death of Artemio Cruz*. Referring to the loss of faith in the "great legitimizing narratives of emancipation and enlightenment," studied by Foucault and Lyotard, Said observes that circularity in narrative is one of the ways in which the linear path of narrative is blocked: "There is nothing to look forward to: we are stuck within our circle."[69] Radical questioning is another possible outcome of the sense of closure thus described: the narrative of failure may come out of a sense of utopian perfectibility.

Critics have compared the structure of *The Green House* with a kaleidoscope that generates moving images.[70] Operating on a system of fragmentation, it juxtaposes different narrative times and plots: five different story lines and constant shifts in their temporal *dispositio* produce the experience of multiplicity. Not surprisingly, this effect rests upon a meticulously orchestrated organizational design that is anything but chaotic.[71]

Furthering the force of the decentered plot is Vargas Llosa's work on voice, which is heteroglossic in the broadest sense: aside from the primacy of dialogue, there is a handling of narration that tries to lose itself in the political unconscious of a community. Here is the author's account of his effort to achieve this effect:

The idea was this: the story of Anselmo and Antonia would be narrated not as it really happened (this we could never know), but according to how the *mangaches* supposed or desired that it happen. The existence of this sentimental adventure would hold in the novel the same vacillating and subjective tone as that of the first "green house." It occurred to me then—in truth it was after throwing many drafts into the garbage that it started to take shape—to introduce a voice, distinct from that of the narrator, that would represent the conscience or soul of Mangachería and that would literally proceed to order, by means of commands, the love lives of Anselmo and Toñita . . . it would be a sort of liquidity, a certain atemporality.[72]

This striving for fluidity and dispersion is the politics of form at work in *La casa verde*: it allows the novel to fictionalize a world of hallucinatory qualities without explaining them away, retaining their mesmerizing power even though they had been the materials of earlier novels.

Aside from the thematic reworking of earlier works, Vargas Llosa is drawing on an established repertory of narrative form furnished by his fascination with *novelas de caballerías* (such as Martorell's *Tirant lo blanc*), with Westerns and other action films, with the spy novel and police thrillers. In this sense—and without the trappings of magical realism—this novel produces a kind of cinematic kinetics propelled by surprise, by the struggle between essential good and evil, by tales of bandits and rapes, duels and theft—all under the mantle of atrocity. The effect is not unlike that produced by *One Hundred Years of Solitude* despite the marked differences in form. Urban readers (whether Peruvian, Latin American, North American, or European) were to be fascinated and terrified by its extremes of meaning, which attain a kind of derealization of the real. I can think of no better example than the final scenes of Fushía's decomposition, as leprosy has eaten at his body and all that is left is the stench of "el montoncito de sangre viva y sangrienta" that makes even his friend Aquilino recoil in disgust.

And what about the world his writing was evoking, manipulating, transforming, and reworking? It was one that sat heavily upon the colonial and the postcolonial imagination. Here again we see the boom novelist revisiting the historical archive. The intricate plot sweeps over the first five decades of the twentieth century and a multitude of characters whose lives are touched by world events they may or may not be aware of. The text's deliberate dislocation and plurality is, as we have seen, a formal treatment of a perceived world; it also makes for manifold connections within each area, between areas, and, importantly, between the nation and the metropolis. In *One Hundred Years of Solitude* these international relations were represented through the Banana Company; in *The Death of Artemio Cruz*,

Artemio's business empire led to associations with North American busi-
nessmen. Here we have Fushía and Reátegui's smuggling schemes designed
to sell rubber to the Axis during World War II, when Peru supported (and
sold rubber to) the Allies. Why evoke a trip Vargas Llosa took in 1958
through a novel that locates the action in the early 1940s? The answer to this
question need not trap us into the problematic sphere of authorial intention; instead, it may throw light on the logic of plot as it relates to verisimilitude and the historical context.

As it happens, Vargas Llosa had to locate the action during the
1939–45 war so as to reignite the rubber trade's capacity to engender horror,
for by the end of World War I the Peruvian Amazon area had lost its hold
on the rubber trade to the plantations in Ceylon and Malaya developed by
the British with seeds from Latin America. This history is narrated in the
novel, made to provide the context within which the logic of fiction obtains. We find it in a passage devoted to the conversations between Reátegui
and Jum—mediated by a translator—about Jum's attempt to start a coop-
erative and trade rubber without Reátegui's intervention. The governor tells
his men that the troubles in Amazonia were caused by outsiders:

the outsiders brought on the trouble, Captain. The last time it had been foreigners,
some Englishmen, with some story about botanical research; they'd gone into the
jungle and come out with seeds from rubber trees, and one fine day the world was
full of rubber from the British colonies, cheaper than Peruvian and Brazilian rubber, that had been the rumination of the Amazon region, Captain, and he: it was
true, Señor Reátegui, that opera companies used to come to Iquitos and that rubber growers lit their cigars with banknotes? Julio Reátegui smiles, his father had a
chef for his dogs, just imagine, and the Captain smiles, the soldiers smile. (147, *203*)

As we shall see, Reátegui's father, like Julio César Arana, belonged to the
era of the rubber boom narrated in *La vorágine* and denounced by Roger
Casement. This later plot that spins out of the Japanese Fushía and his
partnership with Julio Reátegui and their corrupt dealings with Indians,
state officials, and the German-Japanese alliance, derives its credibility from
the war in the Pacific and the difficulty that the Allies encountered obtain-
ing rubber, thereby raising prices and intensifying the margin of greed.
Like the tentacular waterways that only Aquilino manages to navigate, the
historical threads underpinning these connections are intricate and far
reaching. Tracing them may take us back in time and even out of the Amazon: doing so may be justified in the interest of displaying the network of

connections activated by one of the boom's most totalizing novels. It is also an illustration of the challenges of any postcolonial literature in its coming to terms with the unremitting traces of the colonial legacy.

Long before globalization occupied the center of critical attention, the rubber trade—developed after Charles Goodyear's invention of vulcanization in 1839—produced an intricate system of connections across the globe. These involved a densely layered set of social and economic relations between and among imperial crowns (such as Queen Victoria and King Leopold II), Belgian, British, and American rubber companies, "independent" nation-states, local civil and military authorities, trading companies as mediators and partners, explorers and *prácticos* (like Adrián Nieves and Aquilino in *The Green House*, or Clemente Silva in *La vorágine*), smugglers and entrepreneurs of every ilk, and the natives living along the rivers, whose job it was to extract rubber in exchange for such things as knives and trinkets. There were individuals such as Roger Casement and Robert Cunninghame Graham who moved between these different worlds and whose discourse of denunciation is embedded in the historical imaginary of the rubber trade.[73] There were also powerful partnerships such as the one between Peruvian Julio César Arana and the British in the Amazon River Company, headquartered in Iquitos and financed by British banks. And there were corrupt businessmen-turned-governors like Julio Reátegui, who governed the area around Santa María de Nieva in the 1950s, at the time when an Indian named Jum was the head of the Urakusa people, and when Vargas Llosa's first trip to the area took place.[74] To strengthen the reach of the nation state into the jungle areas, a Plan de Educación was devised to remove children from their Indian families in order to teach them what were considered to be civilized ways.

Four decades before Vargas Llosa wrote his novel, the rubber-trading world ensconced itself in the shocked contemplation of the metropolitan audiences through a series of articles published in 1909 by the London magazine *Truth*. Rife with dread and awe, they bore the title "The Devil's Paradise: A British Owned Congo."[75] Julio C. Arana's corruption and brutal mistreatment of the Indians were denounced for abuses that echoed those King Leopold had been notoriously known for in his rubber-rich Congo Free State. Furthering the appalling discoveries was a report commissioned by the Foreign Office, and which led to Roger Casement's presentations before the House of Commons in 1912 and 1913. Rivera's *La vorágine* is a Colombian rendition of the atrocities narrated by Casement, and in the novel the character of Arana is as historical as is Julio Reátegui in *The Green House*. There was thus an aura of shock surrounding the subject, probably heightened by its location. Vargas Llosa himself acknowledges that this combination exerted a powerful hold on his imagination:

> Now I understand it better, but a few years ago I was still embarrassed to admit it. On the one hand, all that barbarism infuriated me: the backwardness, the injustice, and the ignorance of my country were obvious. On the other hand, it fascinated me: what great material to be able to narrate. At that time I started to discover this hard truth: the best material for literature is not happiness but human unhappiness, and writers, like vultures, feed off of carrion.[76]

Carrion it may be, but it makes for spectacular reading, enriched by the echoes of a preexisting archive.

The thing to be noticed is the sheer historical and geographical momentum of this novel, and the extent to which it is informed by a changing system of representation. Gone, of course, is Conrad's formulation of the tragic predicament of the imperial enterprise. Gone, as well, is the nation- and subject-based vision of Rivera's novel. In *La vorágine*, Colombian-ness is a principle of order, even though the nation is in the grip of the likes of Arana and Barrera. When Cova and his men meet Clemente Silva, the fact that they are all Colombian has the reassuring effect of anagnorisis, as a return to the fold. The search for the law is translated into the search for a Colombian consul in the area in which the borders between Peru and Colombia were still awaiting final definition.[77] And while the consul in Iquitos is Arana himself in the novel, and nowhere to be found, Clemente Silva's journey in search of the Consul in Manaus does eventually bear its—belated—fruit. No such guarantee of national legitimacy remains in *The Green House*: don Julio Reátegui and don Fabio Cuesta, the governors, are there simply to manipulate the army and the rubber industry to their advantage. A distant Lima, as was noted above, might offer jail space or domestic employment for the former boarders at the mission in Santa María de Nieva. Perhaps nothing forces us to recognize the impossibility of national legitimacy and cohesion more forcefully than the words uttered by Jum as he is hanged from his extremities, tortured, and humiliated so as to put an end to his attempts at independent trade. Jum yells, *"piruanos, piruanos,"* naming that alien nationality that represents his sense of outrage. The officer in charge states what recourse to the state might yield: "he could always write to Lima, make some requests to the Ministry, maybe the Bureau of Indian Affairs, to indemnify him" (185, *249*). The matter is solved with a *papelito firmado* with which Jum is deceived once more: the state and its institutions can be metonymically inscribed in this faked document.

Nor does the love plot confer meaning to the characters' lives. While other boom novels (most notably, *One Hundred Years of Solitude*) draw on the family and the love plot as narrative models, *The Green House* carries out an unremitting assault on them: the only married couple in the novel, Lituma and Bonifacia, begin their relationship after he rapes her; they also provide the final scene in the brothel, where the money she makes helps keep Lituma and his cronies. Gender, then, becomes one of the carriers of the crisis of masculinity that is at work in this system of representation. Here again a comparison with *La vorágine* proves instructive: Arturo Cova, melodramatic and generally ineffective though he may be, does return to be reunited with Alicia, and, for better or for worse, they march united into the devouring jungle. In *The Green House* women are objects of exchange and circulation, much like the rubber along the riverways. Bonifacia may offer the most dramatic example, but Lalita and Antonia do not fare any better. The latter, loved though she may have been by Anselmo, dies in childbirth; the former is forced to move from man to man (Fushía, then Nieves, and finally el Pesado) as brushes with the authorities remove two of them from the scene. The ruling symbol of the brothel extends beyond the identification of the jungle with Anselmo's "green house" and his green harp: it is also the signifier for the gender system. And while Vargas Llosa's own cheerful account of the historical counterparts of the *inconquistables* in Piura—together with one critic who is as disconcerting as she is unconvincing[78]—may claim there are benign bonds of friendship among them, the plot yields the overwhelming impression that meaningful male effort is absent from this novelistic world. Not even Anselmo and Aquilino, who are not totally immune to ethical considerations, forego harm: Anselmo is the brothel owner who causes Antonia's death; Aquilino helps Fushía in his river exploits. In the jungle, young Indian women are raped without restraint, taken much as the rubber is drawn from the trees. Only La Chunga seems to be in control of her fate, as she ruthlessly runs the second "green house."

The logic of promiscuity rules the novel's world: like the brothel that names it, circulation is out of control. This is true of the powerful river system, which not even the *práctico* Nieves and the experienced Anselmo can control. Rubber is smuggled; women are taken out of their native lands and made to circulate from the convent to domestic employment or to prostitution; Indians are captured and sent into the army. Those who do not circulate, the *inconquistables*, are marooned in a morass of unemployment and drink. The Church is represented by the unforgiving *madrecitas* (whose expulsion of Bonifacia ultimately sends her on her way to La Chunga's place) and by Father García's uncontrolled wrath. In her perceptive analysis of the novel, Sara Castro-Klarén points out that chance plays an important role in the worldview of *The Green House*.[79] Certainly, the characters are obsessed with bad luck, chance's stern face, and they fail to understand the workings of the external mechanisms that dominate them. As noted above, the rhizomatic plot configuration (fluid and intractable, like the Amazon system) underscores such randomness. And yet, the novel's sweep in time and space, its sheer connectedness with history and geography, produce a compelling, variegated vision of the forces that regulate the sphere of possible agency in the periphery of an interconnected world.

To bring these reflections on time and space, ends and beginnings to a close, I will consider briefly the most urban of the boom's novels, Julio Cortázar's *Rayuela* (*Hopscotch*): no jungles, no plains, no swamps or deserts—no vast sweeps of national territory to be cartographically and economically amassed.

"Julio Cortázar at Home"

So claims a 1968 article in *Primera Plana*.[80] Oddly enough, though, the notion of being *at home* is resolutely alien to the world he imagines in his novels and, most certainly, in *Hopscotch*. This novel is rife with questions of space, but like its title it lacks the notion of rootedness that is associated with a home. Critics have dealt with the metaphysical connotations of words like *mandala*, with emblematic bridges, thresholds, or tents charged with metaphoric force leading toward transcendence. My intention here is to read the metaphors backwards, to bring the novel down to its earthly topography.

A decidedly urban novel, *Hopscotch*'s transnational dimensions offer a different take on the geographical unconscious of the sixties. Its readers are not led into the innermost areas of the nation, or to mysterious expanses of land with which metropolitan curiosity could be aroused. Instead, the book is divided into three *lados* or sides, areas, zones. Extending the system of space deictics, Cortázar builds a system of three by using *allá* (there), *acá* (here), and *de otros lados* (of other places). Cities provide the reference for the first two: Paris is "there"; Buenos Aires, "here." For the third area we have a mixture of the two, as well as free-floating texts such as the "Morellianas" and the notes toward the opus by Ceferino Piriz, "La luz de la paz del mundo," read with mirth by Traveler, Talita, and Oliveira. Significantly, the "here" is Buenos Aires,[81] although the novel was written in Paris. This space marker calls attention, the OED tells us, to a person's presence. I would suggest that the presence in question is the reader in Buenos Aires, who is taken, not to Lévi-Strauss's "perfumes of the tropics," but to Paris, city of desire.[82] From *el lado de allá* of the reader—which is *el lado de acá* of the author—Paris is displayed in a detailed toponymy that bespeaks what I would call an anxiety of location.

As Horacio Oliveira walks the streets of Paris, looking for his lover, or strolling about with her, or on his way to a meeting of the Club de la Serpiente, the text's compunction to specify street names seems to be a desire to "root the fictive in the real," as Barthes would have it.[83] But the meticulous insistence with which streets, bridges, parks, and quartiers are named makes one ponder their "tellability," especially when contrasted with the paucity of place names in the Buenos Aires chapters. Could it be that the readers *del lado de acá*, like Oliveira's friend Traveler, longed to venture out into the world of the North, and most especially, Paris? When Cortázar was writing *Hopscotch*, Paris loomed large in the map of Latin American longing. The city Oliveira roams is named as his steps traverse it: if we consider the first few pages of the novel for the sake of illustration, what Michel de Certeau calls *énonciations piétonnières* articulate the rue de Seine, the Quai de Conti, the Marais, the Boulevard de Sebastopol, the Latin quarter, the Parc Montsouris, the Place de la Concorde, Joinville, the Pont des Arts, the Right Bank, the rue des Lombards, the rue Verneuil, the Pont Saint Michel, the Pont au Change—and the list continues. Paris is the city of proper names organized by the rhetoric of walking; Buenos Aires (with counted exceptions such as the Calles Cachimayo, Trelles, and

Maipú, and the Avenidas San Martín and Corrientes) is a vague city of interior spaces: the rooms rented by Oliveira and Gekrepten in the Pension Sobrales, the circus, the asylum. The *errance du sémantique* that de Certeau identifies with the movement on city streets leads to a striking conclusion: "To walk is to run out of space."[84] Indeed, the proliferation of proper names in Paris creates a series of named locations whose effect on readers was, I would suggest, to offer imaginary voyages. The many toponyms are markers for a desired other place, distant and projected by postcolonial yearnings. Little does it matter to identify the name of a street or a bridge with its precise referent: as De Certeau submits, proper names "detach themselves from the places they were supposed to define and serve as imaginary meetings for voyages."[85] Indeed: the Paris of *Hopscotch* is the space for an imaginary rendezvous—not just with La Maga, but with the Latin American reader as well.[86]

But this city of desire is also the city of homelessness, and in the end the hero does return to "this side," the side of the reader. While in Cortázar's short stories Paris is, as Marcy Schwartz lucidly observes, a locus for "idealized creativity and metafictional potential," in which "ontological alternatives" can be pursued, I would claim that the Paris of *Hopscotch* encapsulates both desire and profound dislocation—one that culminates in deportation.[87] In the *Cuaderno de bitácora de Rayuela*, Cortázar writes a brief "[e]ulogy to the café, where we were immortal for an hour. The café, liberty, . . . "[88] Spaces of freedom for wanderers like Oliveira, La Maga, and their friends, tellingly described in Chapter 132 as "the neutral territory for the stateless of the soul, the motionless center of the wheel from where one can reach himself in full career, see himself enter and leave like a maniac . . . one no-man's-land."[89] However, they are not open, expansive spaces: their freedom often exhales squalor, like La Maga's room: "there was only filth and misery, glasses with stale beer, stockings in a corner, a bed which smelled of sex and hair" (13, *28*).

The novel's Paris is the city of the Algerian war, not entirely recovered from the German occupation and World War II. It is a city of cold, rainy days and nights, of damp, smelly coat collars, of grumpy old concierges and narrow dirty stairways. In it, as he puts it, Oliveira moves *como una hoja seca* (like a dry leaf). Even in the company of La Maga the urban scene is inhospitable: "They were walking along there aimlessly and stopping in the doorways, drizzle after lunch is always bitter and something ought to be done about that frozen dust, against those raincoats smelling of rubber" (27, *45*). And while spatial phrases such as "splashing about in a circle," "spinning with one foot nailed to the ground," "enter into a kibbutz," "colony, settlement, a chosen place to reach the final store," "city rights," and scores of others are to be read metaphorically ("Es una metáfora . . . París es otra metáfora," as Oliveira instructs Gregorovius—and the reader—in one of their heated arguments about metaphysical quests), these metaphors can be read backwards, as noted above. The very concreteness of space in *Hopscotch* has, itself, its own *lado de acá* as both desire and its impossibility. Lucky Oliveira freely roaming the cities of Paris, a reader might have said when the novel came out in 1963—but then one might end up feeling that it is not so great after all. He is no real flâneur, only a Latin American would-be immigrant whose ever-moving body finds no dwelling. The question of where to live is not only metaphysical: it is concretely enacted in the novel as the anxious interrogation of the modern Latin American subject whose expanding world has foreclosed topophilia without arresting his longing to explore distant places in the North.[90]

And what about the Buenos Aires Oliveira returns to after plumbing the depths of abjection as he reenacts Heraclitus's descent on the banks of the Seine? Here Cortázar's choice of places and people is marked by cunning and artifice. Which of the many city territories at his imagination's disposal was he to locate the plot in? How would he build a community to act as the *porteño* counterpart to the cosmopolitan Club de la Serpiente? How, indeed, would he fold the two *lados* into one another, so that their *dispositio* would be true to the logic of form? Bringing his character back home (so to speak) posed the challenge of drawing the all-too-familiar Buenos Aires into the fictive polis. Rather than constructing a system of equivalences to the initial *lado de allá*, Cortázar turns it inside out, like a glove. He works by displaying the folds of difference and repetition, by producing echoes and then changing the tune. To the exilic errancy of the Parisian chapters, he juxtaposes the stasis of the Buenos Aires ones: in the sultry summer days of the Southern Hemisphere—hardly more enticing than the damp, gray days of the Parisian winter—Oliveira and the Travelers are lodged in small hotel rooms, staring at each other from window to window. If the novel of walking (with its Joycean traces) is invoked in the Parisian chapters, the novel of confinement is the model in the Buenos Aires ones. The allegorical hopscotch is present in both, though more insistently drawn in the episodes located in the asylum. The spatial properties of the return have less to do with cityscapes than with the interior architecture of a circus or an asylum; their vertical axes are elaborated in their metaphysical implications (the circus tent opening up to the zenith; the morgue at the asylum reaching into the underworld; the higher floors from which to contemplate the courtyard, the hopscotch and the possibility of death). Oliveira is not represented as a walker in his city: only a pizzería on Corrientes, or the bridge over Avenida San Martín make a momentary appearance or two. The novel's interpretive momentum suggests the *huis clos* as the ruling paradigm for reading these images. It would not be otiose to also note that this was a solution to a problem of representation: how to portray a city so well known to his readers without rewriting Mallea, Sábato, Marechal, Mujica Láinez, or even Borges, and without falling prey to the all-too-familiar urban topography of his sophisticated readers. But this city of desire is also the city of homelessness, and in the end the hero does return to "this side," the side of the reader. *Hopscotch*'s geographic sweep offers a vision that expands and then contracts, back into the fold. The circle in this case is Oliveira's round trip. His Parisian existence enacts freedom (no job, no family ties) within nomadic space: the interior spaces are cafés, hotel rooms, smoke-filled pieds-à-terre for the Club de la Serpiente—no homes to settle in.

Avoiding the obvious, then, led him to a *pensión* on Cachimayo Street, to a circus, to an asylum or *loquero*. In keeping with his delight in the humorous parodies of the petit bourgeois mannerisms that have been discussed in Chapter Three, Cortázar opted for a community that readers could laugh at, such as la Cuca Ferraguto, la señora de Gutusso, don Crespo, and Gekrepten. Traveler and Talita would play variations on Oliveira and La Maga, enlarging the connotative resonances of the double as displacement and condensation. Thus, he defamiliarized the familiar in Buenos Aires by imagining eccentric interior locales, and a humorously portrayed community of ostensibly well-meaning simpletons who understand none of the cultural distinctions dazzlingly paraded in the heated discussions of the Club de la Serpiente. And traversing all places, the ever-vigilant subjectivity of Oliveira, so tantalizingly close to the authorial persona Cortázar's readers had grown to expect. Thus, *Hopscotch* brought Paris up close and then offered ethnographic peeks into life in the Buenos Aires *barrios* whose inhabitants would never be the *lectores cómplices/machos* to whom the novel was offered. Those readers could find a veritable encyclopedia of the latest in cultural taste in *del lado de allá,* and then, in *del lado de acá,* an amusing mimicry of a social world they were glad to make fun of. Oliveira's downward mobility in Buenos Aires allows for a different kind of exploration of space.

Read in conjunction with the other boom novels discussed above, *Hopscotch* seems to eschew the sweeping universal reach of national space and time, of transnational networks of power and agency represented in *One Hundred Years of Solitude, The Death of Artemio Cruz,* and *The Green House.* What are we to make of Oliveira's meticulous detachment, his flaunting of disoccupation (either as sheer inaction, or as action in pursuit of purposelessness, as in bending nails or tying strings) when juxtaposed with the feverish pursuits of the Buendías, or with the driven ambition of Artemio Cruz or Fushía? And what about the nation-state and its history in the context of the world system? Etienne tries to exact some solidarity with the Algerian cause from Oliveira, only to afford us the opportunity to read more about the delusions of causes. In Buenos Aires, rumors about uprisings in Campo de Mayo produce a detached unease not much greater than the summer heat. Cortázar's musings about capitalism *en su última carrera* (in its final race) jotted down in his *Cuaderno de bitácora de Rayuela* are not translated into a worldview in *Hopscotch.* That was to come later, as was argued in Chapter Three. In *Hopscotch,* instead, the political unconscious of the sixties takes on a different, more elusive form, and it does so by way of character development.

Horacio Oliveira, faults and all, is a model of humanity that was being worked out in the wake of existentialism, of course. But perhaps we need more than Sartre to understand Oliveira's function in the boom's imaginary. He is the man who opts out, whose critical consciousness hovers at a threshold, as if he were on the verge of becoming. He has the analytical vigilance and honesty of a "new man" who has not yet made the leap into political commitment. Indeed, Oliveira is like a Che Guevara who cannot embrace action: they share the spirit of adventure, a longing for a different world and self-deprecating sense of humor, a defiance of family ties and bourgeois ways. To state the obvious, unlike Che, Oliveira vigilantly eschews political commitment.[91] He is placed at the center of a novelistic world in which neither the family nor the love plot—the cornerstones of the bourgeois novel—are allowed to prevail. The family is at a distance or emblematically killed off with baby Rocamadour's death; the love plot is set up so as to display its failure: finding La Maga would have cornered the character into an unlikely happy ending. Instead, Cortázar opts for the undecidability of the window scene in Chapter 56, when the possibility that he might jump off may lead to an end or to a different beginning. Here again the intimations of utopia and change are derived from the critical stance relentlessly pursued by *Hopscotch*. The other novels under consideration reach that point in different ways, but they all reveal the structure of feeling of a decade that saw itself as both critical and inaugural.

A great deal has been written about *Hopscotch*'s technical originality, its famous *Tablero de direcciones,* its design for different kinds of readings, and its calling into question of the book as a finished product. It is all in keeping with the boom's displays of modern technical virtuosity, of formal flourish and command of form. Like *The Green House, Hopscotch* opts for scrambling fragments so as to have the reader do his[92] own cut and paste; like *The Death of Artemio Cruz*, it relies on the unifying force of one character to structure the fragments. Regardless of the patterns of two (such as Oliveira-Traveler) or of the triangulations (Traveler-Oliveira-Talita, Traveler-Oliveira-Gregorovius, Oliveira-La Maga-Pola, or Oliveira-La Maga-Talita; *del lado de acá, del lado de allá, de otros lados;* and so on), *Hopscotch* is based on the fragment as a system of composition. In fact, the novel began with the fragment that deals with Talita on the board, between Oliveira and her husband, in what could be said to work as a principle that is replicated in all one hundred and fifty-five fragments/chapters.[93] As refined as the elaboration of narrative voice and point of view may be, it is not a novel that foregoes unity: it flaunts fragmentation, and yet it is the story of one character's search for meaning and transcendence, conceived as the singular, "authentic" reality that lies beyond the disperse plurality of appearances, tucked away in a metaphysical fold.

And, like the other novels considered in this chapter, *Hopscotch* has one blind spot that trips up its revolutionary potential: gender. The dominant fictions of patriarchy discussed in Chapter Five are in full force in Oliveira's world: in the homosocial triangulations of desire (La Maga-Gregorovius-Oliveira; Talita-Traveler-Oliveira), in the Club de la Serpiente, in the tug and pull between Oliveira and Traveler. As Gabriela Nouzeilles has shown, women in *Hopscotch* are the objects of playful scorn or of sexual violence,[94] regardless of their function as operators of alterity and—perhaps—transcendence.

The yearnings for change leave the gender system intact, and thus reveal the limitations of the revolutionary projects—be they political or artistic. Like the *amigotes* evoked by Donoso in his *Historia personal del "boom,"* the Club de la Serpiente reinforces male bonds by relegating women to a decidedly inferior sphere. Here was a category that the sixties was unable to revise, and yet it returns in today's rereadings, unsettling the luminous architecture of its monumental works.

Conclusion

How can closure be reached in a study of this kind? As I indicated at the outset, "the sixties" have been taken as a heuristic and rhetorical category more than as a chronological one, so the mere shift to the seventies will not produce the sense of an ending. And the penchant for change that characterized the modernizing impetus of the decade contained the impulses that would lead to its own supersession. The denouement of the decade is surprising, and yet it is the result of the very forces at play in all utopian moments, which never yield their anticipated outcomes. But we are still the heirs of the sixties, and they are still with us in significant ways.

What about the surprising outcome? In social, political, and economic terms, Latin America was faced with upheavals of the greatest magnitude. Hardly any nations were spared the twin horrors of clandestine violence and state repression, from Pinochet's Chile to Colombia's protracted civil wars. Castro's Cuba, in Jean Franco's words, has gone from "representing the revolutionary vanguard to evoking nostalgia for the lost revolutionary ideal."[1] The drive for political liberation often led to violence and the commitment to disputing power at the barrel of a gun—at the other end of which stood a repressive apparatus fueled by a fierce determination not to yield. Ideological differences escalated into stark polarizations with violent outcomes. The utopian longing for liberation turned into the nightmare of repression, and many Latin American nations are still struggling to recover from the trauma of the upheavals of disappearances and torture.

The economic boom of the sixties turns out to have been a stage in the move from a transnational to today's global economic order, characterized by the dynamics of capitalism's uneven development, with pronounced disparities in income and ever-expanding margins of disenfranchised citizens. The economic indicators for Latin America reveal that the percentage of the population living in poverty is on the rise, and that the worst crisis of its economic history has been raging since the 1980s.[2] The consequences are the stuff our contemporary scene is made of: hardship, anger, disenchantment.

In the literary and cultural world, the apparatus of production and distribution has been drastically changed: gone are the *editoriales culturales* of the sixties, and in their stead loom powerful publishing houses like Planeta, Anagrama, and Alfaguara, which massively control the book industry from their Spanish vantage point. Now the preboom situation described by José Donoso (with *chasquis* bringing books to Santiago de Chile from Buenos Aires or Mexico City) repeats itself in its neoliberal avatar, and a novel by, say, Mario Bellatín that is massively distributed in Mexico by Anagrama is hard to come by in a bookshop in Bogotá or Montevideo.

The sphere of symbolic production also entered a phase of retrenchment in the seventies. Creativity was not spent, but it was expressed in a minor key, often with an embrace of popular culture as in the novels of Argentine Manuel Puig, or Mexican *Onda* members such as Gustavo Sainz. Slippery forms of nomenclature such as "postboom" reveal the anxiety of change more than a uniform aesthetic shift, but even boom writers were trying their hand at a kind of writing that embraced lighter, popular forms such as the detective novel (Fuentes's *La cabeza de la hydra* of 1978 or Donoso's *La misteriosa desaparición de la marquesita de Loria* of 1980 would be cases in point) or the soap opera (as in Vargas Llosa's *La tía Julia y el escribidor* of 1977). Women gained entrance into the republic of letters, and names such as Isabel Allende, Luisa Valenzuela, Elena Poniatowska, Cristina Peri Rossi, or Rosario Ferré commanded the attention of the reading public. The novel itself lost considerable ground to *testimonio*, a nonfictional form that put forward the politics of collective subjectivities in the space hitherto occupied by the auratic author whose construction we traced in Chapter Five. In the cultural economy of the seventies and eighties, the political thrust was captured by *testimonio* and the substantial academic criticism that unpacked its implications. Not surprisingly, its rise coincided with repressive regimes that no longer made it possible for streets to be occupied and for protest to be freely expressed. Here it may be necessary to aver that many general readers come to the Latin American sixties through paths provided by *One Hundred Years of Solitude*. By doing so, they frequently essentialize magical realism as the passport to a culture perceived as strange and exotic. But they miss everything out of which the novel was created. Reading it together with the other chapters of this book should do nothing to diminish our admiration for the novel. I would hope, rather, to have placed it in the realm of negotiation and exchange that characterized the decade.

So, we must ask, what is left of the sixties, aside from the kind of nostalgia that bespeaks absence? A lot is left, even in our times of retrenchment into the private sphere. In very general terms, one of the period's enduring legacies is experimentation, and the will to break the bonds of tradition. Change and speed remain firmly ensconced in the cultural habitus. More important, Latin American culture stands on the firm ground established by the great figures of the decade. The contemporary writer stands on soil that was indelibly enriched by the work of her or his 1960s predecessors.

A little tale may encapsulate this enduring presence: when in 1996 a group of young writers prepared an anthology of recent stories from Peru, Mexico, Spain, Argentina, Uruguay, Chile, Ecuador, Colombia, Costa Rica, and Ecuador, they chose a name that reveals the anxiety of influence: *McOndo*.[3] But they also took distance from the model invoked, as can be seen in the playfully deliberate deformation of the toponym.[4] They were responding to their discomfort with the pressures exerted by the impact of the great boom novels in foreign audiences, who (in the incarnation of a North American editor) resisted writing that dispensed with magical realism. In a preface that proclaims a "new," hybrid, nonessentialist Latin American identity representing no specific nation or ideology, the editors summarize the changes in the cultural landscape of the late seventies, the eighties, and the early nineties. In it, Mercedes Sosa, Ricky Martin, and Julio Iglesias co-exist in mixtures that also gather Borges, Comandante Marcos, Latin MTV, Televisa, NAFTA and Mercosur, Miami, Madrid, and Havana. Only an outlandish gesture could begin to displace the power of the boom predecessors.

As to this book, reaching closure may be helped by taking stock of the aims sketched out at the beginning. This is decidedly not a complete or comprehensive cultural or literary history—many such books have been written—but, rather, an exercise in recapturing the intensity of significant scenes in the making of a new culture. It has entailed rereading the scholarship produced over the last forty-odd years, and stepping back to see it and its object of study with the hindsight of the twenty-first century, which allows us to trace both goals and outcomes, pondering the distance between one and the other, and maybe locating a few hidden trajectories. Reading the past from its realized future also allows a panoramic view of the configuration of the world system within which Latin American culture was operating back then, thus offering a sense of a more variegated network of relations today.

Were the aspirations of the sixties within reach, one wonders wistfully in 2007, with the ironic distance of hindsight. Utopian and uncompromising, the era's desire for a future to end all futures was caught in the double bind of apocalypse and invention. But its spectacular expectations have left the energy of excessive desire, libidinal creativity, and liberating energies. In the shift from its high-modernist aesthetic to the ensuing postmodern condition, the decade's ongoing momentum keeps it before us as nostalgia or—more auspiciously—as hope.

REFERENCE MATTER

Notes

INTRODUCTION

1. Raymond Williams, "The Analysis of Culture," *The Long Revolution* (London: Penguin, 1961), 63.

2. Walter Benjamin, "Theses on the Philosophy of History," in *Illuminations*, ed. Hannah Arendt, trans. Harry Zohn (London: Fontana/Collins, 1977), 257. By "the sixties" I do not mean a strict chronological category—the 1960–70 decade— but a heuristic one. In Latin America it makes sense to start in 1959, and to end in the early 1970s. Two momentous political events could operate as boundaries: the Cuban Revolution and the fall of Salvador Allende, which took place in September 1973.

3. The notion of utopia is a fraught concept that inscribes tensions between aspirations for the common good and restrictions to individual freedom. The political and ideological processes one can discern in the sixties actually trace those tensions, especially as regards the repressive turn of the Castro government in the seventies. But it is remarkable that in More's dialogue, Raphael Hythloday's critique of individual property and his views on the common good have a great deal in common with the decade's ideological leanings. More's *Utopia*, while echoing some of Plato's, Aristotle's, and Cicero's ideas about the ideal commonwealth, can be said to be a small compendium of all the questions posed by the topic. I have consulted the 2002 Cambridge University text edited by G. M. Logan and R. M. Adams.

4. I take "world literature" in the sense presented by David Damrosch in his *What Is World Literature?* (Princeton, NJ: Princeton University Press, 2003). See especially his introduction and conclusion.

5. See Jean Franco, *The Decline and Fall of the Lettered City: Latin America in the Cold War* (Cambridge, MA: Harvard University Press, 2002). This remarkable book is the most comprehensive study of the period between the 1930s and the 1990s, and it could be considered the continuation of her important earlier literary histories, *The Modern Culture of Latin America: Society and the Artist*, and *An Introduction to Latin American Literature*. I cannot think of a more powerful account of the relationships between Latin American culture and the ever-present tensions

of the Cold War environment. Unlike Franco, I have worked with a smaller historical sweep, framing my chapters not only within the stretch of one decade, but also along the organizing principle of the scene or productive moment as exemplary of the imbrication of material and symbolic forces.

6. In Michel Foucault, *Remarks on Marx: Conversations with Duccio Trombadori*, trans. R. J. Goldstein and J. Cascaito (New York: Semiotext[e], 1991). Foucault develops the notion that between 1968 and 1970 France was in the midst of intense changes: facing the end of the colonial period, there was dissensus on the left and on the right, since the Communist party's adherence to the anticolonial struggles in Algeria was at best ambivalent. Foucault claims that this was the time in which it was important to find a new vocabulary for the right and for the left: "Certainly it wasn't easy to formulate this new critical position, precisely because the right vocabulary was missing, given that no one wanted to take up the one formulated with categories of the right" (111). It is in this sense that crisis and creation were intertwined.

7. See Max Horkheimer and Theodor W. Adorno, *Dialectic of Enlightenment*, trans. J. Cumming (New York: Continuum, 1999), 85.

8. See Eric Hobsbawm, *The Age of Extremes: A History of the World, 1914–1991* (New York: Pantheon Books, 1994), 257–86, for an overview of the extraordinary economic expansion that took place between the fifties and early seventies. Although the developed capitalist economies were the ones that could consider these years truly golden, the then-called Third World also witnessed profound economic changes during this period, marked among other factors by what Hobsbawm calls "the death of the peasantry" in a dramatic move to urban centers. For an account of the growth of corporations, see John K. Galbraith, *The New Industrial State*, 3rd. ed. (Boston: Houghton & Mifflin, 1978), 75–90. According to Galbraith, the most dramatic growth of corporations in the United States occurred between 1955 and 1974.

9. Daniel Bell's now classic *The Cultural Contradictions of Capitalism* (New York: Basic Books, 1976) pointed to another contradiction of the times: the disjunction between the way in which the corporate world in advanced capitalism encourages hedonistic consumption even as it relies on a work ethic dependent on the postponement of gratification.

10. For more on this, see Daniel Bell, "The Post-Industrial Society," in *Technology and Social Change*, ed. E. Ginzberg (New York: Columbia University Press, 1964), 44–59; Massimo Teodori, *The New Left: A Documentary History* (Indianapolis: Bobbs-Merrill, 1969), 90; and Alain Touraine, *The Post-Industrial Society*, trans. L. Mayhew (New York: Random House, 1971), 220–22. According to Rick Wolff, publications such as the magazine *Monthly Review* and books such as Paul Baran and Paul Sweezy's *Monopoly Capital: An Essay on the American Economic and Social Order* (1966), André Gunder Frank's *Capitalism and Underdevelopment in Latin America* (1967), and Ernest Mandel's *Marxist Economic Theory*

(1968) "did much to put an explicit Marxian economic analysis back on the intellectual map of Americans." See his "Economics," in *60s Without Apology*, eds. S. Sayres, A. Stephanson, S. Aronowitz, and F. Jameson (Minneapolis: University of Minnesota Press, 1986), 329–30.

11. Even children were to be saved from the seductive interpellations of the capitalist system. One very popular work of the period was Ariel Dorfman and Armand Mattelart's *Para leer al Pato Donald: comunicación de masa y colonialismo* (Mexico City: Siglo XXI, 1972), which astutely read the *Donald Duck* comic strip and its ideology, showing the varied ways of the "autocolonización de la imaginación adulta" that begins with the child. In a much later book, Sergio Pitol studies not only "La sociedad de los jóvenes" but also "Utopías de la infancia." See his *La década rebelde: los años 60 en la Argentina* (Buenos Aires: Emecé, 2002).

12. Totalitarian (most notably, fascist) regimes had worked on the ideological seduction of youth in their rallies and marches, but it was not until the sixties that the category of youth occupied the predominant place in the political and cultural imaginary of an era.

13. Edgar Morin has developed the notion of youth as a new historical actor reaching ascendancy in the middle of the twentieth century—not as a social class, but as a new class of age. Previous incarnations of this human type (Athenian youths, medieval scholars, the suffering Werther) would be notable predecessors, but, unlike them, the youth of the sixties were not marginal. Morin identifies several reasons for the ascendancy of youth at this time—among which are the lengthening of education, the liberalization of families and educational institutions, the accelerating rhythms of change (technological, cultural, social)—that fostered an ideology privileging youth and speed. As Morin notes, "Le sage vieillard est devenu le petit vieux retraité; l'homme mûr, le croulant." See his "Jeunesse" in *L'Esprit du temps*, vol. 2 (Paris: Grasset, 1975), 205–21. This is also the decade when Erik H. Erikson worked out the notion of the identity crisis of youth as the crucial time in a human being's development. See his *Young Man Luther: A Study in Psychoanalysis and History* (New York: Norton, 1962). See also Philippe Ariès *L'Enfant et la vie familiale sous l'Ancien Régime* (Paris: Tlon, 1960) for a discussion of another "class of age" that also deals with generational categories.

14. In "Olimpíada y Tlatelolco," in Octavio Paz, *El laberinto de la soledad: Postdata* (Mexico City: Fondo de Cultura Económica, 1992), 270. English translation: "Olympics and Tlatelolco," *The Labyrinth of Solitude and Other Writings*, trans. L. Kemp, Y. Milos, and R. Phillips Belash (New York: Grove Press, 1985), 222. Published translations have occasionally been amended.

15. The sense of alienated youth is admirably captured in Antonioni's 1966 film *Blow Up*, in which the main character (played by David Hemmings) is both immersed in the speed of "swinging London" and almost paralyzed by a detached sense of alienation from his feverish surroundings.

16. The first French edition (*Les Damnés de la terre*) was published by F. Maspero in 1961; the first English translation appeared in 1963. For a compelling and revisionary introduction to the 2004 edition of *The Wretched of the Earth*, see Homi Bhabha's preface to the new translation by Richard Philcox published by Grove Press.

17. For more on the European avatars of Marxism in the second half of the twentieth century, see Perry Anderson, *In the Tracks of Historical Materialism* (Chicago and London: University of Chicago Press, 1984). Anderson discusses the crisis of Marxism and its relationship to the "double disappointment" of the Chinese and West European alternatives to the disastrous Soviet regime.

18. For more on this, see Kaja Silverman, "The Dominant Fiction," *Male Subjectivity at the Margins* (New York and London: Routledge, 1992), 15–51.

19. In Horkheimer and Adorno, *Dialectics of Enlightenment*.

20. Theodor Adorno, *Aesthetic Theory*, trans. Robert Hullot-Kentor (Minneapolis: University of Minnesota Press, 1997), 84 (previous passage) and 85.

21. Roland Barthes, *La Chambre claire: note sur la photographie* (Paris: Gallimard, 1980), 49 and 150.

22. See Fredric Jameson, "Periodizing the Sixties," *6os Without Apology*, eds. S. Sayres, A. Stephanson, S. Aronowitz, and F. Jameson (Minneapolis: University of Minnesota Press, 1984), 181.

CHAPTER I: THE CUBAN REVOLUTION AND CHE GUEVARA

1. In *Dialectic of Enlightenment*, Horkheimer and Adorno refer to "reconciliation" as a radical change in society that would modify the relation of man and nature, and move beyond the alienation of the subject. But at the time of the first edition of 1947, the possibility of such reconciliation seemed unlikely as long as the instrumental principles of both the bourgeois and the totalitarian state held sway. Even language was impoverished by the dominant forces of society in the views of the Frankfurt School. Like few other philosophical works of the postwar period, *Dialectic of Enlightenment* expresses the profound pessimism of a Europe that had even lost its belief in the principles Kant identified with the Enlightenment, seeing them as harmful in their having led to totalitarianism, the destruction of nature, and the reduction of the multiplicity of forms to the destructive schematizations of the universal. Reading these essays, one can get a clearer sense of what the stunning reversals brought about by the early years of the Revolution may have meant to the sense of stasis and exhaustion that held sway in European thought. See especially "The Concept of Enlightenment" (3–42). It is important to bear in mind that the possibilities of actual praxis attaining change were perceived by Adorno as slim. By the early 1950s he had reached the melancholy conclusion that philosophy's moment of realization had been missed. For more on

this see Martin Jay, *The Dialectical Imagination* (Boston and London: Little, Brown, 1973), chap. 8. The young fighters who began their struggle in the Sierra Maestra and took power in early 1959 could be seen as reinstating the possibility of praxis while articulating a utopian program for change.

2. In Barthes, *Mythologies*, 148–59.

3. In Hannah Arendt, *On Revolution* (New York: Viking, 1963), 13.

4. Ibid.: 27.

5. Although the notion of *aura* was most fully articulated in Walter Benjamin's now famous essay "The Work of Art in the Age of Mechanical Reproduction," in *Illuminations*, ed. Hannah Arendt, trans. Harry Zohn (London: Fontana/Collins, 1973), 219–54, it appears in 1930 in a text on hashish. It is developed in "Petite histoire de la photographie," where Benjamin comments on a photograph of Kafka, in *Poésie et révolution*, trans. M. de Gandillac (Paris: Denoel, 1971): 15–36. For a useful discussion of this concept in Benjamin, see Rainer Rochlitz, *Le Désenchantment de l'art: la philosophie de Walter Benjamin* (Paris: Gallimard, 1992), esp. "Destruction de l'aura: photographie et film," 174–94.

6. For the opening up of limits produced by revolutionary dislocation, see Ernesto Laclau, *New Reflections for a Revolution of Our Time* (London: Verso, 1990). Laclau reminds us that dislocation is "the very form of possibility" (42) and that it is a feature of the group of phenomena linked to Marx's notion of "permanent revolution" (45). The early 1960s were steeped in the notions of possibility and emancipation. In the later *Emancipations* (London: Verso, 1996), Laclau addresses the effects of the 1990s' assault on the totalizing ideologies of the Cold War period, which is the period of focus of the present book. Laclau's later work deals with the crisis that followed the very absence of the ruling notions of the 1960s: the tensions between two systems ("the free world" and "communist society") both aspiring to "global human emancipation."

7. Two very cogent articles that chart the relationships between the boom, the Cuban Revolution, the Cold War, and the narrative and the social-scientific imagination are Tulio Halperin Donghi's "Nueva narrativa y ciencias sociales hispanoamericanas en la década del sesenta," *Hispamérica* 9, no. 27 (Dec. 1980): 3–18; and Neil Larsen's "The 'Boom' Novel and the Cold War in Latin America," *Modern Fiction Studies* 38, no. 3 (Autumn 1992): 771–84.

8. A few women—Haydée Santamaría, Vilma Espín, Celia Sánchez Melba Hernández, Clodomira Acosta Ferrales, and Lidia Esther Doce Sánchez—played a central role in the revolutionary movement, as auxiliaries and liaisons. Haydée Santamaría founded Casa de las Américas; Vilma Espín was instrumental in the foundation of the Federación de Mujeres Cubanas (FMC) in 1960, and remained as its head; Celia Sánchez handled Castro's personal schedule and played the unofficial role of benefactress, responding to personal appeals for help of various kinds. The place of women in Cuban power remains a vexed question: "At one

level women played their traditional roles as helpers—raising money, giving shelter, teaching, nursing. As couriers they exploited the stereotypical image of women as innocent and incompetent and were thus able to foil the dictator's police. But women also played more central roles, occupying key positions in the urban underground and in the Sierra. . . . Women never pressed their positions, however, nor were properly rewarded, perhaps in part because they themselves underestimated their contribution. Even Vilma Espín, a significant participant in the struggle, thought of herself as 'a sergeant, not a leader.' When the rebellion triumphed and the task turned to implementing a social and political revolution, its architects were men." See Lois M. Smith and Alfred Padula, *Sex and Revolution: Women in Socialist Cuba* (New York: Oxford University Press, 1996), 22–23. The authors trace the contribution of women to the Castro government, as well as the advances gained by them since 1959. Their conclusions highlight the phallocentric power of the leader, imbued with the values of *machismo-leninismo* and symbolized by the redeeming machete, the national phallus par excellence. Castro did understand that the Revolution needed to harness the support and energy of women, and through Vilma Espín made the FMC an agent for change, promoting women's work and organizing programs in health, education, work, and child care. Yet the FMC enjoined women to be "feminine, not feminist," as Espín put it, and to defend interests defined by the male elite. In the halls of power, women were mostly absent.

9. This term came onto the scene of world politics after 1952, when it was created by French demographer Alfred Sauvy. He meant it to echo the French "third estate" made up of commoners, but it also conveniently demarcated nonaligned countries in the polarized Cold War era. It gained currency in the later years of the 1950s, when even a journal bore the name *Tiers Monde*. "Tricontinental" was a roughly equivalent name, denoting Asia, Africa, and Latin America as three continents joined in the liberation struggles of the sixties. Nowadays, the term has limited coinage.

10. For an insightful account of U.S. perceptions of Castro and his Revolution, see Van Gosse, *Where the Boys Are: Cuba, Cold War America, and the Making of the New Left* (London: Verso, 1993). I thank my colleague Nancy Cott for leading me to this book.

11. Ibid., 55.

12. For more on this, see José Lezama Lima, *Imagen y posibilidad* (Havana: Letras Cubanas, 1981).

13. In Albert O. Hirschman, *Retóricas de la intransigencia* (Mexico City: Fondo de Cultura Economica, 1991).

14. In Rafael Rojas, *Isla sin fin: contribución a la crítica del nacionalismo cubano* (Miami: Universal, 1998). For his part, Gustavo Pérez Firmat notes the specificity of the "Cuban condition" as founded in a state of "incompletion or imperfection" that leads to a culture of *translation*. See his *The Cuban Condition* (Cambridge,

UK: Cambridge University Press, 1989). In their different ways, both Rojas and Pérez Firmat argue for a specifically Cuban national disposition derived from insularity—either as an urge to invent, or as a drive toward translation understood as creative repossession.

15. In More's *Utopia* the merits of insularity are such that Utopus decides to change the original geography of the land and to have a channel cut to separate what was at first an isthmus from the mainland. See "Book II" in the Cambridge University Press 1989 edition of *Utopia* (Cambridge Texts in the History of Political Thought), edited by G. M. Logan and R. M. Adams.

16. Although Herberto Padilla's poetry was celebrated by the revolutionary government early on, he gradually distanced himself from it. His imprisonment in 1971 created quite an international stir: distinguished European intellectuals such as Sartre, De Beauvoir, Moravia, and Resnais signed a letter demanding that Castro's government explain what appeared to be a turn toward Soviet-style repression. Among Latin American intellectuals, this *caso* marked a profound schism between those such as Cortázar and García Márquez, who continued to support Castro, and those such as Vargas Llosa and Paz, who broke with him. Padilla was eventually allowed to leave for the United States, where he accepted a teaching post at Auburn University in Fort Worth, Texas. He died in 2000.

17. See Nadia Lie, *Transición y transacción: la revista cubana Casa de las Américas, 1960–1976* (Gaithersburg, MD, and Leuven: Hispamérica/Leuven University Press, 1996), 22.

18. See, for example, the issues devoted to Chile (nos. 69, 83, 92), Puerto Rico (nos. 70, 93), Panamá (no. 72), Guatemala (no. 84), and Uruguay (no. 97).

19. *Casa de las Américas* 35 (1966): 87. (Henceforth, the volume and page number of journal citations will appear within parentheses.)

20. Another important publication for understanding the relationship between literary expansion and the early years of the revolution was the short-lived *Lunes de Revolución*, which came out between March 1959 and November 1961. See William Luis, *Lunes de Revolución: literatura y cultura en los primeros años de la revolución cubana* (Madrid: Verbum, 2003). As powerful as its early impact was, it was obviously very limited. It was closed down after the famous conflicts surrounding *P.M.*, the short film made by Sabá Cabrera Infante and Orlando Jiménez-Leal. The story of this literary magazine encapsulates the shift from initial expansion to repression that characterized the later years of the decade in Cuba. Emblematic of this is Fidel Castro's 1962 speech "Palabras a los intelectuales," delivered shortly after the closing of *Lunes de Revolución*.

21. The first conference on Solidarity With Peoples of Africa, Asia, and Latin America was held in Havana in January 1966. Out of it came the *Revista Tricontinental*, originally published in Spanish, French, English, and Arabic; and OSPAAL, the Organization of Solidarity with Peoples of Africa, Asia, and Latin America,

which became well known for its artistic posters aiming at outreach within the Third World.

22. As is well known, by the early 1970s only those who adhere to the political lines drawn by Fernández Retamar remain on board, with the obvious reduction in plurality of inflections.

23. José Enrique Adoum, "La Revolución Cubana: cuando lo insólito se vuelve cotidiano," in *Cultura y revolución: a cuarenta años de 1959*, ed. Eduardo Heras León (Havana: Casa de las Américas, 1999), 26.

24. Alma Guillermoprieto, "The Harsh Angel," *Looking for History: Dispatches from Latin America* (New York: Pantheon Books, 2001), 72.

25. My friend and colleague Doris Sommer offered an astute observation about the Argentines at work in reading and writing: Che, Cortázar, and I. There is an undeniable national affiliation. Needless to say, I have not remained immune to the seduction exerted by Che and Cortazar.

26. In Ernesto Guevara Lynch, *Mi hijo el Che* (Barcelona: Planeta, 1981), 255.

27. Jean-Michel Palmier, *Magazine Littéraire* 18 (May 1968): 14.

28. His hands were cut off and sent to Havana; they are kept in a monument at the Plaza de la Revolución. In their desire to prove Che's death, his killers set off a process that both fragmented and sacralized his body. His remains were finally found in 1997, and sent to Cuba.

29. Eric Hobsbawm has written about this in his *Primitive Rebels: Studies in Archaic Forms of Social Movement in the 19th and 20th Centuries* (New York: Norton, 1959).

30. See Jorge Castañeda, *Compañero: The Life and Death of Che Guevara* (London: Bloomsbury, 1997), xiii–xvii.

31. For more on this, see David Kunzle, *Che Guevara: Icon, Myth and Message* (Los Angeles: UCLA Fowler Museum of Cultural History in collaboration with the Center for the Study of Political Graphics, 1998).

32. In his *Lectures on the Philosophy of History* quoted by R. Koselleck, *Futures Past: On the Semantics of Historical Time*, trans. K. Tribe (Cambridge, MA: MIT Press, 1985), 128.

33. See Michael Waltzer, *The Revolution of the Saints: A Study of the Origins of Radical Politics* (New York: Atheneum, 1968).

34. Two other works on gender and the guerrillas are Ileana Rodríguez's *Women, Guerrillas and Love: Understanding War in Central America* (Minneapolis: University of Minnesota Press, 1996), and María Josefina Saldaña Portillo's *The Revolutionary Imagination in the Americas and the Age of Development* (Durham, NC: Duke University Press, 2003). My approach differs in that rather than arguing for a feminization of the guerrillas, I study it as the circulation of homosocial energy, which is characteristic of male-only groups in the patriarchal order.

35. Christianity, Ernesto Laclau reminds us, provided the classical emancipatory discourse: "A discourse of radical emancipation emerged for the first time

with Christianity, and its specific form was *salvation*. With elements partly inherited from Jewish apocalypse, Christianity was going to present the image of a future humanity—or post-humanity—from which all evil would have been eradicated." See Laclau, *Emancipations*, 8.

36. In Ernesto Che Guevara, *Escritos y discursos*, vol. 2 (Havana: Ediciones de Ciencias Sociales, 1977), 228.

37. Interview with Jean Daniel in Algeria, on July 25, 1963, in Ricardo Efrén González, *El Che en la revolución cubana*, vol. 4 (Havana: Ediciones del Ministerio de la Industria Azucarera, 1966), 346.

38. Ernesto Che Guevara, *Escritos y discursos*, vol. 4, 85.

39. Ernesto Che Guevara, "El socialismo y el hombre en Cuba," *Escritos y discursos*, vol. 8, 270, 271.

40. Herbert Marcuse, *One-Dimensional Man: Studies in the Ideology of Advanced Society*, 2nd ed. (London: Routledge, 1991), 252.

41. *Verde Olivo* was founded in April 1959 as the Revolutionary Army's official magazine, replacing other publications such as *El Cubano Libre*, and expressing the views of the left wing of the M26 movement. Originally, it was financed with collections from the rebel army. Che wrote many articles for this magazine, often using it as a platform for the articulation of his political ideas. The first piece appeared on February 26, 1961. It is noteworthy that the title of the pieces in *Verde Olivo* is "Pasajes de nuestra guerra revolucionaria," where the collective *our* underscores the sense of shared undertaking and commitment. The pieces in *Verde Olivo* have numerous photographs of the places mentioned by Che, as well as of his comrades in arms.

42. *Verde Olivo* is an illustrative example: together with articles that proclaim the blend of progress and happiness attained by agrarian reform, literacy campaigns, or the construction of holiday resorts for workers, one finds interspersed numerous articles focused on the looming danger of Eisenhower's and Kennedy's administrations. A reader would turn a page and find herself confronted by a jarring disjunction between a sense of joyful, all-powerful community, and the dire need to be prepared to die in the process of protecting the Revolution.

43. Among other instances of this writing of history as a legacy for future activists, one could cite the writings of Leon Trotsky, *De la Révolution d'Octobre à la paix de Brest-Litovsk* (Geneva: Edition de la revue "Demani," 1918), and Jean Jaurès's five-volume *Histoire Socialiste de la Révolution Française* (Paris: Editions de la Librairie de l'Humanité, 1922).

44. Che began writing these *pasajes* shortly after being named Minister of Industry, in February 1961.

45. Ernesto Che Guevara, *Reminiscences of the Cuban Revolutionary War*, trans. Victoria Ortiz (New York and London: Grove Press, 1968), 29. Spanish edition: *Pasajes de la guerra revolucionaria* (Havana: Ediciones de la Unión de Escritores y Artistas de Cuba, 1963), 5. (Henceforth, citations of this work will appear within

parentheses; page numbers in italics refer to the Spanish edition.) There are remarkable echoes between Che's statement and Herodotus's at the beginning of his account of the Persian Wars, where he also mentions the need to avoid the inevitable blurring of memory brought about by the passing of time. In 1998 the Editora Política of Havana brought out a considerably enlarged version of the *Pasajes*, which approximates a critical edition and contains maps, photographs, additional texts, and notes. In their presentation, the editors (Iraida Aguirrechu, María Cristina Zamora, and Nora Madan) note:

> En esta nueva edición ampliamente anotada e ilustrada, la obra ha sido complementada de diversas formas para una mejor comprensión del lector. Así al final de cada artículo aparece la fuente donde fue publicado inicialmente. Se incluyen notas al pie en las páginas donde se complementan nombres, se amplían informaciones y datos mencionados, se precisan frases que pueden ser desconocidas para quien se acerca al libro. Igualmente aparece un índice de nombre de todas las personas que se mencionan en el texto y un glosario de algunos combatientes del Ejército Rebelde y del Llano citados por el Che, con pequeños apuntes biográficos. (16)

Between 1963 and 1998 the work became part of the Cuban canon, not only for historico-political reasons but also for literary ones; from a slim volume it was turned into a major work enlarged by related texts and a scholarly apparatus.

46. Among the former rebels who joined him in this effort were Fernández Mell, Zayas, Villegas, Castellanos, Pardo, Iglesias, and Acevedo. See Paco Ignacio Taibo II, *Guevara, Also Known as Che*, trans. M. M. Roberts (New York: St. Martin's Press, 1997), 321.

47. The Cuban public's reception was very enthusiastic, and as the later numbers appeared, they were immediately sold out. It was published in book form by the Cuban Writers Union toward the end of 1963, and such was the interest in the subject that there were lines in bookstores to snatch up copies. Che waived his royalties from socialist country editions. Ibid., 370–71.

48. In the original publication of the first *pasaje*, entitled, as is the case in the book version, "Alegría del Pío," there is a telling *Nota de la redacción* at the end. It underscores the extent to which Che's writing is both a memoir and an invitation—the beginning of a collective history. As an invitation, it has the burden of exemplarity. Here it is in full:

> Invitamos a otros actores de este momento de la Revolución, a que envíen sus colaboradores a *Verde Olivo* para enriquecer el panorama de aquel primer combate rebelde. Además, extendemos nuestra invitación a todos los que quieran colaborar en recuerdos, tales como el desembarco del "Granma", el 30 de noviembre, fecha gloriosa de Santiago de Cuba y otras manifestaciones de lucha contra la dictadura . . . El "Che" se propone contar en

números próximos sus recuerdos del combate de La Plata y siguientes, con algún orden cronológico. (*Verde Olivo* 2, nos. 8, 26 [Feb. 1961])

49. In Maurice Halbwachs, *Les Cadres sociaux de la mémoire* (Paris: Albin Michel, 1994), 148–49.

50. See Paul Ricoeur, *La Mémoire, l'histoire, l'oubli* (Paris: Seuil, 2000), 97.

51. For a study of stories of men at war in the literature of Great Britain and the United States, see Samuel Hynes's *The Soldiers' Tale: Bearing Witness to Modern War* (New York: Allen Lane/Penguin Press, 1997). Hynes makes the point that violence is a *rite de passage* for soldiers and revolutionaries: the weaver of the soldier's tale cannot claim his hands are untouched by violence. Che, however, does not explicitly address the thorny question of violence—not because he is squeamish about narrating battles, but because he adopts a generally detached stance when he reports combat encounters, as if he took it for granted that dying and killing were the inevitable business of war.

52. In an early study of the work, César Leante observes: "Tengo la convicción de que el Che escribió [la obra] pensando en ofrecer el costado humano de la lucha guerrillera a los nuevos combatientes que inevitablemente se alzarían." See his "Los *Pasajes* del Che," *Casa de las Américas* 8, no. 46 (Jan.–Feb. 1968): 155. The didactic purpose is also noted in the same issue by Graziella Pogolotti in her "Apuntes para el Che escritor," 152–55.

53. In a different register, Cintio Vitier's poem "Escasez" sings the praises of scarcity and want, turning to poetry as a behavior-modeling system:

> Lo que no hay
> primero brilla como una estrella altiva,
> después se va apagando
> en el espacio vacío, consolador y puro
> de lo que hay.
> (*Testimonios* [Havana: Unión, 1968], 288)

54. Efraín Barradas points out a dichotomy between the *guerrillero* and the doctor that traverses the book and that is resolved as the *des-doctorización* of the narrator. See his "El Che, narrador: apuntes para un estudio de *Pasajes de la guerra revolucionaria*," in Rose S. Minc, ed., *Literatures in Transition: The Many Voices of the Caribbean Area* (Gaithersburg, MD: Hispamérica and Montclair State College, 1982), 143.

55. In a passage devoted to the contribution of the urban leaders to the revolutionary struggle, Che pays tribute to the role played by three women from the city, "conocidas hoy por todo el pueblo de Cuba": Vilma Espín, Haydée Santamaría, and Celia Sánchez (37–38). Later editions feature "Retratos de revolucionarios" including a section entitled "Lidia y Clodomira," who joined the revolutionaries in 1957 to work as messengers. In 1958 the Batista police discovered their Havana

hiding place; they were tortured and killed, and their bodies were thrown into the sea. The rest of the book is devoted to the activities of the male rebels.

56. Che noted that women would take on duties that, as he put it "are scorned by [those] men who perform them; they are constantly trying to get out of those tasks in order to enter into forces that are actively in combat." In Ernesto Che Guevara, *Obras, 1957–1967*, vol. 1 (Paris: Documentos Latinoamericanos, 1970), 107. Quoted in Smith and Padula, *Sex and Revolution*, 30.

57. In the original publication of the *Pasajes de nuestra guerra revolucionaria*, which, as has been noted, contained many photographs; a big, pensive portrait of Fidel appears in several of the pieces, as if the leader's face ratified the erasure of Che, the scribe.

58. Originally, this was a letter addressed to Carlos Quijano, published in *Marcha* on March 12, 1965. It was reprinted in vol. 8 of Ernesto Che Guevara, *Escritos y discursos*, 256.

59. In Guillermo Cabrera Infante, *Mea Cuba*, trans. Guillermo Cabrera Infante and Kenneth Hall (New York: Farrar, Straus & Giroux, 1994), 313.

60. After this chapter's writing was completed, I read Ricardo Piglia's suggestive "Ernesto Guevara, rastros de lectura," in his *El último lector* (Buenos Aires: Anagrama, 2005), 103–38, and found many points of agreement. In the very recent past there has been a remarkable blossoming of the Che myth: in December 2005, the International Institute of Photography in New York devoted an exhibition to the marketing of Che's photographic images; in the summer of 2006 the Victoria and Albert Museum of London produced a similar show. In July 2006 the New York Public Theater staged a play written by José Rivera (who wrote the script for Walter Salles's *Motorcycle Diaries*) about Che Guevara's final days in Vallegrande. Héctor Cruz Sandoval made a film about the Korda photographs (*Kordavision*) in 2004; it was shown in the Rio de Janeiro Film Festival in 2005. During a Mercosur meeting in Argentina in July 2006, both Hugo Chávez and Fidel Castro made their way up to Alta Gracia, Cordoba, to visit the house where Che and his family lived, which was turned into a museum in 2001.

61. See an insightful article by Aníbal González Pérez, "Revolución y alegoría en 'Reunión,' de Julio Cortázar," in *Los ochenta mundos de Julio Cortázar: ensayos*, ed. Fernando Burgos (Madrid: EDI-6, 1987), 93–109.

62. Mario Goloboff, *Julio Cortázar: la biografía* (Buenos Aires: Seix Barral, 1998), 124.

63. Julio Cortázar, "Julio Cortázar: el escritor y sus armas políticas" (Diálogo con Francisco Urondo), *Panorama* (Buenos Aires, Nov. 24, 1970): 44–50. Quoted in ibid., 128.

64. In "Los dichos y los hechos," *Marcha* (Montevideo) 1265 (Mar. 11, 1966): 29. For more on this see Goloboff, *Julio Cortázar*, chap. 11, and María Eugenia Mudrovcic, *Mundo Nuevo: cultura y Guerra Fría en la década del sesenta* (Rosario: Beatriz Viterbo, 1997).

65. Letter to Antón Arrufat of 23 March 1963, in Julio Cortázar, *Cartas 1937–1963*, ed. Aurora Bernárdez (Buenos Aires: Alfaguara, 2000), 544–45.

66. Ibid., 547.

67. I am referring to Dorrit Cohn's *The Distinction of Fiction* (Cambridge, MA: Harvard University Press, 1999).

68. See González Pérez, "Revolución y alegoría," 99–100.

69. "Reunión," in Julio Cortázar, *All Fires the Fire*, trans. Suzanne Jill Levine (New York: Pantheon Books, 1973), 52. Spanish edition: *Todos los fuegos el fuego* (Madrid: Alfaguara, 1984), 66. The first edition of this collection came out in Sudamericana of Buenos Aires in 1966. (Henceforth, citations of this work will appear within parentheses; page numbers in italics refer to the Spanish edition.)

70. For an analysis of these relationships, see Howard Eilberg-Schwartz, "Homoeroticism and the Father-God: An Unthought in Freud's *Moses and Monotheism*," *American Imago* 51, no. 1 (1994): 127–59. Eilberg-Schwartz also notes Carl Jung's claim in *Memories, Dreams, Reflections*, ed. Aniela Jaffe, trans. Richard Winston and Clara Winston (New York: Pantheon Books, 1963), 127: "The sexual libido took over the role of a deus absconditus, a hidden or concealed god . . . Yahweh and sexuality remained the same."

71. Slavoj Žižek, "The Spectre of Ideology," in *Mapping Ideology*, ed. S. Žižek (London: Verso, 1994), 21.

72. "Mensaje al hermano," *Casa de las Américas* 8, no. 46 (1968): 6.

73. See his conversation with Francisco Urondo in *Panorama* quoted above.

74. Adorno, *Aesthetic Theory*, 81. The German original appeared in 1970, and it can be said to represent some of the most forward-looking ideas about art in the alienated, disenchanted ethos of the post–World War II period.

75. In Jacques Derrida, *Specters of Marx: The State of the Debt, the Work of Mourning, and the New International*, trans. Peggy Kamuf (New York: Routledge, 1994).

76. An article about the rise of *hispanos* in the United States in Buenos Aires's *La Nación* bears the title "Hispanos: la apuesta fuerte de Hollywood," and it mentions *Motorcycle Diaries* as well as Penélope Cruz, Antonio Banderas, Salma Hayek, Andy García, and other famous names in what is being called the Latin American film boom: "In the mecca of cinema, the Hispanic presence is no longer just a fad: there is an increasing number of Hispanic American actors and directors who, with beauty and especially with talent, are making their way into the most standout productions" (Aug. 22, 2004).

77. The seductive omission of fighting and killing in this particular context was not lost on a much earlier film analyzed by Van Gosse in his *Where the Boys Are*, a CBS News film made by Robert Taber in May 1957, entitled "Rebels of the Sierra Maestra: The Story of Cuba's Jungle Fighters." Gosse points out that "the Sierra Maestra became for Taber and CBS News the platform for a morality play about kids finding themselves through an otherworldly defiance and being rather

than doing: there is no fighting in 'Rebels of the Sierra Maestra,' no contact with anything outside the jungle, nor even any discussion of Cuban history and how Batista's tyranny had driven the rebels to take up arms" (83).

78. See http://www.indiewire.com/biz/biz_040929boxoffice.html.

79. In Laclau, *Emancipations*, 75–76.

80. My reading owes much to Derrida's *Specters of Marx*, where the historical and the political inhabit the terrain of constitutive undecidability, of an experience of the impossible that "opens up access to an affirmative thinking of the messianic and emancipatory promise as promise" (74–75).

81. At the 2004 Cannes Film Festival, a number of Latin American directors presented films of note. Among them are Lucrecia Martel and Lisandro Alonso (Argentina), Patricio Guzmán and Andrés Wood (Chile), Fernando Eimbcke (Mexico), Sebastián Cordeo (Ecuador), and Juan Pablo Rebella and Pablo Stoll (Uruguay). The terms in which these directors' work is reviewed are reminiscent of those deployed to refer to the novels of the sixties.

82. In an interview in *Sight and Sound*, Salles presents his views on Che's political significance:

> Guevara has resonance today because his quest never ended. His desire to unveil the unknown was present in every moment of his life. . . . When he was 23 he did this journey through Latin America at a time when people from his social class were more interested in Europe. We live in an age when people are blinded by cynicism and here you have a true idealist. We were tired of the rhetoric about the death of ideology and we wanted to make this film in order to believe in something again. (Nick James, "Against the Current," *Sight and Sound* 14, no. 9 [Sept. 2004]: 8–9)

CHAPTER 2: TLATELOLCO 1968

1. As quoted by Larry Rohter in "20 Years After a Massacre, Mexico Still Seeks Healing for Its Wounds," *New York Times* (Oct. 2, 1988): sec. 1, 16.

2. In Julio Scherer García and Carlos Monsiváis, *Parte de guerra II: los rostros del 68* (Mexico City: Nuevo Siglo Aguilar, 2002), 29.

3. For the notion of the premodern dimension of this kind of spectacular form of punishment, see Louis Marin's discussion with respect to the absolute power of the king in his *Le Portrait du roi* (Paris: Minuit, 1981), and Michel Foucault, *Surveiller et punir: naissance de la prison* (Paris: Gallimard, 1975). Carlos Monsiváis has called October 2, 1968, "uno de los momentos medievales de la Era del PRI." See Scherer García and Monsiváis, *Parte de guerra II*, 31.

4. See Jacques Derrida, "Force of Law: The 'Mystical Foundations of Authority,'" *Cardozo Law Review* 11, no. 5–6 (1990): 997.

5. Ibid.

6. Roderic A. Camp's *Intellectuals and the State in Twentieth-Century Mexico* (Austin: University of Texas Press, 1985) charts the forms of affiliation constructed by the governments that came after the Mexican Revolution in order to negotiate the consent and support of artists and intellectuals. Vasconcelos's efforts in this regard are well known; he represents a leading figure in what was to be a series of mediators who established different forms of state-sponsored employment for distinguished artists and writers such as Rivera, Orozco, Reyes, Paz, and, after 1968, Fuentes.

7. Among the recent ones of note are Sergio Aguayo Quezada, *1968: los archivos de la violencia* (Mexico City: Grijalbo, 1998); Scherer García and Monsiváis, *Parte de guerra II*; and Enrique Krauze, *Mexico: Biography of Power; A History of Modern Mexico, 1810–1996*, trans. Hank Heifetz (New York: HarperCollins, 1997). At the yearly commemorative events, the motto constantly repeated is, "2 de octubre no se olvida" (October 2 is not forgotten).

8. For the concept, see Paul Ricoeur, *Freud and Philosophy: An Essay on Interpretation*, trans. Denis Savage (New Haven, CT: Yale University Press, 1970).

9. Walter Benjamin, "Critique of Violence," in *Reflections*, ed. Peter Demetz, trans. Edmund Jephcott (New York: Harcourt, Brace, Jovanovich, 1978), 287.

10. There were violent government responses to student movements all over Latin America. A particularly bloody one was the Argentine "Cordobazo," which took place on May 29, 1969. Unlike the events at Tlatelolco, the Cordobazo began with a march of electrical workers, and only later did the students join in. It was an instance of labor unrest with subsequent student support. After two days of collective violence, the labor leaders involved were arrested. The casualties amounted to anywhere between sixteen and sixty, depending on the sources. A succinct account can be found in Antonius C. G. Robben, *Political Violence and Trauma in Argentina* (Philadelphia: University of Pennsylvania Press, 2005), 44–59.

11. For a more detailed account of the events, see Krauze, "Gustavo Díaz Ordaz," in *Mexico: Biography of Power*, 715–31, and Scherer and Monsiváis, *Parte de guerra II*.

12. Carlos Fuentes, *Paris: la revolución de mayo* (Mexico City: Era, 1968).

13. Ibid., 14; my translation.

14. For a general account of the global student movements, see Ronald Fraser et al., eds. *1968: A Student Generation in Revolt* (London: Chatto & Windus, 1988), and George Katsiaficas, *The Imagination of the New Left: A Global Analysis of 1968* (Boston: South End Press, 1987). For the French movements, see the revisionary book by Kristin Ross, *May '68 and Its Afterlives* (Chicago: University of Chicago Press, 2002), and the early book by Alain Touraine, *Le Mouvement de mai ou le communisme utopique* (Paris: Seuil, 1968). In a very different vein from Touraine's politically committed views, see Jean Pierre LeGoff, *Mai 68: l'héritage impossible* (Paris: Découverte, 1998); and Luc Ferry and Alain Renaut's two books on the

subject: *La Pensée 68: essai sur l'anti-humanisme contemporain* (Paris: Gallimard, 1985); and *68–86: itinéraires de l'individu* (Paris: Gallimard, 1987).

15. See Ross, *May 68 and Its Afterlives*, 8–9:

> [The] political culture was also manifest in the recurrent outbreaks of worker unrest in French factories throughout the mid-1960s, in the rise of an anti-Stalinist, critical Marxist perspective available in countless journals that flourished between the 1950s and the 1970s. The immediate political context in France was in fact one of triumphant Marxism: in large sectors of the workers movement, in the university in the form of Althusserianism, in small groups of Maoist, Trotskyist, and anarchic militants, and in a dominant frame of reference for work conducted in philosophy and the human sciences since World War II.

16. The title of Michel de Certeau's book on 1968 admirably conveys the practical and symbolic dimensions of the actions I am referring to. See his *La Prise de la parole: pour une nouvelle culture* (Paris: Seuil, 1994), originally published in 1968 by Desclee De Brouwer.

17. "My real fear was of a provocation that would have incited us to arms. . . . To maintain order, we needed to avoid leaving police units alone on the field, because, if provoked, they risked, in a fear reflex, opening fire." Maurice Grimaud, interview in *L'express* 2437 (May 19–25 1998: 86–87).

18. "We once again found ourselves in agreement with Georges Pompidou that we needed to let the student movement die its own death, which earned us a reproach of laxity." *Ibid.*, 87.

19. In Elaine Scarry, *The Body in Pain: The Making and Unmaking of the World* (New York and Oxford: Oxford University Press, 1985), 111.

20. In Marin, *Le Portrait du roi*, 11.

21. Ibid., 12; English translation: *Portrait of the King*, trans. Martha M. Houle (Minneapolis: University of Minnesota Press, 1988), 7.

22. Hannah Arendt, *Between Past and Future* (New York: Viking, 1968), 92–93.

23. See Derrida, "Force of Law," 937.

24. In December 2001 a set of photographs sent anonymously to a Mexican journalist in Spain provided the first proof that the government had lied about the role of the Olympia Battalion. The photographs show the white-gloved members of the battalion rounding up students, as well as young men being beaten. They were published in *Proceso* issue number 1310 on December 8, 2001, bearing the title "Tlatelolco 68: las fotos ocultas." Some of the photographs appeared in *The Guardian*, *New York Times*, and *El Mundo* of Madrid; in all cases they led to important articles about the memory of the massacre and the need to confront the responsibility of government actors. In issue number 1311, *Proceso* published the declarations of Florencio López Osuna, one of the speakers at the meeting when

the crowd was attacked on October 2. His account of events gave the Batallón Olimpia a central role in the massacre. López Osuna appeared dead in a hotel room in Mexico City on December 20, 2001; according to official reports, he had been accompanied by a prostitute, who was never located. See Scherer García and Monsiváis, *Parte de Guerra*, 20–22.

25. Further, one could argue that Paz and Poniatowska occupy two very different but central positions in the complex scene of Mexican letters. Paz, the Nobel Prize winner, is the master as *letrado*, the representative of high culture whose voice conveys authority. Poniatowska has fashioned herself as a journalist interested in the voice of others, and prefers to account for her novelistic efforts as the result of her interest in the experience of usually marginalized sectors of the Mexican population, as can clearly be seen in *Hasta no verte, Jesús mío*.

26. On October 3, Paz resigned from his post as Mexican ambassador to India in protest of the violence perpetrated against his fellow citizens the previous day. He sent a poem (dated October 3, in New Delhi) entitled "México: Olimpíada 1968" together with a letter in which he refused to participate in an "Encuentro Mundial de Poetas." The following verses were frequently quoted at the time:

> Si
> Una nación entera se averguenza
> Es león que se agazapa
> Para saltar.

27. Octavio Paz, *The Labyrinth of Solitude*, trans. Lysander Kemp, Yara Milos, and Rachel Phillips Belash (New York: Grove Press, 1985), 292. Spanish edition: *El laberinto de la soledad: Postdata* (Mexico City: Fondo de Cultura Economica, 1981), 327. For an annotated, later edition, see *El laberinto de la soledad: Postdata*, ed. Enrico Mario Santí (Madrid: Cátedra, 1993). (Henceforth, citations of this work will appear within parentheses; page numbers in italics refer to the Spanish edition.) Most of the critical works on the subject focus on *El laberinto de la soledad*. For studies that deal more specifically with *Postdata*, see Enrico Mario Santí, *El acto de las palabras: estudios y diálogos con Octavio Paz* (Mexico City: Fondo de Cultura Económica, 1997); Lisa Aronne-Amestoy, "El umbral prohibido: relectura de Octavio Paz," *Quaderni Ibero-Americani* 59–60 (1985–86): 93–104; Rima de Valbona, "Octavio Paz: prosa en movimiento," *Kanina: Revista de Artes y Letras de la Universidad de Costa Rica* 6, no. 1–2 (1982): 60–66; Floyd Merrell, "Some Considerations of the Notion of 'Otherness' in Octavio Paz's *Postdata*," *Kentucky Romance Quarterly* 24 (1977): 163–74.

28. For an overview of these debates see Carlos Fuentes's "Mexico and Its Demons," *New York Review of Books* 20, no. 14 (1973): 16–21.

29. Friedrich Nietzsche, "Twilight of the Idols," fragment 24, in *The Portable Nietzsche*, trans. Walter Kaufmann (New York: Penguin, 1976), 470.

30. To date, one of the main comprehensive studies of Poniatowska's work is Beth Jorgensen's *The Writing of Elena Poniatowska: Engaging Dialogues* (Austin: University of Texas Press, 1994). See also Sara Poot Herrera, "Las crónicas de Elena Poniatowska," *La Colmena* 11 (1996): 17–22; Ana María Amar Sánchez, "Las voces de los otros: el género de no-ficción en Elena Poniatowska," *Filología* 25, no. 1–2 (1990): 161–74; Elzbieta Sklodowska, *Testimonio hispanoamericano: historia, teoría, poética* (New York: Peter Lang, 1992); David William Foster, "Latin American Documentary Narrative," *PMLA* 99, no. 1 (1984), 41–55.

31. See Georges Bataille, *Inner Experience* (Albany: State University of New York Press, 1988).

32. Foucault, *Remarks on Marx*, 31.

33. Elena Poniatowska, *Massacre in Mexico*, trans. Helen R. Lane (Columbia and London: University of Missouri Press, 1991), 229, 236. Spanish edition: *La noche de Tlatelolco* (Mexico City: Biblioteca Era, 1971), 189, 196. (Henceforth, citations of this work will appear within parentheses; page numbers in italics refer to the Spanish edition.)

34. Poniatowska explains that she gained access to the prisons in the course of the two years that followed the massacre of October 2. See *La noche de Tlatelolco*, 164.

35. Octavio Paz, "A cinco años de Tlatelolco," in *El ogro filantrópico: historia y política* (Mexico City: Joaquín Mortiz, 1979), 143–52.

36. An article that makes this case eloquently is Doris Sommer's "'Not Just a Personal Story': Women's *Testimonios* and the Plural Self," in *Life Lines: Theorizing Women's Autobiography*, eds. Bella Brodzki and Celeste Schenck (Ithaca, NY: Cornell University Press, 1988), 107–30. For the growing literature on *testimonio* we refer the reader to the comprehensive bibliography at the end of George M. Gugelberger, ed. *The Real Thing: Testimonial Discourse and Latin America* (Durham, NC, and London: Duke University Press, 1996). Other comprehensive works on the subject are John Beverley and Hugo Achugar, eds., *La voz del otro: testimonio, subalternidad y verdad narrativa* (Guatemala City: Universidad Rafael Landívar, 2002); special issue of *Revista de crítica literaria latinoamericana* 36 (1992); René Jara and Hernán Vidal, eds. *Testimonio y literatura* (Minneapolis: Institute for the Study of Ideologies and Literature, 1986); and Margaret Randall, *Testimonios: A Guide to Oral History* (Toronto: Participatory Research Group, 1985).

37. Elaine Scarry, *On Beauty and Being Just* (Princeton, NJ: Princeton University Press, 1999): 101–9.

38. See Jean François Lyotard, *Le Différend* (Paris: Minuit, 1983): 47–48. English translation: *The Differend*, trans. Georges Van Den Abbeele (Minneapolis: University of Minnesota Press, 1988).

39. Ibid., xii–xiii; French edition, 11.

40. Elaine Scarry posits a useful etymological relationship in German between *fair, to join, to unite*, and *to pact* that helps bridge the notions of beauty and justice.

My concern here is with the workings of textuality in *La noche de Tlatelolco* as they open the consideration of the bridge between beauty and justice.

41. For this notion see Louis Mink, "Narrative Form as a Cognitive Instrument," in *The Writing of History: Literary Form and Historical Understanding*, ed. R. H. Canary and H. Kozicki (Madison: University of Wisconsin Press, 1978), 129–49, and "History and Fiction as Modes of Comprehension," in *New Literary History* 1 (1970): 514–58.

42. See Jorgensen, *The Writing of Elena Poniatowska*.

43. It is no coincidence that this term should be used by Margarita Isabel. The word *happening* gained currency in the sixties, and it had to do with the desire to move theatricality into everyday life by increasing participation and undermining the boundary between stage and audience.

44. The library on Tlatelolco is vast. Following are some of the works that deal with the traumatic events of October 2, 1968: Dolly Young, "Mexican Literary Reactions to Tlatelolco 1968," *Latin American Research Review* 20, no. 2 (1985): 71–85; Jean Franco, "The Critique of the Pyramid and Mexican Narrative after 1968," in Rose Minc, ed. *Latin American Fiction Today* (Takoma Park, MD: Hispamerica, 1982), 49–60; Carlos Fuentes, "Mexico and Its Demons," a review of *The Other Mexico: Critique of the Pyramid* by Octavio Paz, in *New York Review of Books* 20, no. 14 (1973): 16–21, and *Tiempo mexicano* (Mexico City: Joaquín Mortiz, 1971); Jorge Volpi, *La imaginación y el poder: una historia intelectual de 1968* (Mexico City: Era, 1998); José Revueltas, *México 1968: Juventud y revolución* (Mexico City: Era, 1968); Sergio Zermeño, *México: una democracia utópica; el movimiento estudiantil de '68* (Mexico City: Siglo XXI, 1978); Ramón Ramírez, *El movimiento estudiantil de México* (Mexico City: Era, 1969); Luis González de Alba, *Los días y los años* (Mexico City: Era, 1976); Salvador Hernández, *El PRI y el movimiento estudiantil de 1968* (Mexico City: El Caballito, 1971); Carlos Monsivais, *Días de guardar* (Mexico City: Asociados, 1970); Evelyn P. Stevens, *Protest and Response in Mexico* (Cambridge, MA: MIT Press, 1974); Rosalío Wences Reza, *El movimiento estudiantil y los problemas nacionales* (Mexico City: Nuestro Tiempo, 1971); Gilberto Baham, *Reflexiones de un testigo* (Mexico City: Lenasa, 1969); Roberto Blanco Moheno, *Tlatelolco, historia de una infamia* (Mexico City: Diana, 1969); Herberto Castillo, *Libertad bajo protesta* (Mexico City: Federación Editorial Mexicana, 1973); Juan Miguel de Mora, *Tlatelolco 1968: por fin toda la verdad* (Mexico City: Asociados, 1973); Víctor Flores Olea, *La rebelión estudiantil y la sociedad contemporánea* (Mexico City: UNAM, 1973); Gilberto Guevara Niebla, *La democracia en la calle: crónica del movimiento estudiantil mexicano* (Mexico City: Siglo XXI, 1988); Gonzalo Martré, *El movimiento popular estudiantil de 1968 en la novela mexicana* (Mexico City: UNAM, 1998); and Paco Ignacio Taibo II, *'68* (Mexico City: Planeta, 1998). Aside from these memoirs and essays, there are many poems—some even collected in special anthologies—and novels that take the events of October 2 as

their point of departure. A useful study of novels based on the massacre can be found in Cynthia Steele's *Politics, Gender and the Mexican Novel 1968–88: Beyond the Pyramid* (Austin: University of Texas Press, 1992).

CHAPTER 3: FROM DIASPORA TO AGORA IN CORTÁZAR

1. Julio Cortázar, *Textos políticos* (Barcelona: Biblioteca Letras del Exilio, 1985), 141–42. In the monumental bibliography on Cortázar there is a growing number of articles on the question of his political positions. Such a *mise au point* is beyond the scope of this study. See, among many others, Hernán Vidal, "Julio Cortázar y la nueva izquierda," *Ideologies and Literature* 2, no. 7 (May–June 1978): 45–67 and his *Literatura hispanoamericana e ideología liberal: surgimiento y crisis* (Buenos Aires: Ediciones Hispamérica, 1976); David Viñas, *De Sarmiento a Cortázar: literatura argentina y realidad política* (Buenos Aires: Centro Editor de América Latina, 1982); Miguel Alascio Cortázar, *Viaje alrededor de una silla* (Buenos Aires: La Ciudad, 1971); and Jaime Alazraqui, "Imaginación e historia en Julio Cortázar," in *Hacia Cortázar: aproximaciones a su obra* (Barcelona: Anthropos, 1994). For a lucid and daring reading of *Rayuela* in the context of the New Left and the Cuban revolution, see Santiago Colás, "Toward a Latin American Modernity: *Rayuela*, the Cuban Revolution," in *Postmodernity in Latin America: The Argentine Paradigm* (Durham, NC: Duke University Press, 1994).

2. In *Argentina: años de alambradas culturales* (Buenos Aires: Muchnik, 1984), 40. For more on this, see Karl Kohut, "El escritor latinoamericano en Francia: reflexiones de Julio Cortázar en torno al exilio," *INTI* 22–23 (1985–86): 263–80. For more on the question of exile, see Ernesto González Bermejo, *Conversaciones con Cortázar* (Barcelona: Edhasa, 1978) and Omar Prego, *La fascinación de las palabras* (Barcelona: Muchnik, 1985).

3. See Michel Foucault, "What Is an Author?" in *Textual Strategies*, ed. Josué V. Harari (Ithaca, NY: Cornell University Press, 1979), 141–60.

4. For a comparable meditation on the hostility to strangers in means of transportation, see the following passage in Hans Magnus Enzensberger, *Civil Wars: From L.A. to Bosnia* (New York: New Press, 1994):

> Two new passengers open the compartment door. From this instant, the status of those who entered earlier changes. Only a moment ago, they were the intruders; now, all at once, they are natives. They belong to the sedentary clan of compartment-occupants and claim all the privileges the latter believe are due to them. The defense of an "ancestral" territory that was only recently occupied appears paradoxical. The occupants do not empathize with the newcomers, who have to struggle against the same opposition and face the same difficult initiation which they recently underwent. Curious, the rapidity with which one's own origin is concealed and denied. (106)

Enzensberger is dealing here with the hostility generated by migration in the body politic; one can see how Cortázar's story suggests the ways in which the civil sphere can mobilize dangerously aggressive feelings toward those deemed to be outsiders.

5. Adam Ferguson, *An Essay on the History of Civil Society*, ed. Fania Oz-Salzberger (Cambridge, MA: Cambridge University Press, 1995). Ferguson's essay first appeared in 1767. Echoing Montesquieu and the Renaissance thinkers who equated virtue and citizenship, Ferguson observed: "Candour, force, and elevation of mind are the props of democracy; and virtue is the principle of conduct required to its preservation" (67). Moreover, Ferguson believes that individual happiness lies in the pursuit of the common good: "It would seem, therefore, to be the happiness of man, to make his social dispositions the ruling spring of his occupations; to state himself as the member of a community, for whose general good his heart may glow with an ardent zeal" (56).

6. Julio Cortázar, *Bestiary: Selected Stories*, trans. Alberto Manguel et al.; selected and with an introduction by Alberto Manguel (London: Harvill Press, 1991), 23; Spanish edition: *Cuentos completos*, vol. 1 (Madrid: Alfaguara, 1994), 144. (Henceforth, citations of this work will appear within parentheses; page numbers in italics refer to the Spanish edition.)

7. Juan's confession in *El examen* evokes Marcelo's disgusted observation of the "monsters": "Te voy a decir una cosa horrible cronista. Te voy a decir que cada vez que veo un pelo negro lacio, unos ojos alargados, una piel oscura, una tonada provinciana, me da asco." Julio Cortázar, *El examen* (Buenos Aires, Sudamericana, 1986), 90.

8. See his interview with Rosa Montero, "El camino de Damasco de Julio Cortázar," in *El País* (Mar. 14, 1982): 14 (Suplemento Dominical), in which he explicitly addresses the search for "lo que yo llamo convergencia entre el discurso político y el discurso literario."

9. The Cortázar of these early texts bears striking similarities to the Orwell of *The Road to Wigan Pier* (1937), who claimed: "The fact has got to be faced that to abolish class distinctions means abolishing a part of yourself. . . . It is easy for me to say that I want to get rid of class distinctions, but nearly everything I think and do is a result of class distinctions." Quoted in Gerald Graff, "George Orwell and the Class Racket," *Salmagundi* 70–71 (Spring-Summer 1986), 108–20. Unlike Cortázar, though, Orwell moved away from his identification with the oppressed (marked by his return from Burma in 1927) and toward affirming his own class position.

10. See Pierre Bourdieu, *Distinction: A Social Critique of the Judgement of Taste*, trans. Richard Nice (London: Routledge & Kegan Paul, 1984).

11. See Julio Cortazar, "Las ménades" in *Final del juego* (Buenos Aires: Sudamericana, 1976), 50.

12. For a very lucid reading of "La banda" and "Las ménades" in terms of the historical context of production and Cortázar's response to the changes in the cultural institutions and their audiences brought on by the surge of Peronism, see Marta Morello Frosch, "El discurso de armas y letras en las narraciones de Julio Cortázar," *Coloquio Internacional: lo lúdico y lo fantástico en la obra de Julio Cortázar* (Madrid: Fundamentos/Centre de recherches Latino-Américaines, Université de Poitiers, 1986). I agree with Morello Frosch's view that the character in "Las ménades" has a sense of superiority and distance based on "la certeza de que posee acceso a los códigos de cultura más exigentes; a que comparte incluso, en la calidad de observador, los contratos representacionales que dicha cultura hace con ciertos estamentos en pos de públicos más vastos y celebratorios" (160), but I see no positive connotation whatsoever to the brutal transformation of the audience.

13. Friedrich Nietzsche, *Beyond Good and Evil* (Hamondsworth: Penguin, 1973).

14. In Julio Cortázar, *Deshoras* (Buenos Aires: Nueva Imagen, 1983), 77.

15. Julio Cortázar, *The Winners*, trans. Elaine Kerrigan (New York: Pantheon Books, 1965), 30. Spanish edition: *Los premios* (Madrid: Alfaguara, 1983), 48. (Henceforth, citations of this work will appear within parentheses; page numbers in italics refer to the Spanish edition.)

16. "¿Hubo un accidente, hubo?," or "A la final" are just two of numerous examples illustrating Cortázar's impostation of a working-class, uneducated Argentine Spanish sprinkled with barbarisms of Italian origin. Such expressions locate the characters in the sphere of the *mersa* or *grasa*, which provides many an opportunity for parody.

17. It is not insignificant that most of the *mersas* have Italian names, while the others have names of Spanish origin such as López, Medrano, Costa. There is a patrician name as well: Lavalle. The division here would be centered on the relatively recent immigrant, with residues of faulty linguistic acquisition resulting from *barrio* life in areas such as Pacífico, Villa Crespo, La Paternal. For a most incisive exposition of the connections between the characters in *Los premios* and the area of the city of Buenos Aires that they inhabit, see José Amícola, *Sobre Cortázar* (Buenos Aires: Escuela, 1969), 136ff.

18. Bourdieu, *Distinction*, 2.

19. A great deal could be added about the ways in which *Los premios* elaborates on the nation as failure. I have deliberately suspended that particular discussion in the attempt to move away from the discourse about the nation and toward the space of civil society.

20. Julio Cortázar, *A Manual for Manuel*, trans. Gregory Rabassa (New York: Pantheon Books, 1978). Spanish edition: *Libro de Manuel* (Barcelona: Edhasa, 1977). (Henceforth, citations of this work will appear within parentheses; page numbers in italics refer to the Spanish edition.)

21. The very choice of the group's name is eloquent, even if we take into account that the name has to help mask its underground activities. Note, though,

the definition of "Joda" in the *Nuevo Diccionario de Americanismos* (Bogota: Instituto Caro y Cuervo, 1993):

1. (Coloq.) Broma o chiste que se hace a alguien con la intención de divertirse.
2. (Coloq.) Juerga, diversión informal, generalmente con baile, bebida y canto.
3. (Coloq.) Acontecimiento molesto o desagradable. Hacer a alguien objeto de bromas o burlas.

The prevailing connotation suggests playful disruption as opposed to serious purposive activity. La Joda's exploits remind us of some of the activities of the cronopios in *Historias de cronopios y de famas*, such as having everything on the radio translated into Rumanian, or wreaking havoc in the garden hose factory and at the post office.

22. For an enlightening and similar account of a woman's participation in the oppositional politics of this period, see Ana Maria Araujo, *Tupamaras: Des Femmes de L'Uruguay* (Paris: Des Femmes, 1980).

23. See *Julio Cortázar*, "Noticias del mes de mayo," *Ultimo Round* (Mexico City: Siglo XXI: 1984–85), and "Homenaje a una torre de fuego," *Julio Cortázar al término del polvo y el sudor* (Montevideo: Biblioteca de Marcha, 1987). For a lucid discussion of the political debates preceding the publication of *Libro de Manuel*, and Cortázar's involvement in the Padilla affair, see Steven Boldy, *The Novels of Julio Cortázar* (Cambridge, MA: Cambridge University Press, 1980), chap. 4.

24. See Certeau, *La Prise de la Parole*.

25. Julio Cortázar, *Ultimo round* (Mexico City: Siglo XXI, 1969), 88–119.

26. One of the characters (Ludmilla) herself posits the connection: "Pensar que todo empezó con unos fósforos usados y un pingüino, decime si no parece un happening" (*303*).

27. This disjunction is discussed by Walter Benjamin in his essay on surrealism: see *Reflections*, ed. Peter Demetz, trans. Edmund Jephcott (New York: Harcourt, Brace, Jovanovich, 1978), esp. 189.

28. One particularly optimistic view of the future to be attained through the mediation of culture is Kant's. In his *Anthropology from a Pragmatic Point of View*, trans. V. L. Dowdell (Carbondale: Southern Illinois University Press, 1978), Kant presents culture as the scene in which great humanists are the sublime practitioners who guide and preserve the species, leading it to higher levels of "species gifts." In his writings about intellectuals and their function, Cortázar shows traces of this messianic thrust.

29. In Edward Said, *Representations of the Intellectual: The 1993 Reith Lectures* (London: Vintage, 1994), 39.

30. Ibid., 10.

31. In Oscar Collazos, Julio Cortázar, and Mario Vargas Llosa, *Literatura en la revolución y revolución en la literatura: polémica* (Mexico City: Siglo XXI, 1970), 76.

32. Mario Benedetti, "Sobre las relaciones entre el hombre de acción y el intelectual," in *Letras del continente mestizo*, 3rd ed. (Montevideo: Arca, 1974), 29. It was first read at the Congreso Cultural de la Habana in January 1968.

33. Ibid., 30.

34. "El boom entre dos realidades," in Benedetti, *Letras del continente mestizo*, 39. Like the above-cited piece by Benedetti, this one was written in 1968.

35. In Herbert Marcuse, *Negations* (Boston: Beacon Press, 1968), 130.

36. See Herbert Marcuse, *Essay on Liberation* (Boston: Beacon Press, 1969), 30: "If, now, in the rebellion of the young intelligentsia, the right and the truth become the demands of political action, if surrealistic forms of protest and refusal spread throughout the movement, this apparently insignificant development may indicate a fundamental change in the situation. The political protest, assuming a total character, reaches into a dimension that, as aesthetic dimension, has been essentially apolitical." When the "human sensibility" is freed from "repressive reason," it will invoke "the sensuous power of the imagination."

37. Julio Cortazar, *Argentina: años de alambradas culturales* (Buenos Aires: Muchnik, 1984). This is a text that Cortázar was compiling at the time of his death, and which Saúl Yurkievich completed.

38. Julio Cortazar, *Nicaragua tan violentamente dulce* (Managua: Nueva Nicarágua/Monimbo, 1983).

39. This is an interesting text for the purposes of the present discussion, for it stages the problematics in question. While on the one hand Cortázar narrates his experiences at the Tribunal Bertrand Russell II in 1975, on the other hand he constructs a collage including a comic-strip Fantomás trying to capture mysterious international book thieves who have taken works by such figures as Susan Sontag, Alberto Moravia, Octavio Paz, and Juan Carlos Onetti as well as ITT documents showing the corporation's involvement in the overthrow of Allende, and various newspaper clippings designed to show the United States' nefarious involvement in Latin American affairs. It is hard to establish the right reading stance for this little text, for the farcical account of Fantomás's adventures is in jarring contrast with the dealings of the Tribunal Bertrand Russell II and the political affairs alluded to in the text. *Fantomás* contains some of the contradictory subject positions I am attempting to chart. See Julio Cortazar, *Fantomás contra los vampiros multinacionales* (Buenos Aires: Gente Sur, 1989).

40. Julio Cortazar, "El lector y el escritor bajo las dictaduras en América Latina," *Argentina años de alambradas culturales*, 84. This text was sent by Cortázar to a PEN Club conference that took place in Stockholm in 1978.

41. For more on the power of orality, see Walter Ong, SJ, *Interfaces of the Word: Studies in the Evolution of Consciousness and Culture* (Ithaca and London: Cornell University Press, 1977). Ong underscores precisely the participatory power of orality that obtains in Cortázar's speeches: "Oral utterance thus encourages a sense of continuity with life, a sense of participation, because it is itself participatory" (21).

42. In Said, *Representations of the Intellectual*, 33.

43. See Julio Cortázar's "Acerca de la situación del intelectual latinoameri-cano," *Ultimo Round*, vol. 2 (Mexico City: Siglo XXI, 1969), 265ss. This piece also appears in *Textos políticos*.

44. Ibid., 270.

45. Julio Cortázar, "Las palabras violadas" (paper presented at a meeting of the Comisión Argentina de Derechos Humanos in Madrid, 1981), in *Argentina: años de alambradas*, 63–70.

46. In Julio Cortázar, "Literatura e identidad" (paper presented at a UNESCO meeting in Mexico, 1982), in *Argentina: años de alambradas*, 74.

47. In "El escritor y su quehacer en América Latina" (paper prepared for the Seminario sobre Política Cultural y Liberación Democrática en América Latina, held in Sitges, 1982), Cortázar reformulates the transformation of culture: "We must overcome the old notion of culture as a fixed asset and try to turn it into a movable asset, into an element of daily life to be offered and given, to be bartered and modified, just as we do with consumer goods, with bread and bicycles, and shoes" (100).

48. In "América Latina y sus escritores" (included in the catalogue of an exhi-bition entitled "Expression libre de l'art latinoaméricain," organized by Hipólito Solari Irigoyen at the Hotel de Ville de Bondy in 1979), in Cortázar, *Argentina*, 77.

49. In Emmanuel Lévinas, *Totality and Infinity* (Pittsburgh, PA: Duquesne University Press, 1961), 156. For Lévinas, existence and dwelling are interjoined.

CHAPTER 4: TOWARD A TRANSNATIONAL REPUBLIC OF LETTERS

1. In the field of European letters, one could draw a parallel with the changes toward a market culture that took place at the end of the eighteenth and begin-ning of the nineteenth centuries, when the rise of the middle classes dramatically increased the demand for reading material, and new literary forms and institutions emerged to meet such demand. This was the time of the rise of the novel, of re-views and periodicals, of lending libraries. In Latin America, one can discern an equally dramatic growth in the reading public and in the number of books and pe-riodicals made available to it in the 1960s. For a European (mostly German and English) discussion, see Mary Woodmansee, *The Author, Art and the Market: Rereading the History of Aesthetics* (New York: Columbia University Press, 1994).

2. In *La globalización imaginada* (Buenos Aires: Paidós, 1999), Néstor García Canclini argues for a three-stage process toward globalization: the first one, inter-nationalization, coincides with the early transoceanic navigations; the second stage, transnationalization, is located around the middle of the twentieth century, when technological innovations and faster communications articulate markets in a worldwide fashion, creating interdependent relationships but without undermin-ing the nation-state. Globalization, the third stage, would be characterized by the

deterritorialization produced by recourse to electronic communications and information systems, and the attendant development of systems of worldwide reach. For García Canclini the concentration of power in multinational corporations and their flow of capital, together with the effects of massive migratory movements and international transactions, made it possible at the end of the twentieth century to produce and put into circulation what he calls "global symbolic products," which range from television programs to films, videogames, and music. In the sixties, I would contend, we witness transnationalization as the growing integration of the Latin American cultural markets combined with a powerful modernizing drive that dramatically modifies the consumption of cultural goods, but the nation-state continues to provide the boundary conditions.

3. In Angel Rama's "El 'Boom' en perspectiva," in *Más allá del Boom: literatura y mercado*, eds. David Viñas, Angel Rama, Jean Franco, et al. (Mexico City: Marcha, 1981), 51–110.

4. I insist on the masculine pronoun because, as explained in Chapter Five, authorship remains essentially masculine in the sixties.

5. In Carlos Fuentes, *La nueva novela hispanoamericana* (Mexico City: Joaquín Mortiz, 1969), 97. He proceeds less convincingly: "Un físico nuclear británico se parece a un campesino indígena tzotzil en que ambos han sido marginados por el avance astronómico, inalcanzable, de la tecnología norteamericana."

6. In a prescient article written for *Carteles* in 1931, Alejo Carpentier had decried the lack of *oficio*, the weakness of the *métier* of Latin American writers, and urged his fellow novelists to strive to "llegar al fondo de las técnicas" in order to render the admirable raw material they drew on in sophisticated ways. See his "América ante la joven literatura europea," in *Carteles* (June 28, 1931), reprinted in *La literatura latinoamericana en vísperas de un nuevo siglo y otros ensayos* (Mexico City: Siglo XXI, 1981), 51–57. By the 1960s, what Angel Rama aptly called *la tecnificación narrativa* had been attained. See his "La tecnificación narrativa," in *Hispamérica* 10, no. 30 (1980), 29–82.

7. See Pierre Bourdieu, *The Field of Cultural Production*, ed. Randal Johnson (New York: Columbia University Press, 1993), 74ff.

8. I have chosen a small group of such "stories" among other possibilities. The decade was rich in periodical publications, and a full account of them is beyond the aims of this chapter. Other significant ones are *Libre, Siempre!, Bohemia, La Rosa Blindada*, and *Los Libros*. In Argentina, there were several magazines comparable to *Primera Plana*, such as *Confirmado* and *Análisis*.

9. These publishing houses were based in the major urban centers of the subcontinent, and they included Fondo de Cultura Económica, Siglo Veintiuno, Era, and Joaquín Mortiz in Mexico; Alfa and Arca in Uruguay; Monte Avila in Caracas; Nascimento and Zig-Zag in Santiago de Chile; and Eudeba, Losada, Sudamericana, Emecé, and other smaller ones in Buenos Aires. Seix Barral, Lumen, and Anagrama were in Barcelona, but they had enormous influence on the shaping of

the boom. For more on them and their evolution, see Rama, "El 'Boom' en perspectiva," 66–73.

10. See Danny J. Anderson, "Creating Cultural Prestige: Editorial Joaquín Mortiz," *Latin American Research Review* 31, no. 2 (1996): 3–41. This article charts the strategies of affiliation, visibility, and distinction that ensured this publishing house's prestige, and its centrality in the boom.

11. The fact that many of the "cultural publishers" of the sixties were taken over by large conglomerates like Planeta (which Joaquín Mortiz joined in 1983, and which dismissed the director in 1995) and Anagrama is important for our understanding of the profound changes affecting the publishing industry in recent decades.

12. For an understanding of the ways in which the Instituto Di Tella played a central role in the cultural scene of the sixties, see John King, *El Di Tella y el desarrollo cultural argentino en la década del sesenta*, trans. C. Gardini (Buenos Aires: Arte Gaglianone, 1985), and Patricia Rizzo, *Instituto Di Tella: experiencias '68* (Buenos Aires: Fundación Proa, 1998).

13. Domingo F. Sarmiento, *Obras completas* (Buenos Aires: Luz del Día, 1953), 1, 58–59.

14. Two short-lived *segunda época*'s were launched between 1983 and 1985, and then again in 1990.

15. In Maite Alvarado and Renata Rocco-Cuzzi, "*Primera Plana*: el nuevo discurso periodístico de la década del '60," *Punto de Vista* 22 (1984): 27–30.

16. María Elena Walsh delighted *caffé-concert* audiences with her song:

El mundo nunca ha sido para todo el mundo
pero hoy al parecer es de un señor
que en una escalerita de aeropuerto
cultiva un maletín pero ninguna flor.
Sonriente y afeitado para siempre
trajina para darnos la ilusión
de un cielo en tecnicolor donde muy poquitos
aprenden a jugar al golf.
Qué vivos son los ejecutivos
que vivos que son del sillón al avión
del avión al salón, del harem al eden . . .
(María Elena Walsh, *Las canciones* [Buenos Aires: Seix Barral, 1994])

17. In an interview, Tomás Eloy Martínez describes the configuration of *Primera Plana*'s style: "Todo estaba planeado como una gran diversión, en que contaba el desafío de saber quién inventaba o encontraba adjetivos, sustantivos o modos de decir las cosas que fuesen muy precisos y a la vez insólitos para el lector. La actitud general de la revista era provocar la complicidad con el lector a través de la sorpresa. ¿De qué manera?: mediante la explotación del esnobismo porteño, sujeto a

modas." In Jorge B. Rivera and Eduardo Romano, *Claves del periodismo argentino actual* (Buenos Aires: Tarso, 1987), 61–62.

18. *Primera Plana* 225 (Apr. 18, 1967): 69.

19. *Primera Plana* 223 (Apr. 10, 1967): 110.

20. In *Primera Plana* 237 (July 10–17, 1967) and 306 (Nov. 1968): 72.

21. See Guy Debord, *La Societé du Spectacle* (Paris: Editions Champ Libre, 1971), 22.

22. *Primera Plana*, 306 (Nov. 1968): 72.

23. Ibid.

24. *Primera Plana* 238 (July 24–31, 1967): 73.

25. In Fuentes, *La nueva novela hispanoamericana*, 22.

26. *Primera Plana* 238 (July 18, 1967).

27. The Congress was founded in 1950 by Michael Josselson and Melvin Lasky. One of its central aims was to counterbalance the activities of the Communist Information Bureau, founded in 1947. For a very helpful account of this aspect of Cold War propaganda, see Jean Franco's *The Decline and Fall of the Lettered City: Latin America in the Cold War* (Cambridge, MA: Harvard University Press, 2002), 30ff.

28. *Mundo Nuevo* 1 (July 1966): 4.

29. Ibid.

30. In Franco's *Decline and Fall of the Lettered City* (which I read after this chapter was written), she notes a useful distinction between universalism and cosmopolitanism. While the earlier *Cuadernos por la libertad de la cultura* valued universalism as shorthand for European values and a way out of the debates over national identity and the shortcomings of the national project, the later cosmopolitanism aimed at what she describes as an "internationally viable" style.

31. In *Mundo Nuevo* 1, no. 1 (July 1966): 5.

32. Ibid., 7.

33. For an overview of *Mundo Nuevo*'s affiliations with the Congress for Cultural Freedom, and with the CIA, see Peter Coleman, *The Liberal Conspiracy: The Congress for Cultural Freedom and the Struggle for the Mind of Postwar Europe* (New York: Free Press, 1989), and María Eugenia Mudrovcic, *Mundo Nuevo: cultura y Guerra Fría en la década del sesenta* (Rosario, Argentina: Beatriz Viterbo, 1997).

34. Guillermo Cabrera Infante, "Desde el Swinging London," *Mundo Nuevo* 14 (Aug. 1967): 45–53.

35. Parts of *One Hundred Years of Solitude* appeared in several other periodical publications before Sudamericana published it in 1967. *Amaru* published "Subida al cielo en cuerpo y alma de la bella Remedios Buendía"; *Marcha* brought out "Diluvio en Macondo." These fragments were accompanied by anticipations of the novel's future success.

36. García Márquez had already given to *Mundo Nuevo* the chapters to be published when he learned that the CIA financed the Congreso por la Libertad de la

Cultura. He then sent a letter to Emir Rodríguez Monegal that the latter did not publish, but which appeared in *Encuentro Liberal*: "En estas condiciones, señor Director, no me sorprendería que usted fuera el primero en entender que no vuelva a colaborar en *Mundo Nuevo*, mientras esa revista mantenga cualquier vínculo con un organismo que nos ha colocado a usted y a mí, y a tantos amigos, en esta abrumadora situación de cornudos." Quoted in Mudrovcic, *Mundo Nuevo*, 38.

37. Promotional materials on *One Hundred Years of Solitude* appear since the moment of the novel's publication; all of these excerpts are taken from *Mundo Nuevo* 14 (Aug. 1967): 7.

38. *Mundo Nuevo* 1 (July 1966): 1.

39. Pablo Neruda's presence at the P.E.N. Club Meeting in New York was seen with great disapproval by the Cuban intellectuals gathered around *Casa de las Américas*.

40. "Papel del escritor en América Latina," *Mundo Nuevo* 5 (Nov. 1966): 35.

41. The present-day "constitution of Empire," to borrow a phrase from Hardt and Negri, has replaced such dual tensions by "the idea of a single power that overdetermines them all, structures them in a unitary way, and treats them under one common notion of right that is decidedly postcolonial and postimperialist." See Michael Hardt and Antonio Negri, *Empire* (Cambridge, MA: Harvard University Press, 2000), 9.

42. A similar story could be told about a short-lived journal of the seventies, *Libre*, which brought together consecrated writers such as Juan Goytisolo, Mario Vargas Llosa, Julio Cortázar, Carlos Fuentes, and Jorge Edwards as well as other Spaniards such as Jorge Semprún, José Goytisolo, and Manuel Vázquez Montalbán. *Libre* was launched after the demise of *Mundo Nuevo*, in 1971, and it strove to articulate progressive politics with the independence of the creative imagination. Like *Mundo Nuevo*, and even though it was decidedly supportive of antibourgeois politics, it was unable to steer clear of conflicts with Cuba. It closed after four issues, in 1972. For an account of its aims and the debates around them, see Claudia Gilman, *Entre la pluma y el fusil: debates y dilemas del escritor revolucionario en América Latina* (Buenos Aires: Siglo XXI, 2003): 278–306.

43. The most complete account of these exchanges appears in Peter Coleman's *The Liberal Conspiracy*. For its repercussions on *Mundo Nuevo*, see Mudrovcic, *Mundo Nuevo*, chap. 1.

44. The journal continued until issue numbers 57–58 with Horacio Daniel Rodríguez at the helm. A bitter letter sent by Rodríguez Monegal to Cabrera Infante in September 1968 offers a glimpse of the strains that existed within the intellectual camps:

> El nuevo *Mundo Nuevo* es una pifia que no leerán ni los lectores de pruebas. Qué triunfo para los Ramas, Fernández Retamar, Lisandro Oteros, Díaz Lastra y Julio (Gardel) Cortázar: que le saquen una revista incómoda

de las manos sus propios enemigos y que le pongan ese supositorio tran-
quilizante a la conciencia siempre alerta y revolucionaria de la alerta y revolucionaria izquierda intelectual de América Latina. Lo que hice o traté de
hacer en *Mundo Nuevo* era demasiado lúcido para este continente de beatas,
maricas y revolucionarios.

See "Carta a Guillermo Cabrera Infante" (Sept. 24, 1968). Emir Rodríguez Mone-
gal's Papers, Princeton University Libraries, Princeton, NJ. Quoted in Mudrovcic,
Mundo Nuevo, 110. For more on the conflicts surrounding the end of Rodríguez
Monegal's direction of the journal, see also Ernesto Sierra, "Réquiem para *Mundo
Nuevo*," *Casa de las Américas* 213 (Oct.–Dec. 1998): 135–39.

45. José Donoso, *The Boom in Spanish American Literature: A Personal History*,
trans. Gregory Kolovakos (New York: Columbia University Press, 1977), 104.
Spanish edition: Historia personal del "boom" (Barcelona: Anagrama, 1987), 122.

46. Initially, *Marcha*'s editorial policy strove to steer clear of both Soviet cen-
tralism and North American capitalism. In the late sixties, as the political debates
intensified, the spirit of solidarity with Cuba became more pronounced.

47. Angel Rama, "La construcción de una literatura," *Marcha* 1040 (Dec. 26,
1960): 22–24.

48. *Marcha* 273 (Mar. 9, 1945): 15. Cited in Pablo Rocca, *35 años en Marcha:
crítica y literatura en Marcha y en el Uruguay 1939–74* (Montevideo: Intendencia
Municipal de Montevideo, 1992): 49.

49. Quoted in Rocca, *35 años en Marcha*, 164–65.

50. Ibid., 176.

51. Angel Rama, "El sometimiento intelectual," *Marcha* 1209 (June 12, 1964): 46.

52. For a thorough account of the events that led to the closure of *Marcha*, see
Jorge Ruffinelli, "La censura contra *Marcha*," in *Marcha y América Latina*, eds.
Mabel Moraña and Horacio Machín (Pittsburgh, PA: Instituto Internacional de
Literatura Iberoamericana, Biblioteca de América, 2003), 349–76.

53. Jorge Luis Borges, "Problemas de la traducción," *Sur* 338–39 (Jan.–Dec.
1976): 120.

54. Victoria Ocampo, "El premio María Moors Cabot," *Sur* 297 (Nov.–Dec.
1965): 6. Quoted in John King, *Sur: A Study of the Argentine Literary Journal and
Its Role in the Development of a Culture, 1931–1970* (Cambridge, UK, and London:
Cambridge University Press, 1986), 174.

55. María Luisa Bastos and then Enrique Pezzoni led the magazine with vision
and acuity, attracting younger members such as Edgardo Cosarinsky and Sylvia
Molloy, who had just completed her doctorate in France. Although several issues
of very high quality came out in the late 1960s, Victoria Ocampo's discouragement
with the changing times, coupled with financial worries, led her to suspend regular publication of *Sur*.

56. For the Spanish reading public, Spanish American literature in the fifties
remained as poorly known as—to put it in Joaquín Marco's words—"exotic as

could be, at the time, Japan." See his "Entre España y América," in *La llegada de los bárbaros*, eds. Joaquín Marco and Jordi Gracia (Barcelona: Edhasa, 2004), 19–39. In an article published in *Insula* 175 (June 1961), Jorge Campos decried the fact that Borges's books barely made it to the stands; a year later in the same publication, Francisco Rico greeted the publication of *El hacedor* ruefully: "Quizá ésta que saludamos hoy—impresa en los días finales de 1960—no sea ya la última obra de Borges (el lamentable retraso con que se reciben aquí los libros hispanoamericanos obliga a ser muy cauto en afirmaciones de índole pareja)." Both quoted in Jesús Ferrer Sola and Carmen Sanclemente, "De orígenes y recelos (1960–1966)," in Marco and Gracia, *La llegada de los bárbaros*, 87.

57. I am indebted here to Alejandro Herrero-Olaizola's article "Publishing Matters: Francoist Censorship and the Latin American Book Market," *Literary Research/Recherche Littéraire* 19, no. 37–38 (2002): 21–28.

58. For a discussion of how the boom was "sold" in Spain through categories such as the exotic, the different, and the avant garde, see Burkhard Pohl, "Vender el boom: el discurso de la difusión editorial," in Marco and Gracia, *La llegada de los bárbaros*, 165–88.

59. For helpful tables indicating the proportion of translated texts published in Spain in the decade, see Mario Santana, *Strangers in the Homeland* (Lewisburg, PA: Bucknell University Press, 2001), 47.

60. In *Los españoles y el "boom,"* eds. F. Tola de Habich and P. Grieve (Caracas: Tiempo Nuevo, 1971), 17.

61. Ibid., 18.

62. José María Castellet, "La actual literatura latinoamericana vista desde España," *Panorama actual de la literatura latinoamericana* (Madrid: Fundamentos, 1971), 55–56. Quoted in Santana, *Strangers in the Homeland*, 57.

63. Most of the Catalan poets participated in an *Homenaje a Cuba* published in Paris by *Ruedo Ibérico* to commemorate the Revolution's resistance at Bay of Pigs in 1962.

64. See Carme Riera's excellent *La Escuela de Barcelona* (Barcelona: Anagrama, 1988).

65. A telling detail about cultural values in Franco's Spain: a positive review by José María Castellet of de Beauvoir's *The Second Sex* caused quite a scandal in the Spanish press: Castellet was seen as attacking the family and the Church. For more on this see ibid., 127.

66. Also significant in the presentation of Spanish American authors in Spain was the Editorial Salvat, which launched RTVE, a "colección popular," in 1970. Directed by Joaquín Marco, it published authors such as Miguel Angel Asturias, Arturo Uslar Pietri, Carlos Fuentes, and Mario Vargas Llosa in small, inexpensive volumes that reached massive circulation.

67. In Carlos Barral, *Años de penitencia* (Madrid: Alianza Editorial, 1975), 201.

68. Ibid., 202.

69. While I focus here on Carlos Barral and his work, it should be averred that another important cultural agent of the time was Carmen Balcells, who started her business as literary agent in 1959 but who had made her way into the field initially by working closely with Barral.

70. In the case of the Escuela de Barcelona, this social consciousness had a definitively leftist inflection with roots in the Republican cause.

71. Bourdieu, *The Field of Cultural Production*, 106.

72. In his "Entre dos tierras: Carlos Barral y la unidad cultural latinoamericana," *Carlos Barral y la edición latinoamericana* (Salamanca: Ediciones Universidad de Salamanca, 2004), 427–35, Burkhard Pohl quotes documents that reveal Barral's conception of Hispanism as a series of horizontal bonds among different national cultures, removed from the hegemony of Franco's Spain. This extended to linguistic variations:

> A mí me parece que del mismo modo que el castellano moderno está constituido por un mosaico de formas dialectales equidistantes del conjunto de formas habladas en la época de la conquista, las literaturas hispánicas constituyen un conjunto de literaturas dialectales equidistantes de los clásicos del Barroco. En ese sentido, a mí me parece que el castellano de Santiago de Compostela, . . . el de Santiago de Cuba, el de Santiago de Chile y el de Santiago del Estero están aproximadamente a una misma distancia de una lengua teórica que ninguno de nosotros ha oído nunca . . . existe una literatura matizada, en primer lugar, por la tonalidad dialectal y, en segundo lugar, por lo que yo llamaría la regionalidad de la experiência. (*Catálogo de la producción editorial barcelonesa* [Barcelona: Diputación Provincial, 1973], 51–57, 54)

73. Carlos Barral, *Los años sin excusa* (Barcelona: Barral, 1978), 248.

74. Ibid., 239–72.

75. In her *The World Republic of Letters* (Cambridge, MA: Harvard University Press, 2004), Pascale Casanova argues for the importance of translation for international consecration. This was most certainly the case for the boom novelists. In the case of the Formentor group one can also see Europe's search for exotic new voices to satisfy the ever-growing need for the new of advanced capitalist societies.

76. Other prestigious prizes that honored Spanish American writers (such as Vargas Llosa and Colombia's Manuel Mejía Vallejo and Eduardo Caballero Calderón) were the Premio Eugenio Nadal offered by Editorial Destino, and the Premio de la Crítica. By far the most significant one was Miguel Angel Asturias's 1967 Nobel Prize, which coincided with the publication of *One Hundred Years of Solitude*. 1967 could certainly be seen as a pivotal year for the sense of culmination and arrival in Latin American literature.

77. For the many difficulties that had to be overcome for this book to be published in the face of objections from the Spanish censors, see Nuria Prats Fons, "La

censura ante la novela hispanoamericana," in Marco and Gracia, *La llegada de los bárbaros*: 200–204.

78. Carlos Barral, *Cuando las horas veloces* (Barcelona: Tusquets, 1988), 79.

79. Ibid., 80.

80. The delicacy of these negotiations increased when it was time to adjudicate the *Prix International des Editeurs*, when the thirteen editors came to the table with national and linguistic agendas that required intricate juggling acts. A case in point is the award to Jorge Semprún of the *Prix* in 1963, defeating the advocates of the 1962 Premio Biblioteca Breve, *La ciudad y los perros*, in part because Semprún had written *Le grand voyage* in French, and was favored by Monique Lange (Juan Goytisolo's wife) of Gallimard. Against the Peruvian was also the fact that the 1962 *Prix* had gone to another Spanish-language novel, Juan García Hortelano's *Tormenta de verano*.

81. The two first winners were *La casa verde* in 1967, and *One Hundred Years of Solitude* in 1972.

82. For a compelling account of the very real danger posed by Franco's censors, see Carlos Barral's *Los años sin excusa*, 265ff.

83. Juan Goytisolo, "La novela española contemporánea," *Libre* 2 (Dec. 1971–Feb. 1972): 33–40.

84. An important contribution to the question of censorship is by Nuria Prats Fons, "La censura ante la novela hispanoamericana," in Marco and Gracia, *La llegada de los bárbaros*, 189–220.

85. Barral, *Cuando las horas veloces*, 84–85.

86. Paul de Man, "A Modern Master," *New York Review of Books* (Nov. 19, 1964).

87. Pedro Orgambide, "Jorge Luis Borges," *La Gaceta Literaria* 20 (May 1960): 23. Quoted in María Luisa Bastos, *Borges ante la crítica argentina, 1923–1960* (Buenos Aires: Hispamérica, 1974), 303.

88. Quoted in Bastos, *Borges ante la crítica*, 146.

89. Néstor Ibarra, *La nueva poesía argentina: ensayo crítico sobre el ultraísmo, 1921–1929* (Buenos Aires: Imprenta Molinari, 1930), 128.

90. See *Megáfono* 11 (Aug. 1933): 25–30.

91. For more on this, see Diana Sorensen, *Facundo and the Construction of Argentine Culture* (Austin: University of Texas Press, 1996).

92. For an overview, see John King's *Sur*.

93. The very first translation into French ("El acercamiento a Almotásim") may have been by Néstor Ibarra, who published it in *Mesures* in 1939. In 1944, while still in Buenos Aires, Caillois had commissioned Néstor Ibarra to translate "La lotería en Babilonia" and "La biblioteca de Babel," and had published them in *Lettres Françaises* 14. This journal was sponsored by *Sur*, and its mission was to facilitate the publication of French writers during the Vichy years. Other stories appeared in *Confluences* and *La Licorne* in 1946 and 1947. When *Fictions* appeared in

La Croix du Sud in 1952, Borges was therefore not entirely unknown to the French public. For a detailed account of the early publications and reviews, see Sylvia Molloy, *La diffusion de la littérature hispano-américaine en France au XXe siècle* (Paris: Presses Universitaires de France, 1972), 206ff. As early as 1925, Valéry Larbaud had written an article about *Inquisiciones*.

94. This important series published mostly prose works. Aside from Borges, authors included Ciro Alegría, Enrique Amorim, José María Arguedas, Miguel Angel Asturias, Lydia Cabrera, Guillermo Cabrera Infante, Alejo Carpentier, Rosario Castellanos, Julio Cortázar, Rómulo Gallegos, Ricardo Guiraldes, Martín Luis Guzmán, Juan Rulfo, Ernesto Sábato. See Molloy, *La diffusion*, 177ff.

95. For an insightful reading of what it means to read Kafka in "translation," see Casanova, *World Republic of Letters*, 269–74.

96. Amado Alonso had written one of the first academic articles on Borges's narrative work in 1935. See his "Borges narrador," in *Sur* 14 (Nov. 1935): 105–15. *Megáfono* had devoted an entire issue to Borges in 1933, but its focus had obviously been his earlier work, up to *Discusión. Sur* published an important analysis by Pezzoni in 1952, devoted to *Otras inquisiciones*: "Aproximación al último libro de Borges," *Sur* 217–18 (1952): 101–23. Only later in the decade would the academic critical momentum gain strength in Argentina. Two crucial studies were Ana María Barrenechea's *La expresión de la irrealidad en la obra de Borges* (Mexico City: El Colegio de Mexico, 1957) and Raimundo Lida's "Notas a Borges" in his *Letras hispánicas* (Mexico City and Buenos Aires: Fondo de Cultura Económico, 1958): 280–83.

97. *Les Temps modernes* 83 (Sept. 1952), and *Hygiène des lettres*, vol. 2: *Littérature dégagée* (Paris: Gallimard, 1955). Quoted in Molloy, *La Diffusion*, 210.

98. The 1950s were a period of considerable stasis—not to say crisis—in French letters. Writing about the aims of *La Ligne générale*, integrated by the likes of Georges Perec, Roger Kléman, and Claude Burgelin, Perec notes:

> Ce projet est né d'une colère, d'une exaspération devant ce que propose cette fin des années cinquante: la littérature engagée, dans sa version sartrienne comme dans sa version communiste, se révèle une impasse; la production romanesque, abondante, apparaît lourdement frivole et inconsistante, parfois assez aggressivement réactionnaire comme avec les 'Hussards' (Blondin, Nimier); l'humanisme blessé de Camus(. . .); et on conçoit que la 'révolution' du Nouveau Roman, telle que Robbe-Grillet l'orchestre, n'ait pu que rencontrer l'hostilité d'un groupe qui avait des exigences de renouveau autrement fortes. (Georges Perec, *L. G. Une aventure des années soixante* [Paris: Seuil, 1992], 12)

99. Maurice Blanchot's *Le Livre à venir* (Paris: Gallimard, 1959) has a section of Chapter Two ("La Question Littéraire") devoted to works by Borges: "L'Infini littéraire: L'aleph." The previous section ("Le Secret du golem") deals with Borges and "Casares" (Bioy). In Blanchot, Borges keeps company with Virginia Woolf,

Gide, Musil, Mann, Broch, Kafka, James, Duras, Robbe-Grillet, Hesse, and Beckett. This could be seen as a version of the literary canon of the early sixties in Europe, as seen through a French lens.

100. Michel Foucault, *The Order of Things: An Archaeology of the Human Sciences* (New York: Vintage Press, 1973), xv. French edition: *Les Mots et les choses* (Paris: Gallimard, 1966), 7. Foucault goes on to quote a passage from "El idioma analítico de John Wilkins."

101. de Man, "A Modern Master."

102. Letter from Robert MacGregor to Donald Yates, February 23, 1968. New Directions Publishing Corporation Records, box 2021, Houghton Library, Harvard University. MacGregor is referring to James Irby's introduction, which appears to have delayed publication of *Labyrinths*.

103. Letter from Donald Yates to Robert MacGregor, February 9, 1968. Here Yates is discussing a copyright request from L. A. Murillo for his translation of "La escritura del dios." New Directions Corporation Records, box 2021.

104. See New Directions, folder 21.

105. For more on this, see Carlos Rincón, "Modernidad periférica y el desafío de lo postmoderno: perspectivas del arte narrativo latinoamericano," *Revista de Crítica Literaria Latinoamericana* 15, no. 29 (1989): 61–104. Rincón includes references to Borges's postmodernity in works by Gerald Graff, John Barth, Brian McHale, and D. Fokkema.

CHAPTER 5: THE ANXIOUS BROTHERHOOD

1. See http://nobelprize.org/literature/laureates/1982/marquez-lecture-e.html

2. Gabriel García Márquez, *One Hundred Years of Solitude*, trans. G. Rabassa (New York: HarperCollins, Perennial Classics, 1998), 448.

3. In Paul de Man, *Blindness and Insight: Essays in the Rhetoric of Contemporary Criticism* (Minneapolis: University of Minnesota Press, 1983): 148.

4. H. Blumenberg, *The Legitimacy of the Modern Age* (Cambridge, MA: MIT Press, 1985), 116.

5. Nietzsche articulated this impossibility as follows: "For we are inevitably the result of earlier generations and thus the result of their mistakes, their passions, their aberrations, even of their crimes; it is not possible to loosen oneself entirely from this chain." In *Werke* I, ed. Karl Schlechta (Munich: Carl Hanser, 1954), 230. Quoted in de Man, "Literary History," *Blindness and Insight*, 149.

6. See Roland Barthes, "The Death of the Author," *Image, Music, Text* (New York: Hill & Wang, 1977), 142, 143. The essay was written in 1968.

7. Here I must differ with Idelber Avelar's generally perceptive *The Untimely Present: Postdictatorial Latin American Fiction and the Task of Mourning* (Durham, NC, and London: Duke University Press, 1999). In the chapter "Oedipus in Post-Auratic Times" (22–38), he avers that book sales made it possible for boom writers

to gain financial autonomy. This meant, he argues, foregoing state sponsorship, and turning to the aesthetic as a separate social sphere: as the concomitant loss of aura is mourned for, aesthetics stands in for politics. It is hard to agree with the notion that only in the sixties does state sponsorship for writers come to an end. In fact, such sponsorship was at best elusive in the history of Latin American letters: except for writers who held—often temporary—official posts in government or educational institutions, even in the nineteenth century the question of earning a living was one of pressing concern. A look at Domingo F. Sarmiento's many articles about the importance of buying newspapers and keeping the frail *prensa periódica* afloat, written in the 1840s, would reveal the extent to which writing meant facing financial insecurity. The *modernistas* of the late nineteenth century knew only too well what it meant to lack state sponsorship, as can be seen in Rubén Darío's "El rey burgués" or "El velo de la reina Mab." Further, the relationship between aesthetics and politics in the boom writing, as I will try to show, is not one of substitution, or aesthetization of politics. It is a complex one in which the logic of substitution is not at work: rather, one discerns complex efforts to address major political questions while deploying complex narrative techniques, attempting to operate a self-conscious retrieval of the political through technical virtuosity and narrative strategy. Nor do their novels have a uniquely urban focus: their sweep is such that they produce figurations of the nation that include both the country and the city.

8. For more on the category of the author in the Latin American novel of the time, see Jean Franco, "Narrador, autor, superestrella: la narrativa latinoamericana en la era de la producción de masas," *Revista Iberoamericana* 47, no. 115–16 (1981): 129–48.

9. Fuentes, *La nueva novela hispanoamericana*, 32.

10. See Carpentier, "América ante la joven literatura europea," 56.

11. First published in 1972 by Anagrama in Barcelona, the *Historia personal del "boom"* was brought out again in 1987 with two significant appendixes: "El 'boom' doméstico" by María Pilar Donoso, and "Diez años después" by Donoso himself. I have worked with the 1998 Alfaguara edition, published in Chile. English translation: *The Boom in Spanish American Literature: A Personal History*, trans. Gregory Kolovakos (New York: Columbia University Press, 1977). (Henceforth, citations of this work will appear within parentheses; page numbers in italics refer to the Spanish edition.)

12. See Alone's *Historia personal de la literatura chilena, desde Don Alonso de Ercilla hasta Pablo Neruda* (Santiago: Zig-Zag, 1954). The very first page contains a "*Nota sobre el título*" that clarifies the choice of the word *personal*. There is, also, a disclaimer in this *Nota*: "Otros en la historia ven las masas, las corrientes, los imponderables sociológicos; nosotros vemos ante todo, seres humanos."

13. See Sigmund Freud, *Group Psychology and the Analysis of the Ego*, trans. J. Strachey (New York: Liveright, 1949).

14. *Masculine Domination*, trans. Richard Nice (Stanford, CA: Stanford University Press, 2001), 40. French edition: Pierre Bourdieu, *La Domination masculine* (Paris: Seuil, 1998), 46.

15. See Gilles Deleuze, *Masochism: An Interpretation of Coldness and Cruelty*, trans. J. McNeil (New York: George Braziller, 1971).

16. See Barbara Johnson, "Muteness Envy," *The Feminist Difference* (Cambridge, MA: Harvard University Press, 1998), 153.

17. See Freud, *Group Psychology*.

18. José Donoso, *The Garden Next Door*, trans. Hardie St. Martin (New York: Grove Press, 1992). Spanish edition: *El jardín de al lado* (Barcelona: Editorial Seix Barral, 1981). (Henceforth, citations of this work will appear within parentheses; page numbers in italics refer to the Spanish edition.)

19. Numerous studies have been written about this novel. I will mention only those that I have found most relevant: R. Gutiérrez Mouat, "Aesthetics, Ethics and Politics in Donoso's *El jardín de al lado*," *PMLA* 106, no. 1 (1991): 60–70; Oscar Montero, "*El jardín de al lado*: la escritura y el fracaso del éxito," *Revista Iberoamericana* 49, no. 123–24 (1983): 449–67; E. Barraza Jara, "Las dos escrituras en *El jardín de al lado*, de José Donoso," *Estudios Filológicos* 25 (1990): 131–41; F. González, "The Androgynous Narrator in José Donoso's *El jardín de al lado*," *Revista de Estudios Hispánicos* 23, no. 1 (1989): 99–113; J. M. Lemogodeuc, "Las máscaras y las marcas de la autobiografía: la cuestión del narrador en *El jardín de al lado* de José Donoso," *Convergences et Divergences* 1 (1996): 57–75; L. Kerr, "Authority in Play: José Donoso's *El jardín de al lado*," *Criticism* 25, no. 1 (1983): 41–65; R. García Castro, "Epistemología del closet de José Donoso (1921–1996) en *Conjeturas sobre la memoria de mi tribu* (1996), *El jardín de al lado* (1981) y 'Santelices,'" *Revista Iberoamericana* 68, no. 198 (2002): 27–48; P. Meléndez, "Writing and Reading the Palimpsest: Donoso's *El jardín de al lado*," *Symposium* 41, no. 3 (1987): 200–212; Rosemary Geisdorfer Feal, "Veiled Portraits: Donoso's Interartistic Dialogue in *El jardín de al lado*," *MLN* 103, no. 2 (1988): 398–418; D. Kadir, "Next Door: Writing Elsewhere," *The Review of Contemporary Fiction* 12, no. 2 (1992): 60–69; L. N. Echeverría, "El exilio en *El jardín de al lado* de Donoso," *Confluencia* 10, no. 2 (1995): 67–75; and M. I. Millington, "Out of Chile: Writing in Exile/Exile in Writing—José Donoso's *El jardín de al lado*," *Renaissance and Modern Studies* 34 (1991): 64–77.

20. In Geisdorfer Feal, "Veiled Portraits," 400.

21. Ibid., 401.

22. These are the years when the names of Allende, Valenzuela, Poniatowska, Traba, Peri-Rossi, Ferré, and others were gaining a reading public of their own, although writers like Peri-Rossi had been publishing for years.

23. Most illuminating is a notebook Donoso kept as he was writing *El lugar sin límites*, and that offers valuable insights into Donoso's own writerly tribulations, very much à la Julio Méndez. Aside from keeping a log on his daily fears about the

value of his efforts and the dark menace of writer's block, Donoso speculates on the nature of La Manuela's wish to "torcerlo" a Pancho, "demostrando que no es tan hombre como cree." Even Pancho is tempted, according to Donoso's notes. We read on page 107 of this notebook: "Fascinación de Pancho al sentir que está fascinado con un hombre, sexualmente hablando. Danger y compulsión y asco." This notebook is held with other Donoso papers at the University of Iowa. I thank Professor Daniel Balderston for having facilitated access to these papers.

24. Judith Butler, *Gender Trouble: Feminism and the Subversion of Identity* (New York and London: Routledge, 1990), 7.

CHAPTER 6: REREADING "BOOM" NOVELS
IN THE TWENTY-FIRST CENTURY

1. In Nigeria, which gained independence in 1960, these are the years when Achebe and Soyinka published some of their great works: Achebe's *Things Fall Apart* appeared in 1958, followed by *No Longer at Ease* (1960), *Arrow of God* (1964), and *A Man of the People* (1966). Soyinka wrote the narrative work *The Interpreters* in 1965. In Egypt, Mahfouz's *Cairo Trilogy* came out in the 1950s, and while he remained productive for decades after that, he brought out the acclaimed *Miramar* in 1967, *The Thief and the Dogs* in 1961, and *The Children of Gebelaawi* in 1959. Like the boom novels, these works are characterized by an intense accumulation of historical and geographic materials derived from the cultural universes they represent. Mahfouz, for example, has been called the "Egyptian Balzac."

2. Gilles Deleuze and Félix Guattari, *Anti-Oedipus: Capitalism and Schizophrenia*, trans. R. Hurley, M. Seem, H. Lane (New York: Viking Press, 1977), 62.

3. I use the terms *North* and *South* metonymically, to refer to the first as the metropolitan centers of advanced capitalism in Europe and North America, and to the second as its southern counterpart in Latin America. Needless to say, the "South" includes other continental masses that are not the subject of my study.

4. *Transition* 21 (1932): 115.

5. Ibid.

6. Ibid., 116.

7. *Transition* 27 (1938): 8.

8. In *Transition* 25 (1936): 16.

9. In *Transition* 23 (1935): 52–53.

10. In *Transition* 25 (1936): 23.

11. The title alludes to a text by Breton: "Un Triple V, au nom de la victoire et de la Vue, démultipliée, 'totale,' qui puisse prendre en compte l'avènement de mythes nouveaux." See *André Breton: la beauté convulsive* (Paris: Editions du Centre Georges Pompidou, 1991), 352.

12. In *VVV* 1 (1942): 20. This is in fact the inaugural essay of the journal.

13. Ibid., front page.

14. Ibid., 35.

15. For more on this see James Clifford, "On Ethnographic Surrealism," and "On Collecting Art and Culture," *The Predicament of Culture: Twentieth-Century Ethnography, Literature and Art* (Cambridge, MA: Harvard University Press, 1988), 117–51, 215–52.

16. This may be seen as a dangerous marriage of convenience for artistic forms of cultures hitherto poorly studied, for they entered the metropolitan museums via the rubric of ethnography, and with their status as works of art subordinated to their ethnographic interest. This remains a hotly debated question in the art-historical field.

17. Lucid accounts of it have been formulated by Roberto González Echevarría in *Myth and Archive: A Theory of Latin American Narrative* (Cambridge and London: Cambridge University Press, 1990), and by Jean Franco in *The Decline and Fall of the Lettered City: Latin America in the Cold War* (Cambridge, MA: Harvard University Press, 2002).

18. His article is part of the catalogue for the celebrated exhibition of pre-Columbian art (the first of its kind to receive such popular interest) organized by Georges-Henri Rivière in 1930. See Jean Babelon et al., *L'art précolombien* (Paris: Les Beaux Arts, 1930).

19. For a discussion of the anthropological inflections of *¡Ecue-Yamba-O!*, see Amy Fass Emery, "The 'Anthropological Flaneur' in Paris: *Documents, Bifur* and Collage Culture in Carpentier's *¡Ecue-Yamba-O!*," in her *The Anthropological Imagination in Latin American Literature* (Columbia and London: University of Missouri Press, 1996): 24–42.

20. Another important figure in the emergent field of Mayan Studies at the time was Joseph-Louis Capitan, who was affiliated with the Collège de France.

21. Cited in Susan Buck-Morss, "Benjamin's *Passagenwerk*," *New German Critique* 29 (1983): 211–40.

22. This story appears in "Realismo mágico," in Arturo Uslar Pietri's *Godos, insurgentes y visionarios* (Barcelona: Seix Barral, 1986), 133–40.

23. One might place the boom writing in the larger context of the multiple sources of novelistic power outside Europe or the United States, and which include Arab and African writing (Mahfouz's *The Cairo Trilogy*, for example, belongs to this era). One might then posit a postimperial imaginary within which the Latin American novel of the sixties would be located.

24. The needs of this outside world may be illustrated by the fascination with Tarzan: in the sixties, Tarzan and his books underwent a revival, as "the man in the lion skin [became] a projection of the man in the pinstripe suit or on the assembly line, caught in a system he had not created and could not control." Indeed, the relationship between the English-language novels of the decade and the location of the male subject within the social fabric posits a very different scope for meaningful action in the world: unlike Tarzan, the male characters of the novels written

by Updike, Bellows, or Cheever in the 1960s were only too aware of their very limited powers vis-à-vis the establishment. Tarzan's appeal to primeval energy should not be located too far from the interest in the mysterious and seductive powers of that other "dark" continent—Latin America. See Marianna Torgovnick, *Gone Primitve: Savage Intellects, Modern Minds* (Chicago: University of Chicago Press, 1990), 43.

25. In Alejo Carpentier, *The Lost Steps*, trans. Harriet de Onís (New York: Knopf, 1956), 94. Spanish edition: *Los pasos perdidos* (Madrid: Cátedra, 1985), 160. (Henceforth, citations of this work will appear within parentheses; page numbers in italics refer to the Spanish edition.)

26. See Clifford Geertz's "The Cerebral Savage: On the Work of Claude Lévi-Strauss," *The Interpretation of Cultures* (London: Fontana Press, 1993), 347. Geertz describes the structure of *Tristes Tropiques* as following the quest scheme in the following way: "the precipitate departure from ancestral shores grown familiar, stultifying, and in some uncertain way menacing . . . ; the journey into another, darker world, a magical realm full of surprises, tests and revelations . . . ; and the return, resigned and exhausted, to ordinary existence . . . with a deepened knowledge of reality and the obligation to communicate what one has learned to those who, less adventurous, have stayed behind."

27. Quoted by Geertz, ibid., 347.

28. In Claude Lévi-Strauss, *Tristes tropiques* (New York: Pocket Books, 1973), 45.

29. See Adorno, *Aesthetic Theory*.

30. For the relationship between *El libro de la Gran Sabana* and *Los pasos perdidos*, see Roberto González Echevarria, "The Parting of the Waters," *Alejo Carpentier: The Pilgrim at Home* (Ithaca and London: Cornell University Press, 1977), 155–212.

31. Lévi-Strauss, *Tristes Tropiques*, 469.

32. Ibid.: 473–74.

33. Significantly enough, 1949 is also the date of publication of Asturias's *Hombres de maíz*.

34. In his reading of Carpentier's "De lo real maravilloso americano," Roberto González Echevarría proposes a distinction between two versions of magical realism, "the first, stemming from Roh's book, is phenomenological; the second is ontological and of Surrealist background" (*The Pilgrim at Home*, 113). He locates the ontological version in the surrealist movement given its claims to the existence of a subconscious sphere whose order of reality was more profound than the conscious one. This seems to be a specious distinction; if, as González Echevarría notes, "Carpentier's essay affirms that the marvelous still exists in Latin America" (123), it needs to be located in the codes of traditional, mostly rural-based cultures that the writer appropriates and transforms. From a literary perspective, the mira-

cles that some believe in constitute the rich cultural repertory that he draws on, without necessarily subscribing to their ontological status. Hence it is perhaps unnecessary to pose the question, "Where does Carpentier stand?" (126), since his novels eschew by definition the need for provable truth.

35. Alejo Carpentier, "De lo real maravilloso americano," *Guerra del tiempo* (Santiago: Orbe, 1969), 16–17.

36. Ibid., 18.

37. The following works can be consulted for the vexed question of defining *realismo mágico*: Luis Leal, "El realismo mágico en la literatura hispanoamericana," *Cuadernos Americanos* 26, no. 153 (1967), 200–206; Howard Fraser, "Techniques of Fantasy: Realismo Mágico and Literatura Fantástica," *Chasqui* 1, no. 2 (1972): 20–23; Floyd Merrell, "The Ideal World in Search of Its Reference: An Inquiry into the Underlying Nature of Magical Realism," *Chasqui* 4, no. 2 (1975): 5–17; Lucila Inés Mena, "Hacia una formulación teórica del realismo mágico," *Bulletin Hispanique* 77, 3–4 (1975): 395–407; Enrique Anderson Imbert, *El realismo mágico y otros ensayos* (Caracas: Monte Avila, 1976); Albert Dessau, "Realismo mágico y nueva novela latinoamericana: consideraciones metodológicas e históricas," *Actas del simposio internacional de estudios hispánicos* (Budapest: Editorial de la Academia de Ciencias de Hungría, 1978), 351–58; Juan Barroso, *"Realismo mágico" y "lo real maravilloso" en El reino de este mundo y El siglo de las luces* (Miami: Universal, 1977); Emir Rodríguez Monegal, "Surrealism, Magical Realism, Magical Fiction: A Study in Confusion," in *Surrealismo/surrealismos: Latinoamérica y España*, eds. Peter G. Earle and Germán Gullón (Philadelphia: Center for Inter-American Relations, 1977; Julio Escoto, "Cuenta regresiva al realismo mágico," *Revista de Estudios Hispánicos* 8 (1981): 49–53; Angel Flores, ed. *El realismo mágico en el cuento hispanoamericano* (Mexico City: Premiá, 1985); Graciela Ricci Della Grisa, *Realismo mágico y conciencia mítica en América Latina* (Buenos Aires: Fernando García Cambeiro, 1985); Alexis Márquez Rodríguez, "El surrealismo y su vinculación con el realismo mágico y lo real maravilloso," in *Prosa hispánica de vanguardia*, ed. Fernando Burgos (Madrid: Orígenes, 1986): 77–96; Antonio Planells, "El realismo mágico hispanoamericano ante la crítica," *Chasqui* 17, no. 1 (1988): 9–23; José L. Sánchez Ferrer, *El realismo mágico en la novela hispanoamericana* (Madrid: Anaya, 1990); Julio Barella, "El realismo mágico: un fantasma de la imaginación barroca," *Cuadernos Hispanoamericanos* 481 (1990): 69–78; Gloria Bautista Gutiérrez, *Realismo mágico, cosmos latinoamericano: teoría y práctica* (Bogotá: Latina, 1991); Charles Perrone, "Guimaraes Rosa Through the Prism of Magical Realism," *Tropical Paths: Essays on Modern Brazilian Literature* (New York and London: Garland, 1993); César A. Ayuso, *El realismo mágico* (Valencia, Spain: El Toro de Barro, 1995); Lois Parkinson Zamora and Wendy B. Faris, eds., *Magical Realism: Theory, History, Community* (Durham, NC, and London: Duke University Press, 1995); Edna Aizenberg, "The Famished Road: Magical Realism and the Search for Social Equity,"

Yearbook of Comparative and General Literature 43 (1995): 25–30; Erik Camayd-Freixas, "Magical Realism as Primitivism: An Alternate Verisimilitude," *Romance Languages Annual* 9 (1998): 414–23; Alberto Moreiras, "The End of Magical Realism: José María Arguedas's Passionate Signifier (*El zorro de arriba y el zorro de abajo*)," *Journal of Narrative Technique* 27, no. 1 (1997): 84–112; Abdón Ubidia, "Cinco tesis del 'realismo mágico,'" *Hispamérica* 26, no. 78 (1997): 101–7; Román de la Campa, "Magical Realism and World Literature: A Genre for the Times?" *Revista Canadiense de Estudios Hispánicos* 23, no. 2 (1999): 205–19; and Andrei Kofman, "El problema del realismo mágico en la literatura latinoamericana," *Cuadernos Americanos* 14, nos. 4, 82 (2000): 63–72.

38. In "Isla a su vuelo fugitiva: Carpentier y el realismo mágico," *Revista Iberoamericana* 40, no. 86 (Jan.–Mar. 1974): 18.

39. See Gabriel García Márquez, *Vivir para contarla* (Buenos Aires: Sudamericana, 2002), 438–40.

40. In "The Storyteller," *Illuminations*, trans. Harry Zohn (Glasgow: Fontana/Collins, 1973), 84.

41. For more on this see Fredric Jameson, "Periodizing the Sixties," in *The 60s Without Apology*, eds. S. Sayres, A. Stephanson, S. Aronowitz, and F. Jameson (Minneapolis: University of Minnesota Press, 1984), 178–209.

42. Franco Moretti, *Modern Epic: The World System from Goethe to García Márquez* (London: Verso, 1996), 233.

43. See Michael Taussig, *Shamanism, Colonialism, and the Wild Man: A Study in Terror and Healing* (Chicago and London: University of Chicago Press, 1987), 10.

44. Gabriel García Márquez, *One Hundred Years of Solitude*, trans. Gregory Rabassa (New York: Perennial Classics, 1998), 100. Spanish edition: *Cien años de soledad* (Barcelona: Argos Vergara, 1981), 80. (Henceforth, citations of this work will appear within parentheses; page numbers in italics refer to the Spanish edition.)

45. See Tom Gunning, "The Cinema of Attractions: Early Film, Its Spectator, and the Avant-Garde," in *Early Cinema: Space, Frame and Narrative*, eds. T. Elsaesser and A. Barker (London: BFI, 1990).

46. I am here appropriating Barthes on Sadian eroticism as a combinatory in order to read García Márquez's combinatory of violence and body parts. See Roland Barthes, *Sade, Fourier, Loyola*, trans. R. Miller (New York: Hill & Wang, 1976), 15–37.

47. In a personal communication (July 2004), Gerald Martin has told me that García Márquez actually saw this happen in his childhood.

48. See Angel Rama, *García Márquez: edificación de un arte nacional y popular* (Montevideo: Universidad de la República, 1987). Rama reviews some of García Márquez's predecessors, such as Luis Carlos López and Jorge Félix Fuenmayor. He argues convincingly that the Caribbean coast was able to incorporate the literary renewal swept in by writers such as Faulkner, Joyce, Woolf, or Hemingway precisely because of its relative lack of established traditions. This paucity is, according to Rama, the very platform for its renewal.

49. In *Vivir para contarla*, García Márquez notes that his fictionalized version of the 1928 massacre of the banana plantation workers ended up overpowering the historical record. Having checked press documents and official records, he came to the conclusion that it was simply not possible to ascertain how many people had been killed at the square. Some claimed to remember over one hundred victims; others (*los conformistas*) asserted that there had been no deaths at all. True to the power of his imagination, he avers that he came up with the figure of three thousand in order to be congruent with the epic proportions of the narrative. To his amazement, his fictionalized account slipped into the realm of historical knowledge: "la vida real terminó por hacerme justicia: hace poco, en uno de los aniversarios de la tragedia, el orador de turno en el Senado pidió un minuto de silencio en memoria de los tres mil mártires anónimos sacrificados por la fuerza pública" (*80*). This is an indication of the power exerted by this novel on the political unconscious of its reading public.

50. Fredric Jameson, "The End of Temporality," *Critical Inquiry* 29 (Summer 2003), 701.

51. Ibid., 699.

52. In his *Myth and Archive*, Roberto González Echevarría argues forcibly for the primacy of the anthropological paradigm in the Latin American writing of the twentieth century.

53. The studies that focus on the family in *One Hundred Years of Solitude* are numerous, yet the most lucid one remains Josefina Ludmer's early *Cien años de soledad: una interpretación* (Buenos Aires: Tiempo Contemporáneo, 1972).

54. Gabriel García Márquez, "Nobel Address 1982," http://nobelprize.org/literature/laureates/1982/marquez-lecture-e.html.

55. In Gerald Martin, *Journeys Through the Labyrinth: Latin American Fiction in the Twentieth Century* (London: Verso, 1989), 228. Martin makes a persuasive case in his study, also establishing parallels between the sense of euphoria he detects in the novel—"particularly in its final pages"—and the hopes opened up by the early years of the Cuban Revolution.

56. In Henri Lefebre, *The Production of Space* (Oxford: Blackwell, 1991), 408.

57. Carlos Fuentes, *The Death of Artemio Cruz*, trans. Alfred MacAdam (New York: Farrar, Straus & Giroux, 1991), 307. Spanish edition: *La muerte de Artemio Cruz* (Mexico City: Fondo de Cultura Económica, 1962), 316. (Henceforth, citations of this work will appear within parentheses; page numbers in italics refer to the Spanish edition.)

58. See Paul Julian Smith, *The Body Hispanic: Gender and Sexuality in Spanish and Spanish American Literature* (Oxford: Clarendon Press, 1989), 183ff.

59. Félix Guattari develops this sense of transversal analysis in *Chaosmose* (Paris: Galilée, 1992). He works out the notion in the framework of the *machines sémiotiques* that includes the codes of the "natural" world and their spatial range of operation, the linearity of biological as well as phonological chains, the semiological

linearity of structural meaning, and the "overlinearity" (*surlinéarité*) of a-signifying substances of expression of nondiscursive materiality. Through these myriad indications, Guattari concludes, we reach the following form of being: "Et, là encore, il nous appartient de redécouvrir une façon d'être de l'Être—avant, après, ici et partout ailleurs –, sans être cependant identique à lui-même; un Être processuel, polyphonique, singuralisable aux textures infiniment complexifiables, au gré des vitesses infinies qui animent ses compositions virtuelles" (77). Vargas Llosa's enunciative relativism in *La casa verde* creates the fiction of this kind of semiotic machine, marked by relativity, and by displacements of space, time, and subjectivity.

60. See Mario Vargas Llosa, *Historia secreta de una novela* (Madrid: Tusquets, 1971).

61. In the English-speaking world, Vargas Llosa acknowledges his debt to Faulkner (a forefather claimed by all the boom writers), but we know that Conrad had a powerful influence on Faulkner, Hemingway, and Fitzgerald. So notes Harold Bloom: "The cosmos of *As I Lay Dying*, *The Sun Also Rises*, and *The Great Gatsby* derives from *Heart of Darkness* and *Nostromo*." See Bloom's "Introduction" to his edition of *Joseph Conrad* (New York and Philadelphia: Chelsea House, 1986), 3.

62. See Roland Barthes, *La Préparation du roman I et II: cours et séminaires au Collège de France, 1978–1979 et 1979–1980*, ed. Nathalie Léger (Paris: Seuil/IMEC, 2003), 363ff.

63. Vargas Llosa, *Historia secreta de una novela*, 62.

64. For more on this concept, see Yi-Fu Tuan, *Topophilia: A Study of Environmental Perception, Attitudes, and Values* (New York: Columbia University Press, 1974).

65. Mario Vargas Llosa, *The Green House*, trans. Gregory Rabassa (New York: Harper & Row, 1969), 41. Spanish edition: *La casa verde* (Mexico City: Alfaguara, 2000), 64–65. (Henceforth, citations of this work will appear within parentheses; page numbers in italics refer to the Spanish edition.)

66. For a lucid analysis of the natural scenery in the novel, see Michael Moody, "Paisajes de los condenados: el escenario natural de *La casa verde*," *Revista Iberoamericana* 47, no. 116–17 (1981): 127–36.

67. Deleuze's *Mille Plateaux*, the second volume of *Capitalisme et Schizophrénie* (Paris: Minuit, 1980), offers highly suggestive reflections, eschewing the arboreal configuration for the sake of multiple connections that do not loop back to the one (one city, be it London or Bogotá in the case under consideration). To illustrate this, they choose a comparison borrowed from Ernst Jünger. It is particularly evocative for the study of the novel and its authorial design:

> "Les fils ou les tiges qui meuvent les marionnettes—appelons-les la trame. On pourrait objecter que *sa multiplicité* réside dans la personne de l'acteur qui la projette dans le texte. Soit, mais ses fibres nerveuses forment à leur tour une trame. Et elles plongent à travers la masse grise, la grille, jusque

dans l'indifferencié . . . Le jeu se rapproche de la pure activité des tis-
serands, celle que les mythes attribuent aux Parques et aux Normes." Un
agencement est précisément cette croissance des dimensions dans une
multiplicité qui change nécessairement de nature à mesure qu'elle aug-
mente ses connexions. (15)

68. It is hard to convey the sense of these phrases in English, which has no exact equivalent for *lignes de fuite*. They connote a sense of movement and dispersion away from a center of containment and unity.

69. Edward Said, *Culture and Imperialism* (New York: Alfred Knopf, 1993), 26.

70. Among them, see W. A. Luchting, "Los mitos y lo mitizante en *La casa
verde*," *Mundo Nuevo* 43 (1970): 56–60; G. McMurray, "The Novels of Mario Vargas Llosa," *MLQ* 29, no. 3 (1968): 329–40; J. M. Oviedo, *Mario Vargas Llosa: la invención de una realidad* (Barcelona: Barral, 1970), 143–63; and J. E. Pacheco, "Lectura de Vargas Llosa," *RUM* 22, no. 8 (Apr. 1968): 27–33.

71. A helpful study of the narrative design can be read in J. M. Oviedo's book,
cited above. To remind readers already familiar with the novel, the five story lines
are the following: (1) Anselmo's foundation of the brothel in Piura, (2) the *inconquistables* in Piura, (3) the Sargento Lituma and Bonifacia in Santa María de
Nieva, (4) Jum, the Urakusas, and the rubber trade, and (5) Fushía the smuggler
and Aquilino along the Amazon river system.

72. Vargas Llosa, *Historia secreta de una novela*, 56.

73. There is a fascinating story (marvelously told by Michael Taussig), en-
veloping Roger Casement and his involvement in both the Congo and the Putumayo rivers as British consul. Casement denounced the Congo atrocities to the
British Foreign Office. In that capacity, he met Conrad in 1890. Conrad wrote
about him to his dear Robert Cunnighame Graham: "I have always thought that
some particle of Las Casas' soul had found refuge in his indefatigable body." Casement offers a link between the two worlds of atrocities: he wrote a document to
Sir Edward Grey in 1913, in which he recorded the brutality he had witnessed in
the rubber belt:

> The number of Indians killed either by starvation—often purposively
> brought about by the destruction of crops over whole districts or inflicted
> as a form of death penalty on individuals who failed to bring in their quota
> of rubber—or by deliberate murder by bullet, fire, beheading, or flogging
> to death, and accompanied by a variety of atrocious tortures, during the
> course of these 12 years, in order to extort these 4,000 tons of rubber, can-
> not have been less than 30,000, and possibly came to many more.

See Roger Casement, "Correspondence Respecting the Treatment of British Colonial
Subjects and Native Indians Employed in the Collection of Rubber in the Putumayo
District," *House of Commons Sessional Papers* 68 (Feb. 14, 1912–Mar. 1913), 64–66.
Quoted in Michael Taussig, *Shamanism, Colonialism, and the Wild Man: A Study in*

Terror and Healing (Chicago and London: University of Chicago Press, 1987), 20. I am indebted to Michael Taussig for his research into Roger Casement and Julio César Arana. As to Conrad's friend Robert Cunninghame Graham, he furthers the network of connections with Latin America: not only did he spend a good part of his youth in his family's cattle ranch in Argentina (where he was known as "don Roberto," a name Conrad liked to use in his correspondence with him), but he also wrote several books about Latin American figures such as Antonio Conselheiro, Valdivia, Solano López, Páez, Cortés, and Hernando de Soto. Like Casement—an Irishman—and Conrad, Cunninghame Graham was an outsider to the English system, not only because of the years he spent abroad but also because he struggled for Scottish independence and for workers' civil and economic rights. The latter causes resulted in several prison terms. These three men were able to expose the darker side of the imperial enterprise by straddling several areas of the globe and attaining a vision that was conditioned by the sites in which it was located. When it was Conrad's turn to write about South America in *Nostromo* (1904), he wrote about mining, not about rubber. And yet the same relationships between greed, external financial powers, and internal political struggles rule the fictive universe. Costaguana (based, it is believed, on Conrad's trip to Colombia in 1877) bears in its name the trace of the word *guano*, which, like rubber, controlled the fate of Peru's economy at the end of the nineteenth century and the beginning of the twentieth.

74. Piura, the other economic center of *The Green House*, was equally dependent on the ups and downs of the world economy. Its importance as a cotton-producing area grew during the American Civil War, and again in the early years of the twentieth century. Cotton export relied on British-built and British-controlled railroads. The poverty in the Mangachería district of Piura (in which the *inconquistables* flaunt their disenfranchisement in lives of aimless debauchery) can be explained by the unemployment generated by the arrival of mechanized cotton production. A helpful account of the economic history of both areas can be found in M. J. Fenwick, *Dependency Theory and Literary Analysis: Reflections on Vargas Llosa's The Green House* (Minneapolis: Institute for the Study of Ideologies and Literatures, 1981). See especially chap. 2, "The Historical Background for *The Green House*."

75. A full account of these revelations and their impact can be read in Taussig's *Shamanism, Colonialism, and the Wild Man*. See esp. chaps. 1–4.

76. Vargas Llosa, *Historia secreta de una novela*, 46.

77. This was, in good measure, due to Arana's exploits: in 1899 he had purchased the land north of Iquitos, which is where the Peru-Colombia border disputes existed. Arana had started his empire in the Manaus area of Brazil, so that his holdings spanned three national territories.

78. See J. Jones, "Vargas Llosa's *Mangachería*: The Pleasures of Community," in *Revista de Estudios Hispánicos* 20, no. 1 (1986): 77–89.

79. See Sara Castro-Klarén, "Fragmentation and Alienation in *La casa verde*," *MLN* 87 (1972): 286–99. In her "Memoria, narración y repetición: la narrativa hispanoamericana en la época de la cultura de masas," in A. Rama, D. Viñas, et al., eds. *Más allá del Boom: literatura y mercado* (Mexico City: Marcha, 1981): 111–43, Jean Franco notes a parallel between Fushía's island, its demise, and the failures of Artemio Cruz and Larsen (in Onetti's *Juntacadáveres*), observing the failure of the spirit of individual enterprise common to several of the novels of the boom. Her conclusion speaks to precisely the kind of worldview I am attempting to address: "Así pues, el proyecto individual, esencialmente discontinuo y fragmentado, se plasma en el vacío dejado por los fracasos del capitalismo dependiente y por la desaparición de las viejas comunidades cuyas huellas persisten todavía en la cultura y en la imaginación popular" (120).

80. *Primera Plana* 308 (Nov. 19, 1968): 109–10.

81. In the *Cuaderno de bitácora de Rayuela*, edited by Ana María Barrenechea (Buenos Aires: Sudamericana, 1983) we learn that the initial plan was to begin the novel in Buenos Aires. The switch did not affect the "here" of Buenos Aires, which remained as the vantage point.

82. The role of Paris in the Argentine political and literary imagination is discussed in David Viñas, *De Sarmiento a Cortázar* (Buenos Aires: Siglo XXI, 1971).

83. In "Introduction à l'analyse structurale du récit," *L'Analyse Structurale du recit, Communications* 8 (Paris: Seuil, 1981).

84. Michel de Certeau, *L'Invention du quotidien: 1. Arts de faire* (Paris: Gallimard, 1990), 155.

85. Ibid., 157.

86. Héctor Zampaglione has retraced Oliveira's itinerary and photographed the places mentioned in the novel. The result is an entire book of beautifully photographed Parisian streets, boulevards, cafés, squares, bridges, and parks. Many of them are in the Left Bank, but the range of locations is varied, and it covers points north, south, east, and west. No such photographic re-creation would be possible with actual Buenos Aires locations in *Hopscotch*'s geography. See *El Paris de Rayuela: homenaje a Cortazar* (Barcelona: Lunwerg, 1997).

87. See her *Writing Paris: Urban Topographies of Desire in Contemporary Latin American Fiction* (Albany: State University of New York Press, 1999). Chapter Two offers a very suggestive reading of Paris in Cortázar's short fiction.

88. Cortázar, *Cuaderno de bitácora*, 169.

89. Julio Cortázar, *Hopscotch*, trans. Gregory Rabassa (New York: Pantheon Books, 1966), 510–11. Spanish edition: *Rayuela* (Madrid: Punto de Lectura, 2002), 647. (Henceforth, citations of this work will appear within parentheses; page numbers in italics refer to the Spanish edition.)

90. Critics have given considerable attention to Cortázar's Paris as the locus of desire. In the short fiction, Paris is a space marker (as is the case of "Las babas del

diablo," "El ídolo de las cícladas," or "La autopista del sur"), or it marks one of the poles of narrative tension, as in the case of "El otro cielo."

91. In *Postmodernity in Latin America: The Argentine Paradigm* (Durham, NC, and London: Duke University Press, 1994), Santiago Colás proposes a daring connection between the leap Oliveira may be taking at the end of the second part, in Chapter 56, and Che Guevara's *foco* theory: "During the period of the Cuban revolutionary war itself, what was to be theorized as *foquismo* or *foco* theory best embodies the kind of material participation—the leap—that *Rayuela* seems to put forth" (68). Without subscribing to the particulars of this formulation, I agree that there is a sense of utopian search, an almost revolutionary consciousness that was to be developed later on in Cortázar's life as a writer.

92. In light of Chapter 79, I deliberately avoid the location of the "lectora hembra."

93. In a personal communication, Aurora Bernárdez has told me that Cortázar worked on the novel on the basis of disperse texts that were gathered together by the capacious generic protocols of the novel. Thanks to Ana María Barrenechea's edition of the *Cuaderno de bitácora de Rayuela* we also know that the genesis of the episode narrated in Chapter 41 is a text entitled "La araña" that was left out of *Rayuela* and published separately in *Revista Iberoamericana*, 84–85 (July–Dec. 1973): 388–98. In it Cortázar notes: "existían ya diversos textos breves . . . que estaban buscando aglutinarse en torno a un relato" (397). The structure of the novel has been charted by Ana María Barrenechea in her "La estructura de *Rayuela* de Julio Cortázar," in *La nueva novela latinoamericana*, ed. J. Lafforgue (Buenos Aires: Paidós, 1972), 222–47.

94. See Gabriela Nouzeilles, "La rayuela del sexo según Cortázar," in *Cánones literarios masculinos y relecturas transculturales*, ed. Ileana Rodríguez (Barcelona: Anthropos, 2001), 63–83. The scenes of sexual violence involving Oliveira, La Maga, and Pola make for difficult reading unless one were to buy into the notion that women's bliss depends on male aggression.

CONCLUSION

1. Franco, *Decline and Fall of the Lettered City*, 108.

2. See Jorge Castañeda, *La utopía desarmada: intrigas, dilemas y promesa de la izquierda en América Latina* (Mexico City: Joaquín Mortiz/Planeta, 1993), 12.

3. Alberto Fuguet and Sergio Gómez, eds. *McOndo* (Barcelona: Grijalbo Mondadori, 1996).

4. This deformation is explained thus by the editors: "Sobre el título de este volumen de cuentos no valen dobles interpretaciones. Puede ser considerado una ironía irreverente al arcángel San Gabriel, como también un merecido tributo" (14).

Bibliography

Adorno, Theodor W. *Aesthetic Theory*. Ed. and trans. Robert Hullot-Kentor. Minneapolis: University of Minnesota Press, 1997.

Adoum, José Enrique. "La Revolución Cubana: cuando lo insólito se vuelve cotidiano." In *Cultura y revolución: a cuarenta años de 1959*, 25–27. Ed. Eduardo Heras León. Havana: Casa de las Américas, 1999.

Aguayo Quezada, Sergio. *1968: los archivos de la violencia*. Mexico City: Grijalbo, 1998.

Aizenberg, Edna. "*The Famished Road*: Magical Realism and the Search for Social Equity." *Yearbook of Comparative and General Literature* 43 (1995): 25–30.

Alascio Cortázar, Miguel. *Viaje alrededor de una silla*. Buenos Aires: La Ciudad, 1971.

Alazraqui, Jaime. "Imaginación e historia en Julio Cortázar." In *Hacia Cortázar: aproximaciones a su obra*. Barcelona: Anthropos, 1994.

Alone (Hernán Díaz Arrieta). *Historia personal de la literatura chilena: desde Don Alonso de Ercilla hasta Pablo Neruda*. Santiago de Chile: Zig-Zag, 1954.

Alonso, Amado. "Borges narrador." *Sur* 14 (Nov. 1935): 105–15.

Alvarado, Maite, and Renata Rocco-Cuzzi. "*Primera Plana*: el nuevo discurso periodístico de la década del '60." *Punto de Vista* 22 (1984): 27–30.

Amar Sánchez, Ana María. "Las voces de los otros: el género de no-ficción en Elena Poniatowska." *Filología* 25, no. 1–2 (1990): 161–74.

Amícola, José. *Sobre Cortázar*. Buenos Aires: Escuela, 1969.

Anderson, Danny J. "Creating Cultural Prestige: Editorial Joaquín Mortiz." *Latin American Research Review* 31, no. 2 (1996): 3–41.

Anderson, Jon Lee. *Che Guevara: A Revolutionary Life*. London: Bantam, 1997.

Anderson, Perry. *In the Tracks of Historical Materialism*. Chicago: University of Chicago Press, 1984.

Anderson Imbert, Enrique. *El realismo mágico y otros ensayos*. Caracas: Monte Avila, 1976.

———. *Megáfono* 11 (Aug. 1933): 25–30.

Antonioni, Michelangelo. *Blow Up*. Film. Burbank, CA: Warner Brothers Entertainment, distributed by Warner Home Video, 2004.

Araujo, Ana Maria. *Tupamaras: Des Femmes de L'Uruguay*. Paris: Des Femmes, 1980.

Arendt, Hannah. *Between Past and Future*. New York: Viking, 1968.

———. *On Revolution*. New York: Viking, 1963.

Ariès, Philippe. *L'Enfant et la vie familiale sous l'Ancien Régime*. Paris: Tlon, 1960.

Aroche Parra, Miguel. *53 poemas del 68 mexicano*. Mexico City: Editora y Distribuidora Nacional, 1972.

Aronne-Amestoy, Lisa. "El umbral prohibido: relectura de Octavio Paz." *Quaderni Ibero-Americani* 59–60 (1985–86): 93–104.

Asturias, Miguel Angel. *Hombres de maíz*. Buenos Aires: Losada, 1949.

Avelar, Idelber. *The Untimely Present: Postdictatorial Latin American Fiction and the Task of Mourning*. Durham, NC: Duke University Press, 1999.

Ayuso, César A. *El realismo mágico*. Valencia, Spain: El Toro de Barro, 1995.

Babelon, Jean, et al. *L'art précolombien*. Paris: Les Beaux Arts, 1930.

Baham, Gilberto. *Reflexiones de un testigo*. Mexico City: Lenasa, 1969.

Baker, Robert. "Historical Time, Narrative Time and the Ambiguities of Nostalgia in *Cien años de soledad*." *Siglo* 13, no. 2 (1995): 137–59.

Banco Nacional de Comercio Exterior. *Mexico 1968: Facts, Figures and Trends*. Mexico City: Banco Nacional de Comercio Exterior, 1968.

Barbey, Bruno, et al. *Mai 68 ou l'imagination au pouvoir*. Paris: La Différence, 1998.

Barella, Julio. "El realismo mágico: un fantasma de la imaginación barroca." *Cuadernos Hispanoamericanos* 481 (1990): 69–78.

Barradas, Efraín. "El Che, narrador: apuntes para un estudio de *Pasajes de la guerra revolucionaria*." In *Literatures in Transition: The Many Voices of the Caribbean Area*, 137–45. Ed. Rose S. Minc. Gaithersburg, MD: Hispamérica and Montclair State College, 1982.

Barral, Carlos. *Años de penitencia*. Madrid: Alianza, 1975.

———. *Los años sin excusa*. Barcelona: Barral, 1978.

———. *Cuando las horas veloces*. Barcelona: Tusquets, 1988.

Barraza Jara, E. "Las dos escrituras en *El jardín de al lado*, de José Donoso." *Estudios Filológicos* 25 (1990): 131–41.

Barrenechea, Ana María. "La estructura de *Rayuela* de Julio Cortázar." In *La nueva novela latinoamericana*, 222–47. Ed. J. Lafforgue. Buenos Aires: Paidós, 1972.

———. *La expresión de la irrealidad en la obra de Borges*. Mexico City: El Colegio de Mexico, 1957.

Barroso, Juan. *"Realismo mágico" y "lo real maravilloso" en El reino de este mundo y El siglo de las luces*. Miami: Universal, 1977.

Barthes, Roland. *La Chambre claire: note sur la photographie*. Paris: Gallimard, 1980.

———. "The Death of the Author." In *Image, Music, Text*, 142–48. Trans. Stephen Heath. New York: Hill & Wang, 1977.

———. "Intoduction à l'analyse structurale du récit." In *L'Analyse Structurale du récit, Communications 8*. Paris: Seuil, 1981.

———. *Mythologies.* Trans. A. Lavers. St. Albans, Granada: Paladin, 1973.

———. *La Préparation du roman I et II: cours et séminaires au Collège de France, 1978–1979 et 1979–1980.* Ed. Nathalie Léger. Paris: Seuil/IMEC, 2003.

———. *Sade, Fourier, Loyola.* Trans. R. Miller. New York: Hill & Wang, 1976.

Bastos, María Luisa. *Borges ante la crítica argentina (1923–1960).* Buenos Aires: Hispamérica, 1974.

Bataille, Georges. *Inner Experience.* Trans. Leslie Anne Boldt. Albany: State University of New York Press, 1988.

———. "L'Amérique disparue." *Cahiers de la République des letters, des sciences et des arts,* numéro consacré a l'art précolombien (Paris: Les Beaux Arts, 1928).

Bautista Gutiérrez, Gloria. *Realismo mágico, cosmos latinoamericano: teoría y práctica.* Bogotá: Latina, 1991.

Bell, Daniel. *The Cultural Contradictions of Capitalism.* New York: Basic Books, 1976.

———. "The Post-Industrial Society." In *Technology and Social Change,* 44–59. Ed. E. Ginzberg. New York: Columbia University Press, 1964.

Bell, Michael. *Gabriel García Márquez: Solitude and Solidarity.* London: Macmillan, 1993.

Benedetti, Mario. *Letras del continente mestizo.* Montevideo: Arca, 1974.

Benjamin, Walter. *Illuminations.* Ed. Hannah Arendt. Trans. Harry Zohn. London: Fontana/Collins, 1977.

———. "Petite histoire de la photographie." In *Poésie et révolution,* 15–36. Trans. M. de Gandillac. Paris: Ed. Denoel, 1971.

———. *Reflections.* Ed. Peter Demetz. Trans. E. Jephcott. New York: Harcourt Brace Jovanovich, 1978.

Berger, Mark. *Under Northern Eyes: Latin American Studies and U.S. Hegemony in the Americas 1898–1990.* Bloomington: Indiana University Press, 1995.

Beverley, John, and Hugo Achugar, eds. *La voz del otro: testimonio, subalternidad y verdad narrativa.* Guatemala City: Universidad Rafael Landívar, 2002.

Bhabha, Homi. "Preface." In *The Wretched of the Earth,* by Frantz Fanon. Trans. Richard Philcox. New York: Grove Press, 2004.

Blanchot, Maurice. *Le Livre à venir.* Paris: Gallimard, 1959.

Blanco Moheno, Roberto. *Tlatelolco: historia de una infamia.* Mexico City: Diana, 1969.

Bloom, Harold, ed. *Gabriel García Márquez.* New York: Chelsea House, 1989.

———. "Introduction." In *Joseph Conrad.* New York: Chelsea House, 1986.

Blumenberg, Hans. *The Legitimacy of the Modern Age.* Cambridge, MA: MIT Press, 1985.

Boldy, Steven. *The Novels of Julio Cortázar.* Cambridge, UK: Cambridge University Press, 1980.

Borges, Jorge Luis. *Ficciones.* Buenos Aires: Sur, 1944.

———. *Ficciones.* Trans. Anthony Kerrigan. New York: Grove Press, 1962.

Bourdieu, Pierre. *Distinction: A Social Critique of the Judgement of Taste*. Trans. Richard Nice. London: Routledge & Kegan Paul, 1984.

―――. *La domination masculine*. Paris: Seuil, 1998.

―――. *The Field of Cultural Production*. Trans. Randal Johnson. New York: Columbia University Press, 1993.

―――. *Masculine Domination*. Trans. Richard Nice. Stanford, CA: Stanford University Press, 2001.

Bracamonte, Jorge. *"Rayuela y La Casa verde*: teorías del texto, teorías de lo real." *Revista de Crítica Literaria Latinoamericana* 27, no. 54 (2001): 91–109.

Breton, André. *André Breton: la beauté convulsive*. Paris: Editions du Centre Georges Pompidou, 1991.

Brooks, Brian. "Self-distributed 'Guiana 1838' Shatters BOT Record; 'Motorcycle Diaries' also B.O. Tour de Force" (Sept. 29, 2004). Available at http://www.indiewire.com/biz/biz_040929boxoffice.html.

Brown, Colin. "The Motorcycle Diaries: Walter Salles' stirringly compassionate road movie is far more than a conventional topic." *Screen International* (Jan. 23, 2004): 34.

Brustein, Robert. *Revolution as Theater: Notes on the New Radical Left*. New York: Liveright, 1971.

Buck-Morss, Susan. "Benjamin's *Passagenwerk*." *New German Critique* 29 (1983): 211–40.

Bunck, Julie Marie. *Fidel Castro and the Quest for a Revolutionary Culture in Cuba*. University Park: Pennsylvania State University Press, 1994.

Butler, Judith. *Gender Trouble: Feminism and the Subversion of Identity*. New York: Routledge, 1990.

Cabrera Infante, Guillermo. "Desde el Swinging London." *Mundo Nuevo* 14 (Aug. 1967): 45–53.

―――. *Mea Cuba*. Trans. Kenneth Hall with Guillermo Cabrera Infante. New York: Farrar, Straus & Giroux, 1994.

Cahiers du cinema (Paris: l'Etoile, 1951–).

Camayd-Freixas, Erik. "Magical Realism as Primitivism: An Alternate Verisimilitude." *Romance Languages Annual* 9 (1998): 414–23.

Camp, Roderic A. *Intellectuals and the State in Twentieth-Century Mexico*. Austin: University of Texas Press, 1985.

Campa, Román de la. *"Memorias de subdesarrollo*: novela/texto/discurso." *Revista Iberoamericana* 56, no. 152–53 (July 1990): 1039–54.

Campos, Marco Antonio. *Poemas sobre el movimiento estudiantil de 1968*. Mexico City: Pueblo Nuevo, 1980.

Carpentier, Alejo. "América ante la joven literatura europea." *Carteles* (June 28, 1931). Reprinted in *La literatura latinoamericana en vísperas de un nuevo siglo y otros ensayos*, 51–57. Mexico City: Siglo XXI, 1981.

―――. *The Lost Steps*. Trans. Harriet de Onís. New York: Knopf, 1956.

————. *Los pasos perdidos*. Madrid: Cátedra, 1985.

————. "De lo real maravilloso americano." In *Guerra del tiempo*. Santiago de Chile: Orbe, 1969.

————. *El reino de este mundo*. Mexico City: Edición y Distribución Iberoamericana de Publicaciones, 1949.

Casa de las Américas (Havana: Casa de las Américas, 1960–).

Casanova, Pascale. *The World Republic of Letters*. Cambridge, MA: Harvard University Press, 2004.

Casement, Roger. "Correspondence Respecting the Treatment of British Colonial Subjects and Native Indians Employed in the Collection of Rubber in the Putumayo District." *House of Commons Sessional Papers* (Feb. 14, 1912–Mar. 1913): 64–66.

Castañeda, Jorge. *Compañero: The Life and Death of Che Guevara*. London: Bloomsbury, 1997.

————. *La utopia desarmada: intrigas, dilemas y promesa de la izquierda en América Latina*. Mexico City: Joaquín Mortiz/Planeta, 1993.

Castillo, Herberto. *Libertad bajo protesta*. Mexico City: Federación Editorial Mexicana, 1973.

Castro, Fidel. *Fidel Castro y la Revolución Cubana*. Mexico City: Era, 1975.

————. *La Historia me absolverá*. Gijón, Cuba: Júcar, 1984.

Castro-Klarén, Sara. "Fragmentation and Alienation in *La casa verde*," *MLN* 87 (1972): 286–99.

————. "The Space of Solitude in *Cien años de soledad*." *Working Paper* 18. Washington, DC: Wilson Center, 1978.

Caute, David. *The Year of the Barricades: A Journey through 1968*. New York: Harper & Row, 1988.

Celis, Roger E. "Erotismo y muerte: Georges Bataille y Julio Cortázar." *Chasqui* 31, no. 1 (May 2002): 38–49.

Certeau, Michel de. *L'Invention du quotidien: 1. Arts de faire*. Paris: Gallimard, 1990.

————. *La Prise de la parole: pour une nouvelle culture*. Paris: Desclée de Brouwer, 1968.

————. *La Prise de la parole*. Paris: Seuil, 1994.

Chatzivasileiou, Litsa. "Rereading *Rayuela*: Hypergraphy, Hermaphrodism, and Schizophrenia." *Revista Canadiense de Estudios Hispánicos* 25, no. 3 (Spring 2001): 397–423.

Clifford, James. *The Predicament of Culture: Twentieth-Century Ethnography, Literature and Art*. Cambridge, MA: Harvard University Press, 1988.

Cócaro, Nicolás et al. "El joven Cortázar." Reviewed by Miguel Herráez. *Cuadernos Hispanoamericanos* 583 (Jan. 1999): 141–43.

Cohn, Dorrit. *The Distinction of Fiction*. Cambridge, MA: Harvard University Press, 1999.

Colás, Santiago. *Postmodernity in Latin America: The Argentine Paradigm*. Durham, NC: Duke University Press, 1994.

Coleman, Peter. *The Liberal Conspiracy: The Congress for Cultural Freedom and the Struggle for the Mind of Postwar Europe.* New York: Free Press, 1989.

Collazos, Oscar, Julio Cortázar, and Mario Vargas Llosa. *Literatura en la revolución y revolución en la literatura (polémica).* Mexico City: Siglo XXI, 1970.

Colombí de Albero, Beatriz. "La casa de Julio Cortázar." *Inti* 55–56 (Spring–Fall 2002): 165–66.

Conrad, Joseph. *Heart of Darkness.* London: Penguin, 1989.

———. *Nostromo.* New York: Harper, 1904.

Cortázar, Julio. *All Fires the Fire.* Trans. Suzanne Jill Levine. New York: Pantheon Books, 1973.

———. "La araña." *Revista Iberoamericana,* 84–85 (July–Dec. 1973): 388–98.

———. *Argentina: años de alambradas culturales.* Buenos Aires: Muchnik, 1984.

———. *Cartas, 1937–1963.* Ed. Aurora Bernárdez. Buenos Aires: Alfaguara, 2000.

———. "Cartas 1, 1937–1963; Cartas 2, 1964–1968; Cartas 3, 1969–1983." Ed. Aurora Bernárdez. Reviewed by Carles Alvarez Garriga. *Cuadernos Hispanoamericanos* (Jan. 2001): 125–28.

———. "Cartas desconocidas de Julio Cortázar." Ed. Mignon Domínguez. Reviewed by Miguel Herráez. *Cuadernos Hispanoamericanos* 583 (Jan. 1999): 141–43.

———. *Cuaderno de bitácora de Rayuela.* Ed. Ana María Barrenechea. Buenos Aires: Sudamericana, 1983.

———. *Cuentos completos.* Madrid: Alfaguara, 1994.

———. *Deshoras.* Buenos Aires: Nueva Imagen, 1983.

———. *End of the Game and Other Stories.* Trans. Paul Blackburn. New York: Pantheon Books, 1967.

———. "El escritor y su quehacer en América Latina." Seminario sobre Política Cultural y Liberación Democrática en América Latina, Sitges, Spain, 1982.

———. *El examen.* Buenos Aires: Sudamericana, 1986.

———. *Fantomás contra los vampiros multinacionales.* Buenos Aires: Gente Sur, 1989.

———. *Final del juego.* Buenos Aires: Sudamericana, 1976.

———. "Homenaje a una torre de fuego." In *Julio Cortázar al término del polvo y el sudor.* Montevideo: Biblioteca de Marcha, 1987.

———. *Hopscotch.* Trans. Gregory Rabassa. New York: Pantheon Books, 1966.

———. "Julio Cortázar: el escritor y sus armas políticas" (Diálogo con Francisco Urondo). *Panorama* (Buenos Aires; Nov. 24, 1970): 44–50.

———. *Libro de Manuel.* Barcelona: Edhasa, 1977.

———. *A Manual for Manuel.* Trans. Gregory Rabassa. New York: Pantheon Books, 1978.

———. "Mensaje al hermano." *Casa de las Américas* 8, no. 46 (1968): 6.

———. *Nicaragua tan violentamente dulce.* Managua: Nueva Nicaragua/Monimbo, 1983.

———. *Los premios.* Madrid: Alfaguara, 1983.

———. *Rayuela.* Buenos Aires: Sudamericana, 1963.

———. *Rayuela*. Madrid: Punto de Lectura, 2002.

———. *Textos políticos*. Barcelona: Biblioteca Letras del Exilio, 1985.

———. *Todos los fuegos el fuego*. Madrid: Alfaguara, 1984.

———. *Ultimo round*. Mexico City: Siglo XXI, 1969.

———. *The Winners*. Trans. Elaine Kerrigan. New York: Pantheon Books, 1965.

Damrosch, David. *What Is World Literature?* Princeton, NJ: Princeton University Press, 2003.

De la Campa, Román. "Magical Realism and World Literature: A Genre for the Times?" *Revista Canadiense de Estudios Hispánicos* 23, no. 2 (1999): 205–19.

de Man, Paul. *Blindness and Insight: Essays in the Rhetoric of Contemporary Criticism*. Minneapolis: University of Minnesota Press, 1983.

———. "A Modern Master." *New York Review of Books* (Nov. 19, 1964).

Debord, Guy. *La Societé du Spectacle*. Paris: Editions Champ Libre, 1971.

Deleuze, Gilles. *Masochism: An Interpretation of Coldness and Cruelty*. Trans. J. McNeil. New York: George Brazilier, 1971.

———. *Mille Plateaux*. Paris: Minuit, 1980.

———, and Félix Guattari. *Anti-Oedipus: Capitalism and Schizophrenia*. Trans. R. Hurley, M. Seem, and H. Lane. New York: Viking, 1977.

Derrida, Jacques. "Force of Law: The 'Mystical Foundations of Authority.'" *Cardozo Law Review* 11, no. 5–6 (1990): 919–1045.

———. *Specters of Marx: The State of the Debt, the Work of Mourning, and the New International*. Trans. Peggy Kamuf. New York: Routledge, 1994.

Desnoes, Edmundo. *Memorias de subdesarrollo*. Buenos Aires: Galerna, 1968.

Dessau, Albert. "Realismo mágico y nueva novela latinoamericana: consideraciones metodológicas e históricas." In *Actas del simposio internacional de estudios hispánicos*, 351–58. Budapest: Academy de Sciences of Hungary, 1978.

Deveny, John J., and J. M. Marcos. "Women and Society in *Cien años de soledad*." *Journal of Popular Culture* 22, no. 1 (Summer 1988): 83–90.

"Los dichos y los hechos." *Marcha* no. 1265 (Mar. 11, 1966): 29.

Donoso, José. *The Boom in Spanish American Literature: A Personal History*. Trans. Gregory Kolovakos. New York: Columbia University Press, 1977.

———. *The Garden Next Door*. Trans. Hardie St. Martin. New York: Grove Press, 1992.

———. *Historia personal del "boom."* Barcelona: Anagrama, 1972.

———. *Historia personal del "boom."* Barcelona: Anagrama, 1987.

———. *Historia personal del "boom."* Santiago de Chile: Alfaguara, 1998.

———. *El jardín de al lado*. Barcelona: Seix Barral, 1981.

———. *Notebook*. University of Iowa papers, Iowa City.

Donoso, María Pilar. "El 'boom' doméstico." In *Historia personal del "boom,"* by José Donoso. Santiago de Chile: Alfaguara, 1998.

Dorfman, Ariel, and Armand Mattelart. *Para leer al Pato Donald: comunicación de masa y colonialismo*. Mexico City: Siglo XXI, 1972.

Earle, Peter. *Gabriel García Márquez: el escritor y la crítica*. Madrid: Taurus, 1981.

———. "Utopía, Universópolis, Macondo." *Hispanic Review* 50, no. 2 (1982): 143–57.

Echeverría, L. N. "El exilio en *El jardín de al lado* de Donoso." *Confluencia* 10, no. 2 (1995): 67–75.

Efrén González, Ricardo. *El Che en la revolución cubana*. Havana: Ediciones del Ministerio de la Industria Azucarera, 1966.

Eilberg-Schwartz, Howard. "Homoeroticism and the Father-God: An Unthought in Freud's *Moses and Monotheism*." *American Imago* 51, no. 1 (1994): 127–59.

Emery, Amy Fass. "The 'Anthropological Flaneur' in Paris: *Documents, Bifur*, and Collage Culture in Carpentier's *¡Ecue-Yamba-O!*" In *The Anthropological Imagination in Latin American Literature*. Columbia: University of Missouri Press, 1996.

Enzensberger, Hans Magnus. *Civil Wars: From L.A. to Bosnia*. New York: New Press, 1994.

Erikson, Erik H. *Identity: Youth and Crisis*. New York: Norton, 1968.

———. *Young Man Luther: A Study in Psychoanalysis and History*. New York: Norton, 1962.

Escoto, Julio. "Cuenta regresiva al realismo mágico." *Revista de Estudios Hispánicos* 8 (1981): 49–53.

Etiemble, René. *Littérature dégagéé, 1942–1953*. Paris: Gallimard, 1955.

———. "Un homme à tuer: Jorge Luis Borges, cosmopolite." *Les Temps modernes* 83 (Sept. 1952).

Fanon, Frantz. *Les Damnés de la terre*. Paris: Maspero, 1961.

Farías, Victor. *Los manuscritos de Melquíades: Cien años de soledad; burguesía latinoamericana y dialéctica de la reproducción ampliada de negación*. Frankfurt: Verlag Klaus Dieter Vervuert, 1981.

Fenwick, M. J. *Dependency Theory and Literary Analysis: Reflections on Vargas Llosa's The Green House*. Minneapolis: Institute for the Study of Ideologies and Literatures, 1981.

Ferguson, Adam. *An Essay on the History of Civil Society*. Ed. Fania Oz-Salzberger. Cambridge, UK: Cambridge University Press, 1995.

Fernández, Jesse. "La ética del trabajo y la acumulación de la riqueza en *Cien años de soledad*." *Hispamérica* 13, no. 37 (1984): 73–79.

Fernández Retamar, Roberto. "On Cuban Literature, 1959–81." *Pacific Quarterly* 8, no. 3 (1983): 106–9.

Ferry, Luc, and Alain Renaut. *La Pensée 68: essai sur l'anti-humanisme contemporain*. Paris: Gallimard, 1985.

———. *68–86: itinéraires de l'individu*. Paris: Gallimard, 1987.

Feuer, Lewis. *The Conflict of Generations: The Character and Significance of Student Movements*. New York: Basic Books, 1969.

Fiddian, Robin, ed. *García Márquez*. London and New York: Longman, 1995.

Flores, Angel, ed. *El realismo mágico en el cuento hispanoamericano*. Mexico City: Premiá, 1985.

Flores Olea, Víctor. *La rebelión estudiantil y la sociedad contemporánea*. Mexico City: UNAM, 1973.

Foster, David William. "Latin American Documentary Narrative." *PMLA* 99, no. 1 (1984): 41–55.

Foucault, Michel. *Les Mots et les choses*. Paris: Gallimard, 1966.

———. *The Order of Things: An Archaeology of the Human Sciences*. New York: Vintage Books, 1973.

———. *Remarks on Marx: Conversations with Duccio Trombadori*. Trans. R. J. Goldstein and J. Cascaito. New York: Semiotext(e), 1991.

———. *Surveiller et punir: naissance de la prison*. Paris: Gallimard, 1975.

———. "What Is an Author." In *Textual Strategies*, 141–60. Ed. Josué V. Harari. Ithaca, NY: Cornell University Press, 1979.

Franco, Jean. *An Introduction to Latin American Literature*. London: Cambridge University Press, 1969.

———. "The Critique of the Pyramid and Mexican Narrative after 1968." In *Latin American Fiction Today*, 49–60. Ed. Rose Minc. Takoma Park, MD: Hispamérica, 1982.

———. *The Decline and Fall of the Lettered City: Latin America in the Cold War*. Cambridge, MA: Harvard University Press, 2002.

———. "Memoria, narración y repetición: la narrativa hispanoamericana en la época de la cultura de masas." In *Más allá del boom: literatura y mercado*, 111–43. Eds. A. Rama et al. Mexico City: Marcha, 1981.

———. *The Modern Culture of Latin America: Society and the Artist*. London: Pall Mall, 1967.

———. "Narrador, autor, superestrella: la narrativa latinoamericana en la era de la producción de masas." *Revista Iberoamericana* 47, no. 115–16 (1981): 129–48.

———, John Beverley, and Eliseo Colón, trans. "Narrador, autor, superestrella: la narrativa latino-americana en la época de la cultura de masas." *Revista Iberoamericana* 47, no. 114–15 (Jan.–June 1981): 129–48.

Fraser, Howard. "Techniques of Fantasy: Realismo Mágico and Literatura Fantástica." *Chasqui* 1, no. 2 (1972): 20–23.

Fraser, Ronald, et al., eds. *1968: A Student Generation in Revolt*. London: Chatto & Windus, 1988.

Freud, Sigmund. *Group Psychology and the Analysis of the Ego*. Trans. J. Strachey. New York: Liveright, 1949.

———. *Totem and Taboo: Resemblances Between the Psychic Lives of Savages and Neurotics*. New York: Moffat, Yard, 1918.

Fuentes, Carlos. *The Death of Artemio Cruz*. Trans. Alfred MacAdam. New York: Farrar, Straus & Giroux, 1991.

———. "Mexico and Its Demons: Review of The Other Mexico; Critique of the Pyramid by Octavio Paz." *New York Review of Books* 20, no. 14 (1973): 16–21.

———. *La muerte de Artemio Cruz.* Mexico City: Fondo de Cultura Económica, 1962.

———. *La nueva novela hispanoamericana.* Mexico City: Joaquín Mortiz, 1969.

———. *Paris: la revolución de mayo.* Mexico City: Era, 1968.

———. *La región más transparente.* Mexico City: Fondo de Cultura Económica, 1958.

———. *Tiempo mexicano.* Mexico City: Joaquín Mortiz, 1971.

Fuguet, Alberto, and Sergio Gómez, eds. *McOndo.* Barcelona: Grijalbo Mondadori, 1996.

Galbraith, John K. *The New Industrial State,* 3rd ed. Boston: Houghton & Mifflin, 1967.

———. *The New Industrial State.* Boston: Houghton & Mifflin, 1978.

García Canclini, Néstor. *La globalización imaginada.* Buenos Aires: Paidós, 1999.

García Carranza, Araceli. *Bibliografía cubana del Comandante Ernesto Che Guevara.* Havana: Ministerio de Cultura, 1987.

García Castro, R. "Epistemología del closet de José Donoso (1921–1996) en *Conjeturas sobre la memoria de mi tribu* (1996), *El jardín de al lado* (1981) y 'Santelices.'" *Revista Iberoamericana* 68, no. 198 (2002): 27–48.

García Márquez, Gabriel. *Cien años de soledad.* Barcelona: Argos Vergara, 1981.

———. *La hojarasca.* Madrid: Alfaguara, 1979.

———. "Nobel Lecture 8 December 1982: The Solitude of Latin America." In *Nobel Lectures, Literature, 1981–1990.* Eds. Tore Frängsmyr and Sture Allén. Singapore: World Scientific, 1993. Available at http://nobelprize.org/literature/laureates/1982/marquez-lecture-e.html.

———. *One Hundred Years of Solitude.* Trans. Gregory Rabassa. New York: HarperCollins, Perennial Classics, 1998.

———. *Vivir para contarla.* Buenos Aires: Sudamericana, 2002.

Geertz, Clifford. "The Cerebral Savage: On the Work of Claude Lévi-Strauss." In *The Interpretation of Cultures.* London: Fontana Press, 1993.

Geisdorfer Feal, Rosemary. "Veiled Portraits: Donoso's Interartistic Dialogue in *El jardín de al lado.*" *MLN* 103, no. 2 (1988): 398–418.

Giacoman, Helmy F., ed. *Homenaje a Gabriel García Márquez: variaciones interpretativas en torno a su obra.* New York: Las Américas, 1972.

Gilman, Claudia. *Entre la pluma y el fusil: debates y dilemas del escritor revolucionario en América Latina.* Buenos Aires: Siglo XXI, 2003.

Goloboff, Mario. *Julio Cortázar: la biografía.* Buenos Aires: Seix Barral, 1998.

González, F. "The Androgynous Narrator in José Donoso's *El jardín de al lado.*" *Revista de Estudios Hispánicos* 23, no. 1 (1989): 99–113.

González de Alba, Luis. *Los días y los años.* Mexico City: Era, 1976.

González Bermejo, Ernesto. *Conversaciones con Cortázar.* Barcelona: Edhasa, 1978.

González Echevarría, Roberto. "*Cien años de soledad*: The Novel as Myth and Archive." *MLN* 90, no. 2 (1984): 358–80.

———. "Isla a su vuelo fugitiva: Carpentier y el realismo mágico." *Revista Ibero-americana* 40, no. 86 (Jan.–Mar. 1974).

———. *Myth and Archive: A Theory of Latin American Narrative.* Cambridge, UK: Cambridge University Press, 1990.

———. "The Parting of the Waters." In *Alejo Carpentier: The Pilgrim at Home*, 155–212. Ithaca, NY: Cornell University Press, 1977.

González Pérez, Aníbal. "Revolución y alegoría en 'Reunión,' de Julio Cortázar." In *Los ochenta mundos de Julio Cortázar: ensayos*, 93–109. Ed. Fernando Burgos. Madrid: EDI-6, 1987.

Gosse, Van. *Where the Boys Are: Cuba, Cold War America and the Making of the New Left.* London: Verso, 1993.

Goytisolo, Juan. "La novela española contemporánea." *Libre* 2 (Dec. 1971–Feb. 1972): 33–40.

Graff, Gerald. "George Orwell and the Class Racket." *Salmagundi* 70–71 (Spring–Summer 1986): 108–20.

Greer, Germaine. *The Female Eunuch.* New York: McGraw-Hill, 1970.

Grimaud, Maurice. "Interview." *L'Express* 2437 (May 19–25, 1998): 86–87.

Guattari, Félix. *Chaosmose.* Paris: Galilée, 1992.

Guevara, Ernesto Che. "Carta a Carlos Quijano." *Marcha* (Mar. 12, 1965).

———. *Escritos y discursos.* Havana: Ciencias Sociales, 1977.

———. *The Motorcycle Diaries: Notes on a Latin American Journey.* Ed. and trans. Alexandra Keeble. Melbourne: Ocean Press, 2003.

———. *Obras, 1957–1967.* Paris: Documentos Latinoamericanos, 1970.

———. *Obras completas 1957–1967.* Havana: Casa de las Américas, 1970.

———. *Pasajes de la guerra revolucionaria.* Havana: Ediciones de la Unión de Escritores y Artistas de Cuba, 1963.

———. *Reminiscences of the Cuban Revolutionary War.* Trans. Victoria Ortiz. New York: Grove Press, 1968.

Guevara Lynch, Ernesto. *Aquí va un soldado de América.* Mexico City: Planeta, 1989.

———. *Mi hijo el Che.* Barcelona: Planeta, 1981.

———. *Mi hijo el Che.* Buenos Aires: Sudamericana, 1984.

Guevara Niebla, Gilberto. *La democracia en la calle: crónica del movimiento estudiantil mexicano.* Mexico City: Siglo XXI, 1988.

Gugelberger, George M., ed. *The Real Thing: Testimonial Discourse and Latin America.* Durham, NC: Duke University Press, 1996.

Guillermoprieto, Alma. "The Harsh Angel." In *Looking for History: Dispatches from Latin America*, 73–86. New York: Pantheon Books, 2001.

Gunning, Tom. "The Cinema of Attractions: Early Film, Its Spectator, and the Avant-Garde." In *Early Cinema: Space, Frame and Narrative.* Eds. T. Elsaesser and A. Barker. London: BFI, 1990.

Gutiérrez, Mouat, Ricardo. "Aesthetics, Ethics and Politics in Donoso's *El jardín de al lado.*" *PMLA* 106, no. 1 (1991): 60–70.

———. "*Cien años de soledad* y el mito farmacopéiyico del realismo mágico." *Revista de Estudios Hispánicos* 91, no. 17–18 (1990–91): 267–79.

Halbwachs, Maurice. *Les cadres sociaux de la mémoire.* Paris: Albin Michel, 1994.

Halperin Donghi, Tulio. "Nueva narrativa y ciencias sociales hispanoamericanas en la década del sesenta." *Hispamérica* 9, no. 27 (Dec. 1980): 3–18.

Hardt, Michael, and Antonio Negri. *Empire.* Cambridge, MA: Harvard University Press, 2000.

Hernández, Salvador. *El PRI y el movimiento estudiantil de 1968.* Mexico City: El Caballito, 1971.

l'Herne. *Volume Dedicated to Borges.* Paris: l'Herne, 1964.

Herrera-Olaizola, Alejandro. "Publishing Matters: Francoist Censorship and the Latin American Book Market." *Literary Research/Recherche Littéraire* 19, no. 37–38 (2002): 21–28.

Hirschman, Albert O. *Retóricas de la intransigencia.* Mexico City: Fondo de Cultura Económica, 1991.

Hobsbawm, Eric. *The Age of Extremes: A History of the World, 1914–1991.* New York: Pantheon Books, 1994.

———. "1968—A Retrospect." *Marxism Today* (May 1978): 130–45.

———. *Primitive Rebels: Studies in Archaic Forms of Social Movement in the 19th and 20th Centuries.* New York: Norton, 1959.

———. *Revolutionaries: Contemporary Essays.* New York: Random House, 1973.

Hodges, Donald. *The Legacy of Che Guevara: A Documentary Study.* London: Thames & Hudson, 1977.

Horkheimer, Max, and Theodor W. Adorno. *Dialectic of Enlightenment.* Trans. John Cumming. New York: Continuum, 1999.

Hynes, Samuel. *The Soldiers' Tale: Bearing Witness to Modern War.* New York: Allen Lane/Penguin Press, 1997.

Ibarra, Néstor. *La nueva poesía argentina: ensayo crítico sobre el ultraísmo, 1921–1929.* Buenos Aires: Molinari, 1930.

Iznaga Beira, Diana. "Che Guevara y la literatura de testimonio." *Universidad de la Habana* 232 (n.d.): 149–66.

Jackson, Rebecca. *The 1960s: An Annotated Bibliography of Social and Political Movements in the U.S.* Westport, CT: Greenwood Press, 1992.

James, Nick. "Against the Current." *Sight and Sound* 14, no. 9 (Sept. 2004): 8–9.

Jameson, Fredric. "The End of Temporality." *Critical Inquiry* 29 (Summer 2003).

———. "Periodizing the 60s." In *The 60s Without Apology*, 178–209. Eds. S. Sayres et al. Minneapolis: University of Minnesota Press, 1984.

Jammes, Robert. "Introduction." In *Cuba: Les Etapes d'une libération; Hommage à Juan Marinello*. Toulouse: Université de Toulouse-Le Mirail, 1979–80.

Janes, Regina. *One Hundred Years of Solitude: Modes of Reading*. Boston: Twayne, 1991.

Jara, René, and Jaime Mejía Duque. *Las claves del mito en García Márquez*. Valparaíso: Ediciones Universitarias de Valparaíso, 1972.

Jara, René, and Hernán Vidal, eds. *Testimonio y literatura*. Minneapolis: Institute for the Study of Ideologies and Literature, 1986.

Jaurès, Jean. *Histoire socialiste de la Révolution française*. Paris: Editions de la Librairie de l'Humanité, 1922.

Jay, Martin. *The Dialectical Imagination*. Boston: Little, Brown, 1973.

Johnson, Barbara. "Muteness Envy." In *The Feminist Difference*, 129–53. Cambridge, MA: Harvard University Press, 1998.

Jones, J. "Vargas Llosa's *Mangachería*: The Pleasures of Community." *Revista de Estudios Hispánicos* 20, no. 1 (1986): 77–89.

Jorgensen, Beth. *The Writing of Elena Poniatowska: Engaging Dialogues*. Austin: University of Texas Press, 1994.

Jung, C. G. *Memories, Dreams, Reflections*. Ed. Aniela Jaffe. Trans. Richard Winston and Clara Winston. New York: Pantheon Books, 1963.

Kadir, D. "Next Door: Writing Elsewhere." *The Review of Contemporary Fiction* 12, no. 2 (1992): 60–69.

Kant, Immanuel. *Anthropology from a Pragmatic Point of View*. Trans. V. L. Dowdell. Carbondale: Southern Illinois University Press, 1978.

Katsiaficas, George. *The Imagination of the New Left: A Global Analysis of 1968*. Boston: South End Press, 1987.

Kerr, L. "Authority in Play: José Donoso's *El jardín de al lado*." *Criticism* 25, no. 1 (1983): 41–65.

King, John. *El Instituto Di Tella y el desarrollo cultural argentino en la década del sesenta*. Trans. C. Gardini. Buenos Aires: Ediciones de Arte Gaglianone, 1985.

———. *Sur: A Study of the Argentine Literary Journal and Its Role in the Development of a Culture, 1931–1970*. Cambridge, UK: Cambridge University Press, 1986.

Kirby, Michael. *Happenings: An Illustrated Anthology*. New York: Dutton, 1965.

Klawans, Stuart. "Styles of Radical Will." *The Nation* (Oct. 4, 2004): 32–36.

Kofman, Andrei. "El problema del realismo mágico en la literatura latinoamericana." *Cuadernos Americanos* 14, nos. 4, 82 (2000): 63–72.

Kohut, Karl. "El escritor latinoamericano en Francia: reflexiones de Julio Cortázar en torno al exilio." *INTI* 22–23 (1985–86): 263–80.

———. "Las polémicas de Julio Cortázar en retrospectiva." *Hispamérica* 29, no. 87 (Dec. 2000): 31–50.

Korol, Claudia. *El Che y los argentinos*. Buenos Aires: Sudamericana/Planeta, 1994.

Koselleck, Reinhart. *Futures Past: On the Semantics of Historical Time*. Trans. K. Tribe. Cambridge, MA: MIT Press, 1985.

Kovacs, Susan. "Revolutionary Consciousness and Imperfect Cinematic Forms." *Humanities in Society* 4, no. 1 (Winter 1981): 101–12.

Krauze, Enrique. *Mexico: Biography of Power; A History of Modern Mexico, 1810–1996.* Trans. Hank Heifetz. New York: HarperCollins, 1997.

Kunzle, David. *Che Guevara: Icon, Myth and Message.* Los Angeles: UCLA Fowler Museum of Cultural History, in collaboration with the Center for the Study of Political Graphics, 1998.

Laclau, Ernesto. *Emancipations.* London: Verso, 1996.

———. *New Reflections for a Revolution of Our Time.* London: Verso, 1990.

Lafforgue, Martin, et al. *AntiBorges.* Barcelona: Vergara, 1999.

Laing, R. D. *The Politics of Experience.* New York: Pantheon Books, 1967.

Larsen, Neil. "The 'Boom' Novel and the Cold War in Latin America." *Modern Fiction Studies* 38, no. 3 (Autumn 1992): 771–84.

Leal, Luis. "El realismo mágico en la literatura hispanoamericana." *Cuadernos Americanos* 26, no. 153 (1967): 200–206.

Leante, César Leante. "Los *Pasajes* del Che." *Casa de las Américas* 8, no. 46 (Jan.–Feb. 1968): 155.

Lefebre, Henri. *The Production of Space.* Oxford: Blackwell, 1991.

LeGoff, Jean Pierre. *Mai 68, l'héritage impossible.* Paris: La Découverte, 1998.

Lemogodeuc, J. M. "Las máscaras y las marcas de la autobiografía: la cuestión del narrador en *El jardín de al lado* de José Donoso." *Convergences et Divergences* 1 (1996): 57–75.

Levinas, Emmanuel. *Totality and Infinity.* Pittsburgh, PA: Duquesne University Press, 1961.

Levine, Suzanne Jill. *El espejo hablado: un estudio de Cien años de soledad.* Caracas: Monte Avila, 1975.

Lévi-Strauss, Claude. *Tristes Tropiques.* New York: Pocket Books, 1973.

Lezama Lima, José. *Imagen y posibilidad.* Havana: Letras Cubanas, 1981.

Lida, Raimundo. "Notas a Borges." In *Letras hispánicas*, 280–83. Mexico City: Fondo de Cultura Económico, 1958.

Lie, Nadia. *Transición y transacción: la revista cubana Casa de las Américas, 1960–1976.* Gaithersburg, MD, and Leuven: Hispamérica/Leuven University Press, 1996.

López Mejía, Adelaida. "Debt, Delirium and Cultural Exchange in *Cien años de soledad.*" *Revista de Estudios Hispánicos* 29, no. 1 (1995): 3–25.

Luchting, W. A. "Los mitos y lo mitizante en *La casa verde.*" *Mundo Nuevo* 43 (1970): 56–60.

Ludmer, Josefina. *Cien años de soledad: una interpretación.* Buenos Aires: Tiempo Contemporáneo, 1972.

Luis, William. *Lunes de Revolución: literatura y cultura en los primeros años de la revolución Cubana.* Madrid: Verbum, 2003.

Lukács, Georg. *History and Class Consciousness: Studies in Marxist Dialectics.* Trans. Rodney Livingstone. Cambridge, MA: MIT Press, 1971.

Lyotard, Jean-François. *Le Différend.* Paris: Minuit, 1983.

———. *The Differend.* Trans. Georges Van Den Abbeele. Minneapolis: University of Minnesota Press, 1988.

Magnum Photos. *1968, Magnum dans le monde.* Paris: Hazan, 1998.

Mahfouz, Naguib. *The Cairo Trilogy.* Trans. William Maynard Hutchins et al. Cairo: American University in Cairo Press, 2001.

Mao Tse Tung. *Quotations from Chairman Mao Tse Tung.* Ed. S. Schram. New York: Praeger, 1967.

Marcha (Montevideo, 1939–74).

Marco, Joaquín, and Jordi Gracia, eds. *La llegada de los bárbaros.* Barcelona: Edhasa, 2004.

Marcos, Juan Manuel. "Mujer y violencia social en *Cien años de soledad.*" In *Violencia y literatura en Colombia,* 91–95. Ed. J. Titler. Madrid: Orígenes, 1989.

Marcuse, Herbert. *Counterrevolution and Revolt.* Boston: Beacon Press, 1972.

———. *Essay on Liberation.* Boston: Beacon Press, 1969.

———. *Negations.* Boston: Beacon Press, 1968.

———. *One-dimensional Man: Studies in the Ideology of Advanced Society,* 2nd ed. London: Routledge, 1991.

Marin, Louis. *Le Portrait du roi.* Paris: Minuit, 1981.

———. *Portrait of the King.* Trans. Martha M. Houle. Minneapolis: University of Minnesota Press, 1988.

Márquez Rodríguez, Alexis. "El surrealismo y su vinculación con el realismo mágico y lo real maravilloso." In *Prosa hispánica de vanguardia,* 77–96. Ed. Fernando Burgos. Madrid: Orígenes, 1986.

Martin, Gerald. *Journeys Through the Labyrinth: Latin American Fiction in the Twentieth Century.* London: Verso, 1989.

Martré, Gonzalo. *El movimiento popular estudiantil de 1968 en la novela mexicana.* Mexico City: UNAM, 1998.

———. *Los símbolos transparentes.* Mexico City: Cinco Siglos, 1978.

Maturo, Gabriela. *Claves simbólicas de García Márquez.* Buenos Aires: García Cambeiro, 1977.

McGuirk, Bernard, and R. Cardwell, eds. *Gabriel García Márquez: New Readings.* Cambridge, UK: Cambridge University Press, 1987.

McLuhan, Marshall. *Understanding Media.* New York: Signet, 1964.

———, and Q. Fiore. *The Medium Is the Message.* New York: Bantam Books, 1967.

McMurray, G. "The Novels of Mario Vargas Llosa." *MLQ* 29, no. 3 (1968): 329–40.

Meléndez, P. "Writing and Reading the Palimpsest: Donoso's *El jardín de al lado.*" *Symposium* 41, no. 3 (1987): 200–212.

Mena, Lucila Inés. "Hacia una formulación teórica del realismo mágico." *Bulletin Hispanique* 77, no. 3–4 (1975): 395–407.

Merrell, Floyd. "The Ideal World in Search of Its Reference: An Inquiry into the Underlying Nature of Magical Realism." *Chasqui* 4, no. 2 (1975): 5–17.

————. "Some Considerations of the Notion of 'Otherness' in Octavio Paz's *Postdata*." *Kentucky Romance Quarterly* 24 (1977): 163–74.

Millett, Kate. *Sexual Politics*. New York: Doubleday, 1970.

Millington, M. I. "Out of Chile: Writing in Exile/Exile in Writing—José Donoso's *El jardín de al lado*." *Renaissance and Modern Studies* 34 (1991): 64–77.

Mink, Louis. "History and Fiction as Modes of Comprehension." *New Literary History* 1 (1970): 514–58.

————. "Narrative Form as a Cognitive Instrument." In *The Writing of History: Literary Form and Historical Understanding*, 129–49. Eds. R. H. Canary and H. Kozicki. Madison: University of Wisconsin Press, 1978.

Molloy, Sylvia. *La diffusion de la littérature hispano-américaine en France au XXe siècle*. Paris: Presses Universitaires de France, 1972.

Monsivais, Carlos. *Días de guardar*. Mexico City: Asociados, 1970.

Montero, Oscar. "*El jardín de al lado*: la escritura y el fracaso del éxito." *Revista Iberoamericana* 49, no. 123–24 (1983): 449–67.

Montero, Rosa. "El camino de Damasco de Julio Cortázar." *El País* (Suplemento Dominical; Mar. 14, 1982): 14.

Moody, Michael. "Paisajes de los condenados: el escenario natural de *La casa verde*." *Revista Iberoamericana* 47, no. 116–17 (1981): 127–36.

Mora, Juan Miguel de. *Tlatelolco 1968: por fin toda la verdad*. Mexico City: Asociados, 1973.

More, Thomas. *Utopia*. Ed. and with an Introduction by George M. Logan and Robert M. Adams. Cambridge Texts in the History of Political Thought. Cambridge, MA: Cambridge University Press, 1989.

Moreiras, Alberto. "The End of Magical Realism: José María Arguedas's Passionate Signifier (*El zorro de arriba y el zorro de abajo*)." *The Journal of Narrative Technique* 27, no. 1 (1997): 84–112.

Morello Frosch, Marta. "El discurso de armas y letras en las narraciones de Julio Cortázar." Coloquio Internacional: lo lúdico y lo fantástico en la obra de Julio Cortázar, Centre de Recherches Latino-Américaines, Université de Poitiers. Madrid: Fundamentos, 1986.

Moretti, Franco. *Modern Epic: The World System from Goethe to García Márquez*. London: Verso, 1996.

Morin, Edgar. "Jeunesse." In *L'Esprit du temps*, vol. 2, 205–21. Paris: Grasset, 1975.

"Motorcycle Diaries Shoot Underway." *Screen International* (Nov. 1, 2002): 5.

Mudrovcic, María Eugenia. *Mundo Nuevo: cultura y Guerra Fría en la década del sesenta*. Rosario, Argentina: Beatriz Viterbo, 1997.

Mundo Nuevo (Paris: Instituto Latinoamericano de Relaciones Internacionales, 1966–71).

New Directions Publishing Corporation Records (Houghton Library, Harvard University, Cambridge, MA).

Nietzsche, Friedrich. *Beyond Good and Evil.* Trans. R. J. Hollingdale. Harmondsworth: Penguin, 1973.

———. *The Portable Nietzsche.* Trans. Walter Kaufmann. New York: Penguin, 1976.

———. *Werke* I. Ed. Karl Schlechta. Munich: Carl Hanser, 1954.

Nouzeilles, Gabriela. "La rayuela del sexo según Cortázar." In *Cánones literarios masculinos y relecturas transculturales*, 63–83. Ed. Ileana Rodríguez. Barcelona: Anthropos, 2001.

Nuevo Diccionario de Americanismos (Bogota: Instituto Caro y Cuervo, 1993).

Ocampo, Victoria. "El premio María Moors Cabot." *Sur* 297 (Nov.–Dec. 1965): 6.

Ong, Walter. *Interfaces of the Word: Studies in the Evolution of Consciousness and Culture.* Ithaca, NY: Cornell University Press, 1977.

Orgambide, Pedro. "Jorge Luis Borges." *La Gaceta Literaria* 20 (May 1960): 23.

Ortega, J., ed. *Gabriel García Márquez and the Powers of Fiction.* Austin: University of Texas Press, 1988.

———. "Para una mapa de Borges." *Revista Iberoamericana* 100–101 (1977): 745–50.

Orwell, George. *The Road to Wigan Pier.* London: Gollancz, 1937.

Oviedo, J. M. *Mario Vargas Llosa: la invención de una realidad.* Barcelona: Barral, 1970.

Pacheco, J. E. "Lectura de Vargas Llosa." *RUM* 22, no. 8 (Apr. 1968): 27–33.

Palencia-Roth, Michael. "Los pergaminos de Aureliano Babilonia." *Revista Iberoamericana* 49, no. 123–24 (Apr.–Sept. 1983): 403–17.

Palmier, Jean-Michel. *Magazine Littéraire* (May 18, 1968): 14.

Paz, Octavio. "A cinco años de Tlatelolco." In *El ogro filantrópico: historia y política*, 143–52. Mexico City: Joaquín Mortiz, 1979.

———. *El laberinto de la soledad.* Mexico City: Cuadernos Americanos, 1950.

———. *El laberinto de la soledad: Postdata.* Mexico City: Fondo de Cultura Económica, 1981.

———. *El laberinto de la soledad: Postdata.* Ed. Enrico Mario Santí. Madrid: Cátedra, 1993.

———. *The Labyrinth of Solitude and Other Writings.* Trans. Lysander Kemp, Yara Milos, and Rachel Phillips Belash. New York: Grove Press, 1985.

Pera, Cristóbal. "Alienación (europeización) o introversión (incesto): Latinoamérica y Europa en *Cien años de soledad*." *Chasqui* 22, no. 2 (Nov. 1993): 85–93.

Perec, Georges. *L. G.: Une Aventure des années soixante.* Paris: Seuil, 1992.

Pérez Firmat, Gustavo. *The Cuban Condition.* Cambridge, UK: Cambridge University Press, 1989.

Perrone, Charles. "Guimaraes Rosa Through the Prism of Magical Realism." In *Tropical Paths: Essays on Modern Brazilian Literature.* Ed. Randal Johnson. New York: Garland Publishing, 1993.

Pezzoni, Enrique. "Aproximación al último libro de Borges." *Sur* 217–18 (1952): 101–23.

————. *El texto y sus voces*. Buenos Aires: Sudamericana, 1986.

Piglia, Ricardo. "Ernesto Guevara, rastros de lectura." In *El último lector*, 103–38. Buenos Aires: Anagrama, 2005.

Pinillos, María de las Nieves. "La novela de la guerrilla iberoamericana." *Cuadernos Hispanoamericanos* 400 (Oct. 1983): 174–82.

Pitol, Sergio. *La década rebelde: los años 60 en la Argentina*. Buenos Aires: Emecé, 2002.

Planells, Antonio. "El realismo mágico hispanoamericano ante la crítica." *Chasqui* 17, no. 1 (1988): 9–23.

Pogolotti, Graziella. "Apuntes para el Che escritor." *Casa de las Américas* 8, no. 46 (Jan.–Feb. 1968): 152–55.

Pohl, Burkhard. "Entre dos tierras: Carlos Barral y la unidad cultural latinoamericana." In *Carlos Barral y la edición latinoamericana*, 427–35. Salamanca, Spain: Ediciones Universidad de Salamanca, 2004.

Poniatowska, Elena. *Hasta no verte, Jesús mío*. Mexico City: Era, 1969.

————. *Massacre in Mexico*. Trans. Helen R. Lane. Columbia: University of Missouri Press, 1991.

————. *La noche de Tlatelolco*. Mexico City: Era, 1971.

Poot Herrera, Sara. "Las crónicas de Elena Poniatowska." *La Colmena* 11 (1996): 17–22.

Prado Salmón, Gary. *Guerrilla inmolada: The Defeat of Che Guevara*. Trans. John Deredita. New York: Praeger, 1990.

Prego, Omar. *La fascinación de las palabras*. Barcelona: Muchnik, 1985.

Prieto, Adolfo. *Borges y la nueva generación*. Buenos Aires: Letras Universitarias, 1954.

Primera Plana (Buenos Aires: Danoti, 1962–90).

Quintero Herencia, Juan Carlos. "La 'Casa de las Américas' (1960–71): el imaginario institucional de una revolución." *DAI* (Princeton University) 56, no. 3 (Sept. 1995): 955A.

Rama, Angel. "El 'Boom' en perspectiva." In *Más allá del Boom: literatura y mercado*, 51–110. Eds. David Viñas et al. Mexico City: Marcha, 1981.

————. "La construcción de una literatura." *Marcha* 1040 (Dec. 26, 1960): 22–24.

————. *García Márquez: edificación de un arte nacional y popular*. Montevideo: Universidad de la República, 1987.

————. "El sometimiento intelectual." *Marcha* 1209 (June 12, 1964): 46.

————. "La tecnificación narrativa." *Hispamérica* 10, no. 30 (1980): 29–82.

Ramírez, Ramón. *El movimiento estudiantil de México*. Mexico City: Era, 1969.

Randall, Margaret. *Testimonios: A Guide to Oral History*. Toronto: Participatory Research Group, 1985.

Reader, Keith. *The May 1968 Events in France*. New York: St. Martin's, 1993.

Revista de crítica literaria latinoamericana 36 (Lima, 1992).

Revista Tricontinental (Havana; 1966, 1967).

Revueltas, José. *México 1968: juventud y revolución*. Mexico City: Era, 1968.

Ricci Della Grisa, Graciela. *Realismo mágico y conciencia mítica en América Latina*. Buenos Aires: Fernando García Cambeiro, 1985.

Ricoeur, Paul. *Freud and Philosophy: An Essay on Interpretation*. Trans. Denis Savage. New Haven, CT: Yale University Press, 1970.

———. *La Mémoire, l'histoire, l'oubli*. Paris: Seuil, 2000.

Riera, Carme. *La Escuela de Barcelona*. Barcelona: Anagrama, 1988.

Rincón, Carlos. "Modernidad periférica y el desafío de lo postmoderno: perspectivas del arte narrativo latinoamericano." *Revista de Crítica Literaria Latinoamericana* 15, no. 29 (1989): 62–204.

Rivera, Jorge B., and Eduardo Romano. *Claves del periodismo argentino actual*. Buenos Aires: Tarso, 1987.

Rivera, José Eustasio. *La vorágine*. Santiago de Chile: Empresa Letras, 1936.

Rizzo, Patricia. *Instituto Di Tella: experiencias '68*. Buenos Aires: Fundación Proa, 1998.

Robben, Antonius C. G. *Political Violence and Trauma in Argentina*. Philadelphia: University of Pennsylvania Press, 2005.

Rocca, Pablo. *35 años en Marcha: crítica y literatura en Marcha y en el Uruguay 1939–74*. Montevideo: Intendencia Municipal de Montevideo, 1992.

Rochlitz, Rainer. *Le Désenchantment de l'art: la philosophie de Walter Benjamin*. Paris: Gallimard, 1992.

Rodríguez, Ileana. "Principios estructurales y visión circular en *Cien años de soledad*." *Revista de Crítica Literaria Latinoamericana* 5, no. 9 (1979): 79–97.

———. *Women, Guerrillas and Love: Understanding War in Central America*. Minneapolis: University of Minnesota Press, 1996.

Rodríguez Monegal, Emir. "Carta a Guillermo Cabrera Infante." *Rodríguez Monegal's Papers* (Sept. 24, 1968). Princeton, NJ: Princeton University Libraries.

———. "Papel del escritor en América Latina." *Mundo Nuevo* 5 (Nov. 1966): 35.

———. "Surrealism, Magical Realism, Magical Fiction: A Study in Confusion." In *Surrealismo/surrealismos: Latinoamérica y España*. Eds. Peter G. Earle and Germán Gullón. Philadelphia: Center for Inter-American Relations, 1977.

Rohter, Larry. "20 Years After a Massacre, Mexico Still Seeks Healing for Its Wounds." *New York Times* (Oct. 2, 1988): sec. 1, 16.

Rojas, Rafael. *Isla sin fin: contribución a la crítica del nacionalismo cubano*. Miami: Universal, 1998.

Romano, Vicente. *Cuba en el corazón*. Barcelona: Anthropos, 1989.

Rosa, Nicolás. "Borges y la crítica." In *Los fulgores del simulacro*, 259–315. Santa Fe, Argentina: Universidad Nacional del Litoral, 1987.

Ross, Kristin. *May '68 and Its Afterlives*. Chicago: University of Chicago Press, 2002.

Ruffinelli, Jorge. "La censura contra *Marcha*." In *Marcha y América Latina*, 349–76. Eds. Mabel Moraña and Horacio Machín. Pittsburgh, PA: Instituto Internacional de Literatura Iberoamericana, Biblioteca de América, 2003.

Said, Edward. *Culture and Imperialism.* New York: Knopf, 1993.

———. *Representations of the Intellectual: The 1993 Reith Lectures.* London: Vintage, 1994.

Saldaña Portillo, María Josefina. *The Revolutionary Imagination in the Americas and the Age of Development.* Durham, NC: Duke University Press, 2003.

Sánchez Ferrer, José L. *El realismo mágico en la novela hispanoamericana.* Madrid: Anaya, 1990.

Santana, Mario. *Strangers in the Homeland.* Lewisburg: Bucknell University Press, 2001.

Santí, Enrico Mario. *El acto de las palabras: Estudios y diálogos con Octavio Paz.* Mexico City: Fondo de Cultura Económica, 1997.

Sarmiento, Domingo F. *Obras completas.* Buenos Aires: Luz del Día, 1953.

Sayres, Sohnya, et al., eds. *The 60s Without Apology.* Minneapolis: University of Minnesota Press, 1984.

Scarry, Elaine. *On Beauty and Being Just.* Princeton, NJ: Princeton University Press, 1999.

———. *The Body in Pain: The Making and Unmaking of the World.* New York: Oxford University Press, 1985.

Scherer, Fabiana. "Hispanos: la apuesta fuerte de Hollywood." *La Nación: Revista* (Buenos Aires; Aug. 22, 2004).

Scherer García, Julio, and Carlos Monsiváis. *Parte de guerra II: los rostros del 68.* Mexico City: Nuevo Siglo Aguilar, 2002.

Schwartz, Marcy. *Writing Paris: Urban Topographies of Desire in Contemporary Latin American Fiction.* Albany: State University of New York Press, 1999.

Sierra, Ernesto. "Réquiem para *Mundo Nuevo.*" *Casa de las Américas* 213 (Oct.–Dec. 1998): 135–39.

Sigal, Silvia. *Intelectuales y poder en la década del sesenta.* Buenos Aires: Puntosur, 1991.

Silverman, Kaja. *Male Subjectivity at the Margins.* New York: Routledge, 1992.

Sklodowska, Elzbieta. *Testimonio hispanoamericano: historia, teoría, poética.* New York: Peter Lang, 1992.

Smith, Lois M., and Alfred Padula. *Sex and Revolution: Women in Socialist Cuba.* New York: Oxford University Press, 1996.

Smith, Paul Julian. *The Body Hispanic: Gender and Sexuality in Spanish and Spanish American Literature.* Oxford: Clarendon Press, 1989.

Sommer, Doris. "'Not Just a Personal Story': Women's *Testimonios* and the Plural Self." In *Life Lines: Theorizing Women's Autobiography,* 107–30. Eds. Bella Brodzki and Celeste Schenck. Ithaca, NY: Cornell University Press, 1988.

Sommier, Isabelle. *La Violence politique et son deuil: l'après 68 en France et en Italie.* Rennes: Presses Universitaires de Rennes, 1998.

Sorensen, Diana. *Facundo and the Construction of Argentine Culture.* Austin: University of Texas Press, 1996.

Spota, Luis. *La plaza*. Mexico City: Grijalbo, 1977.

Steele, Cynthia. *Politics, Gender and the Mexican Novel 1968–88: Beyond the Pyramid*. Austin: University of Texas Press, 1992.

Stevens, Evelyn P. *Protest and Response in Mexico*. Cambridge, MA: MIT Press, 1974.

Sur (Buenos Aires, 1931–92).

Sweig, Julia. *Inside the Cuban Revolution: Fidel Castro and the Urban Underground*. Cambridge, MA: Harvard University Press, 2002.

Taibo, Paco Ignacio, II. *Guevara, Also Known as Che*. Trans. M. M. Roberts. New York: St. Martin's, 1997.

———. *'68*. Mexico City: Planeta, 1998.

Tartakowky, Danielle. *Le Pouvoir est dans la rue*. Paris: Aubier, 1998.

Taussig, Michael. *Shamanism, Colonialism, and the Wild Man: A Study in Terror and Healing*. Chicago: University of Chicago Press, 1987.

Teodori, Massimo. *The New Left: A Documentary History*. Indianapolis: Bobbs-Merrill, 1969.

Terán, Oscar. *Nuestros años sesentas*. Buenos Aires: Puntosur, 1991.

Todorov, Tzvetan. "Macondo en París." *Texto Crítico* 11 (1978): 36–45.

Tola de Habich, Fernando, and Patricia Grieve, eds. *Los españoles y el 'boom.'* Caracas: Tiempo Nuevo, 1971.

Torgovnick, Marianna. *Gone Primitve: Savage Intellects, Modern Minds*. Chicago: University of Chicago Press, 1990.

Toro, Alfonso de, and Fernando de Toro, eds. *Jorge Luis Borges: pensamiento y saber en el siglo XX*. Madrid: Iberoamericana, 1999.

Touraine, Alain. *Le Mouvement de mai ou le communisme utopique*. Paris: Seuil, 1968.

———. *The Post-Industrial Society*. Trans. L. Mayhew. New York: Random House, 1971.

Transition (Paris, 1927–38).

Trotsky, Leon. *De la Révolution d'Octobre à la paix de Brest-Litovsk*. Geneva: Edition de la revue "Demani," 1918.

Tuan, Yi-Fu. *Topophilia: A Study of Environmental Perception, Attitudes, and Values*. New York: Columbia University Press, 1974.

Ubidia, Abdón. "Cinco tesis del 'realismo mágico.'" *Hispamérica* 26, no. 78 (1997): 101–7.

Uslar Pietri, Arturo. "Realismo mágico." In *Godos, insurgentes y visionarios*. Barcelona: Seix Barral, 1986.

Valbona, Rima de. "Octavio Paz: prosa en movimiento." *Kanina: Revista de Artes y Letras de la Universidad de Costa Rica* 6, no. 1–2 (1982): 60–66.

Vargas Llosa, Mario. *La casa verde*. Mexico City: Alfaguara, 2000.

———. *García Márquez: historia de un deicidio*. Barcelona: Barral, 1971.

———. *The Green House*. Trans. Gregory Rabassa. New York: Harper & Row, 1969.

————. *Historia secreta de una novela.* Madrid: Tusquets, 1971.

Verde Olivo (Havana: FAR, 1959–).

Vidal, Hernán. "Julio Cortázar y la nueva izquierda." *Ideologies and Literature* 2, no. 7 (May–June 1978): 45–67.

————. *Literatura hispanoamericana e ideología liberal: surgimiento y crisis.* Buenos Aires: Hispamérica, 1976.

Viñas, David. *De Sarmiento a Cortázar.* Buenos Aires: Siglo XXI, 1971.

————. *De Sarmiento a Cortázar: literatura argentina y realidad política.* Buenos Aires: Centro Editor de América Latina, 1982.

Vitier, Cintio. *Testimonios.* Havana: Unión, 1968.

Volpi, Jorge. *La imaginación y el poder: una historia intelectual de 1968.* Mexico City: Era, 1998.

VVV (New York, 1942–44).

Walsh, María Elena. *Las canciones.* Buenos Aires: Seix Barral, 1994.

Waltzer, Michael. *The Revolution of the Saints: A Study of the Origins of Radical Politics.* New York: Atheneum, 1968.

Wences Reza, Rosalío. *El movimiento estudiantil y los problemas nacionales.* Mexico City: Nuestro Tiempo, 1971.

Williams, Raymond. *The Long Revolution.* London: Penguin, 1961.

Wolff, Rick. "Economics." In *The 60s Without Apology.* Eds. S. Sayres et al. Minneapolis: University of Minnesota Press, 1986.

Woodmansee, Mary. *The Author, Art and the Market: Rereading the History of Aesthetics.* New York: Columbia University Press, 1994.

Wright, Thomas C. *Latin America in the Era of the Cuban Revolution.* New York: Praeger, 1991.

Yates, Donald. "Letter to Robert MacGregor: February 9, 1968." New Directions Publishing Corporation Records, Folder 2021. Cambridge, MA: Houghton Library, Harvard University.

Young, Dolly. "Mexican Literary Reactions to Tlatelolco 1968." *Latin American Research Review* 20, no. 2 (1985): 71–85.

Zamora, Lois Parkinson, and Wendy B. Faris, eds. *Magical Realism: Theory, History, Community.* Durham, NC: Duke University Press, 1995.

Zampaglione, Héctor. *El París de Rayuela: homenaje a Cortázar.* Barcelona: Lunwerg, 1997.

Zermeño, Sergio. *México: una democracia utópica; el movimiento estudiantil de '68.* Mexico City: Siglo XXI, 1978.

Žižek, Slavoj. "The Spectre of Ideology." In *Mapping Ideology*, 1–33. Ed. S. Žižek. London: Verso, 1994.

Index

Abril, Xavier, 168
Acevedo Díaz, Eduardo, 136
Adorno, Theodor, 4, 5, 9–10, 50, 105, 173
Adoum, José Enrique, 23
Aesthetics: and the novel, 8, 160, 185;
    and politics, 12; and ethics, 54, 62,
    69–77, 179; and exile, 100; surrealist,
    101; socialist, 125
Agustín, Jose, 110
Alborta, Freddy, 25
Alcalde, Ramón, 137
Alegría, Ciro, 110
Algerian war, 4, 103
Allende, Isabel, 209
Alone (Hernán Díaz Arrieta), 147
Alonso, Amado, 138
Althusser, Louis, 2, 7
Amis, Kingsley, 166
Anderson Imbert, Enrique, 137
Anderson, Benedict, 111
Anderson, Danny, 110
Antonioni, Michelangelo, 119
Apocalypse, apocalyptic, 4, 8, 46, 143,
    180, 187–89, 211
Arciniegas, Germán, 116
Arenas, Braulio, 168
Arendt, Hannah, 15, 16, 61
Arguedas, José María, 14, 123, 190
Aridjis, Homero, 110
Arrufat, Antón, 21, 22, 43, 44
Artaud, Antonin, 118
Asturias, Miguel Angel, 134–35, 170–71
Aura, 16, 76, 105; and Che, 11, 27, 51;

and Fidel Castro, 38, 40; and the
    "boom," 142, 145, 151, 158, 198, 209
Authorship, 13; and Poniatowska, 69–70;
    and the "boom" novelists, 107–8, 146,
    147, 161–62

Bachelard, Gaston, 139
Baker, Josephine, 169
Balcells, Carmen, 159
Banderas, Antonio, 51
Barral, Carlos, 129, 130–35, 150
Barrenechea, Ana María, 138
Barthes, Roland, 10, 14, 15, 115, 145, 170,
    182, 191, 201
Bataille, Georges, 67–8, 139, 170
Batista, 15, 19, 20–21, 29, 33–34, 123
Baudelaire, Charles, 119, 130, 166
Beatles, the, 119
Beauvoir, Simone de, 25, 124, 130
Beckett, Samuel, 136, 139
Bellatín, Mario, 209
Bello, Andrés, 124, 125
Benedetti, Mario, 22, 101–2; and Casa de
    las Américas, 23
Benet, Juan, 133
Benjamin, Walter, 2, 29, 35, 54, 54–55,
    56, 61–62, 67, 105, 119, 171, 178
Bergerac, Cyrano de, 139
Bianco, José, 127, 138
Blackburn, Paul, 45
Blake, William, 166
Blanchot, Maurice, 139, 140
Blumenberg, H., 144

Body, the: and Che Guevara, 25–27, 36–37, 49; politic, 27–28, 41, 60, 68, 75, 76; social, 85, 93–94, 97–99; and writing, 145, 181–82, 195, 203
Bolívar, Simon, 23
Bonnefoy, Yves, 131
"Boom," 8, 12, 13–14, 20, 107, 114, 117–18; and gender, 13, 17, 148–63; and invention, 15; and continental consciousness, 127; and international connections, 128–42; and tension between destruction and beginnings, 143–63; and re-reading in the 21st century, 164–207. *See also* Donoso, José; Donoso, María Pilar
Bordaberry, Juan María, 126
Borges, Jorge Luis, 23, 110, 119, 124, 125, 127, 131, 188, 204, 210; and *Ficciones*, 134, 138, 141; and international acclaim, 135–42; and the "boom," 145
Bourdieu, Pierre, 84, 88, 109, 132, 156–57
Brando, Marlon, 6, 18
Breton, André, 96, 117–18, 167–68, 169
Buber, Martin, 167
Burgess, Anthony, 166
Burroughs, William S., 146
Butler, Judith, 162

Cabellero Calderón, Eduardo, 110
Cabrera Infante, Guillermo, 42, 44, 117, 119, 134
Cáceres, Jorge, 168
Caillois, Roger, 138
Calvino, Italo, 107, 146
Campos, Haroldo de, 121
Canon formation, 98, 107, 121, 124–25, 131, 132, 136–37, 140, 154–55
Capitalism, 2, 5, 9, 20, 205, 209; and Frankfurt School, 4, 17; print, 109–42
Carpentier, Alejo, 23, 126, 134, 147, 191; and the "boom," 145, 167, 170–71; and *The Lost Steps*, 172–74; and *El libro de la Gran Sabana*, 172–73; and "De lo real maravilloso en América," 174–75; and *El reino de este mundo*, 174, 176

Carroll, Lewis, 139
Cartographic (imagination), 13, 190–91, 193, 200
Casa de las Américas, 21, 22, 23, 31, 43–44, 49, 116, 124, 127–28, 130
Casement, Roger, 196, 197
Caso Padilla. See Padilla Affair
Castañeda, Jorge, 25
Castellanos, Rosario, 110
Castellet, José María, 130, 131
Castro, Fidel, 11, 17–20, 27, 28, 33, 36–42, 45, 46–48, 53, 208
Castro-Klarén, Sara, 200
Catholic Church, 2, 3
Cela, Camilo José, 131
Censorship, 11, 31, 57, 104, 120, 126; and Franco, 129–30, 134, 166
Centro, 137, 138
Certeau, Michel de, 74, 96, 201–2
Césaire, Aimé, 101, 168
Chanady, Amaryll, 176
Chaskel, Pedro, 26
Chiriboga, Marcelo, 160
Cienfuegos, Camilo, 34
Civil society, 55, 62, 67, 68, 70, 79, 80, 82, 87–88, 92–93, 102, 188
Cold War, 3, 107, 116, 120, 121, 122
Coleman, Alexander, 141
Coleman, Peter, 126
Collazos, Oscar, 49, 101
Collective memory, 31, 58, 62, 75, 77
Comas, Juan, 191
Community, 7; and Cuban Revolution, 11, 12, 17, 18, 20–21, 27–28, 34–35, 39, 40–41; and capitalism, 17–18; intellectual, 23; imagined, 27, 116; and memory, 30, 31; international, 59; and Tlatelolco, 60, 67, 74–76; and Cortázar, 81, 85, 98, 100, 203, 204; cosmopolitan, 113; of novelists, 157, 160; and political unconscious, 178, 194; national, 190
Congreso Cultural de la Habana, 21, 22
Conrad, Joseph, and *Heart of Darkness*, 190–92, 193, 198

Consumer society, 5, 58–59, 93, 107, 108, 115, 127, 128

Contorno, 137, 138

Cortázar, Julio, 12, 13, 22, 78–105, 110, 113–14, 115, 117, 120; and "Reunión," 11, 42–50, 151; and *Casa de las Américas*, 23, 43–44, 49; and short stories, 79–82, 83–85; and *Rayuela*, 82, 85, 91, 92, 97, 119, 153, 199–207; and *Libro de Manuel*, 82, 85, 92–100, 102; and *El examen*, 84; and *Final de juego*, 85–86; and *Los premios*, 86–92, 110; and *Argentina: años de alambradas culturales*, 102–4; and the "boom," 145–46, 149, 150, 158; and *Blow Up*, 153

Cosmopolitanism, 51, 113, 115, 117–18, 139–40, 142, 151, 169, 188, 203

Cruz Sandoval, Héctor, 26

Cuban Revolution, 3, 7, 10, 12, 15–53, 102–3, 123, 125, 127, 186; and invention, 15; and international scope, 16, 129; and literature, 126, 130. *See also* Casa de las Américas; Guevara, Ernesto Che

Cultural history, 1, 107, 144

Cunninghame Graham, Robert, 197

De la Serna, Rodrigo, 51

De Man, Paul, 135, 141, 144

Dean, James, 6

Debord, Guy, 113, 114

Debray, Regis, 22

Decolonization, 13, 17, 58, 98, 178, 190

Deleuze, Gilles, 158, 165, 193–94

Derrida, Jacques, 50, 55–56, 170

Di Giovanni, Norman Thomas, 141

Díaz Arrieta, Hernán. *See* Alone

Díaz Gutiérrez, Alberto. *See* Korda

Díaz Ordaz, Gustavo, 56, 57–58, 60–62, 75

Distinction, 84–85, 89, 103, 112, 204

Donoso, José, 13, 122, 134, 209; and *El obsceno pájaro de la noche*, 8; and *Historia personal del "boom,"* 17, 23, 147–63, 207; and *El jardín de al lado*, 155, 158–63; and *El lugar sin límites*, 162

Donoso, María Pilar, 154, 160; and "El 'boom' doméstico," 154–58

Dostoevsky, Fyodor, 87

Droguet, Carlos, 134

Drummond de Andrade, Carlos, 123

Echeverría, Luis, 56

Einaudi, Giulio, 132

Eisenhower, Dwight D., 18

Eisenstein, Sergei, 75

Eliot, T. S., 124

Elizondo, Salvador, 110

Ernst, Max, 167

Ethnography, 13; in literature, 83, 172–74, 204; in periodicals, 168–70

Etiemble, René, 139, 140

Existentialism, 118, 166, 205

Family in the novel, 8–9, 11, 22–23, 27, 79, 82, 91, 98, 105, 147, 150, 154, 180, 185, 190, 199, 204, 205

Fanon, Frantz, 7, 103

Fantastic, the, 17, 43, 80, 82, 83, 100, 118, 139, 175, 176–77

Faulkner, William, 124, 148, 177

Feltrinelli, Giacomo, 25

Ferguson, Adam, 82

Fernández Moreno, César, 121

Fernández Retamar, Roberto, 22, 23, 43, 103, 123, 126, 128

Fernández Santos, Francisco, 130

Ferré, Rosario, 209

Flaubert, Gustave, 157

Flores, Angel, 176

Fondo de Cultura Económica, 57

Foucault, Michel, 4, 67–68, 80, 140, 170, 194

Fouchet, Christian, 60

Fox, Vicente, 54

Fraga Iribarne, Manuel, 129

Franco, Francisco, 128, 129

Franco, Jean, 208

Frankfurt School, 3, 17, 25, 29, 50

Franqui, Carlos, 158
Freud, Sigmund, 2, 9, 46–47, 48, 81, 152, 160
Frobenius, Leo, 166
Fuentes, Carlos, 13, 23, 56, 58–59, 107, 110, 115, 117–19, 120, 121, 127, 134, 209; and *The Death of Artemio Cruz*, 8, 9, 186, 188–90, 193, 194, 195–96, 205, 206; and the "boom," 145, 149, 150–52, 154, 160; and *La nueva novela hispano-americana*, 146–47; and *La región más transparente*, 150, 153

Galeano, Eduardo, 125; and *Las venas abiertas de América Latina*, 7
Gallegos, Romulo, and *Doña Bárbara*, 8
Gallimard, Claude, 132
García Bernal, Gael, 51–52
García Hortelano, Juan, 133–34
García Márquez, Gabriel, 13, 134; and *One Hundred Years of Solitude*, 8, 19, 110, 115, 120, 135, 153, 165, 178–86, 187, 188, 189, 190, 192, 194, 195, 199, 205, 210; and Nobel Prize, 143, 155, 186; and the "boom," 145–46, 149, 150, 154, 157, 158, 160; and *La hojarasca*, 177
García Márquez, Mercedes, 157, 158
García Ponce, Juan, 110
Garro, Elena, 110
Gautier, Eric, 51, 52
Geertz, Clifford, 172
Geisdorfer Feal, Rosemary, 161
Gender and gender system, 9, 10, 62, 94–96; and revolution, 11, 28; and the "boom," 13, 148–49, 152, 154–55, 161, 162, 199, 206–7
Genette, Gérard, 140
Gil de Biedma, Jaime, 131
Gilbert, Stuart, 167
Globalization, 107, 113, 197. *See also* Internationalization; Transnational
González de Mendoza, Pedro, 170
González Echeverría, Roberto, 176–77
González, Aníbal, 45–46
Goodyear, Charles, 197

Gorkin, Julián, 116
Goytisolo, José Agustín, 131
Goytisolo, Juan, 134
Goytisolo, Luis, 134, 152–53
Granaderos, 57, 58, 60, 61–62, 75
Granado, Alberto, 51
Grass, Günter, 117, 134
Graves, Robert, 131
Grimaud, Maurice, 60
Guattari, Félix, 165, 190, 193–94
Guerra, Eutimio, 40–41
Guevara, Ernesto Che, 6, 20, 24–42, 59, 101, 115, 205; and myth, 11, 25–27, 37, 51; and *Pasajes de la guerra revolucionaria*, 11, 29–42, 52; and fiction, 42–50; and film, 50–53. *See also* "New man"
Guillermoprieto, Alma, 24
Gunning, Tom, 181

Habermas, Jürgen, 100
Halbwachs, Maurice, 31
"Happening," 13, 74, 93, 97, 108, 166
Hare, David, 170
Hauser, Arnold, 123
Hegel, Georg Wilhelm Friedrich, 26, 73, 191
Hemingway, Ernest, 124
Hernández, Felisberto, 124
Hirschman, Albert O., 19
History. *See* Cultural history; Literary history
Hobbes, Thomas, 85
Holbein, Hans, 76
Hollywood, 9, 51
Hombre Nuevo. See "New man"
Horkheimer, Max, 4, 5, 10
Huston, John, 18
Huxley, Aldoux, 118

Ibargüengoitia, Jorge, 110
Ibarra, Néstor, 136–37, 138
Identity, 1, 38, 60–61, 66, 132, 149, 185, 191; national, 14, 55, 67, 104, 118, 135; continental, 21, 52, 102, 104, 106, 210; transnational, 24; and gender, 27,

161–62; collective, 31, 81; and memory, 67; and writing, 145
Iglesias, Julio, 210
Illia, Arturo Umberto, 115
Internationalization, 104, 136, 138. *See also* Globalization; Transnational
Irby, James, 141

Jameson, Fredric, 184
Jitrik, Noé, 123, 128, 137, 138
Johnson, Barbara, 159
Jolas, Eugène, 170
Jorgensen, Beth, 74
Joyce, James, 139, 148, 167, 177, 203

Kafka, Franz, 124, 138, 139, 148, 167
Kant, Immanuel, 10
Kazan, Elia, 18
Kerrigan, Anthony, 131, 141
King, Martin Luther, 59
Korda (Alberto Díaz Gutiérrez), 25–26
Koselleck, Reinhard, 40

La Lupe, 119
Lacan, Jacques, 2, 8, 9, 42, 48
Laclau, Ernesto, 52
Lawrence, D. H., 118
Leal, Luis, 176
Leclaire, Serge, 9
Ledig-Rowohlt, Heinrich, 132
Lefebvre, Henri, 188
Leiris, Michel, 169
Leñero, Vicente, 110, 134
Letra y Línea, 138
Lévinas, Emanuel, 105
Lévi-Strauss, Claude, 8, 9, 146, 164–65, 168–70, 172, 173–74, 201
Lévy-Bruhl, Lucien, 169
Lewis, Oscar, 57
Lezama Lima, José, 145
Liberation, 2–3, 5, 9, 12, 17, 18, 19, 21, 22, 27, 81, 92, 105, 114, 124, 208
Libre, 44
Lida, Raimundo, 138
Lima, Lezama, 19

Literary history, 13, 134–35, 144–45, 147, 152, 159, 165–66, 211
Literary marketplace, 13, 120, 123, 127, 135
London, Jack, 44
López Mateos, Adolfo, 57
Lowry, Malcolm, 118
Lugones, Leopoldo, 119
Lukács, Georg, 17–18
Lyotard, Jean-François, 71, 194

Macedo, Rita, 150, 151–52
MacGregor, Robert, 141
Machado, Antonio, 131
Magical realism, 13, 16–17, 171, 174–77, 195, 210
Mallarmé, Stéphane, 130
Mallea, Eduardo, 110, 204
Mann, Thomas, 148
Marcha, 41, 101, 111, 122–26, 127–28
Marcuse, Herbert, 96, 102; and *Reason and Revolution*, 4; and *Eros and Civilization*, 4; and *One-Dimensional Man*, 4, 24–25, 29
Marechal, Leopoldo, 204
Marin, Louis, 60–61
Marra, Nelson, 126
Marsé, Juan, 133
Martí, José, 19, 22, 24, 29, 31
Martin, Gerald, 186
Martin, Ricky, 210
Martorell, Joanot, 195
Marx, Karl, 2, 16, 49
Marxism, 2, 4, 8; and Marxist theory, 8, 166; and revolution, 19
Masculinity: and the Cuban Revolution, 38, 40; and the "boom," 149, 152, 155, 156, 161, 199. *See also* Phallocratic bonds
Matta, Eduardo, 168
Maurois, André, 141
Mauss, Marcel, 169, 170
Mendillín Conference, 2
Messianic, 16, 19, 48, 52, 79, 102, 104–5
Mia, Gianni, 51

Michaux, Henri, 118
Miller, Arthur, 121
Monsiváis, Carlos, 55, 56, 73
Montero, Oscar, 161
Moravia, Alberto, 146
Moretti, Franco, 179
Mujica Láinez, Manuel, 204
Müller-Bergh, Klaus, 176
Mundo Nuevo, 43, 116–22, 123, 124, 126, 127–28
Murena, H. A., 138

Narrative voice, 36, 38, 45, 153, 155, 156, 160, 177–78, 180, 182, 185, 206
Neruda, Pablo, 23, 49, 121
New Left, 2, 5
"New man," 2, 11, 14, 18, 20, 92, 98, 101, 205; and Che Guevara, 24–42, 125
Nietzsche, Friedrich, 65, 85
Nosotros, 136
Nouzeilles, Gabriela, 206
Número, 124

Ocampo, Victoria, 121, 127, 138
Odría, Manuel, 20
Onetti, Juan Carlos, 123, 124, 126
Orfila Reynal, Arnaldo, 57
Orgambide, Pedro, 136
Ortega, Julio, 128
Ortiz, Fernando, 167
Orwell, George, 124
Oviedo, José Miguel, 123

Pacheco, José Emilio, 110
Padilla Affair, 20, 21, 44, 135, 158
Palance, Jack, 51
Palés Matos, Luis, 167
Palmier, Jean-Michel, 25
Parra, Nicanor, 121
Partido Revolucionario Institucional (PRI), 12, 54–55, 62, 63–64
Patriarchy, 8, 9, 27, 96, 156–57, 206
Paz, Octavio, 6, 12, 44, 48, 54, 55, 68, 77, 127, 146; and *Postdata*, 56, 62–67; and *El laberinto de la soledad*, 63–65, 67, 119

Pérez Jiménez, Marcos, 20
Peri Rossi, Cristina, 125, 209
Perón, Juan, 20, 115, 123; and Peronism, 91
Pezzoni, Enrique, 138
Phallocratic bonds: and Cuban Revolution, 17, 27, 28, 39–42; and the "boom" novels, 148–63, 206–7
Picasso, Pablo, 169
Pinochet, Augusto, 208
Plot, 1, 8, 11, 32–33, 86, 149, 160, 181, 184, 186–87, 189–90, 194–95, 199–200, 203, 205–6; and logic of, 13, 79, 96, 161, 173, 191, 196
Poe, Edgar Allan, 138, 139
Pompidou, Georges, 60
Poniatowska, Elena, 12, 54, 55, 56, 209; and *La noche de Tlatelolco*, 62, 67–77
Prebisch, Raúl, 2
Prieto, Adolfo, 137, 138
Primera Plana, 109, 111–16, 126, 127, 165, 200
Prizes, 21, 24, 125, 131–35, 136, 139, 140–41, 154–55, 170
Proust, Marcel, 124
Publishing houses, 114; and Joaquín Mortiz, 110, 129; Eudeba, 110; Jorge Alvarez, 115; and the Cold War, 120–22; and new houses, 125, 209; in Spain, 128–30; and prizes, 131–34, 136; Alfred Knopf, 151
Puig, Manuel, 129, 134, 209

Quant, Mary, 119
Quijano, Carlos, 122, 126
Quiroga, Horacio, 124

Rama, Angel, 23, 107, 109, 110, 123, 124, 125–26, 128, 183
Raynaud, George, 170
Read, Herbert, 167
Reading public, 102, 135, 136, 155, 209; in Europe, 3, 166; in North America, 3; in Latin America, 107–9, 113, 121, 124, 127, 130, 145, 187; in Spain, 129, 130,

134; in France, 138; in England, 141; international, 176
Redemption, redemptive, 2, 7, 9, 19, 20, 29, 41, 48–49, 52, 104, 189
Redford, Robert, 51
Reed, Alastair, 131
Rein, Mercedes, 125, 126
Republic of letters, 1, 106, 115, 117, 122, 129, 135, 138, 147, 152, 158, 161, 209
Revolution: and May 1968, 4, 25, 60, 102; and gender, 11; American, 16; French, 16; Hungarian, 18; October, 22; and masculine camaraderie, 27–29; Nicaraguan, 78, 102–3; Mexican, 189. *See also* Cuban Revolution; Student movements; Tlatelolco massacre
Revueltas, José, 56
Reyes, Alfonso, 167
Ribemont Dessaignes, Georges, 170
Ricardou, Jean, 139
Ricoeur, Paul, 31, 146
Rimbaud, Arthur, 96, 130
Ríos, Juan, 168
Rivera, José Eustasio, 51, 91, 194; and *La vorágine*, 183, 192, 196, 197–99
Rivet, Paul, 169
Robbe-Grillet, Alain, 107
Robles Piquer, Carlos, 134
Rodó, José Enrique, 124
Rodríguez Monegal, Emir, 43, 116–22, 123, 124, 125–26, 128, 176
Roh, Franz, 176
Rojas Pinilla, Gustavo, 20
Rojas, Rafael, 19–20
Rosa, Guimaraes, 120
Ross, Kristin, 59
Ruffinelli, Jorge, 126
Rulfo, Juan, 134; and *Pedro Páramo*, 8, 9, 110; and the "boom," 145

Sábato, Ernesto, 123, 134
Said, Edward, 77, 100, 103, 194
Sainz, Gustavo, 110, 209
Salazar Bondy, Sebastián, 123
Salinas, Jaime, 131, 133

Salles, Walter, and *Motorcycle Diaries*, 11, 50–53
Sánchez, Néstor, 113
Santamaría, Haydée, 21, 43
Sarmiento, Domingo Faustino, 111, 137, 193
Sartre, Jean-Paul, 4, 7, 8, 25, 130, 137, 139, 140, 205
Scarry, Elaine, 60, 70, 76
Schwartz, Marcy, 202
Sebreli, Juan José, 137
Seix Barral, 129–35
Seix, Victor, 131
Seligman, Kurt, 169
Shariff, Omar, 51
Shelley, Percy Bysshe, 104–5
Sierra, Barros, 57
Silverman, Kaja, 9
Smith, Paul Julian, 189
Sollers, Philippe, 139
Sontag, Susan, 117, 119, 146
Sosa, Mercedes, 210
Spark, Muriel, 166
Spectrality, 25, 48, 50, 52, 61, 149–50, 162
Stalin, Joseph, 18
Stein, Gertrude, 167
Structure of feeling, 9, 10, 16, 17, 107, 159, 169, 206
Student movements, 8, 11, 26, 55, 56–61, 71, 72, 74, 96
Styron, William, 107
Sur, 124, 127–28, 129, 137–38
Surrealism, 4, 13, 101, 102, 117–18, 175–76; and Cortázar, 79, 92, 94, 96–97, 105; and Surrealist magazines, 166–70

Taussig, Michael, 179
Tel Quel, 170. *See also* Sollers, Philippe
Testimonios, 62, 68–70, 75, 76. *See also* Poniatowska, Elena
Third World, 2, 7, 8, 18, 19, 22, 58, 59, 119, 164, 179
Timmerman, Jacobo, 112
Tlatelolco massacre, 12, 54–78
Transition, 165–70

Transnational, the, 3, 13, 17, 19, 23, 59, 106, 107, 109, 119, 128, 130–31, 132, 140, 144, 150, 165, 201, 205, 209; and identity, 1, 24; and economy, 5, 108; and the literary, 13, 108, 138; and audience, 21, 164. *See also* Globalization; Internationalization

Trauma, 54–55, 62, 67, 75, 77, 208

Trombadori, Duccio, 4

Trotsky, Leon, 96

Trujillo, Rafael, 21

Ultimo Round, 96

Urondo, Francisco, 43

Uslar Pietri, Arturo, 171

Utopia, 1, 2, 3–4, 5, 8, 9, 208, 211; and the Cuban Revolution, 11, 15–53, 130; and 1968, 77; and Cortázar, 78, 96, 104–5, 206; and periodicals, 116, 121; and the novel, 143, 144, 186, 187, 189, 194

Valbeuna Briones, Angel, 176

Valcárcel, Luis, 167

Valenzuela, Luisa, 209

Vallejo, César, 23

Vallejo, Demetrio, 57

Vargas Llosa, Mario, 13, 22, 101, 110, 120, 121, 123, 134, 190–200, 209; and *Casa de las Américas*, 23; and *La ciudad y los perros*, 132–33, 134, 153; and the "boom," 145, 149, 157, 158; and *The Green House*, 8, 186, 190, 191–99, 205, 206

Vargas, Fernando, 51

Verde Olivo, 29, 36

Verdevoye, Paul, 138

Verne, Jules, 139

Viñas, Ismael and David, 137, 138

Violence, 1, 7, 12, 18, 36, 54–77, 92, 175, 179–80, 182, 185, 206, 208; and myth, 25; and aesthetics, 54, 62, 179

Vraisemblable, 79, 96

VVV, 166–70

Walsh, María Elena, 112

Walzer, Michael, 26, 29

Weber, Andrew Lloyd, 51

Weber, Max, 90

Woolf, Virginia, 148

World literature, 3, 156, 171

Yates, Donald, 141

Youth culture, 33, 45, 51–53, 127; and generation, 5–6, 58–59, 94; and revolution, 15, 32; and Tlatelolco, 75; and revolts, 102; and novelists, 112–13, 117, 155; and the "boom," 163

Žižek, Slavoj, 48

Cultural Memory | in the Present

Hubert Damisch, *A Childhood Memory by Piero della Francesca*

Asja Szafraniec, *Beckett, Derrida, and the Event of Literature*

Sara Guyer, *Romanticism After Auschwitz*

Alison Ross, *The Aesthetic Paths of Philosophy: Presentation in Kant, Heidegger, Lacoue-Labarthe, and Nancy*

Gerhard Richter, *Thought-Images: Frankfurt School Writers' Reflections from Damaged Life*

Bella Brodzki, *Can These Bones Live? Translation, Survival, and Cultural Memory*

Rodolphe Gasché, *The Honor of Thinking: Critique, Theory, Philosophy*

Brigitte Peucker, *The Material Image: Art and the Real in Film*

Natalie Melas, *All the Difference in the World: Postcoloniality and the Ends of Comparison*

Jonathan Culler, *The Literary in Theory*

Michael G. Levine, *The Belated Witness: Literature, Testimony, and the Question of Holocaust Survival*

Jennifer A. Jordan, *Structures of Memory: Understanding German Change in Berlin and Beyond*

Christoph Menke, *Reflections of Equality*

Marlène Zarader, *The Unthought Debt: Heidegger and the Hebraic Heritage*

Jan Assmann, *Religion and Cultural Memory: Ten Studies*

David Scott and Charles Hirschkind, *Powers of the Secular Modern: Talal Asad and His Interlocutors*

Gyanendra Pandey, *Routine Violence: Nations, Fragments, Histories*

James Siegel, *Naming the Witch*

J. M. Bernstein, *Against Voluptuous Bodies: Late Modernism and the Meaning of Painting*

Theodore W. Jennings, Jr., *Reading Derrida / Thinking Paul: On Justice*

Richard Rorty and Eduardo Mendieta, *Take Care of Freedom and Truth Will Take Care of Itself: Interviews with Richard Rorty*

Jacques Derrida, *Paper Machine*

Renaud Barbaras, *Desire and Distance: Introduction to a Phenomenology of Perception*

Jill Bennett, *Empathic Vision: Affect, Trauma, and Contemporary Art*

Ban Wang, *Illuminations from the Past: Trauma, Memory, and History in Modern China*

James Phillips, *Heidegger's* Volk: *Between National Socialism and Poetry*

Frank Ankersmit, *Sublime Historical Experience*

István Rév, *Retroactive Justice: Prehistory of Post-Communism*

Paola Marrati, *Genesis and Trace: Derrida Reading Husserl and Heidegger*

Krzysztof Ziarek, *The Force of Art*

Marie-José Mondzain, *Image, Icon, Economy: The Byzantine Origins of the Contemporary Imaginary*

Cecilia Sjöholm, *The Antigone Complex: Ethics and the Invention of Feminine Desire*

Jacques Derrida and Elisabeth Roudinesco, *For What Tomorrow . . . : A Dialogue*

Elisabeth Weber, *Questioning Judaism: Interviews by Elisabeth Weber*

Jacques Derrida and Catherine Malabou, *Counterpath: Traveling with Jacques Derrida*

Martin Seel, *Aesthetics of Appearing*

Nanette Salomon, *Shifting Priorities: Gender and Genre in Seventeenth-Century Dutch Painting*

Jacob Taubes, *The Political Theology of Paul*

Jean-Luc Marion, *The Crossing of the Visible*

Eric Michaud, *The Cult of Art in Nazi Germany*

Anne Freadman, *The Machinery of Talk: Charles Peirce and the Sign Hypothesis*

Stanley Cavell, *Emerson's Transcendental Etudes*

Stuart McLean, *The Event and Its Terrors: Ireland, Famine, Modernity*

Beate Rössler, ed., *Privacies: Philosophical Evaluations*

Bernard Faure, *Double Exposure: Cutting Across Buddhist and Western Discourses*

Alessia Ricciardi, *The Ends of Mourning: Psychoanalysis, Literature, Film*

Alain Badiou, *Saint Paul: The Foundation of Universalism*

Gil Anidjar, *The Jew, the Arab: A History of the Enemy*

Jonathan Culler and Kevin Lamb, eds., *Just Being Difficult? Academic Writing in the Public Arena*

Jean-Luc Nancy, *A Finite Thinking*, edited by Simon Sparks

Theodor W. Adorno, *Can One Live after Auschwitz? A Philosophical Reader*, edited by Rolf Tiedemann

Patricia Pisters, *The Matrix of Visual Culture: Working with Deleuze in Film Theory*

Andreas Huyssen, *Present Pasts: Urban Palimpsests and the Politics of Memory*

Talal Asad, *Formations of the Secular: Christianity, Islam, Modernity*

Dorothea von Mücke, *The Rise of the Fantastic Tale*

Marc Redfield, *The Politics of Aesthetics: Nationalism, Gender, Romanticism*

Emmanuel Levinas, *On Escape*

Dan Zahavi, *Husserl's Phenomenology*

Rodolphe Gasché, *The Idea of Form: Rethinking Kant's Aesthetics*

Michael Naas, *Taking on the Tradition: Jacques Derrida and the Legacies of Deconstruction*

Herlinde Pauer-Studer, ed., *Constructions of Practical Reason: Interviews on Moral and Political Philosophy*

Jean-Luc Marion, *Being Given That: Toward a Phenomenology of Givenness*

Theodor W. Adorno and Max Horkheimer, *Dialectic of Enlightenment*

Ian Balfour, *The Rhetoric of Romantic Prophecy*

Martin Stokhof, *World and Life as One: Ethics and Ontology in Wittgenstein's Early Thought*

Gianni Vattimo, *Nietzsche: An Introduction*

Jacques Derrida, *Negotiations: Interventions and Interviews, 1971–1998*, ed. Elizabeth Rottenberg

Brett Levinson, *The Ends of Literature: The Latin American "Boom" in the Neoliberal Marketplace*

Timothy J. Reiss, *Against Autonomy: Cultural Instruments, Mutualities, and the Fictive Imagination*

Hent de Vries and Samuel Weber, eds., *Religion and Media*

Niklas Luhmann, *Theories of Distinction: Re-Describing the Descriptions of Modernity*, ed. and introd. William Rasch

Johannes Fabian, *Anthropology with an Attitude: Critical Essays*

Michel Henry, *I Am the Truth: Toward a Philosophy of Christianity*

Gil Anidjar, *"Our Place in Al-Andalus": Kabbalah, Philosophy, Literature in Arab-Jewish Letters*

Hélène Cixous and Jacques Derrida, *Veils*

F. R. Ankersmit, *Historical Representation*

F. R. Ankersmit, *Political Representation*

Elissa Marder, *Dead Time: Temporal Disorders in the Wake of Modernity (Baudelaire and Flaubert)*

Reinhart Koselleck, *The Practice of Conceptual History: Timing History, Spacing Concepts*

Niklas Luhmann, *The Reality of the Mass Media*

Hubert Damisch, *A Theory of /Cloud/: Toward a History of Painting*

Jean-Luc Nancy, *The Speculative Remark: (One of Hegel's bon mots)*

Jean-François Lyotard, *Soundproof Room: Malraux's Anti-Aesthetics*

Jan Patočka, *Plato and Europe*

Hubert Damisch, *Skyline: The Narcissistic City*

Isabel Hoving, *In Praise of New Travelers: Reading Caribbean Migrant Women Writers*

Richard Rand, ed., *Futures: Of Jacques Derrida*

William Rasch, *Niklas Luhmann's Modernity: The Paradoxes of Differentiation*

Jacques Derrida and Anne Dufourmantelle, *Of Hospitality*

Jean-François Lyotard, *The Confession of Augustine*

Kaja Silverman, *World Spectators*

Samuel Weber, *Institution and Interpretation: Expanded Edition*

Jeffrey S. Librett, *The Rhetoric of Cultural Dialogue: Jews and Germans in the Epoch of Emancipation*

Ulrich Baer, *Remnants of Song: Trauma and the Experience of Modernity in Charles Baudelaire and Paul Celan*

Samuel C. Wheeler III, *Deconstruction as Analytic Philosophy*

David S. Ferris, *Silent Urns: Romanticism, Hellenism, Modernity*

Rodolphe Gasché, *Of Minimal Things: Studies on the Notion of Relation*

Sarah Winter, *Freud and the Institution of Psychoanalytic Knowledge*

Samuel Weber, *The Legend of Freud: Expanded Edition*

Aris Fioretos, ed., *The Solid Letter: Readings of Friedrich Hölderlin*

J. Hillis Miller / Manuel Asensi, *Black Holes / J. Hillis Miller; or, Boustrophedonic Reading*

Miryam Sas, *Fault Lines: Cultural Memory and Japanese Surrealism*

Peter Schwenger, *Fantasm and Fiction: On Textual Envisioning*

Didier Maleuvre, *Museum Memories: History, Technology, Art*

Jacques Derrida, *Monolingualism of the Other; or, The Prosthesis of Origin*

Andrew Baruch Wachtel, *Making a Nation, Breaking a Nation: Literature and Cultural Politics in Yugoslavia*

Niklas Luhmann, *Love as Passion: The Codification of Intimacy*

Mieke Bal, ed., *The Practice of Cultural Analysis: Exposing Interdisciplinary Interpretation*

Jacques Derrida and Gianni Vattimo, eds., *Religion*